A History of the
First Parish Church
Of
Scituate, Massachusetts:
Its Life and Times

⚘

Richard M. Stower

ISBN: 978-0-9858282-5-7
Copyright © Richard M. Stower

Published by:
Converpage
23 Acorn Street
Scituate, MA 02066
www.converpage.com

To Nancy, Jonathan
and the members of First Parish,
past, present and future

The First Parish Communion Cups
Photograph taken by Sarah Ballinger

Since... [the First Parish Church of Scituate's] tranquil life commenced among these scattered farms, what deluges, what earthquakes of change, have swept over the globe, and left it unshaken and untouched! It has witnessed the beginning and the end of the three great social convulsions of the modern world: the English Revolution, the American Revolution, and the French Revolution. It was at least a hundred and forty years old when Napoleon was in his cradle. It was venerable when Washington was born, and vigorous when Cromwell died. These reminiscences indicate, that, if your society has a future, it has also a past. If it has hopes, it has also memories and prejudices, and old and dear traditions.

You notice, sir, that this bare hill looks out upon the open ocean; and the weather-beaten spire above us is one of the surest and most welcome landmarks of the sailor. How many a wary mariner, homeward-bound, has hailed its familiar outlines, descried through storm and mist, with a thrill of joy unutterable! And so may many a bewildered voyager on the sea of life hail this church, under your administrations and those of your successors, as a Pharos of light and hope, set up on the coasts of the last, still haven to which we are all drifting; that haven, which, at best, we see through a glass darkly, and of which we only know that "there the wicked cease from the troubling, and the weary are at rest!"

- Seth Webb, Jr. upon the ordination of the Rev. William G. Babcock as minister of the First Parish of Scituate, September 16, 1860

Introduction

On January 18, 1634 a small group of people huddled together near the warm hearth in a simple house along the edge of Scituate Harbor and to the north of the cold brook, the *Satuit,* that gave the town its Wampanoag name. The house belonged to James Cudworth, a salter, and with him that evening were his wife, Mary, his friend, Timothy Hatherly, and several others who assembled there for a very serious purpose: to gather the first church in the town. Leading them in prayer was the Rev. John Lothrop, newly arrived from London, by way of Boston. Thus was assembled the First Church of Scituate, a settlement in the Plymouth Colony of the Pilgrims.

The Rev. Samuel Deane, in his *History of Scituate, Massachusetts* (1831) wrote, "Few subjects are more agreeable (at least to many minds) than that of contemplating the characters of the men who first broke the soil which we now cultivate, and few things can more excite the imagination, than to muse upon the spot where they lighted their domestic fires, or to walk over the green turf that covers their remains."[1]

This book, the history of the First Parish Church in Scituate, is an account of and a musing on those early planters and all who have come since. There are not many institutions in the United States as old as First Parish in Scituate and it is a testament of the "character, opinions and manners"[2] of all who have been a part of that sacred community that it lives on to the present time. Like Rev. Deane before me, I am grateful not only to "the characters of the men who first broke the soil" but to the historians of the church who have plowed the hardened ground of history, unearthing the activities of men and women which present a rich story of a community, not only

---

[1] Samuel Deane. *History of Scituate, Massachusetts, From Its Settlement to 1831* (1831, reprint 1975), 165.
[2] Deane, 165.

1

of faith, but of action as well. History is the story of all those people who have come before us. We are who we are because of all that happened earlier. So it is with the writing of history. When it comes to the records of First Parish in Scituate, I have walked behind the plow guided by church historians including Rev. Deane, the Rev. Robert Lewis Weis, Margaret Cole Bonney, Jean Cole Strzelecki, as well as Mr. Clarence Waite of the First Trinitarian Congregational Church of Scituate. Margaret Cole Bonney was the social historian of First Parish for most of the twentieth century. She privately published several volumes about Scituate and First Parish. Other essays of hers are used here to give a personal view of the life of the church. Nevertheless, most of what is contained herein has been consolidated for the first time from the journals of First Parish's early ministers kept at the Scituate Town Archives; two volumes containing Annual Meeting minutes and other business matters; the minutes of various committee and women's groups meetings; and photographs.

There are others to thank and acknowledge. The staff at the Southwark Local History Library and the British Library in London which gave me the thrill of holding a four-hundred year old tract written by the Rev. Henry Jacob as I began my research in 2000. The staff at the Massachusetts Historical Society was very helpful and a conversation with Conrad E. Wright set me on the right path. Chris Spiegel of the Ministries and Faith Development Office at the Unitarian Universalist Association helped locate photographs of some ministers. Fran O'Donnell, the curator of manuscripts and archives at the Andover-Harvard Library at the Harvard Divinity School facilitated my research by gathering the files of Scituate's ministers since Rev. Edmund Q. Sewall. Jeffrey S. Cramer of the Thoreau Institute in Lincoln, Massachusetts and the staff of the Huntington Library in San Marino, California guided me through the correspondence and biographies recounting the relationship of Ellen Sewall and John and Henry David Thoreau. The equally compelling stories of the lesser known Rev. Sheldon C. Clark and Rev. Henry W. Pinkham were aided by the staffs at the Joseph Labadie Collection at the Hatcher Library of the University of Michigan in Ann Arbor and the Peace Collection at Swarthmore College's McCabe Library. The folks at the Scituate Historical Society, Betty Miessner and David Ball and, at the Scituate Town Archives, Betty Foster shared their knowledge of Scituate's history. Finally, to this collection of names, I add Yvonne Twomey, a member of First Parish and a trustee of the Scituate Historical Society. Yvonne gave me encouragement every step of the way.

A special acknowledgement goes to my professors of history at the George Washington University many years ago: Roderic Davison, Charles J. Herber, Peter P. Hill, Robert C. Kenney; and, at Harvard Divinity School, C. Conrad Wright and David D. Hall.

In most cases I have modernized spelling and punctuation. For simplicity's sake, the older dates noted here are according to the Julian calendar. England and some other parts of Protestant Europe refused to accept the Gregorian calendar when Pope Gregory XIII decreed it in 1582. England didn't adopt it until 1752. All dates following 1752 follow the Gregorian calendar. Every effort has been made to be accurate in dates and facts. No doubt there are errors herein and those errors are nobody's but mine. The beauty of digital publishing is that corrections can be made in short order in subsequent editions and yet the digital age presents the historian with a problem. As more information becomes digitized and available online, the rabbit hole of research gets deeper and deeper. Professor Herber advised me to stop the research and start writing. I started the writing but occasionally continued to peek at search engine results and found more historical jewels. Nevertheless, the American journalist, Gene Fowler, had it right when he once uttered a timeless statement about writing a book. He said, "A book is never finished, it is abandoned." So, I abandon the book, for now.

Spring 2012
Scituate, Massachusetts

3

Chapter One

Godly Men and Women

The historian, Stephen Foster, writing about Puritanism notes, "American history begins before America."[1] So it is with the history of the First Parish Church in Scituate, Massachusetts. In order to appreciate the early history of the Scituate church we must understand the historical context in which it came to be gathered, first led by the Rev. Henry Jacob in the Southwark borough of London in 1616 and later by his successor, the Rev. John Lothrop, in Scituate in 1634. This means we must start in sixteenth century England with the rise of the Puritan movement; then to the split between the two reformist factions: the Puritans, who believed, hoped and prayed that the Church of England could reform itself, not so much in doctrine, as in ritual and governance; and the Separatists, who had given up all hope that the Church could be changed and who decided to travel on their own path returning the church of Christ to its origins.

When John Lothrop arrived in Scituate in the fall of 1634, he probably knew a good number of the settlers there because, like him, they had come to the Plymouth Colony by way of Kent, England.

---

[1] Stephen Foster. *The Long Argument: English Puritanism and the Shaping of New England Culture, 1570-1700* (1991), xii.

4

Though born in Yorkshire, Lothrop's first parish assignment was at St. James Parish in Egerton, Kent. The connection between Kent and Scituate was strong. Even Lothrop's predecessor in the Southwark church, the Rev. Henry Jacob, was born in Kent and, like Lothrop, served as the minister of a small parish, St. Martin's church in Cheriton.

Kent is one of the more historically important counties in England. Certainly, its importance lies with its location. Twenty-one miles from Egerton, across the English Channel to the southeast, is France. Fifty miles to the northwest from Egerton is London. Kent is blessed with rich, fertile soil, whose farms produced grain, hearty livestock and fruit. In the Middle Ages it was one of the most prosperous regions of England because of a well-established class of crop farmers and sheepherders of moderate means who, as freemen, owned their land. It was this economic independence that allowed, by the sixteenth century, an easing of economic, social and religious practices that persisted in other areas of England.[2] From the late fifteenth century until the mid-seventeenth, Kent was one of the most important of all the counties in England. Its proximity to London placed it at the crossroads of trade and communication with the continent and gave it a competitive advantage in the London markets.[3] After William the Conqueror invaded and ruled England in the eleventh century, Kent had a reputation as an unruly province, a place of periodic unrest, if not outright rebellion. Its acts of resistance gave Kent its motto, "Invictus" (Undefeated).

Non-conformity seems to have appeared naturally in the countryside. The nature of farming, the weakness of manorial authority and the tradition of a life of comparative isolation encouraged individualistic and independent attitudes. One contemporary observer thought there was a clear correlation between the relatively isolated life in the towns of Kent and the

[2] C. W. Chalkin. *Seventeenth Century Kent* (1965), 1.

[3] W. K. Jordan. "Social Institutions in Kent, 1480-1660" in *Essays in Kentish History* ed. by M. Roake and J. Whyman (1973), 85-86.

encouragement of independent thought. Winter weather, with its cold temperatures and drifting snow, may have also played a role as it, too, contributed to the isolation from Anglican clergy and practice.[4] In addition to the farmers, there gradually grew a merchant class trading in textiles and other woven goods. This came about in part during the sixteen century when three waves of skilled Protestant weavers came from the Low Countries on the continent and found refuge in Kent. Their religious views were influential. The clothiers and artificers (manual laborers) of Kent, those who made woolen cloth, excelled at their craft. They dyed their wool before weaving, thus making their cloth renowned for its color and variety.[5] Clothiers traveled to London many times a year and spread their independent social, political and religious views during their commercial dealings with merchants in London who bought their cloth. At home, the weavers, spinners and carders who came to pick up or deliver materials were "easy converts" because their livelihood was dependent on these independent thinkers.

The London borough of Southwark, at the south end of London Bridge, had been a busy section of the city since the early Middle Ages. A survey of London, written in 1598, gives the following description of Southwark: "The Borough of Southwark, which is a ward of London without the walls, consisteth of divers streets, ways and winding lanes, all full of buildings - at a subsidy to the king this borough yieldeth about eight hundred pounds, which is more than any one city in England payeth, except London. Old London Bridge was the only bridge over the Thames at London and all traffic to and from the City and the South of England and hence the continent of Europe passed through Southwark's Borough High Street...." Inns lining the street catered to the many travelers; the Tabard Inn, for example, was used by Chaucer as the starting point for his pilgrims in *Canterbury Tales*." [6]

---

[4] Chalkin, 228-229.
[5] Jordan, 86; Chalkin, 118.
[6] Boast, Mary. *The Mayflower and Pilgrim* Story (1995), 15.

To the citizens of London, Southwark, easily reached by the London Bridge or by the many ferryboats that plied the Thames River, was the place to go for entertainment. It was certainly a place of great vitality. Here, just outside the City of London's jurisdiction, the area had long been known for its bear gardens and the popular sport of bear baiting. It was also notorious for its 'stews' or brothels. By the late sixteenth century, however, the neighborhood became the home of entertainment of a very different kind. Southwark was the theater district of Elizabethan London. Here, the Rose Theatre was built in 1588 and the Globe Theater opened 1599 where many of William Shakespeare's plays were first performed. It was a place of extreme contrasts. Near the Globe Theater were both the bear gardens and the bishop's prison, the Clink, where religious dissenters were sent. All prisons of those days were horrible, unhealthy, overcrowded places, but the Clink was particularly revolting. The prison owed its extreme unpleasantness to its very damp location below the high water mark near the river, the common sewer and the bishop's pond. Southwark in the sixteenth and seventeenth centuries attracted aspects of life, groups of people and ways of thought not favored by London authorities within its own walls. No wonder, then, that it became a center of religious dissent and the birthplace of an Independent Church.[7] Dr. Thomas Binney, an eminent nineteenth century English Congregationalist, wrote that "During the latter half of the 16th century some of the most distinguished Puritan confessors and martyrs found in Southwark a home, a church, a prison and a grave."[8]

When King Henry VIII of England wanted to divorce his wife, Catherine of Aragon, he asked Pope Clement VII to give him papal approval to the dissolution of the marriage. When the pope refused, Henry took matters into his own hands. He not only divorced himself from Catherine, he divorced Rome from any religious matters in England and declared himself the head of the Church of England, independent from the authority of Rome. Unlike

---

[7] Boast, 17.
[8] Boast, 13.

what was happening on the Continent, England's Reformation began as a political matter that affected religious life. In the rest of Europe, it was the reverse. German princes sided with Luther and his call for church reform in their effort to increase their own power, influence and territory at Rome's expense. Yet even with the support of the princes, the continental Reformation was more of a popular religious movement that affected political life rather than England's top-down change. Over time the consequences of the English Reformation were very different than the religious upheaval on the continent. In England, there was no single popular and charismatic leader like Martin Luther or John Calvin. English monarchs went their own ecclesiastical way, in some cases forcing the nation to be whipsawed by returning the nation to Catholicism, then back to Protestantism, then to a blend of the two and finally to a restless Protestantism in the first third of the seventeenth century. The result was decades of civil turbulence and religious unrest culminating in the Royalist-Puritan English Civil War of 1642-1651.

When Henry VIII died in 1547, his son, Edward VI, came to the throne. Having had a Protestant education, Edward was sympathetic to its growing influence as reformers arrived in England from Germany and Poland. One of Edward's first major undertakings was to solidify Protestantism in England with the passage of the Act of Uniformity in 1549. Written by a committee headed by the Archbishop of Canterbury, Thomas Cranmer, the act is primarily known for the creation of the English language *Book of Common Prayer* as the sole legal form of worship in England. Churches in England until 1549 used the Latin missal with slight alterations. The act was highly controversial and hostility to it, in general, and to the new prayer book, in particular, led to rioting in some areas of the country, especially those areas that continued their loyalty to Rome. In response, a new Act of Uniformity was passed in 1552 that introduced a greatly revised Protestant *Book of Common Prayer*. Anyone who attended a service where this liturgy was not used faced six months imprisonment for a first offence, one year for a second offence, and life for a third. Edward VI's reign was a brief six years, but in that short time the form and the spirit of the Church of

England had been "massively altered."[9] It was now a national church that was episcopal, that is, governed by bishops. All English people were obligated to support a church that by royal decree was now Protestant. While the reforms may have been widespread, they were not deep.

There was little opposition to Edward's changes, other than the isolated rebellion against the first edition of the Book of Common Prayer, and yet, there was great enthusiasm for the ascension to the throne of Mary, Edward's half-sister who was a devout Catholic. Mary restored Catholicism as the state church of England and easily persuaded Parliament to repeal most of the church legislation passed under Henry and Edward. She purged the Protestant bishops from the church, some of whom were burned at the stake. She married the Catholic king of Spain, Philip II in 1554. Discontent between the powerful and the powerless in England increased. The marriage was widely unpopular among the people and much of the nobility. Some of the opposition was religiously motivated; others condemned it because they didn't want England to be part of the Spanish Empire. One such dissident, Sir Thomas Wyatt, assembled a following of some four thousand in Kent and a royal army of six hundred was sent from London to battle him. But many of the six hundred defected and joined with Wyatt who advanced on London. But, along the south bank of the Thames by London Bridge in Southwark, Wyatt paused a bit too long and found the gates to London Bridge closed and his forces retreated in disarray. Wyatt was captured and hung a few months later.[10] When Mary died in 1558 her death may very well have been seen among many to be an act of Providence.[11]

Elizabeth I, Mary's half-sister, came to the throne following Mary's death. Elizabeth, in legislation, ecclesiastical appointments, and in her response to the growing threat of Catholic Spain, allied

---

[9] Sidney E. Ahlstrom. *A Religious History of the American People* (1972), 87.

[10] Frank W. Jessup. *Kent History Illustrated* (1966), 112.

[11] Ahlstrom, 87-88.

herself with the Protestant cause. With Elizabeth came a return to Protestantism but there was no sectarian peace. Elizabeth clearly wanted to unify England; however, at one extreme there were those who still upheld the Catholic faith, and at the other, there were those who felt the Reformation had not gone far enough. Toleration of individual religious belief and practice other than that required by the Church of England was not tolerated. Elizabeth believed it was necessary to restrain all forms of religious non-conformity; necessary to require uniformity in worship; and necessary to accept the authority of the Church of England in all ecclesiastical matters in order to fulfill her goal of a united England. The Act of Supremacy of 1558 declared the Queen, "Supreme Head of the Church in England," and that rebellion against the established church was considered as rebellion against the throne, a crime of treason. Some did not heed the threat, no matter the cost.

In 1571, a group of people held in Bridewell Prison conducted worship services led by a minister, the Rev. Richard Fitz. They were "godly men and women who felt constrained to separate from the Church by Law Established." Their crime and the reason for their imprisonment was their refusal to obey the Act of Uniformity imposed by Queen Elizabeth I.[12] They represented a growing movement within England which sought to reform the Church by, among other goals, eliminating the office of bishop and altering the *Book of Common Prayer*. With increased literacy and the wider distribution of the Bible, these reformers looked at how the early Christian church was formed and wanted to recreate that pure church. The people of this movement became known as Puritans.

A treatise titled, *An Admonition to the Parliament* (1572), clearly stated the disappointment Puritans had felt with the middle-road Elizabeth was taking between the significant Catholic population and the radical Protestant reformers. "We in England," the *Admonition* decried, "are so far off, from having a church rightly reformed, according to the prescript of God's word, that as yet we are not come to the outward face of the same." This broadside offered a "detailed

---

[12] Dennis Godfrey. *Clink! The Story of a Forgotten Church*, pamphlet

and comprehensive" indictment of the Church of England. It criticized the liturgy of the worship service, the quality of the clergy, and church discipline (that is, governance). To many like-minded reformers the publication of the *Admonition* was ill timed. It's dissemination came when the new Protestant religious environment was still "thin on the ground" and the Catholic counterattack was beginning.[13]

Carl Bridenbaugh describes the social turmoil in seventeenth century England:

> [T]he religious insecurity of many an Englishman that was felt as a gnawing sense of sin [was] accompanied by a relentless search for religious security and assurance. Men and women were faced with spiritual anxiety that arose in Puritan souls about predestination and temporary faith. The question they might have asked themselves was: 'How can I know I possess saving faith that leads to eternal glory and not simply temporary faith that ends in eternal damnation?'[14]

As is the case with most reform movements, the Puritans did not choose their own name. It was, in the beginning, a term of mockery. As the movement matured and gained more followers, they accepted the name "puritan" as a positive expression of their commitment to obey the will of God as they saw it. This meant that they would observe the Sabbath day more strictly than others; they would look upon the sermon as preaching the word of God; and they also preferred the fellowship of "godly" people like themselves even

---

[13] Foster, 2.

[14] Quoted in Stephen Brachlow. "John Robinson and the Separatist Ideal," in *The Puritan Experiment in the New World*, The Westminster Conference, (1976), 9.

if it meant public ridicule.[15] With the zeal of any reforming group, the Puritans believed that their mission was not just to save souls. The Church of England, they believed, was called to provide England with moral direction; to be the steward of its culture; and to be the standard-bearer of the international Protestant Reformation on English soil. So focused were they on these four inseparable obligations that "anyone who thought they could be so much as conceived separately was [deemed] no Puritan."[16] If there ever was a single Puritan sentiment that summed up its affirmation, it was given in a New England sermon that read, "If you are heedless of your works, if you will live at random according to your hearts desire you may be sure you are no believer." Stephen Foster observed, "Minister or layman, patron and magistrate or humble professor, what made people into Puritans was, first, their own attainment of a sense of purpose, their forsaking of a life 'at random,' and second their perception of how little church and state were doing to give that same sense to England as a whole."[17]

Believing that they had a personal call from God, Puritans still needed doctrine to structure and institutionalize their "prophetic fire." Since the movement's leaders were mostly university graduates and academics, their religious stance, as one historian put it, "is generally marked by careful thought; it is an intellectual tradition of great profundity."[18] At the core of the Puritan's belief was the doctrine of "covenant theology," which held that God's design for humanity's fate was not part of some vast impersonal plan. Quite the contrary, it was very individualized due to the covenant of grace that God made with Abraham. Grace was helped along by one's faith, which was deeply personal. Puritans may have disagreed among themselves about how much a person's destiny was God's work and how much was a man's or woman's, but all agreed that the call of

---

[15] David D. Hall, ed. *Puritans in the New World: A Critical Anthology*, (2004) x.
[16] Foster, 2-3.
[17] Foster, 7.
[18] Ahlstrom, 130.

being God's elect, always initiated by God (the act of grace), would come as a personal encounter with God, therefore more was demanded of a man or woman than just an intellectual understanding of divine mercy. The Puritan believed that faith involved inward, outward and obedient preparation, as well as humility, gratitude and a fundamental commitment to walk in God's way according to His law. [19] From this interpretation of the Bible came the Puritan view of human nature, human obligation, and human destiny; their belief about nature and society; and, their vision of the hereafter. [20]

Many paid a great price for their interpretation of the Bible and Jesus's message. The dark, dank Clink prison in Southwark held a group of religious dissenters. Within the dungeon walls a church was gathered in 1586, led by two former Cambridge University scholars, John Greenwood, a clergyman and Henry Barrow, a lawyer. They asserted the right of religious liberty believing that Jesus Christ was the sole head of the Church, not any monarch or bishop. Greenwood and Barrow shared the rediscovered knowledge of the New Testament brought to the fore by the Protestant Reformation. They were called Independents or Separatists or Brownists (named after the non-conformist Robert Browne) who planted the idea of a gathered church.

Earlier, in 1517, Martin Luther, a German Roman Catholic priest and theologian, became increasingly disaffected with the church in its theology, governance and practices. Luther believed that all humans were subject to the Original Sin of Adam and Eve. The sin was so burdensome that only God's grace could save them. But even so, the sinner could never really be free from sin; even a baptized Christian would sin and sin again. Luther also believed that God's unending mercy rested on the understanding that God saves some human beings in spite of what they are and what they do. Humans remain sinners, but they are justified (accepted) still – not

---

[19] Ahlstrom, 131.
[20] Claudia Durst Johnson. *Daily Life in Colonial New England* (2008), 5.

because *they* are good but because *God* is.[21] Redemption required a deep, inward and personal mystical sense of salvation in Christ. There was no need, according to Luther, to do good deeds and avoid sin. People could even "sin boldly," knowing that salvation is by faith and not by works.[22] For many, Luther's theology and later, John Calvin's ideas for reforming the church, were not radical enough.

Calvin was a French theologian who fled from Catholic France to a more sympathetic Switzerland where he was an equal to Luther in influencing the Protestant Reformation. For the conservative Protestant reformers, like Luther and Calvin, as well as the Roman Catholic Church, the church was God's invention through which God's grace was granted. But for the more radical reformers, like Greenwood and Barrow, and later Henry Jacob and John Lothrop, the church was made up of a body of "saints" who had sought out and received God in an active way, rather than as a passive vessel receiving God's grace. The sacraments might confirm and consolidate a believer's faith, but they did not create it. What mattered to the radicals "was that each individual had received God spiritually rather than materially."[23] An active, personal relationship with God, from the point of view of the crown and crozier, was a threat to their authority.

The English Parliament passed a law in 1592, "An Act for the Punishment of Persons Obstinately Refusing to Come to Church." The act ordered "all persons above the age of sixteen, refusing to come to church, or persuading others to deny her Majesty's authority in causes ecclesiastical, or dissuading them from coming to church, or being *found present at any conventicle or meeting, under pretense of religion*, [emphasis added] shall, upon conviction, be committed to prison without bail till they shall conform, and come to church;" and that, should they refuse to recant, "within three months, they shall abjure the realm, and go into perpetual banishment; and that if they do not

---

[21] Linda Woodhead. *An Introduction to Christianity*, (2004), 170.
[22] Woodhead, 171.
[23] Woodhead, 194.

depart within the time appointed, or if they ever return without the queen's license, they shall suffer death without the benefit of clergy." It was this statute that imprisoned many Separatists including the Rev. John Lothrop and members of his Southwark congregation in 1632.[24] Despite the legal warning, the household was the "basic unit of Puritan religious life," and the Puritans refused to give up homebound religious services.[25] Having Puritan worship in one's home might not have worried the Archbishop of Canterbury but the fear was that household worship would grow into neighborhood meetings.[26]

By the last quarter of the 16th century, the Puritans, believing their "gentle words" were not persuasive sought a more direct course: "The wound groweth desperate.... It is no time to blanch, or to sew cushions under men's elbows."[27] The defenders of the Church responded by accusing the Puritans of being "deluded" in thinking that the Church must 'have the same kind of government that was in the apostles' time...and no other,' and that men might not 'in any [way] retain in the Church anything that hath been abused under the Pope.'"[28] The Puritans were treading on dangerous ground. For centuries religious dissenters from the conformist norm were branded as people who were promoting heresy or schism but Puritans believed themselves to be theologically orthodox and definitely not heretics. Even if they could convince their opponents that they were theologically pure, the Puritans could not avoid being called "schismatics." Very little could be more provocative than to be seen not only as an enemy of the church but of the state also, for which the charge was treason.[29]

---

[24] David Beale. *The Mayflower Pilgrims: Roots of Puritan, Presbyterian, Congregationalist, and Baptist Heritage* (2000), 15.
[25] Foster, 13.
[26] Foster, 13.
[27] *An Admonition to the People of England* (1589), quoted in Daniel Neal, *History of the Puritans, Vol. I* (1863), 121.
[28] Perry Miller. *Orthodoxy in Massachusetts, 1630-1650* (1965), 27.
[29] Miller, 26-28.

The Puritans were also quite concerned with the quality of the local clergy. In Kent, for example, the standard of scholarship and preaching among the clergy was much higher than it had been at the accession of Elizabeth I.[30] Puritans, in Kent agreed with all their fellow Christians that a minister was "first and foremost a man who opened and applied the Bible for his audience."[31] But, for the Puritans, their pastor was more. His ministry was not only to the larger church but also to parish life, the caring for the souls, health and well being of his parishioners. It was because of this relationship between pastor and parishioner that the Puritans wanted to have a say in who was called to be their parish vicar. They saw the ritual of a bishop laying his hands on a man and then ordaining him as a priest as a meaningless relic from the Catholic past. On the other hand, for the elders of a congregation to lay their hands on the man they called as their pastor "affecteth the ordeyners [ordainers], when they feel him for whom they pray; and the ordeyned [ordained] when he feeleth a calling and charge from God (as it were) sensibly coming upon him, and the congregation, when they see him separated from the rest, by whom they shall reap much comfort or grief."[32]

It was with a growing disappointment in the Elizabethan reforms, or lack of them, that gave form and function to the Puritan movement. Clearly any thought or action that wavered from Elizabeth's compelled religious uniformity was dealt with severely. So it was that when Elizabeth died in 1603, and the throne of England transferred from the Tudors to the Stuarts, the Puritans hoped the new monarch, James I, would be more sympathetic to them. Even as James was heading to London from Scotland to be crowned king, Puritans presented to him a document known as the "Millenary Petition," so-called because it was hoped that there would be a thousand signatures on the petition.

---

[30] Chalkin, 222.
[31] Foster, 21.
[32] Foster, 45, quoting *A Demonstration of the Truth of That Discipline Which Christ Hath Prescribed in His Word*, ed. Edwin Arber, 1588.

One of those who signed the petition was the Rev. Henry Jacob, who was to found the Southwark congregation in 1616. Jacob's attitudes on the church were to have an important influence on the development of religious radicalism in London and beyond. Not one to keep his views to himself or to a small circle of like-minded people, he published a treatise, *Reasons taken out of Gods Word and the best humane Testimonies proving a necessitie of reforming our Churches in England* (1604), calling others to support the Millenary Petition.[33] Among the requests put forth in moderate and respectful language, the Puritans asked for changes in church liturgy, such as discontinuing the requirement of the signing of the cross in baptism; changes in clerical dress; a demand that no popish opinion be taught or defended; that no ministers be ordained except scripturally qualified men; that those in the ministry who are unable to preach, be charitably removed; that ministers can marry; that church discipline be administered strictly according to the law of Christ. In response, James convened a conference in January 1604 at Henry VIII's favorite country residence, Hampton Court. This, however, was not a sincere effort on the part of the king who wanted no part of any form of representative church government. As the conference was about to begin and as the outnumbered Puritans sat in a waiting anteroom, James met with the primate of the Church of England, the Archbishop of Canterbury, and other bishops. He confided to those in the room that he had lived among Puritans since his childhood and that he detested their ways.[34] This did not bode well for a productive conference.

When a group of Puritans entered the room and spoke with the king, they expressed concerns in four areas: purity of doctrine, the ministry, reform of church polity [governance], and changes to the *Book of Common Prayer*. During the discussion on church governance, the word "presbytery" was used. Such a form of polity would have included laymen in the governing of the local churches. Even the hint of self-governance threw the king into a rage. James

---

[33] Beale, 30, n. 39.
[34] Beale, 19-20.

said that a presbytery "as well agreeth with a monarchy as God with the Devil." He angrily told the Puritans not to bring the subject up for seven years and only on his deathbed would he give them a hearing. With the conference clearly at an end, the king urged the Puritans to conform under threat of discipline.[35] To the Puritan, Protestant church polity "was every bit as important as Protestant theology." The simplest way, they thought, to bring about the Protestant reformation in England "always seemed to them to be a public debate."[36] John Udall, a Puritan martyr, warned, "Venture your bishoprics upon a disputation, and we will venture our lives, take the challenge if you dare."[37] "For in Puritan eyes the hierarchy stood self-condemned. Its abuses were evident, its pomp and luxury...."[38]

The Millenary Petition conference was not an entire failure. From it came a new translation of the Bible, the King James Version, which made it easier for people to understand what the ministers were preaching since they now, if literate, could read Scripture for themselves. Nevertheless, the price for requesting the conference was high. Almost immediately after the Hampton Court Conference three hundred non-conformist Puritan ministers were silenced, jailed or sent into exile. The fact that there were even three hundred Puritan ministers indicates widespread dissatisfaction with the Church of England. However, a split was widening among the Puritans themselves. Some wanted to *reform* the church; others wanted to *restore* the church to its original, primitive structure. Creating and sustaining independent churches was no easy task as both crown and church were against it. Even those who believed that the English Protestant Reformation did not go far enough were unsure where their dissatisfaction should take them. There were many "false starts and new beginnings" for a period of almost half a century before an Independent church took hold and prospered, even though that church, the congregation of Henry Jacob and John Lothrop, would

---

[35] Beale, 20-21.
[36] Miller, 23-24.
[37] Quoted in Miller, 24.
[38] Miller, 24.

have its share of troubles and schisms. Most who gathered in separatist congregations that failed either went into exile (most went to Holland) or went underground only to emerge in other smaller clutches of congregations.[39] In those first years of the seventeenth century, a growing group of non-separating Puritans was using language virtually indistinguishable from the Separatists. Henry Jacob, one of the group of petitioners, in 1604 expressed the view that a church is formed "by a free mutual consent of Believers joining and covenanting to live as Members of a holy Society together."[40]

The Separatists, always in the minority, were radical Puritans, who shared with the majority of Puritans their aversion to the unchanged Roman Catholic ceremonies and rituals; and to the wearing of sumptuous vestments as well as their antipathy to the authoritarian hierarchy of the Church of England. Where the Separatists went beyond the non-Separatist Puritan position was in repudiating the Church of England as a "false" church. The basis for this view was the Bible. The Separatists saw in the Scriptures the model for a Christian community: small, non-hierarchical and gathered together by a covenant agreed to be members of that community. This "rigid" position of the Separatists was often the reason for their inability to create sustainable congregations since some of their number wanted to keep communion with their Anglican parish, that is, to be free to worship there as well. Not only were the Crown and Church of England hostile to them, hostile enough to jail them; but the Puritans themselves were antagonistic toward the Separatists. Thus, the Separatists were "doomed.... to a sterile isolation among the Protestant radicals in England."[41] Not so in New England, as we will see.

---

[39] Murray Tolmie. *The Triumph of the Saints: The Separate Churches of London, 1616-1649* (1977), 2.
[40] Edmund S. Morgan. *Visible Saints: The History of a Puritan Idea* (1963), 29.
[41] Tolmie, 2.

Henry Jacob, born in 1563, grew up in Cheriton, Kent and received both his BA and MA from Oxford in the 1580s. He was ordained as a minister in the Church of England in Cheriton. Nathaniel Morton, born among the Pilgrims in Holland and later one of the Plymouth Colony's earliest historians, described Jacob as "a man of discretion, courage, and humility...in a time of persecution and danger."[42]

St. Martin's Church, Cheriton, Kent
(the tower was built in the 13ᵗʰ century)

Jacob may have first come to the attention of the crown and the church in 1597 when he questioned the passage in the Apostles' Creed that says that Christ descended into hell following his

---

[42] Nathaniel Morton. *New England Memorial,* (1669), 345.

crucifixion. One bishop had sermonized the literal truth of the statement while others, including Jacob, did not believe it to be so. Jacob bravely printed a series of treatises on the subject. Nevertheless, fearing for his freedom, Jacob left for the safety of Holland where he pastored among English exiles. But even in Holland there was a serious debate among the exiles as to whether the Church of England was a "true church." Jacob at the time believed it was, though it was in need of reform in its governance and worship.[43]

In the early days of his dissent from the doctrine and authority of the Church of England, Jacob was not a Separatist, rather he was described as "a most zealous Puritan,"[44] who had a "Puritan's horror of Separatism,"[45] but he did believe in congregationalism and he may even have coined the term. Over time, Jacob fell under the sway of the radical dissidents, but at that time he only went so far, being known as a "semi-Separatist Puritan." After a 1596 visit to a Separatist where Jacob attempted to convince him of his "errors," Jacob, as a result of the conversation, came to seek a middle way.

The Church of England was under fervent attack by men like Henry Jacob who argued constantly that the church had departed from the apostolic traditions of the ancient church which was not diocesan (hierarchical) but made up of "particular and ordinary congregations." Jacob argued that the New Testament, particularly Paul's letters, showed independent and autonomous churches spread throughout the Mediterranean. The Church of England's governance of churches in a diocesan manner, according to Jacob, corrupted the pure congregationalism of the ancient model. Central to Jacob's argument was the nature of "tradition." Jacob saw a distinction

---

[43] Walter Wilson. *The History and Antiquities of Dissenting Churches, Vol. I* (1808), 37-38.
[44] Wilson, 36.
[45] Michael Watts. *The Dissenters: From the Reformation to the French Revolution* (1978), 51.

between "tradition" and "circumstances." "Tradition" could be found in the Scriptures, i.e., the word and institutions of God, while "circumstances" were human constructs. Jacob did not see the Church as a product of a particular time and place, but as an "immemorial institution" modeled after the first Christian communities.[46]

In 1604 Jacob wrote a treatise, *Reasons Taken Out of God's Word*, which caught the eye of church authorities. In it, he advocated a congregational form of church governance, but within the parishes of the Church of England. The Bishop of London, Richard Bancroft, got word of the pamphlet and sent a messenger to Jacob asking him to come to speak to him. Jacob, suspicious of the reason for the audience, nonetheless went to see the bishop, who promptly arrested Jacob and sent him to the Clink for eight months. This caused his wife and four small children great hardship.[47]

The Clink, built in 1161, over the course of its history jailed a multitude of criminal offenders, religious dissenters, debtors and those who over-indulged in drink in the Bankside section of Southwark.[48] It is hard for us to imagine conditions inside the jail, even as we consider the worst of our modern places of confinement, but we do have some vivid descriptions of conditions in prisons of the time. The following is a contemporary description of one prison in 1604, the year of Jacob's sentencing

> Eighty men and women were huddled together in one filthy dungeon, where they were all chained by the feet to an iron ring in such a manner that they could only just change their position by sitting

---

[46] Charles W. A. Prior. *Defining the Jacobean Church: The Politics of Religious Controversy, 1603-1625* (2005), 82.

[47] Champlin Burrage. *The Early English Dissenters, Vol. I* (1912 r.), 284.
[48] http://www.southwark.gov.uk/DiscoverSouthwark/HistoricSouth wark/SouthwarkPrison.html#Anchor-Despite-43793

standing or lying down. They were eaten up by vermin, and surrounded by filth, which they had no means of removing ... whilst the stench made food loathsome.[49]

Conditions were no better in other jails. Another description is by Robert Southwell, a Jesuit whose father, a favorite of the Royal Court, visited his son in the Gatehouse Prison at Westminster. Southwell found his son "covered with filth, swarming with vermin, with maggots crawling in his sores, his face blistered, and his bones almost protruding through his skin from want of food and nourishment."[50]

After his arrest, Jacob pleaded to the bishop from jail that what he wrote was no affront to the church but, rather, a temperate and reasonable discourse:

I use not therein any distraction or reproach in any way. I do but argue and reason the matter, being no new but an ancient controversy among us. I beseech you weigh with yourself, what evil is there in this wherein nothing is said but only against ecclesiastical unwritten traditions.... I hope it is not unlawful nor new for Christian subjects lowly to desire reformation of such things at Prince's hands.... We are condemned by many and verily we ought so to be as schismatics and contentious persons if we should differ from you and yet give forth unto the world no reasons of our difference.... Last of all as I came to your Lordship freely without commandment when only my servant told me from your messenger that your Lordship would speak with me, so I beseech you deal kindly

---

[49] Robert Edmond Chester Waters. *Parish Registers in England, Their History and Contents with Suggestions for Securing Their Better Custody and Preservation* (1887), 63.

[50] Waters, 63

with me. I beseech you restore me to my poor wife and four small children, who without my enlargement [income] are in much distress.[51]

Nevertheless, the bishop demanded contrition and Jacob acquiesced to signing a document in which he agreed to conform to the authority of church doctrine, "I do here faithfully promise to disperse no more of them [the pamphlets].... Also I do promise that I will not speak against the Church government and orders now among us established by law." The following day, April 5, 1605, after a conversation with the Archbishop of Canterbury, Jacob was released.[52] Two years later, Bancroft, by then the Archbishop of Canterbury, began a broader effort to discipline the Puritan renegades. Fearing another imprisonment, Jacob fled to Middelburg, a Dutch city where many Puritans and Separatist exiles lived. While in Middelburg, Jacob continued to write and publish pamphlets.[53]

In the Netherlands Jacob deepened his convictions about what made a "visible church." The church visible "consists of all those throughout the world that profess the true religion, together with their children." It is called "visible" because its members are known and its assemblies are public. There is a mixture of "wheat and chaff," of saints and sinners. The church *invisible* "consists of the whole number of the elect that have been, are, or shall be gathered into one under Christ, the head thereof." This is a pure society, the church in which Christ dwells. It is the body of Christ. It is called "invisible" because the greater part of those who constitute it are already in heaven or are yet unborn, and also because its members still on earth are not aware of their elect status. The qualifications of membership in it are internal and are hidden. They are unseen except by Him who "searches the heart." "The Lord knoweth them that are his" (2 Timothy 2:19). Jacob believed that each parish congregation was a complete visible church unto itself in which the members

---

[51] Burrage, II, 149-151.
[52] Burrage, I, 284.
[53] Tolmie, 8.

themselves chose the minister, the deacons and who could be excommunicated, if necessary.[54] He argued that "every particular ordinary congregation of faithful people in England is a true and proper visible church."[55]

As anti-Puritan persecution grew, Jacob was moving towards what in essence was separatism. In 1605, he and other Puritans again petitioned the King, this time asking him for permission to assemble and publicly worship in a self-governing congregation. To make sure his intentions were clear and to disassociate himself from the Separatists, Jacob also added in his petition that his congregation would "keep brotherly communion with the rest of our English churches...."[56] No record of a royal response to Jacob exists, and if there was, it likely was negative. Jacob petitioned once more, this time from exile, emphasizing that the gathered church would exist under royal control along with the parish churches and in communion with them. There is no record of a royal response to this petition either.

In another treatise, published in 1606, Jacob argued that the bishops were not following the orders of the king when, if there was a dispute over rituals and church governance, the Bible should be seen as the authority in such matters, not the bishops. Jacobs asserted the bishops were dismissing dissenting ministers by force and they continued forms of worship that were of human, not divine creation. In another treatise Jacob stated, "For it is unlawful to hold any form of a church now which was not then, or hath no pattern for it under the Apostles."[57] Jacob believed that one of the basic tenets of the

---

[54] Tolmie, 8.

[55] Quoted in Watts, p. 52.

[56] Tolmie, 8.

[57] Henry Jacob, *A declaration and plainer opening of certaine points, with a sound confirmation of some other, contained in a treatise [entitled], The divine beginning and institution of Christes true visible and ministeriall church* (1612), 11.

Apostle's doctrine of church formation was that "no pastor should be obtruded [thrust] on a flock against their wills."[58]

The non-Separatist Puritans, sympathetic as they were to many of the Separatist criticisms of the Church of England, would not for one moment agree that the established church of England was not a true church and therefore should be abandoned. Their contention was that the Church of England was the true church of Christ and therefore, Separatism was an impudent and unnecessary expedient.[59] The Separatists, in response, attacked the Puritans with greater passion that they did the Anglicans. The Separatists, for their part, regarded the Church of England as a false church with a false ministry and false sacraments. They believed it was guilty of idolatry and existed without the true knowledge of God. However, according to the Separatists, the Puritans knew what the will of God was, but lacked the commitment to follow it. From the Separatists' point of view it was much less reprehensible to be ignorant of the truth, as were the Anglicans, than to know the truth, as did the Puritans, and then fail to practice it.[60]

In his writings after 1609, Jacob began his shift towards a more intentional separatist position. He began to emphasize the kingly office of Christ as the head of each congregation as a way to free the church away from its acceptance of the primacy of civil authority that is, the crown. In 1612, Jacob published *A Declaration and Plainer Opening of Certain Points* in which he contended "Christian people, whether few or many, joined together in a constant society of one ordinary congregation to serve God according to his word, are a true visible church of Christ...."[61] The most important shift of emphasis, however, came with Jacob declaring that the church

---

[58] Henry Jacob, *An Attestation of many divines that the Church-government ought to bee alwayes with the peoples free consent* (1613), 15-16.
[59] Edward H. Bloomfield. *The Opposition to the English Separatists, 1570-1625* (1981), 115-116.
[60] Bloomfield, 122.
[61] quoted in Tolmie, 9.

government should be exercised with the people's *free* consent. Now, in addition to choosing their own minister and deacons, Jacob was calling for the congregation itself to determine who could join the congregation. Still, he did not want to cut himself and others off from parish congregations.

Jacob's gradual shift towards separatism was due in large part to his friendship with the pastor of the exiled Pilgrims, John Robinson, in Leiden, the Netherlands. What was distinctive about Jacob's position, which brought him to the edge of separatism but not totally accepting it, was his belief that a gathered church didn't have to renounce communion with the established church. Even though Robinson's separatist views were influential on Jacob, his position, although separatist in language, avoided a decisive break with non-separatists.[62] Jacob was still seeking that middle way.

One intriguing question that has challenged scholars is, did Robinson influence Jacob or Jacob, Robinson? In the past some have said that it was Robinson who influenced Jacob to embrace "his sentiments of Discipline and Governance." More recently however others have said it was the other way around with Jacob influencing Robinson.[63] What is likely the case is that both influenced each other. We can only assume that this is the case because there is no written correspondence known to exist between the two. However, William Bradford, a Pilgrim leader and later governor of the Plymouth Colony, noted in his journal that he frequently traveled to Leiden and stayed with Pilgrims and that "some of us knew Mr. [Robert] Parker, Doctor [William] Ames and Mr. Jacob when they sojourned for a time in Leiden and all three for a time boarded together and had their victuals dressed by some of our acquaintance."[64] These three men, Parker, Ames and Jacob, were of great intellect and fervor and friends to each other, yet they struck out on different paths,

---

[62] R. J. Acheson. *Radical Puritans* (1990), 22.
[63] Timothy George. *John Robinson and the English Separatist Tradition* (1982), 161n.
[64] George, 160-161.

indicative of the fluidity of religious views at that time. Ames believed in non-Separating congregationalism; Parker, at first agreed, but then moved to presbyterian (a council of elders) polity. For his part, Jacob shifted from Puritan conformity to congregational independency before returning to London to gather the Southwark congregation in 1616.

In 1610 Jacob defined the form of a church this way: "A true visible and ministerial church of Christ is a number of faithful people joined by their willing consent in a spiritual outward society or body politic, ordinarily coming together into one place, instituted by Christ in his New Testament, and having the power to exercise ecclesiastical government and all God's other spiritual ordinances (the means of salvation) in and for itself immediately from Christ."[65] Such a church was complete unto itself. It could decide who were the saints; who to ordain as ministers; and how and under what circumstances members would be disciplined.[66] Who were these "visible saints" that made up a church? It certainly wasn't a matter of social status for the non-conformists believed that all were equal before God. Later on, in New England, a committee of elders would pass on the "saintliness" of a new member with the primary criteria being a profession of faith and a personal experience of Jesus Christ.

"The year 1616," one historian observed, "has never been regarded as significant in the history of the Puritans in England." Nevertheless, it was. Despite his earlier arrests for religious agitation and his exile in Leiden, Henry Jacob, courageously but quietly returned to England that year. He visited acquaintances from the earlier Puritan battles, included those who had given up the fight. With the approval of his associates and colleagues, he sought to organize a "new kind of Puritan congregation, separate from the

---

[65] Henry Jacob. *Divine Beginnings and Institutions of Christ true Visible ... Church*, 18.
[66] Ahlstrom, 133.

parish churches…."[67]

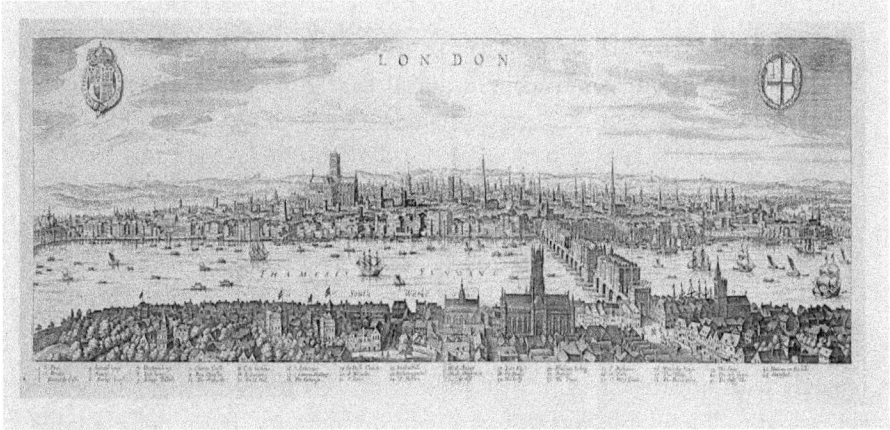

Panorama of London, 1616
(Southwark Cathedral to the lower left of London Bridge)

On an unknown day in 1616 Jacob called a group of followers together for a day of fasting and prayer and to those assembled he proposed gathering a congregation. At the end of the day those who wished to follow Jacob, in a rite of covenant, "joined both hands each with the other Brother and stood in a Ringwise [circle]: their intent being declared, Henry Jacob and each of the rest made some confession and profession of their faith and repentance; some were long and some were brief, they covenanted to "gather to walk in all God's ways as he had revealed or should make known to them.[68] Being an illegal gathering, Jacob and his congregation met in various places, in private homes, fields, ships, and warehouses. Since even before the reign of Elizabeth,

---

[67] Tolmie, 7
[68] Burrage I, 314.

29

Devout men and women had learnt that in a small company of Christian people united to each other by strong mutual affection and a common loyalty to Christ, it was possible to realize in a wonderful way the joy and strength of the communion of saints; and that such an assembly, though it had only a weaver or a wheelwright for its minister, ought have a vivid consciousness of access to God through Christ, and might receive surprising discoveries of the divine righteousness and love.[69]

At the time of the gathering of the congregation in Southwark, Jacob was fifty-three, so the founding of the Southwark church was no act of youthful radicalism. In his youth he rejected separatism, "believing that it was wrong to separate from people who 'in simplicity' partook of corrupt traditions but who were 'true Christians nevertheless.'" Yet what became primary for Jacob, at that moment in his life, was the "absolute purity of church form" giving way "to the consciences of simple believers."

Jacob soon found his "middle way" challenged by those on either side of him. No matter the ambivalence Jacob felt towards separatism, both the crown and the church saw his congregation as separatist. And no matter how Jacob tried to placate the King, his idea of what a congregation should be was, indeed, radical. Nevertheless, as much as it appeared that Jacob's church was separatist in governance it still permitted its members to have communion with Church of England parishes without censure. He believed that communion between his Southwark congregation and neighboring parish churches was both possible and permissible.[70] This meant that members of both congregations could share communion (called specifically, intercommunion) with each other. While this was the model Jacob sought and implemented, the entire congregation did not embrace it. Almost from the beginning Jacob's

---

[69] R. W. Dale, *History of English Congregationalism* (1907), 62.
[70] Acheson, 23.

congregation had been troubled about sharing communion with members of the established Church. Later, in 1630, when a member of the congregation under the leadership of Jacob's successor, Rev. John Lothrop, sought to have his child baptized, not with the Southwark congregation, but in his parish church, the division was clear. Lothrop tried to keep the congregation together by renewing their covenant but a small group of committed separatists left in anger.[71]

At about the same time as his return to London, Jacob published another tract in Middelburg, *A Confession and Protestation of the Faith of Certaine Christians*. In it he continued to implore the King to allow a gathered church. To assuage any concern on the part of James I and the Archbishop of Canterbury, Jacob asked the King to "assign to us some civil magistrate or magistrates qualified with wisdom, learning, and virtue to be...our overseers for our more peaceable, orderly, and dutiful carriage of ourselves, both in our worshipping God, and in all other our affairs."[72] But the King would not allow it. If the King or the Archbishop did not create a parish church with their authority, it was not a sanctioned congregation. For all they cared, no matter the distinctions Jacob was making vis-à-vis the Separatists, what Jacob was asking for was a Separatist, "schismatic" and, therefore, most importantly, an illegal congregation.[73]

At first, the Southwark congregation would also attend their parish church to show their commitment to be in communion with the parish, even though this still was a dangerous act. Soon the Jacob church grew and group worship was no longer practical or wise. Thus the act of intercommunion was left to the discretion of individual members.[74] But what to do with a newborn child? Where to baptize? It was one matter to share communion with the parish church and

---

[71] Acheson, 33.
[72] Tolmie, 10.
[73] Tolmie, 11.
[74] Tolmie, 14.

31

those who did not attend weekly services in the large city of London were barely noticed. But it was required that children be baptized in the parish where the parents lived. The Jacob church itself was not immune to the centrifugal forces affecting Protestant England. The issue of baptism would become an increasingly heated one in the Southwark church. Some members eventually rejected infant baptism and adopt the believer's (that is, adult) baptism.

The historical significance of the Jacob-Lothrop church, as scholars refer to it, is clear. From 1616 until 1641, it "served as a recruiting agency and training school for some of the most important sectarian leaders" of the English Civil War (1642-1651). The Jacob church "harbored within its membership rigid separatists as well as ordinary Independents…. [It] became progressively more tolerant of variant forms [of governance] and by 1642 stood in parental relationship both to strict separatist and, to what would become Baptist congregations."[75] "The Jacob church stood at the very center of a new and complex wave of nonconformity that had burst the bounds of puritan orthodoxy long before the [Civil War] had begun in England."[76]

The English Civil War, actually a series of battles and lulls, took place between 1642 and 1651. The two primary causes were political and religious. King Charles sought to unite the kingdoms of England, Scotland and Ireland. Many in Parliament thought this would dramatically increase the power of the king. In the seventeenth century Parliament was not a permanent part of English government. It was called into session by the monarch and served in an advisory capacity with one major exception the king could raise revenue through taxation only with Parliament's consent.

Charles, in addition to his desire to unite his kingdoms also sought to gain influence on the continent through his participation in Europe's Thirty Years' War (1618-1648). Although the war began as

---

[75] Tolmie, 4.
[76] Tolmie, 12.

a conflict between the Catholic Holy Roman Empire and Protestant German princes, the long war also was a battleground for the conflicting geopolitical interests of Spain, France, Sweden and Denmark. However, England's involvement in the war in Europe was disastrous and costly. Charles called upon Parliament to raise taxes to fund his military campaigns and, although Parliament supported the King's efforts to aid European Protestants, they refused to raise revenue. Parliament did not trust the king, already concerned over his marriage to a French Catholic princess and his desire to control Scotland and Wales. The disputes and distrust led Charles to dissolve Parliament. Without relying on Parliament Charles ruled with a heavy hand. While he raised money by other means, what really upset members of Parliament were his proclamations regarding religious practices. Charles also refused to accept Parliament's proposal of a constitutional monarchy. During one of the periods of armed conflict, Charles was captured, tried for treason and executed in January 1649. This led to the abolition of the monarchy and the creation of the Commonwealth of England followed by the Protectorate, under the leadership of the Puritan, Oliver Cromwell. The monarchy was restored with the return of King Charles II in 1661.

What were the differences between a Separatist congregation and a parish church? Other than the place of worship, a pious visitor might well feel at home. The sacraments of the Lord's Supper and baptism were available to all members who wished it. What was different was that any member (but men only) could preach from Scripture. Below the surface was a new structure. The pastor was supported by voluntary donations rather than the compulsory tithe that also was used to support poor members. "The Jacob church therefore fulfilled all the needs of Christian worship and fellowship for those members who wished to avoid the parish churches, and from the beginning there were members who were in practice complete Separatists."[77]

---

[77] Tolmie, 14.

By the time Jacob left the congregation for Virginia in 1622 even its most conservative members no longer considered the church a Puritan or reformed church within the Church of England.[78] The Jacob church did not ordain a layperson to lead them though they could have under their own sense of church governance. Lay preachers did "edify one another" but after a two-year hiatus, the Rev. John Lothrop, a "man of a tender heart and a humble and meek spirit," was chosen and ordained as pastor.[79]

John Lothrop was a Cambridge University graduate who was the vicar in Egerton, until he renounced his ordination in the Church of England and moved with his family to London. In Egerton, he labored faithfully as long as he accepted the rituals and government of the Anglican Church. But Lothrop got into trouble for ignoring *The Book of Common Prayer* in favor of scripturally based sermons, long ones at that.[80] When he could bear it no longer, he renounced his orders to fulfill the ministry to which his conscience and his heart had called him. In 1623, at the age of thirty-nine, with five children to support -- a sixth died in infancy -- John left the Church of England and subscribed to the teachings of the Separatists.

When King Charles I came to the throne in 1625, he tried as his father James I did, to make all political and religious institutions conform to his will. He found Parliament, with the growing influence of the Puritans, obstinate so he tried to rule without its cooperation. In 1633, Charles chose the Bishop of London, William Laud, to become the Archbishop of Canterbury and empowered him to reform the entire Church of England. Laud was equal to his king in his opposition to the Puritan movement as he sought to root out the Puritan's form of worship. For Laud, uniformity was the rallying cry and he sought to make it "clear once and for all that the Church of England, not the individual (Puritan) conscience,"[81] was the body

---

[78] Tolmie, 15.

[79] Burrage, II, 296.

[80] Acheson, 23.

[81] Antonia Fraser. *Cromwell* (1973), 46.

34

authorized to determine what practice that uniformity would take. Bishop Laud, with the concurrence of King James I and then, Charles I,

Interior of Saint James Parish Church, Egerton, Kent

had rules decreed for the excommunication of all who opposed him and his doctrines and who did not affirm that the Church of England was the true apostolic church. Any persons who separated themselves from the Church "and [took] unto themselves the names of another church not established by law" could be accused of heresy. If a person was arrested repeatedly for this offence they could be put to death. Laud was determined to impose a uniform system of worship in England. He outlawed unadorned buildings and simple services and his subordinates reviewed and licensed all publications. Any books and pamphlets that did not pass the censor were burned with great public fanfare. Laud ordered inspection tours of all parishes to determine the orthodoxy of the clergy and the use of *The Book of Common Prayer*. He directed constables and other authorities to seek out groups who were having religious meetings not in conformity with Anglican liturgy. When the authorities found such private and illegal church gatherings, they arrested all persons involved and kept them in custody for trial. Archbishop Laud prosecuted scores of Puritans in Star Chambers, long unused, revived; branding, nose splitting, amputation of ears, long imprisonments and enormous fines were common punishments. Laud was particularly interested in keeping a special watch on eleven congregations in London, one of which was John Lothrop's group. He dispatched agents to find Lothrop and his congregation in the act of illegal worship.[82]

William Kifton, an early leader of the English Baptists, was a member of the church in Southwark during the pastorate of John Lothrop; he described some of the persecution the non-conformists faced and added details about their meetings:

> I joined myself to an independent congregation, being about twenty-two years of age, with a resolution as soon as it pleased God to open a way to New England, but the Providence of God prevented me; and in a better time it pleased God to provide for me a suitable yokefellow who was with me in judgment and who was joined to the same congregation with me. Being then in the heat of the Bishop's severities we were forced to meet very early in the morning and continue together till night, and amongst them, at their desire, I improved those small abilities God was pleased to give me, and although many times our meetings were disturbed yet I was kept out of the hands of the persecutor.[83]

---

[82] Richard Woodruff Price. *John Lothropp: A Puritan Biography and Genealogy*, http://www.pricegen.com/lothropp.htm
[83] Clarence M., Waite. *Congregationalism in Scituate* (1967), 3.

William Laud
Bishop of London (1628 1633)
Archbishop of Canterbury (1633-1645)

On April 22, 1632 Reverend Lothrop's congregation met for worship as usual, in the house of Humphrey Barnet, a brewer's clerk in the Blackfriars area of London. Suddenly, a group of men led by Tomlinson, Bishop Laud's warrant officer, invaded the room. They overpowered the group and seized forty-two members, including Rev. Lothrop while eighteen escaped. Those who were arrested lingered for months in Clink prison.

On May 3rd John Lothrop, Humphrey Barnet, Henry Dod, Samuel Eaton, William Granger, Sara Jones, Sara Jacob, Pennina Howse, Sara Barbone, and Susan Wilson were brought to trial by the Anglican Church High Commission Court, an ecclesiastical court established to deal with religious dissenters. Made up of the Archbishop of Canterbury, the Bishop of London and other bishops, the High Commission was hostile to the Separatists. The Commission sought to crush the movement with long prison terms. Bishop Laud was very concerned about the Separatist problem in his diocese and the arrest of the Southwark congregation was part of his effort to ferret out their secret meetings. In 1634, in a letter to a friend, Laud described his commitment to this task, "I found in my own Diocese...divers[e] professed Separatists, with whom I shall take the best and most present Order that I can...."[84] The account of the Southwark congregation's trial that follows is taken from the court transcript that reveals the dangers to which religious dissenters were subjected if they did not conform to the practices of the Church of England.[85]

HENRY JACOB'S CHURCH, IN SOUTHWARK, INTERRUPTED BY OFFICERS, AND CARRIED BEFORE THE HOUSE OF LORDS.

The court intended to begin the inquiry by questioning Rev. Lothrop, but "Mr. Lothrop, the Minister, did not appear at the first, but kept himself out of the way awhile." Humphrey Barnet instead was the first questioned and was asked when he last attended an

---

[84] William Prynne. *History of the Troubles and Tryal of the Most Reverent Father in God and Blessed Martyr, William Laud, Lord Arch-Bishop of Canterbury* (1694), 529.

[85] Samuel Rawson Gardiner, ed. *Reports of Cases in the Courts of Star Chamber and High Commission*, (1886), 278 ff.

Anglican Church service. He replied he was at his parish church when the rest of Lothrop's congregation was arrested. He remarked that he used to attend church regularly, but his wife would not go with him.

The Bishop of York asked, "Will you suffer that in your wife?"

Without waiting for a response, the King's Advocate read the charges. Those arrested were in an unlawful conventicle [church service]. "I pray that they may be put to answer upon their oaths to the Articles [of allegiance to the Church of England], and that they set forth what exercises they used, and what were the words spoken by them."

The Advocate then turned to Henry Dod, reminding him that he was warned before at other hearings and released upon the promise that he would no longer engage in such seditious activity. Dod replied, "Good Mr. Advocate, spare that."

Dod was asked if he attended regularly his parish church, to which he replied that he used to go but now preferred to hear the "most powerful ministry."

Bishop William Laud interceded, "And therefore you hear Mr. Lothrop. What ordination hath he?"

Dod replied that he was a minister.

"Did you hear him preach and pray?" asked Bishop Laud, and then continued, "Nay, you yourself and the rest take upon you to preach and to be ministers."

Dod gave a simple "No" to Laud's accusation.

"Yes you do, and you were heard [to] preach and pray," responded Laud.

Henry Dod seemed to get bolder as Laud became more direct. "I shall be ready in this particular to confess my fault, if I am convinced to be in any."

Two of the other prisoners were then asked to take the oath of allegiance, but they asked to be excused at that time so that they might have more time to "consider and be informed of the oath [of conformity]."

The Archbishop of Canterbury, George Abbot, spoke next, "You show yourselves most unthankful to God, to the King and to the Church of England, that when (God be prayed) through his Majesty's care and ours you have been preaching in every church, and men have liberty to join in prayer and participation of the Sacraments and have catechizings and all to enlighten you, and which may serve you in the way of salvation; you in an unthankful manner cast off all this yoke, and in private, unlawfully assemble yourselves together, making rents and divisions in the Church. If anything be amiss, let it be known, if anything be not agreeable to the word of God, we shall be as ready to redress it as you, but whereas it is nothing but your own imaginations, and you are unlearned men that seek to make up a religion of your own heads! I doubt no persuasion will serve [to] turn [you]. We must take this course."

Bishop Laud was quick to point out that this group of Separatists was only a small portion of those who were meeting in the city of London. In addition, he named the other areas of the city where illegal meetings were being held. "Let these be imprisoned," he demanded. He felt they should make an example of those standing before the court.

At last, Reverend Lothrop was brought before the Commission. He was asked by what authority he preached and held religious meetings. Bishop Laud, made a far more insulting remark. "How many women sat crossed-legged upon the bed, whilest you sat on one side and preached and prayed most devotedly?"

John Lothrop was angered: "I keep no such evil company, they were no such women."

The Bishop of London and Archbishop of Canterbury asked him the same question, "Are you a Minister?"

The Bishop of St. David's, Theophilus Field, interrupted with a question about Lothrop's past involvement in the Church of England, which must have caused Rev. Lothrop some pang of conscience: "Were you not Doctor King's, the Bishop of London's [assistant] in Oxford? I take it you were; and you show your thankfulness by this?"

Lothrop's response to these two questions was that he was a minister, to which Laud asked, "How and by whom qualified?"

John Lothrop responded, "I am a Minister of the gospel of Christ, and the Lord hath qualified me." He, like the others, was asked if he would lay his hand on the Bible and take the oath but he refused.

After the court dealt with cases other than those from the Southwark congregation, Samuel Eaton and three women, Sara Jones, Pennina Howes, and Sara Barbone, all members of the Southwark church, returned to the court and were questioned. The high commissioners demanded to know why the defendants were at the forbidden church service when they should have been at Anglican meetings.

"We were not assembled in contempt...." responded Eaton.

"No, it was in contempt of the church of England," Bishop Laud thundered back.

Then Laud brought up new charges against the group, pointing out that they had first been discovered at Lambeth [in central London] and then other places, until they were captured in the Blackfriars area of London. Not only were they meeting illegally but they had in their possession books criticizing the Church of England.

The Archbishop of Canterbury continued the examination of the group of four: "Where were you in the morning before you came hither to this [Barnet's] house?" They responded that they had been with their families. Archbishop Abbot wanted to know what they did with their families that morning.

Samuel Eaton responded, "We read the Scriptures and catechized our families…and may it please this honorable Court to hear us speak the truth, we will show you what was done, and free us of the contempt of authority. We did nothing but what you will allow us to do."

At this response Bishop Laud was incredulous: "Who can free you? These are dangerous men, they are scattered company sown in all the city…. Hold [Give] them the book [the Bible, to swear on]."

Eaton responded that he dared not swear or take the oath, "though I will not refuse it, I will consider it."

Sir Henry Martin, a commissioner, interjected, "Hear, hear, you shall swear but to answer what you know, and as far as you are bound by law. You shall have time to consider of it, and have it read over till you can say it without book if you will, when you have first taken your oath that you will make a true answer."

Still, Samuel Eaton protested, "I dare not, I know not what I shall swear to."

The King's Advocate tried to explain why it was necessary that he take the oath [of conformity], since the charges against them were so serious. "It is to give a true answer to articles put into the Court against you, or that shall be put in touching this conventicle of yours, and [other] heretical tenets, and what words, and exercises you used, and things of this nature."

Once again Eaton responded, "I dare not [take the oath]."

Having no more success with these individuals than all the others, Laud turned his anger on the three principal leaders of the group, Henry Dod, Humphrey Barnet, and Reverend Lothrop. "Henry Dod, you are the obstinate and perverse ringleader of these folks, you had a fair admonition the last Court day, and we have this day assigned you to answer upon your oath."

"I hope we are not so impious, we stand for the truth; for taking the oath I crave your patience, I am not resolved upon it," Dod responded.

Barnett reminded Bishop Laud again that he was at the parish church when the group was arrested at his home on April 22nd, "but for taking the oath I desire to be resolved."

Still failing in his attempt, the persistent Laud turned to Lothrop, again. "Mr. Lothrop, hath the Lord qualified you? What authority; what order have you? The Lord hath qualified you, is that a sufficient answer? You must give a better answer before you and I part."

"I do not know that I have done anything which might cause me justly to be brought before the judgment seat of man, and for this oath I do not know the nature of it," Lothrop responded.

The court then got to the heart of the matter, "The manner of the oath is that you shall answer to that you are accused of, for schism," the King's Advocate charged.

The court's impatience at the whole proceeding became clear when the Archbishop of York threatened, "If he will not take his oath, away with him."

To which Lothrop responded, "I desire that other passage may be remembered; I dare not take this oath."

At this, the court ordered that the defendants be kept "in straight custody, especially Lothrop, for the Bishop of London said he had more to answer for that he knew of."

When it was again demanded of Samuel Eaton that he take the oath, he responded as others before, "I do not refuse it, though I do not take it, it is not out of abstinence, but as I shall answer it at the Last day, I am not satisfied whether I may take it."

Samuel Howe was called to take the oath and answer to the articles, to which he replied, "I have served the King both by sea and by land, and I had been at sea if this restraint had been made upon me and do not know what this oath is."

The King's Advocate replied that the king desired his service in obeying his laws.

Then quickly in succession, twelve of those arrested at Blackfriars were brought in again to testify and take their oath. Bishop Laud asked Pennina Howes, after she again refused to take the oath, "Will you trust Mr. Lothrop and believe him rather than the Church of England?"

"I refer myself to the word of God, whether I may take this oath or not," she stated.

The others each in turn refused to take the oath, and each remarked why they would not take the oath. Elizabeth Melborne's remark is interesting, "I do not know any such thing as a Conventicle, we did meet to pray and talk of the word of God, which is according to the law of the land."

To this remark the Archbishop of York addressed the issue directly, "God will be served publicly, not in your private house."

Bishop Laud then turned to William Granger, apparently one of the more affluent members of the group, "Granger! You look like a man of fashion, will you take your oath to answer to the articles according to your knowledge, and as far as you are bound by law?"

Like many of the others, Granger begged for time. This was the second time most had been required to take their oath, and they still asked for more time.

"I would not have any of the standers-by think that you or any of these have not had time to consider of this, you rent and tear the Church and will not submit yourself to the trial of law. You must know the justice of this Court is limited and you may be driven to adjure the Realm [driven into exile] for your offense," Bishop Laud responded.

Robert Reignolds, when asked to take the oath, expressed his concern for others besides himself. "If I have done anything against the law, let me be accused by the course of the law, if I thought this oath might be taken with a good conscience, I would take it, and I do for the present desire you, though you do not pity me, yet to pity my poor wife and small children."

"Pity your wife and children yourself, and lay your obstinacy to your conscience," replied the Archbishop of York.

Abigail Delemar, "proved to be a spirited, fractious and sharp tongued witness, giving the Court in lip as much as she got in the form of admonishment, argument, and lectures in doctrine." When required to take the oath, she asked if it was the oath of allegiance. When informed by the King's Advocate that it was to answer the truth of the charges against her, she responded, "I neither dare nor will take this oath till I am informed of it, that I may with a good conscience."

Bishop Laud informed the court that this was no ordinary, rebellious Separatist, since her husband was the Queen's servant and a strict Roman Catholic, but "she is a deep Familist and Brownist, and one of the Conventiclers taken at Blackfriars." He complained to the court that a few days earlier the group had held a fast in prison "that they might be delivered out of prison."

Delemar was asked if she would go next Sunday to church, "No, but I will go in the afternoon," she replied. When asked why she would not attend in the morning she expressed her true feeling about certain Anglican doctrine, "Because then I shall hear popish doctrine. I was once in the Whore's bosom, and these horns thrust me in, but God hath delivered me."

"What horns?" the Archbishop of Canterbury asked. "The horns of the beast," Abigail notified him.

"Whores do make horns indeed," Bishop Laud responded.

Archbishop Abbot asked Delemar, who was married to a Frenchman, if she had ever been a "papist."

"Yes, I was once in the whore's lap, and seeing that I am escaped out of it I shall, God willing, take heed how I am thrust in again."

"I see you are an obstinate woman," the Archbishop of Canterbury complained, "as all the rest of your company are."

"You persecute us without a cause. You have sent twenty-six of us to prison, but since we were imprisoned what course have you taken to inform us? Which of you have sent any man to us, or taken any pains to inform us [of the specific charges]?" Abigail protested.

The Court of High Commission continued with the hearing, declaring that several members of Lothrop's congregation were no longer in custody. Sara Barbone, it was reported, had escaped and was in hiding, so her bond was forfeited. In addition, friendly jail keepers had let seven or eight others "of those that were best able to bear it" out of prison. The recommendation was that no more be put in prison until those who were gone were recaptured. The keeper of the prison apologized and promised that he would endeavor to find them again, but Bishop Laud would not take any chances. "Let these women therefore for the honor of the Court be sent to other prisons, and the rest to be removed some to one prison and some to another."

This concluded the hearing before the Court of High Commission as they are recorded in this remarkable document. However, we find in other sources more about the hearings. One of the most valuable sources is the George Gould manuscript, which confirms the prisoners were held in several prisons, "ye space of some two years, some only under Bail, some in hold." Some of the prisoners were even allowed to write. Most prominent among them was Sara Jones, who wrote *The Answers of Mrs. Sara Jones and Some others before the Court of High Commission, Petitions to the King, Mrs. Jones Chronicle of God's remarkable Judgments that Year* and *Mrs. Jones' Grievances*. Sara Jones appears to be a very outspoken, authoritative member of the Southwark congregation.[86] Eight years after being arrested, Jones published "for her own use, *The Relation of a Gentlewoman long under the persecution of the bishops; with some observations passed in the High Commission Court during her bondage*. It certainly was unusual for a woman in the seventeenth century to publish writings and even more unusual to publicly speak on ecclesiastical matters. She firmly believed in a "gathered church." Jones, speaking in front of the High Commission in 1632, and later recounting her testimony in her *Relation*, in order to reach a wider audience, stated that it was her desire of God "that 'the great things of his law may not be a strange thing to us; but having respect to our covenant, that are in covenant together, to walk with him in all his ways, so far as we know or shall know." This is an echo of the Jacob-Lothrop church covenant. Reaffirming the covenant, Jones "believed 'that a company

---

[86] Stephen Wright. "Sarah Jones and the Jacob-Jessey Church: The Relation of a Gentlewoman", (2004)
http://www.bl.uk/eblj/2004articles/pdf/article2.pdf, 1.

of faithful people covenanting together, agreeing in the name of the Lord, make one church, endowed with power and order."'[87]

Jones also reported in *Relation* that in 1632 not only were members of the Southwark congregation arrested but "there were about forty houses burnt up on the [London] Bridge," homes of the non-conformists. Still, in face of all this Sara Jones remained hopeful, "though ye be killed all the day long, stand your ground, where ye be pillars of truth the witnesses shall be set on their feet...."[88]

The most severe treatment by the High Commission was directed at Rev. Lothrop. E. B. Huntington, a Lothrop descendent, wrote of the death of Lothrop's wife, Hannah. While he was confined to prison, "a fatal sickness was preying upon his wife, and bringing her fast toward her end." Huntington continues by quoting the *New England Memorial*, by Nathaniel Morton, published in 1669, "His wife fell sick...of which sickness she died. He procured liberty of the bishop [William Laud, who had become Archbishop in 1633] to visit his wife before her death, and commended her to God by prayer, who soon gave up the ghost. At his return to prison, his poor children, being many, repaired to the bishop at Lambeth, and made known unto him their miserable condition, by reason of their good father's being continued in close durance, who commiserated their condition so far as to grant him liberty, who soon after came over to New England.[89] During 1633, while Lothrop and others were in prison, the membership of the Southwark church increased, so much so as to be a real disadvantage to the welfare of the congregation because of loose lips and the bishop's spies.[90]

The Public Record Office in London records show that Rev. Lothrop was released from prison on April 24, 1634. Henry Jessey,

---

[87] Wright, 3-4.

[88] Jones quoted in Wright, p. 6,

[89] E. B. Huntington, ed. *Genealogical Memoir of the Lo-Lathrop Family* (1884), 25.

[90] Burrage, I 34.

who succeeded John Lothrop as minister of the Southwark congregation, wrote a series of recollections known as the "Jessey Memoranda," which recorded the early years of the congregation. From the memorandum we have a contemporary account of the final days of John Lothrop with his congregation in Southwark:

> At last...there being no hopes that Mr. Lathrop should do them any further Services in ye Church, he having many motives to go to New England if it might be granted after the death of his wife, he earnestly desiring ye Church would release him of that office which (to his grief) he could in no way perform & that he might have their consent to go to New England, after serious consideration had about it, it was freely granted to him.

The discussion with his congregation became a serious threat to Lothrop being arrested again, since he was in violation of his parole. Lothrop went into hiding and warrants for the arrest of Lothrop and Samuel Eaton were issued on three separate occasions.

The final entry in the state papers pertaining to John Lothrop, dated February 19, 1635, noted that the defendants failed to appear on the warrants, and they should be imprisoned again. However, the search by the authorities for John Lothrop was in vain, for he had set sail for the American colonies in late July or early August. He arrived in Boston on September 18, 1634 on the ship *Griffin*.[91] One of his fellow passengers was Anne Hutchinson, who, within a few years after her arrival, was banished from the Massachusetts Bay Colony for heresy and for "traducing" the colony's ministers.

It was on the crossing of the Atlantic Ocean that, according to one account, John Lothrop was reading his Bible and fell asleep when a spark from his candle fell upon an open page and burned a

---

[91] Huntington, 25.

hole through several pages. He repaired the damaged pages and then, according to family tradition, supplied the missing texts from memory, since no other Bible was accessible to him. Today, the Bible is on display in the Sturgis Library in Barnstable, Massachusetts. Although tradition has it that the damage to the Bible was aboard the *Griffin*, Mary Briggs, in her work, *We and Our Kinsfolks*, presents another theory on where the Lothrop Bible was burned. "Either on shipboard, or, as is more probable, in Lambeth Gaol [Jail], a spark from his candle fell upon its open page and burned a ragged hole through many leaves. He patched this neatly with paper on which he supplied the missing words. If, [as] family tradition has it, these restorations of the text were from memory, there being no other Bible accessible, we cannot believe that the accident occurred on shipboard, for such a scarcity of the Word of God in a company including so many church members is no more credible than creditable." [92]

Samuel Deane, in his history of Scituate writes, "From these dissenters, we are descended. They were too conscientious to conform; they were too intrepid to be compelled by the fear of burning at the stake; they were hunted from covert to covert at home and longed, like the panting hart, for shelter and cooling streams...."[93]

---

[92] Keith W Perkins. "John Lothropp"
http://www.cumorah.org/libros/ingles/Regional_Studies_in_LDS_Hi
story_British_Isles_-_Various_authors.html, n. 48
[93] Deane (1825), 11.

Chapter Two

Satuit

The Pilgrim settlement at Plymouth was not the first English-speaking colony in America. In 1584 Sir Walter Raleigh was granted a royal charter by Queen Elizabeth to colonize a portion of what later would become the Virginia Colony and is now North Carolina. By 1590 all the settlers of Roanoke Colony mysteriously disappeared. In April 1606 King James issued a royal charter to the Virginia Company for the purpose of establishing a British colony in Jamestown (present day Virginia). Most of the investors and settlers were highborn landowners and wealthy merchants eager to exploit the resources and bounty of the New World. The settlement at Jamestown in 1607 (and the later Massachusetts Bay Colony) was clearly a commercial enterprise; however, the spread of the Christian gospel was a high priority as well. The Jamestown settlers were primarily Presbyterians from Scotland and Anglicans from England. Both groups were loyal to king and church. In fact, before leaving for Virginia they were required to take the Oath of Supremacy.

The purpose of the Plymouth colony, on the other hand, was singular. It was an "experiment in Christian living." The Pilgrims came to New England to carry on their lives as the first Christians did. To be sure, the Pilgrims who came on the Mayflower and those who followed them to Plymouth sought a better life and economic self-sufficiency. Still, no one can deny that the driving force for this emigration to the New World was "English Puritanism desiring to realize itself." They sought to restore the primitive, apostolic church 'pure and unspotted by human accretions or inventions.'"[1]

Unlike Jamestown, the Plymouth colony was not established by a royal charter. In the absence of a royal charter, the Plymouth colonists initiated their organization of a government and legal structure by creating a "civil body politick."

> In the name of God, Amen. We whose names are underwritten, the loyal subjects of our dread sovereign, Lord King James, by the Grace of God, of Great Britain, France, and Ireland, King, Defender of the faith, etc. Having undertaken for the glory of God, and the advancement of the Christian faith, and the honor of our King and country, a voyage to plant the first colony in the northern parts of Virginia [as the east coast from present day North Carolina to Maine was called]; do by these presents solemnly and mutually, in the presence of God and one another, covenant and combine ourselves together into a civil body politick, for our better ordering and preservation, and furtherance of the ends aforesaid; and by virtue hereof, do enact, constitute, and frame such just and equal laws, ordinances, acts, constitutions, and officers, from time to time, as shall be thought most meet and convenient for the general good of the colony; unto which promise all due submission and obedience.

The Pilgrims were following their theology that people by mutual consent "combine together" to form a governmental structure which gives its due to King James but nevertheless

---

[1] Samuel Eliot Morison. *The Intellectual Life of Colonial New England*, (1980), 6-8.

exacts "laws…for the general good of the colony…." Thus, the Pilgrims expanded their view of their congregations toward a view of government.

Forty-one adult men of the original Plymouth settlers signed this understanding on November 11, 1620, and it provided a first step toward setting up a government that could claim legitimate authority over the conduct of Colony inhabitants.[2] Legal historians often emphasize that the Plymouth Colony applied a combination of English common law and Mosaic Law in regulating the daily affairs of the settlers. This use of religious authority was also beneficial in establishing the Colony's own authority to govern. What they lacked without royal charter was often obtained by invocation of the Colony's service of the greater "glory of God." Interestingly, when Plymouth Colony's General Court later ordered towns to craft ordinances for managing the local, day-to-day affairs of the townspeople, the General Court required that such local regulations be made with fidelity to the laws of the "Govern[ment] of the General Court, and not of England itself…."[3]

The early Plymouth settlers were a mixture of poor and what today would be considered "middle class." They were wool combers and tailors; weavers and coopers; carpenters, tanners and farmers. Later arrivals brought doctors, lawyers and merchants. Life was harsh no matter what one's trade and the early settlers had more immediate concerns than matters of theology. "Men who had to covet, miserly, the kernels of corn for their daily bread, and till the ground, staggering through weakness from the effect of famine, can do but little in settling the metaphysics of faith…."[4] A review of the early records of the coroner show that living in the Plymouth colony was dangerous as well. Death from disease and the elements was common. Of non-natural deaths, many people drowned for the

[2] Edwin Powers. *Crime and Punishment in Early Massachusetts, 1620-1692: A Documentary History* (1966), 27-28.
[3] http://www.histarch.uiuc.edu/plymouth/ccflaw.html#I
[4] George B. Cheever. *The Journal of the Pilgrims* (1849), 112.

ocean, rivers and numerous ponds in the area presented a new and hazardous environment to people who could not swim. Those who went out hunting and fishing were subject to canoe accidents. Sawmills, alcohol, suicide and, in a few cases, murder, also took their toll.[5]

Most, but not all, settlers in the Plymouth colony were churchgoers. Those who did were firm believers in the Puritan ethic that taught that a man or woman could serve God in their chosen calling as much as a minister. Christians, they believed, were meant to engage the world not retreat from it. This doctrine of the calling, that one could serve God by nobly fulfilling a function determined by the conditions of this world, proved one's right to a place in heaven with God and Christ.[6] Being three thousand miles away from England, the Pilgrims and later their Puritan neighbors to the north were able to institute reforms in the church that they would never have been able to do back home. The "Congregational Way" was quite different from the structure of the Church of England and laid the groundwork for the manner in which civil society was governed in the Plymouth Colony. Congregations throughout the colony were a group of equals; each was equal in authority to each other, none being inferior to a higher body. The authority to make decisions on aspects of church governance rested with the congregation alone. Each local church was gathered by a covenant among its members, who, in order to become a member, had to express a conversion experience.

"The Congregational Way" suggested an independence of the individual churches from a superior and centralized authority. But, while the churches governed themselves independently, their similar styles facilitated cooperation and consultation. The Cambridge Platform of 1648, a statement agreed to by many of the Pilgrim/Puritan churches in the Plymouth and Massachusetts Bay colonies, laid out an autonomous congregational organization with a

---

[5] http://www.histarch.uiuc.edu/plymouth/inquest.htm
[6] Morison, 9-10.

communal covenant: to care for each other's (congregation's) welfare; to offer advice on a point of contention within another church; to admonish a neighboring church for straying from doctrine or practice; by permitting members of one church visiting another to share in communion; to recommend members when they move from one community to another and; to assist churches in their time of need. From this beginning arose an association of ministers who would attend ordinations, exchange pulpits and arbitrate disputes between minister and congregation and between separate congregations. As long as these arrangements and councils were just advisory and not authoritative, they provided the best means of keeping doctrine uniform among congregations and their ministers.[7]

Fewer than twenty university-educated men came to Plymouth in its first thirty years and only three remained, all ministers. Because Plymouth was relatively poor it had a hard time attracting clergy of high stature and quality. Oddly, it took nine years to call its first minister and the first few ministers' tenures were brief. By 1665, most communities in the colony had to settle for lay leaders because they could not financially support ministers.[8] Scituate was different on both counts. From the founding ministry of Lothrop to that of Charles Chauncy and Henry Dunster, Scituate's ministers were of great distinction and learning.

On September 18, 1634 John Lothrop, his family and some thirty members of the Southwark church arrived in Boston on the *Griffin*. Within ten days he and the others left Boston for Scituate, where a number of people, "the Men of Kent" had already settled.

---

* The discrepancy between the dates is due to Protestant England's refusal to replace the Julian calendar with the Gregorian calendar as most Catholic countries had done beginning in 1582. In the Gregorian calendar the first day of the new year was March 25th. It was not until 1752 that England adopted the Gregorian calendar with January 1st as the start of the new year.
[7] Francis J. Bremer. *The Puritan Experiment* (1995), 112.
[8] Bremer, 54.

Lothrop's arrival was "long expected" by the Scituate residents.[9] Lothrop may have known Timothy Hatherly who was from Southwark and had settled in Scituate after arriving in Plymouth in 1623. Hatherly made annual trips back to England and considering his status in Scituate and the Plymouth colony, he may have recruited Lothrop to come to Scituate.[10]

Lothrop's records begin in 1634 before the Scituate church was formally gathered. A small group met for a day of humiliation prayer and fasting on November 6, 1634 at James Cudworth's house, and they had another fast on Christmas day before they joined in a formal covenant on January 8, 1634* – during yet another fast. This is the date that is recognized as the gathering of the Scituate congregation. A church covenant was a statement that articulated the initial vision of a religious community. A covenant spoke of a divine relationship with the individual members of the religious community and they to each other.[11] On January 19th the congregation called Rev. Lothrop as its minister and ordained him by the practice of the laying on of the hands by the elders of the congregation.[12]

John Lothrop was born in Etton, Yorkshire in 1584. He founded one of the most distinguished families in American history. Among his descendants are Presidents Ulysses S. Grant, Franklin Delano Roosevelt, George Herbert Walker Bush and George Walker Bush; poet Henry Wadsworth Longfellow and his brother, Unitarian minister, Samuel; Supreme Court Justice Oliver Wendell Holmes, Jr.; artist, Georgia O'Keefe; presidential candidate Adlai Stevenson; banker J. P. Morgan; and Joseph Smith, founder of the Church of Latter Day Saints (Mormon).

---

[9] Letter from James Cudworth to Rev. John Stoughton, December 1634, *New England History and Genealogical Register*, Vol. XIX, 101-104.
[10] Robert Charles Anderson. *The Pilgrim Migration: Immigrants to Plymouth Colony, 1620-1633* (2004), 234.
[11] Weir, 5.
[12] Deane, 59.

Lothrop began his studies at Christ Church College at Oxford in 1601 and then went to Queens' College at Cambridge and graduated with a BA in 1605 and an MA in 1609. The cause of Lothrop's transfer from Oxford to Cambridge may have been the religious climate at both universities. Although Oxford had at one time taken a tolerant position toward the Puritans, by the time Lothrop arrived the mood had changed. Cambridge, on the other hand, was moving toward a more liberal view of dissenters against the Church of England and, as a result, became the intellectual center of this dissension. Although he was to become an Anglican minister, it may have been at Cambridge that Lothrop first developed his Puritan leanings and disposition. When he was twenty-three, he began his church service as a deacon in the Church of England at Bennington, Hertfordshire. By age twenty-five, after receiving his master's degree, he moved to Kent, where he became curate, or minister, at the parish church in Egerton, forty-eight miles southeast of London.

Kent, being the center of religious dissention, was fertile soil for Lothrop to explore his ideas on theology and church governance. For fourteen years he tended to his flock while harboring growing doubts about the authority and authenticity of the Church of England. To be sure, as a parish curate, he had security and status, both financial as well as emotional, but it appears he voluntarily gave that up when he left Egerton for London. In 1624 he replaced Henry Jacob as the pastor of the first Independent congregation in Southwark. There, as we have seen, Lothrop faced poverty, ridicule and prison forcing him and his family to leave for New England.

A prominent historian of the period, Champlin Burrage, points out the significance of the Jacob-Lothrop Southwark congregation for New England,

> The majority of the Puritan churches of New England [in the Massachusetts Bay Colony] did not even know what the church polity of the Plymouth Congregation was, and hence did not derive views

from the congregation of the Pilgrim Fathers [the Leiden church].... While the Plymouth church may at first have differed slightly from more professed followers of Henry Jacob, i.e. the Independent Puritans, it was nevertheless, well leavened with "Jacobite" doctrine. Hence American Congregationalism, as well as that in England, is to be traced back to...the Independent or Congregational Puritanism...[that Jacob helped shape].[13]

Over the course of its history, the Scituate congregation has been known by a variety of names: The Northerly Society in Scituate, The North Precinct, The First Church of Christ and Precinct in the Town of Scituate, The Church of Christ in the North Precinct, The First Church and Parish in Scituate, The First Church and Congregation in Scituate, The First Percent, The First Parish in Scituate, Church and Society of the First Parish in Scituate, The First Parish (Unitarian) Church of Scituate, North Parish in Scituate, First Parish Church of Scituate-Unitarian, and the First Parish Unitarian Universalist Church of Scituate.

Among the early colonial settlements, Scituate might have been the most contentious parish in the Plymouth Colony. It was bound to happen throughout the Plymouth and Massachusetts Bay Colonies that there would be a growing restlessness within the parishes. At first it may have been due to arguments over the location of the meetinghouse or the rates (taxes) to fund it. It may even have been due to which family got to buy which pew. But disagreements between minister and parishioners were rare in the early days. "'Evil speaking against the minister' had carried a heavy penalty in the early years and few had dared."[14] In most places, the minister was held in high regard not only because of his position but also because of his being learned. Not so in Scituate. From the very beginning the

---

[13] Burrage, I, 34.

[14] Ola Elizabeth Winslow. *Meetinghouse Hill, 1630-1783* (1972), 197.

Scituate congregation was in turmoil 0during the ministries of Reverends Lothrop and Chauncy.

Since First Parish Scituate was among the earliest churches to gather, the process of its founding was probably the model for those that came after. As they had in Southwark, men were the "pillars" of the church and would question each other to satisfy themselves that they were "visible saints," all of high character and sound in their beliefs in addition to recounting their religious epiphany. Once chosen, the "pillars" agreed to a covenant and then examined others who sought to become members of the church who, in turn, joined in agreeing to the covenant.[15] Women were allowed to become members of congregations even if their husbands were not and they were most of the "visible saints" in the seventeenth century.[16]

Scituate was fortunate that many of the early settlers were educated, intelligent men and it was expected that their minister would be of the same character.[17] Some of those "pillars" and "visible saints" in the settlement when Lothrop arrived were: Timothy Hatherly, James Cudworth, William Gilson, Anthony Annable, Humphrey Turner, Henry Cobb and Edward Foster.[18] Many of these names are familiar street names in present day Scituate. Timothy Hatherly was born in Devonshire and later became a wealthy felt maker in Southwark. Having commercial connections in Holland, Hatherly became familiar with the Leiden Separatists. It was this association that later may have brought him in contact with Henry Jacob. He arrived in the Plymouth Colony in 1623 aboard the *Anne*, stayed in Plymouth until his home and possessions were destroyed in a fire. He traveled north to the abandoned colony of Wessagusset (now Weymouth) before returning to London to re-establish his fortune. Having earlier explored and traveled the coast from

---

[15] Bremer, 100.

[16] Bremer, 178.

[17] Deane, 92.

[18] Daniel E Damon, "History of Scituate and South Scituate" in *History of Plymouth County, Massachusetts* (1884), p. 405.

Plymouth to Wessagusset, Hatherly and his business partners applied to the Plymouth General Court for a land grant which was approved. He returned to New England in 1632 where he lived in Plymouth for two years before moving to Scituate. There, Hatherly found a village that was built under the direction of his agent and nephew, Edward Foster. The buildings were a "compact cluster of homes" in a "defensive arrangement" along Kent Street, south of the Satuit Brook that gave the village its name.[19] The village was, for the most part, neatly laid out with house lots of four-and five-acres. As the town quickly grew, so did the lots. All paled in comparison to Hatherly's 200-acre farm.[20] In his work, *Early Planters of Scituate*, Harvey Hunter Pratt says that Hatherly, no less than the Plymouth Pilgrim leaders, Governors William Bradford, Edward Winslow and John Carver, was a Separatist "of the most pronounced character".[21] Through his generosity, Hatherly made it possible for the Scituate church to seek out like-minded clergy and sustain them by providing a salary, land and a parsonage.[22] After his arrival, Rev. Lothrop was given land by Hatherly that was located on the southeast side of the Colman's Hills section of the settlement (where the transfer station and the Widow's Walk Golf Course are presently located). Lothrop later sold the twenty-acre lot with "one dwelling house with barn and outhouses, uplands, marsh ground" back to Hatherly in 1640."[23]

In addition to Hatherly, there were others who warmly greeted Lothrop upon his arrival. James Cudworth was born in Somerset and was a salter. He was a loyal supporter of Rev. Lothrop and a friend of Hatherly. Cudworth became a deputy to the Plymouth General Court and served as a general during King Philip's War. William Gilson, a miller, built one of the first windmills in the

---

[19] Stephen R. Valdespino, *Timothy Hatherly and the Plymouth Colony Pilgrims* (1987), 57.
[20] Valdespino, 71 n6.
[21] Harvey Hunter Pratt. *The Early Planters of Scituate* (1929), 20.
[22] Valdespino, 66.
[23] Robert Charles Anderson. *The Great Migration Begins, Vol. II* (1995), 236.

colony and also served in the colonial government.[24] Anthony Annable was born in Kent in 1599. He and his family left Scituate in 1639 with Rev. Lothrop along with the Cudworths (who later returned), the Cobbs as well as other families and founded the town of Barnstable on Cape Cod. Henry Cobb was born in England and was an elder of the Scituate church. Humphrey Turner was born somewhere in England in 1594. He was a tanner by trade and is described as being a "useful and enterprising man."[25] He served the town as constable, surveyor and juryman. As a juryman, Turner, along with Edward Foster sat at the trial of the first white men accused of murdering a Wampanoag. The defendants were found guilty and hung.[26] Although his trade in Scituate is unknown he became a tavern keeper in Barnstable. Foster was born in Kent in 1590 and was Scituate's first lawyer. Though there was not much work for him in those early days, he did serve as agent for his uncle, Timothy Hatherly.

According to Samuel Deane, there was a "cheerful union" between the Southwark people and the Scituate settlers and so it "therefore may safely be concluded that they entertained nearly the same religious sentiments, and agreed in the main, in practice." However, the peace and harmony Lothrop sought in the New World was not to be. As Deane puts it, the church was not "perfectly united."[27] When John Lothrop traveled across the Atlantic he brought not only many parishioners from the Southwark congregation but also a dispute that had caused great concern in Southwark and was to bedevil Lothrop and his successors, particularly Charles Chauncy. Amidst the turmoil and disputes surrounding dogma, the supremacy of the Bible and the authority of the bishops, there arose in England a controversy regarding the mode of baptism. Many radical Puritans and Separatists, relying on the authority of the Bible, saw no biblical example of infant baptism in

---

[24] Deane, 275.

[25] Deane, 360.

[26] Pratt, 315.

[27] Deane, 59.

the Scriptures. They cited Mark 16:16: "He that shall believe and be baptized, shall be saved." Where, they asked, was there a direct instruction in the Bible for the baptism of children? Citing Mark, these radicals accepted as true the "believer's baptism," that is, baptism of an adult who had made an expression of Christian faith. Until the dispute was settled, the definition of who was a member of a congregation hung in the balance but in the meantime the Southwark and Scituate congregations (and their successors in England) were stuck "in a conflict of contradictory loyalties."[28] Baptists* confronted radical Separatists reminding them that they were baptized in the Church of England which the former no longer held was a "true" church. The issue was not settled among the members of the Southwark congregation that came to Scituate with Lothrop and there were people already in Scituate who had differing views. At least in the more liberal Plymouth Colony the dispute could be aired. In the Massachusetts Bay Colony, the more conservative Puritans required orthodoxy, causing Roger Williams, a believer in adult baptism and an early proponent of religious freedom, to be banished for sedition because of his criticism of the Kings James I and Charles I and the church. Williams traveled by foot to the head of Narragansett Bay and founded the Rhode Island colony.

In the midst of the controversy over the manner of baptism another dispute arose. Scituate was growing in population. When Rev. Lothrop arrived in 1634 there were nine houses. Four years later there were fifty-one. It didn't take long for settlers to move further inland, many along the banks of the North River. With the population growing and moving inland there were calls for moving the meetinghouse to a more central location. This added to tensions in Rev. Lothrop's congregation.

The meetinghouse, a town's only public building, stood at its center and was the "most significant mark" the people would make

---

[28] Tolmie, 51.

* The designation, "Baptist" didn't come into use until the 1640s (Burrage I, 26).

on the local landscape. It declared to all that religion was the fundamental purpose of the community and its highest priority.[29] In Scituate, according to Deane's *History*, a meetinghouse had already been erected by the time Lothrop had arrived, but this is not likely, since the founders of the congregation gathered at Cudworth's house on January 18th, 1634. When a meetinghouse was built, probably around 1636, it was about a half-mile from Scituate harbor hill on what is now called Meetinghouse Lane close to the Men of Kent Cemetery. That first meetinghouse stood for the ministries of John Lothrop, Peter Saxton, Christopher Blackwood, Charles Chauncy, Henry Dunster and Nicholas Baker.[30] It probably was like most meetinghouses in the Plymouth colony in style and construction. The building was unheated. It was almost square in area and, in keeping with Puritan simplicity, it's interior was plain with no ornamentation, no statues or stained glass windows. This practice continues today, as it is rare for a Pilgrim/Puritan church that later became a Unitarian church, to have stained glass windows. On the other hand, stained glass windows were common in churches that later became Universalist or were founded as Universalist congregations. There is a belief, not substantiated but plausible, that the clear windows in the meetinghouse had another purpose. For the Pilgrims and the Puritans, the emphasis in worship was not on rituals or ceremony; what was important in their services was the Word of God. Reading the Bible made New England the most literate British Colony. People would bring their Bibles to worship or the Thursday lecture. The clear windows provided as much natural light as possible into the meetinghouse making the reading of Scripture easier. Only ordained ministers gave the sermon and the sermon's source was not the minister's wisdom but Scripture. Not only were sermons given on Sunday they were delivered on every significant occasion in the community.[31] Wooden benches were the pews and were owned by church members or, if one could not afford a family pew, then the

---

[29] Harry S. Stout. *The New England Soul* (1986), 13-14.
[30] Deane, 30.
[31] Stout, 24.

church would assign one to a member. It is most probable that the well-to-do families had the seats closest to the pulpit.

In a New England congregation, the church leaders consisted of the minister, who would visit members and tutor the youth; the "teacher" who was to emphasize doctrine (Scituate never had one); and the elders who were responsible for the discipline of the members of the congregation. Along with the pastor, the elders would visit congregation members and warn those who were misbehaving by not coming to church, or drinking too much, or being ostentatious in clothing and home furnishings.[32] Another officer of the church was the deacon who handled the business affairs of the congregation. Finally, there were the "tithing men" who kept order in the meetinghouse. They would keep members awake by poking them with a long rod with a feather at one end and a ball on the other. Apparently in deference to gender differences, a brush of the feather on their face awakened women, while men were struck on the head with the ball end.[33]

The town of Scituate was granted incorporation by the General Court of Plymouth in late 1636. To mark the occasion, Rev. Lothrop called for a day of humiliation and prayer.[34] Despite his blessings and prayers for the prospering of the town and the growth of the congregation, Lothrop was looking to remove himself from the congregation's contentiousness. Over a period of months Lothrop would call for days of humiliation and prayer to provide guidance's for the congregation to find an answer to its dispute. He noted in his diary on February 22, 1637 that his call for such an occasion was done to ask for two more deacons, "but especially for our removal." When prayer was not enough, Lothrop petitioned the governor and General Court. He wrote to Governor Thomas Prence, "Many grievances attend me, from them which I would be

---

[32] Johnson, 18.

[33] Johnson, 18.

[34] "Scituate and Barnstable Records," *New England Historical and Genealogical Record, Vol. IV.*

freed, or at least have them mitigated, if the Lord see it good." Lothrop asked Prence for permission to move to what is now Rochester, Massachusetts, then known as "Seipican." Court documents indicate that James Cudworth, William Gilson, Anthony Annable, Henry Cobb, Edward Foster, their families and others would join Lothrop in the move.[35]

Seipican was known to be "haunted" by pirates and French privateers along the coast. Hostile natives also were a cause for concern. Scituate's Lawrence Litchfield explored the area to determine the need and extent of defense planning. Almost certainly based on Litchfield's report, Lothrop and the others changed their minds and petitioned the court to move to the safe harbors and valuable salt hay marshes of Mattakeese (now Barnstable on Cape Cod), where Lothrop and a majority of the Scituate congregation removed themselves in 1639.[36]

As he could not resolve the baptism controversy in London, Lothrop couldn't settle it in Scituate either. The new Barnstable congregation was also divided on the matter, so much so that Lothrop felt compelled to publish a treatise in 1644 titled, "A Short Form of Catechism of the Doctrine of Baptism. In Use in These Times That Are So Full of Questions." Barnstable was split three ways with many members holding to immersion, others to adult immersion only and a third party believed in the immersion of both infants and adults.[37]

The fact that the majority of congregants moved to Barnstable with Rev. Lothrop would have consequences for the ministry of Charles Chauncy. Rev. Lothrop, knowing that those who remained in Scituate would be left without a church, sought and received permission from the General Court to gather the remaining

---

[35] Deane, 169-170.
[36] Waite, 9.
[37] Henry Melville King. *The Baptism of Roger Williams* (1897), 48, 52.

members into a new church body.[38] This was an act of kindness and generosity born of Lothrop's sense of responsibility toward the non-conformist cause. Nathaniel Morton, the contemporary chronicler of life in the Plymouth Colony, described Rev. Lothrop as being "a man of … humble heart and spirit – lively in dispensation of the word of God, studious of peace, furnished with godly contentment, willing to spend and be spent for the cause and Church of Christ."[39] Before Lothrop left he gathered those who would remain in Scituate (about eight men) and asked if they agreed to become a church and covenant "to walk together in the ways of God, according to His revealed will." The men agreed to separate from Lothrop's church and become their own.[40]

Though the discord over baptism was muted somewhat (though briefly, as we shall see) with the removal of Lothrop and others, the problem of the church's location remained. Mr. William Vassall, a wealthy member of the Massachusetts Bay Colony, joined the Scituate church in 1636 when he bought a sizable farm along the North River and built a home he called Belle House Neck, near the present intersection of Neal Gate Street and Chief Justice Cushing Highway. Vassall appealed persistently to the Plymouth General Court to create a second Scituate parish that would allow settlers inland and along the North River to gather their own church. But since the population of Scituate was still small and scattered there was little likelihood that Vassall would get his way with the General Court. That is, until the Rev. Charles Chauncy came to Scituate.

The first Scituate thanksgiving was on December 22, 1636:

[I]n ye Meetinghouse, beginning some half an hour before nine & continued until after twelve a clocked, ye day being very cold, beginning with a short prayer, then a psalm sang, then more large in prayer, after

---

[38] Waite, 9.
[39] Deane, 170.
[40] Waite, 9-10.

that an other Psalm, & then the Word taught, after that prayer - & the[n] a psalm, - Then making merry to the creatures, the poorer sort being invited of the richer." The next thanksgiving on October 12, 1637 was "performed much in the same manner aforesaid, mainly for these two particulars. 1. For the victory over the Pequot's, ye 2. For Reconciliation betwixt Mr. Cotton and the other ministers.[41]

The church altogether observed thirty-four days of humiliation and fasting but only nine thanksgivings days between 1634 and 1653. Could this be a sign that those years were particularly harsh; that there was little to be thankful for; and that the more numerous days of humiliation, fasting and prayer were beseeching God for his blessing?

For many years, particularly after the publication of Deane's *History of Scituate,* it was believed that the first minister of the Scituate church was a Giles Saxton (or Sexton). More modern sources have revealed this not to be the case. Even Deane notes that prior to Lothrop's arrival there was no gathered church with a minister, though certainly religious services of some sort were held. Citing Cotton Mather's *Magnalia Christi Americana* (1702), Deane refers to a Mr. Saxton, whose first name was not known but Deane believed it to be "Giles." Deane quotes Mather's description of Saxton as a Yorkshireman and "a studious and learned person, and a great Hebrician." Many historians since Deane have repeated this error that is also etched on the monument at the Men of Kent Cemetery on Meetinghouse Road in Scituate.

The New England Historical and Genealogical Review and the earlier *Thorseby's History of the Church of Leeds* identify *Peter* Saxton as a minister who served the Scituate congregation briefly in 1640. Saxton was born in Bramley, Yorkshire and attended Trinity College

---

[41] "Scituate and Barnstable Records," *New England Historical and Genealogical Record, Vol. IV.*

at Cambridge. He served as rector in Edlington but after years of serving the Anglican Church he began taking on Puritan ideas. He increasingly became alienated from the doctrines and rituals of the church and went so far as to call the surplice, a white vestment with open flared sleeves, "the Whore's smock." Such public pronouncements put his freedom, if not his life, at risk and so in 1640 he fled to New England and came to Scituate. In England Saxton was known to be a "powerful preacher," and "a learned and studious man." But his stay in Scituate was brief due to "some unhappy contention" in the colony, probably the continuing controversy over baptism. Saxton returned to England where all apparently was forgiven. He served a church in Leeds until his death in 1651.[42]

The ministry following Peter Saxton's was another brief one. In 1641, the Rev. Christopher Blackwood served as minister. Blackwood, like Saxton, was born in Yorkshire around 1608. He attended Pembroke College at Cambridge where he received both his BA and MA. He served as vicar at the parish church in Stockbury, Kent in 1631 and came to New England in 1640. He preached briefly in Scituate. When Lothrop left Scituate he sold his home back to Timothy Hatherly, who then sold it to Blackwood. Very little is known of Blackwood's time in Scituate other than his departure. He left New England in 1642 to return to England at the outbreak of the English Civil War, between the Puritan Parliament and King Charles.[43] In England he had a "dramatic" conversion to Baptist views, calling infant baptism, "a human tradition, and that it contained more evil in it than ever I could have imagined." Blackwood served a congregation in Staplehurst, Kent and then was a chaplain in Ireland with Charles Fleetwood, the commander-in-chief of the Parliamentarian forces in Ireland, where Blackwood was

---

[42] *New England Historical and Genealogical Register, Volume XVI* (1860), 123-124.

[43] Susan Hardman Moore. *Pilgrims: New World Settlers and the Call of Home* (2008), 231 n27.

considered the "oracle of the Anabaptists in Ireland."[44] Following his departure, the Scituate congregation called the Rev. Mr. Charles Chauncy.

---

[44] Harry Leon McBeth. *English Baptist Literature on Religious Liberty to 1689* (1980), 75-76.

Chapter Three

"Stand Fast and Learn"

Charles Chauncy was born in Yardleybury, Hertfordshire, England, in 1592 and graduated from Trinity College, Cambridge in 1613. He soon became a fellow of his college and was awarded a Bachelor of Divinity degree in 1624. While in Cambridge he became a highly regarded professor of Hebrew and Greek, earning a reputation for "learning and eloquence, genius and piety."[1] By 1627 Chauncy became vicar of the Ware parish. At first he became well known in the area for his preaching but soon his fame turned to notoriety as his Puritan leanings made him insufferable to his ecclesiastical superiors. He was known to have a hot temper and, at times, quite nervous and at others, fully at ease.[2]

The first incident arousing displeasure was Chauncy's opposition to the *Book of Sports* (1617). King James issued a pronouncement listing the sports that could be played on Sunday (the Sabbath) and other holy days. The pronouncement stated in part, "That for his good people's recreation, his Majesty's pleasure was, that after the end of divine service, they should not be disturbed, letted [forbidden] or discouraged from any lawful recreations, such as

---

[1] William Chauncy Fowler. *Memorials of the Chaunceys* (1868), 10.
[2] Allen French, *Charles I and the Puritan Upheaval (1955)*, 287.

dancing, either men or women, archery for men...or any such harmless recreations..." Prohibited activities were bear-baiting and bowling.[3] Chauncy, along with other Puritans, was critical of this proclamation because he sought to restore, what in his mind, was the biblical requirement to keep the Sabbath holy and not profane it with frivolities, but rather honor it with prayer, reflection and rest from the week's normal routine. "Then it was that our Mr. Chauncy, hearing the drums beat for dances and frolicks on the Lord's day, was, like other good men, afraid that God would break the rest of the kingdom, and cause drums to be beaten up for marches and battles on that very day."[4] Chauncy responded to the *Book of Sports* by catechizing (teaching) his parish on Sunday afternoons. The Church prohibited Sunday afternoon preaching and Bishop Laud saw no difference between preaching and catechizing.

For his views and actions Chauncy was brought before the High Commission to answer thirteen charges in January 1629. The Commission accused Chauncy of asserting in a sermon that "idolatry was admitted into the church," and that there was a need for "men of courage to remind their superiors of their neglect" for allowing atheism, heresy and popery in the church. He was also charged for his refusal to use *The Book of Common Prayer* and to read the Athanasian Creed (affirming the Trinity); his refusal to wear the proper vestments; and his not using the sign of the cross during baptisms. He was also accused of affecting "the name of a Puritan and ...to be reputed one of them." Another accusation stated that Chauncy caused "much strife, heartburning, and dissention in Ware by maintaining that the Sabbath began every Saturday at sunset." Unlike the other charges which he vehemently denied, this accusation Chauncy admitted, noting that his practice was grounded in Scripture. He was moreover charged with claiming that "there were many thousand souls damned in hell for their gaming and reveling in the twelve days of Christmas time, and that such damned souls cursed the birth of our Savior and the Church for instituting the

---

[3] Fowler, 12.
[4] Cotton Mather. *Magnalia Christi Americana*, (1855), 466.

celebration." This, too, he admitted to the astonishment of some and the admiration of others.[5] To the indictments he didn't admit to, his answers were vague and evasive.

The Commission required Chauncy to submit to the authority of Bishop Laud, the same bishop who would later hound Rev. John Lothrop. Laud required Chauncy to make a "submission" (confession) in Latin. This, under the circumstances, probably pleased Chauncy for his parish in Ware would not understand the ancient language, thus minimizing the damage to his ministry. Beginning with a complement to Bishop Laud, Chauncy's submission acknowledged and then retracted his most inflammatory public remarks. Chauncy said that he had not meant to be contemptuous of church practices. He admitted his errors regarding the Sabbath and all the other charges. In short, Chauncy renounced what once were strongly held opinions. Whether Chauncy was intimidated or convinced to abandon his ideas, the result was that he kept his vicarage. Still, in all likelihood, Chauncy continued his opposition to Bishop Laud's control, at first discreetly, but soon, directly and openly.

Chauncy was again brought before the High Commission court in 1635, charged this time with opposing the erection of an altar-rail, which separated the clergy from the people during communion. It was voted by the parish in Ware, with the support of the Bishop of London, to build the rail with a bench around the communion table "to avoid disorder at communion." Chauncy saw it differently. For one thing, it placed a barrier between pastor and parishioner and he called it "a snare to men's consciences." He took it as a personal affront by those who wanted to drive him out as vicar. As long as the rail stayed up, Chauncy would not administer communion. Whether by choice or ultimatum Chauncy transferred to another parish (Marston St. Lawrence) but before leaving he had some choice words. A minister should not leave a parish for personal advancement, he said; nor should he leave for better pay or a nicer

---

[5] French, 287-289.

location. A minister should only leave because of "personal persecution against his ministry." This Chauncy believed was the case. In his last sermon in Ware, Chauncy said, "If anything that is contrary to the conscience of a minister be laid upon him, though in the judgment of others it be a thing indifferent, yet he ought not to wound his conscience.... It is a heavy thing that a people should be willing to be rid of a minister for these small matters, called but 'tales' and trifles by them, but though these be never so small, if he cannot do them without wounding his soul, God gives him leave to depart." As a matter of conscience, Chauncy spoke at his new parish of what he experienced in Ware. Soon, he was on the Bishop of Peterborough's list of "recalcitrant ministers."[6]

This second appearance before the High Commission was due to a suit brought, not by members of his new congregation in Marston St. Lawrence, but by his successor at Ware. For two years Chauncy travelled back and forth to London to appear before the Commission. He wrote later of his "woeful experience, for I have suffered myself heavy things, wasted my estate two whole years together in the High Commission Court.[7] On February 11, 1635, Chauncy, his spirit broken, his money depleted, recanted "with bended knee" his words and actions in front of the High Commission.[8] Once again he disavowed strongly held opinions. Not satisfied with hearing Chauncy recant, Bishop Laud humiliated Chauncy by pronouncing before the court that Chauncy should "carry himself peaccably and conformably to the doctrines, the discipline, and rites and ceremonies of the Church of England; and that in case he should be brought before [the High Commission] again for any similar offence, the court intended to proceed against him with all severity...."[9] Chauncy was suspended from his vicarage in Marston St. Lawrence, imprisoned, and made to pay the significant

---

[6] French, 291-292.
[7] French, 293-294.
[8] French, 295.
[9] Fowler, 13.

costs of the trial. Confinement in the dank, dark and airless prison also took its toll.

In 1637 Chauncy wrote a withdrawal of his recantation titled, *The Retraction of Mr. Charles Chauncy formerly Minister of Ware in Hertfordshire* (later published in 1641 when he was in Massachusetts.) The title page contained these words

> Wherein is proved the unlawfulness and danger of railing in altars or communion tables, written with his own hand before his going to New England, in year, 1637. Published by his own direction for the satisfaction of all such who either are, or justly might be offended with his scandalous submission, made before the High Commission Court, Feb. 11 Anno 1635. London, Printed 1641.[10]

Because he still strongly opposed the authority of the bishops and fearing for his life, Chauncy waited until he left England before he published his provocative statement. Not only did he defend his original position on the railing but Chauncy also took the opportunity to write about his weakness in the face of such an ordeal before Bishop Laud and the High Commission. He couldn't excuse himself and so he "[cried] out his own shame and confusion." He also urged other like-minded people to stand fast and learn from his example.[11] "Few suffered for non-conformity more than he, by fines, by jails, by necessities to abscond, and at last by an exile from his native country," wrote Cotton Mather.[12]

Chauncy arrived in Plymouth with a reputation and good timing for the dramatic. A few days after his disembarking the Great Earthquake of 1638 occurred. Chauncy's intelligence and preaching skills were well known to the people of Plymouth and elsewhere. To the north, Governor John Winthrop of the Massachusetts Bay

---

[10] French, 296n.
[11] French, 297-298.
[12] Mather, 466.

Colony noted in his journal that in Charles Chauncy, Plymouth had procured a "great scholar and godly man." However, Chauncy also had a reputation for being a prickly and stubborn man. It was the original intention of the Plymouth congregation, "desperate" for religious leadership,[13] to hire Chauncy as settled minister and the Rev. John Reynor, the already settled pastor, would become "teacher" an important, but lesser position. A teacher was one who assisted the minister in educating the congregation in the gospel. However, this did not happen because of Chauncy's belief in baptism by immersion or "dipping" (John Robinson, the Pilgrim's spiritual leader in Leiden, was a sprinkler[14]) and celebrating the Lord's Supper in the evening every Sunday. Most in the Plymouth congregation opposed immersion and the evening Lord's Supper. As a result, Chauncy was hired as the congregation's teacher and Reynor remained in his position as pastor.

As it was for John Lothrop, the controversy over the manner of baptism and the emotions it raised within congregations would follow Chauncy for the rest of his life. The governors of the two colonies, Governors Bradford of Plymouth and Winthrop of Massachusetts Bay both recorded the events surrounding the baptism dispute involving Chauncy and the Plymouth congregation. Bradford details the efforts the congregation pursued to settle the matter. Winthrop notes also that churches in his colony received letters from both the Plymouth elders and Rev. Chauncy seeking their support. The Plymouth church elders wrote to neighboring Duxbury as well as churches in Massachusetts Bay and Connecticut for advice. The responses Plymouth received supported the elders' position of baptism by sprinkling. They contended that immersion in the winter months would put the health of an infant at risk, and to delay baptism by immersion until warmer weather was non-scriptural. The Plymouth congregation sought a compromise to calm the waters with Chauncy. Bradford records that the elders agreed that dipping was

---

[13] George F. Willison. *Saints and Strangers* (1945), 346.
[14] Dorothy Carpenter. *William Vassall and Dissent in Early Massachusetts* (2004), http://home.gwi.net/~sscarpen/vassall/Vassall.pdf, 78.

lawful but that, in the cold Plymouth winters, it would not be "convenient." Mr. Chauncy could, when performing baptisms, fully immerse a child; whereas when Mr. Reynor performed the rite he could sprinkle. True to his obstinacy Mr. Chauncy refused the compromise.[15] Chauncy's declaration that sprinkling was unlawful made many anxious about the validity of their own baptism or, as they put it, they feared their baptism was "annihilated."[16] Chauncy was invited by some to leave for Providence, Rhode Island where his views would have been welcomed in the Roger Williams-founded colony. Rev. Thomas Hooker, (founder of the Connecticut Colony and former minister in Cambridge, Massachusetts) wrote to his son-in-law and successor at First Parish Cambridge, the Rev. Thomas Shepard, on November 2, 1640,

> I have of late had intelligence from Plymouth. Mr. Chauncy and the church are to part, he to provide for himself, and they for themselves. At the day of fast, when a full conclusion of the business should have been made, he openly professed he did as verily believe the truth of his opinion as that there was a God in heaven, and that he was as settled in it as that the earth was upon the center. If such confidence find success I miss my mark. Mr. Humphrey, I hear, invites him to Providence, and that coast is most [suitable] for his opinions and practice.[17]

Timothy Hatherly urged Chauncy to come to Scituate instead of Providence[18] where the practice of dipping was accepted, though

---

[15] William Bradford. *Bradford's History of Plymouth Planation*, ed. William A.T. Davis, r.1971, 362-363; John Winthrop. *History of New England, Vol. I* (1825), 330-331.

[16] King, p. 45

[17] Joseph Barlow Felt. *Ecclesiastical History of New England, Vol. I* (1855), 443.

[18] Valdespino, 67.

not unanimously, thus guaranteeing the continuance of the turmoil in the Scituate congregation. Several members of the Scituate congregation knew of Chauncy's view of baptism and were opposed to his call. One group "held to infant sprinkling; another to adult immersion exclusively; and a third, (which included Mr. Chauncy) to immersion of infants as well as adults."[19] Chauncy was adamant on immersion; in fact, he dipped both of his children, though one apparently "swooned" after being immersed in cold water on a winter's day. Still, he did allow children in his parish to be "sprinkled," but by other clergy. A mother concerned that her child would be frightened by immersion asked for the child to be baptized by sprinkling instead. The mother had reason for concern since another child, three years old, about to be dipped, grabbed Chauncy by his coat and nearly pulled the minister into the water. To ease the mother's fear Chauncy wrote a letter to the minister of a Boston church giving his permission that the child be baptized by sprinkling. Others soon did the same thing. The discussion and debate over Chauncy's position swept all over New England.[20]

Why was the mode of baptism important? Why did intelligent, pious men debate the issue, at times vehemently? Because this was a time when religious dissenters from the Church of England were expounding doctrines that were newly formed and fermenting. Small or obscure groups adopted many new ideas that would later fall by the wayside. Other ideas would take hold and be widely embraced which would then lay the foundation for church doctrine. Nevertheless, New England non-conformist predecessors had boxed them in so tightly that the late 16th and early 17th centuries dissenters had to perform theological contortions to fit their ideas into doctrines. Even today, there is no full consensus on the meaning and mode of baptism. In the late 16th and early 17th centuries the discussion of new ideas was percolating up from numerous preachers and teachers. There was little consensus as a multitude of treatises

---

[19] King, 47.
[20] King, 46.

were being printed, discussed and condemned, even by fellow dissenters. Too many chefs were overcooking the stew. Strict separatists were under pressure to justify the validity of the baptism they received by the Church of England. Semi-separatists also had to defend their belief in a gathered church while clinging to the traditional view of baptism.

For those who did believe in adult baptism, what did that mean for their children? In the end, it was "dipping" leading the way to adult baptism that brought an end to the relationship between the Separatists and the traditional church.[21] Since Baptists did not have churches of their own, they first mingled with the other dissenters. But when a child was baptized they silently but openly expressed their opposition. By turning their backs to the minister. Sometimes they would walk out of the meetinghouse in a manner that left the meaning unambiguous.[22] The Separatists looked to the Bible as the authority for all things doctrinal and ecclesiastical. To them John the Baptist established the model for baptism, as they believed he baptized Jesus and others by immersion. Jesus was also an adult, providing another distinction, that of "believer's baptism," favored by nascent Baptists. They believed that the Bible teaches that only persons who have been born again ("regenerate") could be members of a church. This new birth does not come by expressing knowledge of Jesus and his teachings but by a genuine experience of faith in Him brought about, according to the believer, by Jesus' intervention in that person's life. Once a council of elders accepted this expression as sincere the person was accepted into the church and then baptized. Baptists hold that salvation is necessary for baptism, not the other way around. A person must be a disciple of Jesus before they are eligible for baptism and church membership; therefore the baptism of infants was inappropriate since they were unable to confess faith in Christ.

---

[21] Tolmie, 51-52.

[22] David Benedict. *A General History of the Baptist Denomination in America and Other Parts of the World,* (1848), 379

Even before Charles Chauncy came to Scituate, his beliefs and practices provoked opposition in the Scituate congregation, as they had in Plymouth. The most prominent of the critics was William Vassall, described as "a man of discontented spirit always" and the "New England malcontent."[23] He was among the merchant group that established the Massachusetts Bay Company and its colony, coming to New England in 1628. Most of the men of the Massachusetts Bay Company were Puritans, though certainly not hostile to the crown. It is unlikely that King Charles I would have granted them their charter had they been antagonistic to the church, though he probably was under the impression that it was primarily a commercial venture. Nevertheless, Vassall and others wanted reforms in the church and were not pleased with the activities of the High Commission. Vassall was a principled (at least when it came to religious beliefs), but quarrelsome man. It was said of him that he was "a man never at rest...but when in the fire of contention."[24] The Boston Puritans considered him a dangerous radical because of his belief in religious tolerance, and so he left the Massachusetts Bay colony.

Vassall came to Scituate hoping for a quieter life and bought property on the North River in part because his religious views were similar to those of John Robinson's Pilgrims. Soon his claim of the land was challenged and thus began a chain of events that made Vassall's life in Scituate anything but quiet. The legal problem was that the Plymouth court had granted Vassall's claim before the boundaries of the Conihasset Grant were settled.[25] One of the major holders of the grant was Timothy Hatherly. Vassall's claim was also an irritant to the already settled farmers with small lots as his property was an enormous two hundred acre lot. Hatherly's lot might have been the same size, but Vassall was a newcomer and certainly not as highly regarded as Scituate's benefactor.

---

[23] Williston Walker. *The Creeds and Platforms of Congregationalism* (1991), 163, 179.
[24] Deane, 368.
[25] Carpenter, 65.

William Vassall met his match in stubbornness with Charles Chauncy. Each was a nemesis to the other. The tug-of-war between Chauncy and Vassall is significant in colonial history for it raised the questions of church authority, the mode of baptism, and how churches were to manage discord within their congregations. Vassall soon challenged Chauncy on the matters of baptism, church authority, the Lord's Supper and the location of the meetinghouse for public worship in Scituate. Chauncy was a stickler when it came to the Protestant sacrament and the debate over baptism clearly divided the Scituate congregation. This was the primary reason for the second division of the church (the first being Lothrop's departure to Cape Cod); but there were two other issues that roiled the congregation. Chauncy believed the Lord's Supper (communion) should be celebrated every Sunday, specifically in the evening as that was the time of day of Jesus' Last Supper, but communion should only be available to members of the congregation. Vassall, being a champion of religious tolerance, believed that the Scituate congregation should accept Anglicans and other Christians at the communion table. The dispute may also have been based in Vassall's personal dislike for Chauncy for his vacillation in twice recanting his Puritan beliefs before the High Commission. For Chauncy's part, he saw Vassall as being "liberal" (a term with fluid meaning in those days of religious turmoil), since Vassall believed in open communion. Chauncy even accused Vassal of being an Episcopalian[!] Deane notes in his history, "[I] will not attempt to decide this question at this late period...."[26] Nor shall we.

The disputes between these two men were really about the fundamental issue of where authority resided in the Scituate congregation. Chauncy and his supporters accurately claimed a majority of the members of the church called him and that majority was in full sympathy with him and his views as they instituted a new covenant; and those who did not subscribe to the "discipline" of the

---

[26] Deane, 89.

majority and the minister were separating themselves from the Scituate church. Vassall and his supporters, on the other hand, believed that the church left by Rev. Lothrop was the true church of Scituate; that it had its own doctrines (that is, church discipline); and Chauncy's new mandates were unjustified and without proper authority, because Chauncy had established a new covenant, meaning to Vassall, a new congregation.[27] Vassall and others thought that this was a dismissal of the Lothrop-gathered church and declared themselves to be the true congregation in Scituate. For their part, Chauncy, Hatherly and others saw the call for a new covenant as a reaffirmation of the Lothrop congregation under the leadership of a new minister.

Deane's *History of Scituate* contains correspondence from February 1642 to September 1645 between Mr. Vassall and those whose support he sought, as well as Mr. Chauncy's rebuttals.[28] Unfortunately for history, most of the correspondence in Deane's volume is from and to Vassall, with few documents coming directly from Chauncy's hand. True to his nature, William Vassall wrote frequently and passionately about who were members of the "true" church of Scituate and his antipathy towards Mr. Chauncy. A document dated February 2, 1642, probably written by Vassall, reveals the division in the church. Declaring that "their" church had been forsaken by the Chauncy faction, the Vassall group stated,

> We do here now further Covenant, and renew that Covenant that we were formerly in together as a Church, that as a Church of Christ, we, by the gracious assistance of Christ, will walk in all the ways of God that are and shall be revealed to us out of his word, to be his ways, so far as God shall enable us. And to this end, we will do our best to procure and maintain all such officers as are needful, whereby we may enjoy all his ordinances, for the good of the

---

[27] Waite, p. 14; Philip F. Gura. *A Glimpse of Sion's Glory* (1984), 20.
[28] Deane, 66-84.

souls of us and ours; and we shall not refuse into our society such of God's people, whose hearts God shall incline to join themselves unto us, for the furtherance of the worship of God amongst us, and the good of their souls.[29]

Engraved by H W Smith

*Rev. Charles Chauncy**

---

[29] Deane, 61.

* Although Harvard University presents this portrait of Rev. Chauncy, who became the second president of Harvard College, it is possible that the portrait is that of Chauncy's great-grandson and namesake, Rev. Charles Chauncy (1705-1787)

Not surprisingly Chauncy was angry when he heard that Vassall had communicated the above with other churches in Plymouth and Massachusetts Bay seeking their support. Chauncy defended his position in a letter to the elders of the church in Roxbury, led by the Rev. John Eliot, claiming Vassall and his party were in error by proclaiming their church the "true" church of Scituate. Chauncy supported his position by recounting the fact that just prior to Lothrop leaving there was a day of humiliation at Mr. Hatherly's house where those staying in Scituate "entered into covenant with God and Christ and with one another, to walk together in the whole revealed will of God and Christ." Chauncy pointed out that even though the Vassall party cites this as the beginning of the "Vassall church," Vassall and another member of his faction were not present; and those Vassall allies who were there did not affirm the covenant by "word of mouth" (overtly), but agreed to the covenant they said, implicitly. Chauncy disputed the legitimacy of their unspoken assent of the covenant. Furthermore, Chauncy said that when the Vassall faction made their covenant, it was done "surreptitiously", without any notice to the entire church body, without fasting and prayer, and done "during the extremity of the great snow…when few could come without apparent danger." [30] Simply put, Chauncy charged that the Vassall covenant lacked validity.

A few weeks later, Vassall responded to Chauncy's letter "of complaints against us." Someone must have sent the Chauncy-Roxbury letter on to Vassall and his response, addressed to Chauncy, was filled with sarcasm and contempt. Vassall denied considering the meeting at Hatherly's house the founding of the church; he denied that the meeting of his faction was surreptitious because Chauncy had earlier told them they "were not of your church'; that the details Chauncy gave about the suddenness of the meeting and its being held in the midst of an extreme snowstorm amounted to defamation; and the implication that their meeting was "irreligious" because they did not pray and fast was false. Vassall declared that Chauncy's congregation "was no more a church without us than we were

---

[30] Deane, 63.

without you."[31] Writing to the Rev. John Wilson of Boston, Vassall reiterated his claims that his faction represented the old church and Chauncy's was a new one; that there was no schism in the church for Chauncy himself declared Vassall and his party not members of the congregation for their refusal to agree to the covenant; that Chauncy's animosity to him and his allies was due in part because of their opposition to Chauncy being called to Scituate and that was why Chauncy and others were not invited to the Vassall party's discussions for fear "he [Chauncy] might have disturbed our peaceful proceedings." Vassall also mentioned the distance many of the newer Scituate settlers had to travel to get to the meetinghouse, "If all other differences were reconciled, yet it were the undoing of us and them both, if we do not become two congregations, and take in more to them and us."[32]

Vassall was persistent in trying to align ministers in Plymouth and Massachusetts Bay to his cause. Vassall, despite being a man of liberal views, was apparently on good terms with the conservative elders in Boston and so he sought support from them in his contest with Chauncy.[33] Prominent people in Boston treated Vassall with great respect because he was one of the most eminent, if not congenial, men in the area. Not only was he wealthy, but he also had connections in London, including a brother in Parliament.[34] Having great influence, Vassall was determined to agitate for equal rights and liberty of conscience in both the Plymouth and Massachusetts Bay colonies at once, by petitioning both general courts, and in case of failures there, presenting similar petitions to Parliament.

Writing to Rev. John Cotton of Boston in March 1643 Vassall thanked Cotton for his "Christian charity in holding communion" with him and for trying to mediate the differences between him and Chauncy. Chauncy apparently was willing to have a hearing before

---

[31] Deane, 64-65.
[32] Deane, 67-68.
[33] Carpenter, 92.
[34] Carpenter, 93.

the elders from other churches to try to end the controversy, but Vassall complained that Chauncy would not tell Vassall and others what the "faults" were. Vassall noted in a postscript that he wanted to send copies to Revs. Wilson and Eliot but could not, for paper "is so scanty."[35] A month later, Vassall reported to Cotton that there had been attempts to reconcile the two parties, most recently at the home of Rev. Partridge of Duxbury. At the same time Vassall recounted his efforts to call Rev. William Witherell as minister of Vassall's congregation, properly seeking from Mr. Partridge, Witherell's dismissal from the Duxbury church.[36] Vassall followed his communication to Rev. Cotton with a letter to the wider audience of church elders in both Massachusetts Bay and Plymouth. Again Vassall restated his arguments that he represented the true church of Scituate.

Toward the end of 1643 or the beginning of 1644 Vassall got word from the councils. According to Deane, the response from the Massachusetts Bay Colony churches to Vassall has been lost, but the Plymouth response, "of a different tenor," survived; it was clear and Solomon-like, giving something to both parties, but it clearly favored Chauncy's position. First, the Plymouth General Court stated that the congregation left behind by Lothrop was indeed in a true "church state" and that Mr. Vassall's membership had properly been transferred from Mr. Lothrop's church to the Scituate (Chauncy's) church. However, since Mr. Vassall and his party were members of Chauncy's church they were incorrectly denied communion by Rev. Chauncy. The elders of Plymouth judged that Vassall and others did "gather themselves into a new body" in an "irregular" way because they did not seek consent of the Scituate church; they did not consult with other churches; and because their gathering was done "without solemn humiliation." The elders urged both parties to reconcile, but if an agreement could not be found, then, if the Vassall faction requested, they were to be granted an "orderly dismission."[37]

---

[35] Deane, 71-72.

[36] Deane, 72, 77.

[37] Deane, 75-77.

William Vassall received support from the churches and elders in Massachusetts Bay but far less support (if any) in his home jurisdiction of Plymouth. In April 1645 he responded to a letter from Rev. Edward Bulkeley of Marshfield in which Bulkeley asked Vassall to defer any action regarding Mr. Witherell and other matters until elders from Massachusetts Bay could travel to Plymouth for a meeting so that Vassall and his party could be "catechized" about "their work of grace." Vassall, emboldened by the support he was receiving from Massachusetts Bay, refused to wait to call Rev. Witherell. Complicating an already difficult situation was the fact that the Duxbury church refused to dismiss Mr. Witherell for the purpose of becoming the minister of the Vassall church. The Church in Plymouth asked Vassall to "desist" on following through with the call and ordination of Mr. Witherell. Nevertheless, on September 2, 1645, Mr. Witherell was ordained as minister of the "Vassall church," by the laying on of hands by its members, without the consent of the Duxbury church. In attendance were representatives from surrounding churches who, according to Deane, were there to protest rather than assist in Witherell's ordination.[38]

Even with his obstinacy (some would say, his vision) Vassall was a man of principle. Through his desire for religious tolerance, Vassall also sought to expand the idea and process of church membership; and, his actions had an impact on civil affairs as well. Vassall told Governor Bradford of Plymouth he had a written proposition, "to allow and maintain full and free tolerance of religion to all men that would preserve the civil peace and submit unto government," to be presented to the Plymouth General Court. There was to be "no limitation or exception against Turk, Jew, Papist, Arian, Socinian, Nicholaytan, Familist, or any other..." To expand the idea of who could be a church member and who could have a say in civic affairs (that is, only male church members) is laudable from a twenty first century perspective; and American democracy and its freedoms are in debt to men like Vassall. The leaders in New England saw themselves as advancing religious liberty as well, not

---

[38] Deane, 80-83.

only in New England, but in the mother country also. But the Pilgrim/Puritan establishment was caught between a rock and a hard place. Governor Bradford and others expressed concern about the "sad" consequences that would follow if Vassall's petition was voted on, and so Bradford did not even bring Vassall's proposal to a vote despite significant support in the General Court. Nevertheless, they were concerned that if there were radical changes such as those suggested by Vassall their system would come under attack by the King. Therefore, the leaders of the Plymouth and Massachusetts Bay colonies believed it was necessary to strengthen the existing institutions since the Puritan view was under attack back home in the English Civil War between Anglican King Charles I and the Puritan-influenced Parliament.[39]

In 1648, three years after founding his congregation (the Second Parish of Scituate) and many years after the bitter, contentious and divisive fight with Charles Chauncy, William Vassall left Scituate for Barbados, a place of greater religious tolerance, but also a place for greater commercial rewards. He died there in 1655.[40] After Vassall left Scituate there were many attempts at reconciliation between the two congregations. In December 1649 a meeting was held in the home of Deacon Thomas Robinson of the Second, or South Parish. Attending were members of First Parish, Chauncy, Timothy Hatherly, Humphrey Turner and others. From the new church were Witherell, William Hatch, John Stockbridge and others. Once again Chauncy enumerated his accusations and nothing noteworthy was accomplished other than an unusual but mild rebuke of Chauncy from his supporter, Hatherly, when Chauncy once again accused the new church of creating a schism. Hatherly said, "It could be no schism, because we had promised them a dismission whenever they should require it, and sent it to them before they did demand it." Deane points out that while Hatherly appreciated Chauncy's learning and other talents, he was repeatedly "grieved" by Chauncy's "hasty

---

[39] Brooks Adams. *The Emancipation of Massachusetts*, 85; Walker, 165-166.
[40] Carpenter, 234.

and ardent temper."[41] A few years later, Rev. Witherell and the elders of the South Parish church sent Chauncy a letter pleading to "deal faithfully and plainly" with them as brethren "so that we may be brought to the right way towards God," still claiming not to know what "that evil is you see in us." Chauncy responded that it had been "no small grievance of spirit" to him that so long a time had passed since the two groups had been in communion. Still, obstinate as ever, Chauncy said that if Witherell didn't know his and his congregation's error, in spite of many meetings and correspondence, "we cannot hope to do more."[42]

Not wanting to give Chauncy the last word, Witherell, in a barbed letter, responded by accusing Chauncy of not addressing the problem in good faith. Witherell also pointed out to Chauncy an inconsistency in his position. While Chauncy refused to be in communion and associate with members of the Second Parish Church, it did not prevent him from attending the wedding of Second Parish Deacon Thomas Robinson to the widow, Mary Woodey. Witherell noted in his journal, maybe with a gleam in his eye, that when this letter was read by Chauncy in church on July 16, 1653 there was a severe thunderstorm in Scituate with hail "flung on our innocent heads."[43]

Deane notes that Chauncy, like Vassall, also held fast to his principles, never calling Vassall's group a "church" but rather a "society." Chauncy's church was the only one in Scituate and the question as to which was the first church in Scituate never was really resolved. Deane says, "there was certainly much plausibility" in Mr. Vassall's assertion that Chauncy's church seceded from Lothrop's church. But, as Deane noted in 1831, "principles recently settled, [referring to the Dedham case of 1819, formally known as *Baker v. Fales*] decide the question otherwise, and very properly; because it

---

[41] Deane, 84.
[42] Deane, 85-86.
[43] Deane, 87.

was conceded that Mr. Chauncy's Church and Society together, were a majority of 'two or three men,' and retained the Meeting-house."[44]

In 1675, after thirty-three years, the two churches repaired their relationship. The reconciliation between the two Scituate parishes was made easier by the departures of Mr. Vassall and Rev. Chauncy. While not restoring itself as one church, the Rev. Nicholas Baker, then the minister of First Parish, responding to a letter from Mr. Witherell "of our neighbor Church of Christ in [South] Scituate," said that the members of First Parish "do willingly and gladly lay aside all former offences taken up, or ancient disagreements and differences betwixt us…. And in that you desire fellowship with us in the gospel that we may have communion one with another as the Churches of Christ, we do cordially embrace your motion…."[45]

The Chauncy-Vassall controversy had another, even more significant role in colonial history: the manner in which the present First Parish Unitarian Universalist church governs itself in association with other Unitarian Universalist churches. The Pilgrims and Puritans, reformers that they were, could not contain the impulse toward a "free church."[46] With new ideas about church governance and roiling debates about theology and liturgy, even the systematic Puritans had difficulty keeping congregations in some order and discipline. How, for instance, were the Puritan congregations, geographically far from the control of the Church of England, and the Pilgrim congregations, broken away from the Church of England, related to each other within their colony of Massachusetts Bay or Plymouth and with the congregations in the other colony? Concerns about church discipline and order were paramount with the banishments of Roger Williams for his Baptist views and Anne Hutchinson for her criticism of Puritan ministers and their theology. In September 1646, at the request of a number of ministers from

---

[44] Deane, 88.

[45] Deane, 88.

[46] Edwin Gaustad and Leigh Schmidt. *The Religious History of America* (2002), 49.

both colonies, Charles Chauncy among them, a synod was held in Cambridge in August of 1648 which produced a document known as the Cambridge Platform. The signers of rejected the idea of a presbyterian polity with ruling councils of elders (presbyters) for maintaining discipline. Instead they agreed that each of their churches would seek advice from councils along with "admonitory powers," but such councils would not have coercive authority over them, thus preserving each congregation's independence and autonomy. Nonetheless, "heresy, disobedience, and schism were 'to be restrained and punished by *civil* authority (emphasis added).[47] This is the polity model that has characterized the Unitarian, Universalist and Congregational churches to the present day, independent and autonomous of a central authority.

Despite Chauncy's irritable nature, his counsel was often sought even for the most unsavory matters. William Bradford, writing in his journal in 1642, notes with a despairing voice the "wickedness" that was corrupting the Plymouth Colony. Laws and punishment "could not suppress [the] breaking out of sundry notorious sins." Drunkenness, adultery and other sexual misconduct between unmarried and married people were of great concern. "Even sodomy and buggery (things too fearful to name) have broke forth in this land," Bradford wrote. Perhaps, Bradford reflected, it was because the Devil was paying particular attention to the churches whose people were trying so hard to preserve "purity and holiness." Delving into psychology, Bradford thought another reason for sinful behavior in the colony was because the strict laws caused emotions to be so pent up that they released themselves in sinful ways.[48] A letter to Bradford from the governor of the Massachusetts Bay Colony seeking his advice initiated these reflections. Similar letters were sent to the colony magistrates and church ministers and elders on the matter of "heinous offences" that could be a capital crime.[49] Revs. Reynor of Plymouth, Partridge of Duxbury and Chauncy of Scituate

---

[47] Ahlstrom, 155-156.
[48] Bradford, 385-386.
[49] Bradford, 386

responded to Bradford. Chauncy's response was the longest and most detailed with Biblical and legal references. Chauncy was outspoken on sexual assault and the pursuit of "strange flesh." New England, he wrote, was "defiled by such sins" as bestiality.[50]

One question Bradford posed was what sodomitical acts (as well as rape, incest and bestiality) are to be punished by death? Chauncy said that the Ten Commandments and the Mosaic Code are "immutable and perpetual." They, along with the wisdom of the great church teachers, provide that these sins be punished by death. This included "destroying conception in the womb by potions."[51] Chauncy's response was timely. Thomas Granger, a young servant to a Duxbury man, whose parents lived in Scituate, was accused of bestiality with "a mare, a cow, two goats, five sheep, two calves and a turkey." Bradford noted that it was horrible "to mention but the truth of the history requires it." The boy confessed not only to the magistrates in private but in public to the ministers, the jury and the whole court. Granger was executed on September 8, 1642. Bradford commented, "A very sad spectacle it was; for first the mare, and then the cow, and the rest of the lesser cattle [calves], were killed before his [Granger's] face, according to the law [If a man lies with a beast, he shall be put to death; and you shall kill the beast. Leviticus 20:15]. Then Granger was put to death himself."[52]

Chauncy's ministry in Scituate was taking its toll as Deane recorded evidence of Chauncy's unhappiness. There was, after all the contentious feud with William Vassall and the sniping of people who remained at First Parish. Deane saw this as understandable grounds for Chauncy's mood, "The circumstances by which he was surrounded, together with his ardent temperament, make apology in part, for his uneasiness." A studious man endowed with "great talents and eminent learning," Deane says that Chauncy "was too much inclined to accept it as an indignity, that his powers should not keep

[50] Richard Godbeer. *Sexual Revolution in Early America* (2002), 67.
[51] Bradford, 397.
[52] Bradford, 397.

down all opposition...." Deane, understanding the limitations of ministers, compassionately writes of Chauncy,

> There lay his weakness — in not being able to make allowance for the poverty and hardships of his people in the new settlement, and in imagining that his opponents in religious principles and usages, were his personal enemies. He was constantly chafed by the opposition: his Society had become divided and weakened, and his apprehensions in regard to a livelihood were of a most melancholy kind.[53]

To try and soothe the indignities he felt, Chauncy wrote to the Plymouth Colony governor in search of some financial relief, though, as Deane chronicles, there is no record of a satisfactory response. Even in these early days, Deane says, there was a debate about taxes used to support the ministry.[54]

After twelve difficult years in Scituate, Chauncy, in 1654, longed to return to England now that it was under the rule of the Puritan, Lord Protector Oliver Cromwell. Just as he was to set sail for home, representatives of the Board of Overseers of Harvard College offered Chauncy its presidency. He accepted and held the office until his death on February 19, 1671, at the age of eighty-one. Chauncy, due to his firm stance on issues of ministry, his intellect, his leadership, sermons and writings, as well as his presidency of Harvard College, is considered among the most influential men in the early colonial period. He was held in high estimation at Cambridge, and Cotton Mather says that when he had been a year or two in the town "the church kept a whole day of thanksgiving to God for the mercy which they had enjoyed in his being there." Prickly, even at Harvard, he had strong words of admonition to the students. In one of his sermons he speaks of the wearing of long hair as "a heathenish

---

[53] Deane, 174.
[54] Deane, 174.

practice," and as "one of the crying sins of the land."[55] Nevertheless, Cotton Mather said this of the Rev. and President Charles Chauncy, New England "enjoyed such a privilege, and such a president as our Chauncy...."[56]

---

[55] *Appleton's Cyclopedia of American Biography* (1886), 594.
[56] Mather, 475.

Chapter Four

Errors, War and Reconciliation

When Charles Chauncy was elected President of Harvard in 1654 he replaced the Rev. Henry Dunster who, conveniently, if not by pre-arrangement, followed Chauncy as minister of the First Parish in Scituate. Not much is known about the early years of Dunster except that he received a BA and an MA from Emanuel College at Cambridge in 1630 and 1634 respectively. Like Lothrop and Chauncy, Dunster left England to escape persecution for his non-conformity. It is clear from his appointment as Harvard's first president that Dunster was respected for his learning and his piety. He took office on August 27, 1640. Under his leadership Harvard College built the foundation on which it rests today. When Dunster arrived at Harvard, the College was in financial disarray, so much so, that some students left. As president, he oversaw reform of the academic program including the establishment of a requirement for four years of study, and the introduction of a code of conduct for students. He gained funding from the Massachusetts Bay General Court as well as from individual donors, and persuaded former students to return the College. Thomas Shepard, who was the pastor in Cambridge during the first years of Dunster's administration, spoke of him as a "man pious, painful, and fit to teach, and very fit to lay the foundations of the domestical affairs of the College; whom

God hath much honored and blessed."[1] Reverend Jonathan Mitchell, Shepard's successor at Cambridge, a friend and former student of Dunster's, would have a different opinion of him "when he 'fell' into certain 'briars' of dissent from the established creed" on baptism.[2] A biographer, on the other hand, described Dunster as, "A singularly honest mind, which no promises and no persecutions could turn from his convictions…. Firm as a rock in the defense of his principles, he could never be roused to a fight with his adversaries. He was no iconoclast. He was just the opposite. Thoroughly manly and courageous, he was yet gentle and courteous."[3] Dunster never doubted the need for a school to train ministers, but what he came to doubt was the validity of infant baptism for which he found no support in Scripture. He was a respected clergyman, not some fanatic, as some Puritans believed those who were against infant baptism to be.

Henry Dunster refused to baptize his fourth child, born in 1654, and publically announced from the pulpit in Cambridge what he had come to believe in private, that he was opposed to infant baptism, though not to immersion, like Chauncy.* The overseers at Harvard were concerned that Dunster's ideas would "ensnare" the college's students. Fellow members of the Cambridge church "were somewhat vehement and violent" in their dissatisfaction when Dunster refused to baptize his child. But Dunster was also "opposed to controversy and strife." He wrote, "I am not utterly unacquainted with the levity and timidity of my spirit. But slender and feeble reasons they are not, or at least seem not to me, that enforce me to expose myself (that's the least), my family, and all the effects and concernments of us both, viz. the work committed to me, which, I bless God, I esteem more than myself, the peace of the church…." In another letter to a friend in England, Dunster wrote,

---

[1] Alexander Young. *Chronicles of Massachusetts* (1841), 552.
[2] Jeremiah Chaplin. *The Life of Henry Dunster* (1872), iii.
[3] Chapin, iv, vii.
* Though not the minister of First Parish in Cambridge, Dunster, as President of Harvard College, had the privilege of the pulpit.

"Controversies I am unwilling to launch out into, the ocean of contention over swelling with a spring-tide, insomuch that it overflows the banks of conscience, and drowns the pleasant meadows of fruitful love, and all the sweet pastures of piety."[4]

The fact that Dunster took his position against infant baptism as a matter of individual conscience did not prevent other clergy from believing it to be a serious enough matter that called into question the appropriateness of him leading Harvard. Even his friend and former student, Jonathan Mitchell publically opposed Dunster's position on infant baptism, though Dunster almost won Mitchell over to his side. Almost, but Mitchell went on to preach many sermons defending the "comfortable truth" of infant baptism.[5] He once said that he had been "fearful to go needlessly to Mr. Dunster," because he "found a venom and a poison in his insinuations and discourses against paedobaptism, " thinking that "they were from the Evil One."[6]

Alexander McKenzie, an historian of the First Church in Cambridge, gives the following account of the controversy

> Henry Dunster, President of the College, and a member of this church, was, to use the language of Cotton Mather, 'unaccountably fallen into the briars of antipaedobaptism; and being briar'd in the scruples of that persuasion, he not only forebore to present an infant of his own unto the Baptism of our Lord, but also thought himself under some obligation to bear his testimony in some sermons against the administration of baptism to any infant whatsoever.' The brethren of the church were somewhat vehement and violent in the expression of their dissatisfaction

---

[4] Chaplin, 103-104, 117.

[5] http://www.pbministries.org/History/John%20T.%20Christian/vol 2/history2_part1_04.htm

[6] Chaplin, 222.

with the position by one so eminent. They thought that for the good of the congregation, and to preserve abroad the good name of the church, he should cease preaching until 'he had better satisfied himself in the point doubted by him.' The divine ordinance which he opposed was held in the highest veneration by our fathers. It had come to them from the earliest days of the church, and was sanctified before them by all the early associations of life. It connected them with God by his ancient covenant. It was a heavenly boon to the child upon whom parental faith and fidelity bestowed it. Its meaning, value and authority, had been carefully taught by their first ministers, of blessed memory. With the boldness and decision with which they set themselves against all wrong, all encroachment on religious ordinances, they lifted up their voice against one who presumed to contradict what the church had always held, and to deny where Shepard affirmed; and not even his sacred calling, nor his lofty official position could shield him from censure.[7]

The Massachusetts Bay Colony General Court soon got involved. It called upon nine ministers and two church elders to meet with Dunster privately in order to correct him. The two-day meeting was fruitless and Dunster was unyielding, re-affirming his belief that there was nothing in Scripture, nor in the history of the ancient churches, to support the baptism of infants. The uproar became so great that Dunster was "indicted by the grand jury for disturbing the ordinance of infant baptism on the Cambridge church, [and] sentenced to a public admonition...."[8] Most of the ministers in New England would gladly have had Dunster remain in the position if only he would keep quiet about his baptism stance. This he refused

---

[7] Alexander McKenzie. *Lectures on the History of the First Church in Cambridge (1873),* 102, 103.

[8] Josiah Quincy. *History of Harvard University, Vol. I,* (1860), 15-18.

to do and preferred "exile" in the Plymouth Colony in order not to offend his colleagues or his students. Appearing before the General Court Dunster said, "The whole transaction of this business is such which in process of time, when all things come to mature consideration, may very probably create grief on all sides; yours subsequent, as mine antecedent. I am not the man you take me to be."[9] Despite these words the Massachusetts Bay General Court, May 3, 1654, passed the following order:

> Forasmuch as it greatly concerns the welfare of this country that the youth thereof be educated, not only in good literature but sound doctrine, this Court doth therefore commend it to the serious consideration and special care of the Overseers of the College and the selectmen in the several towns, not to admit or suffer any such to be continued in the office or place of teaching, educating, or instructing the youth or child, in the college or school, that have manifested themselves unsound in the faith, or scandalous in their lives, and not giving due satisfaction according to the rules of Christ.[10]

Dunster accepted this statement and tendered his resignation as President of the College. He graciously said,

> I here resign up the place wherein hitherto I have labored with all my heart (Blessed be the Lord who gave it) serving you and yours. And henceforth (that you in the interim may be provided) I will be willing to do the best I can for some weeks or months to continue the work, acting according to the orders prescribed to us; if the Society in the interim fall not

---

[9] Chaplin, 223.
[10] *The Records of the Colony of Massachusetts Bay, Vol. III.* 397.

to pieces in our hands; and what advice for the present or for the future I can give for the public good, in this behalf, with all readiness of mind I shall do it, and daily by the grace of our Lord Jesus Christ, pray the Lord to help and counsel us all.

From the General Court, on May 25, 1654 he received only this curt answer:

In answer to the writing presented to this Court by Mr. Henry Dunster, wherein amongst other things he is pleased to make a resignation of his place as President, this Court doth order that it shall be left to the care and discretion of the Overseers of the College to make provision, in case he persist in his resolution more than one month (and inform the Overseers) for some...person to carry on and end that work for the present.[11]

Rev. Cotton Mather, for his part, wrote the following about Dunster's resignation:

Among those of our fathers, who differed somewhat from his brethren, was that learned and worthy man, Mr. Henry Dunster . . . Wonderfully falling into the errors of Antipaedobaptism, the overseers of the College became solicitous that the students there might not be unawares ensnared in the errors of the President. Wherefore they labored with an extreme agony either to rescue the good man from his own mistake, or to restrain him from imposing them upon the hope of the flock, of both which, fording

---

[11] *The Records of the Colony of Massachusetts Bay, Vol. III*, 353.

themselves to despair, they did as quietly as they could, procure his removal, and provide him a successor in Mr. Charles Chauncy.[12]

Nowhere else in the American colonies, nor possibly elsewhere in the world, was there a more literate culture than in New England. Congregations knew that the clergy were vital to their moral education in matters of doctrine and behavior. Across class lines, from the highest bred to the lowest, New Englanders were "people of the Word," who could read the Bible cover to cover. In most cases it was all they read.[13] The sermon was a way of connecting the world to Scripture. The Puritans (and Pilgrims) believed that God and Satan were in a constant battle in the present life and that everything that happened in daily life, be it death, disease, famine, was directly caused or allowed by God. The role of the clergy was to interpret these things.[14] "Through their multiple private functions as explainers of Scripture, moral teachers and disciplinarians, comforters and guides, and their public roles in affecting community legislation and politics, many prominent clergy took on a mythic stature as protectors of the community...."[15] Any perceived wavering from orthodoxy was seen as a threat to the community, thus the banishment of Roger Williams and Anne Hutchinson; and, in the case of Dunster, it was just as severe, since he was influencing the next generation of ministers.

As a result of Dunster's recalcitrance, a law was passed requiring all teachers at Harvard or in public schools who were "unsound of faith" to be relieved of their duties. Whatever deference was given to Dunster was probably due to the respect of many for his intellect and gratitude for his having saved Harvard from financial ruin. Another factor was his respect for the authority of the magistrates. Though strong willed in his opposition to infant baptism,

---

12 Mather, 406.
13 Stout, 32.
14 Johnson, 27.
15 Johnson, 28.

Dunster publicly and with humility accepted the magistrate's right to decide such matters.[16] Though he kept this matter as a point of personal conviction, he did not lead a Baptist movement, although Baptist historians regard him as a founder of the American Baptist church.[17]

Dunster left Cambridge and the Massachusetts Bay colony, found exile in the more tolerant colony of Plymouth, came to Scituate immediately after his resignation and spent the rest of his life there. His biographer notes that "Scituate deserves honorable mention for its friendly treatment of dissenters." After all, while the Scituate congregation might not have come to an agreement on the mode of baptism, they were not as disturbed by the issue as were the ministers of Massachusetts Bay. Dunster, according to the biographer, "was content, under the circumstances, to remain in fellowship with his Independent [Pilgrim] brethren so long as they did not interfere with his liberty of conscience. It is greatly to the credit of the people of Scituate, that the true doctrine of the rights of conscience had made such progress among them...."[18]

The historian of the First Trinitarian Congregational Church in Scituate, Clarence Waite, raises the question of Henry Dunster's ministerial status. He has always been accorded a place on the list of First Parish church ministers but the evidence indicates that his was simply a cooperative relationship with no definite church connection.[19] "He [Dunster] was doubtless welcomed (in Scituate) as a learned and able minister; and in spite of his antipaedobaptist views he appears to have served the church in Scituate for several years, although not probably in the capacity of pastor...."[20] Harvey Hunter Pratt notes that Dunster came to the Scituate church not as an

---

[16] Darren Staloff. *The Making of An American Thinking Class* (1998), 99-100.

[17] William Gerald McLoughlin. *New England Dissent* (1971), 21-22.

[18] Chaplin, 205.

[19] Waite, 17.

[20] Waite, 18.

ordained preacher of the gospel, but as a "teacher," a difference without much of a distinction from a modern point of view.[21] Whatever the case, the people of Scituate gave him "a hearty welcome to their town and their homes." Dunster was similar to Charles Chauncy in his scholarship and familiarity with ancient languages, but Dunster's temperament was quite different. He was described as a "mild and tolerant" man, something Chauncy was not.[22] James Cudworth had "great esteem and affection" for Dunster shown in a letter written a year before Dunster's death, "Through mercy we have yet among us the worthy Mr. Dunster, whom the Lord hath made boldly to bear testimony against the spirit of persecution."[23] This was in reference to Dunster's defense of the Quakers in the Massachusetts Bay and Plymouth colonies.

Rev. Dunster died in Scituate on February 27, 1659. His body was embalmed and taken to Cambridge for burial. The fact that Dunster appointed the Rev. Mitchell, along with Charles Chauncy, to appraise his library as well as bequeathing some books to them, says much about the character of Dunster, for Mitchell had been one of Dunster's harshest critics on the issue of baptism. Dunster asked to be buried in Cambridge hoping that "time and reflection" would allow his interment to "soften whatever asperity remained." It would take him back to the place that he most cherished and would also show that he had no resentment towards those who had been so harsh to him. As his biographer writes, "All his great services in the cause of the sacred and liberal learning while at Cambridge, were cast quite into the shade by the Christ-like charity and humility which characterized his obscurity at Scituate, and especially his farewell to the world."[24] Jonathan Mitchell was present at the burial and composed an elegy as "a respectful tribute to his memory."[25]

---

[21] Pratt, 72.
[22] Davis, 15.
[23] Chaplin, 209.
[24] Chaplin, 224.
[25] Chaplin, 225.

Scituate's reputation for religious tolerance was manifested by its conduct towards Quakers. The sect, newly founded by George Fox in England in the late 1640s, did not find a warm welcome in Massachusetts Bay. Almost from the beginning Quakers were persecuted, prosecuted, tried, and in the case of Mary Dyer, hung. The reason for persecution, in part, was the Quaker belief that a Christian could have a direct experience with Jesus Christ without the mediation of clergy. Not wanting to be superfluous and without power and influence, the Puritan clergy took great offense and did all they could to drive the Quakers out of the colony. In Scituate, Henry Dunster, Timothy Hatherly, James Cudworth and Isaac Robinson (the son of the pastor to the Pilgrims, John Robinson) stood against the oppressive measures taken in Plymouth against the Quakers. For a while, early colonial historians accused Rev. Dunster of persecuting Quakers living in Scituate. This is a mistake and the record left by Gen. James Cudworth, historian Daniel Damon says, disproves the charge. According to Damon, the two Scituate churches and their pastors were "conspicuous" in standing alone in opposing the persecution of the Quakers.[26] Nathaniel Morton, writing in 1669, says that Dunster was "useful in helping to oppose the abominable opinions of the Quakers."[27]

Principled stands often came at a price. James Cudworth lost his seat in the Plymouth Colony General Court and his views expressed in a letter written to a friend in England didn't help his relations with those in power:

> As to the state and condition of things amongst us, it is sad, and so likely to continue. The antichristian, persecuting spirit is very active, and that in the powers of this world. He that will not lash, persecute and punish men that differ in matters of religion, must not sit on the bench, nor sustain any office in the Commonwealth. Last election, Mr. Hatherly and

[26] Damon, 425
[27] Nathaniel Morton. *New England's Memorial* (1669), 186.

103

myself we left off the bench, and myself discharged of my captainship, because I had entertained some of the Quakers at my house, thereby that I might be the better acquainted with their principles. I thought it better to do so, than with the blind world to censure, condemn, rail at, and revile them, when they neither saw their persons nor knew any of their principles. But the Quakers and I cannot close in diverse things, and so I signified to the Court; but told them withal, that as I was no Quaker, so I would be no prosecutor.[28]

Thomas Lechford was the first professional lawyer in the Massachusetts Bay Colony. He came to Boston in 1638 and his stay was short. He was not sympathetic to the Puritan Colony and even less so to Separatist Plymouth. He was disbarred for trying to influence a jury and returned to England in 1641. The following year Lechford published, *Plain Dealing: or, News from New England*, a volume of observations ranging from the geography, and the flora and fauna of New England as well as comments on civil and religious affairs and practices. Lechford noted that it was common in some New England settlements for a bell to summon people to the daylong worship; other communities had the town crier; but in most towns of New England people were called to worship by the beat of a drum or the sound of a conch shell.

Keeping with their piety, New England church members had two services on Sunday, one in the morning, the other in the afternoon. The service would begin with a prayer, about fifteen minutes long, delivered by the minister. A scriptural reading and an exposition of it followed. Then there was a singing of the psalms done in the forming of "lining out" where the minister would sing the first verse and the congregation would respond with the next and so on. The focus of the service was the sermon, usually hours long.[29]

---

[28] Chaplin, 207-208.
[29] Johnson, 22.

There is no question that with Chauncy and Dunster the members of First Parish listened to sermons of great spiritual value. Sermons in colonial times were received as a means, not only of spiritual development and discipline, but also as a means of intellectual advancement. While literacy was on the rise, the spoken word was used to convey news, science and civic issues. Moreover, the sermons were a reflection of what was on people's minds, their hope and certainly, in a hostile environment, their fears. To those sitting in the pews their highest concern was their personal salvation. What, after all, was the meaning and goal of this earthly life if not to be in "the heaven of God Himself"?

The Puritan society held the spoken word in high regard and a minister would always try to meet that expectation; he would be a "gospel herald" declaring the way to personal salvation through faith in Jesus Christ.[30] To make sure the minister kept to the hour-long sermon an hourglass was beside him on the pulpit although it was reported that on occasion a minister, once the sands of the hourglass reached the bottom chamber, simply turned the hourglass over and kept preaching. The service concluded with a prayer and a blessing. There was no sign of the cross or kneeling, thus rejecting the rituals of the Church of England (and Catholicism).[31]

Worship would resume after lunch at two o'clock with a psalm being sung and the teacher (or minister) giving another sermon. On occasion a baptism would take place. Just before worship ended a deacon would get up and say, "Brethren of the congregation, now there is time left for contribution, wherefore God hath prospered you, so freely offer." The most prominent members of the congregation sitting in the first pews, followed by the Elders and then the "regular" people would come forward to where a deacon was seated and place their contribution into a box. Most contributions were of money but sometimes someone would place other items in the box such as a gilded cup. The money would be

---

[30] Stout, 27.
[31] Johnson, 22-23.

used towards the "maintenance of the ministers and the poor of the church. During the week, particularly on Thursdays, there were lectures in many towns. Poor people would attend as many as two or three a week "to the great neglect of their affairs and the damage of the public," so much so that in Massachusetts Bay the General Court called a meeting with church elders to ask them to shorten and limit the frequency of the church meetings. The elders did not take kindly to this and considered the request "an infringement of their liberties."[32]

The Sabbath which began at sundown on Saturday and lasted until sunset Sunday was the most important day of the week. In fact, it was the only holy day observed in New England. There were no Christmas or Easter celebrations, no Good Friday solemnity. What were observed besides the Sabbath were certain days of fasting and thanksgiving. Fast days were called upon in times of great trial such as disease, internal conflict or battles with Indians.[33] Fast days and weekday sermons were given to gain God's blessings for the founding of a church or to maintain civic order, telling the community who they were and what they must do to gain God's favor.[34] On fast days, normal activities would stop and the community would gather at the meetinghouse to plead for God's mercy and think about the meaning of the event that called for fasting and prayer. For the most part fast days were somber occasions with the small glimmer of hope that by gathering together in humility they were taking the right path toward deliverance.[35] Despite the Puritan's preference for spontaneous fasts and thanksgivings over fixed holidays, there was one day, a civil holiday, that next to the Sabbath was the most important day of the year. It was election day when free men would gather to elect legislators and to nominate members of the Governor's Council. Beginning in the 1630s, election days ended with a sermon.

---

[32] Thomas Lechford. *Plain Dealing* (1867), 48ff.
[33] Johnson, 25.
[34] Stout, 27.
[35] Stout, 28.

The minister was easily the most traveled person in town. He would make frequent calls to his parishioners, go to ministers meetings once a month and attend a colleague's ordination or attend a church council to assist in settling another church's internal dissention. It was rare in colonial times for ministers to be compensated in cash. The minister received most of his salary in commodities such as firewood, grain, cheese, oysters, meat or fowl. Church members and other townspeople would give to the minister what they could, when they could. If a parishioner were a shoemaker, the minister would likely leave after a visit with a new pair of boots. The minister would also likely be a farmer, in good times his yield was as much as his neighbors; in lean times, he had a foretelling of how meager his salary would be. The irregularity of the minister's salary, in whatever form, would often breed exasperation and hardship.[36]

Since formal schooling did not occur until the latter part of the seventeenth century, the Sunday and Thursday sermons, and the discussions they engendered were the intellectual life of the community. Gradually over the decades and for a century and a half, the theological doctrines about human behavior and the Protestant belief in the "priesthood of all believers" laid the seeds for the idea of individual liberty and ultimately, the Declaration of Independence, the Constitution and the American nation.[37]

When people wanted to join a congregation they first met with the church elders in private. They would be asked to make a statement about "the work of grace upon their souls ...." If the elders were satisfied that a person was a true believer and that "they have been wounded in their hearts for their original sin...and that they find their hearts drawn to believe in Christ Jesus," then they were admitted into the congregation assuming no member of the church raised an objection. The whole congregation would give their

---

[36] Winslow, 214.
[37] Winslow, 92, 94-95.

assent by rising and offering their right hand in fellowship to the new member.[38]

According to Lechford, it was the custom at funerals that nothing was read nor a sermon given though the minister was present. There was a tolling of a bell and the deceased would be carried to the grave where friends and neighbors would stand as the deceased was buried "with such gravity and sobriety as those that be present may seem to fear the judgments of God, and to hate sin, which is the cause of death...."[39]

In matters of discipline, for a public offence, such as adultery, the matter would be dealt with in public, otherwise the church elders would deal with it privately. A party would be brought before the congregation for a trial, witnesses to the offence would offer testimony and the congregation would find the person innocent, admonished or, in the most severe case, excommunicated. If the punishment was an admonishment, then the person would abstain from communion for a period of time and then seek the Church's approval to participate in communion again. In the extreme case of excommunication, the person was considered a heathen and was banned from any church activity or ritual, though their spouse, parents and children were allowed to participate.[40]

Marriage was a civil act, not a religious sacrament, and solemnized by civil magistrates, not ministers. John Robinson, pastor to the Pilgrims, in his pamphlet, *A Justification of Separation* (1610), provided the rationale for making marriage a civil act. He cited almost twenty Scriptural references "to prove that the celebration of marriage, the burial of the dead, are not ecclesiastical actions, appertaining to the ministry, but civil, and so to be performed." In the Plymouth Colony, the first marriage was performed on May 12, 1621 by a magistrate. In Massachusetts Bay no law precluded a

---

[38] Lechford, 19, 28.
[39] Lechford, 87-88.
[40] Lechford, 29-33.

minister from performing a marriage for fear of going against the laws of England. Nevertheless, it became the practice for the ceremony to be performed by a magistrate. [41] To this day, in the United States, marriage is a civil act that can only be blessed by clergy.

The Plymouth General Court was struggling to adopt a proper mode of conduct around public worship. These ordinances laid the foundation for the Pilgrim and Puritan reputation as being narrow minded and overly serious. In 1669 constables were charged with making sure no one was sleeping, loitering or playing around the meetinghouse during public worship. A law was passed which fined anyone caught smoking within two miles of the meetinghouse on Sunday. Another ordinance was enacted which prohibited the observance of Christmas Day as a holiday and outlawed any celebrations. As the number of towns grew in Plymouth the practice of financially supporting the church was codified. The Court was mindful of the need for income to supplement the minister's meager wages. In 1657, a statute passed by the General Court provided that in towns where there was "an able Godly Teaching Minister," a tax was levied "upon the estates of the Inhabitants according to their abilities to make up such a convenient maintenance, for his comfortable attendance on his work...."[42] It was the parish that determined the amount needed "for convenient maintenance" of the minister but the duty of collecting it fell on the town. The Court also encouraged seaside towns "where God's providence" caused whales to be beached, that some of the profits of the sale of the oil from the whale would be set aside for the town's minister.[43]

When Rev. Dunster died in 1659, the Rev. Nicholas Baker of nearby Hingham was asked to preach at First Parish in Scituate and soon thereafter, as was the custom, the church ordained and installed him as minister of the First Parish in 1660. Deane and others

---

[41] Lechford, 86-87n.
[42] Waite, 20-21.
[43] Waite, 20.

incorrectly state that Baker lacked a formal education, "Where and when he had qualified himself for the ministry we have not learned; but the probability is, that without a regular education, by the force of his own talents, he had acquired a respectable degree of theological knowledge...."[44] However, Baker did graduate from St. John's College at Cambridge, England (BA, 1631; MA, 1635).[45] Before becoming Scituate's pastor, Baker owned extensive properties in Hull, another small settlement in the Plymouth Colony, and served as a deputy in its General Court.

It was during Mr. Baker's ministry that harmony between the First Church and Parish and the South Society (Second Parish) was accomplished. Members of the South Society sought to reunite the two congregations making one body. They were motivated by the fact that their meetinghouse was in disrepair and the society's minister, Mr. Witherell, was nearly eighty years old and in ill health. While the inhabitants of the town wanted to have one church, the General Court in Plymouth mindful of the decades old controversy, advised against it:

> We...desire to be sensible of your present state, which is as you say, sadly desolate, as concerning the uniting of the two societies together; we look at it...to be the best expedient for the obtaining of mutual strength in the ways of God, in communications of the gifts and graces of his Holy Spirit, for general and special welfare of all, and for the support of ministerial administrations. Notwithstanding, we conceive, by reason of remote distance of place and other considerations, that if it were effected it would not have the tendency to the effecting of the ends proposed to induce unto the same, but rather to the contrary; and therefore our advice is to a continuance

---

[44] Deane, 181.

[45] Baker, Fred A. *Genealogical Record of Rev. Nicholas Baker (1610-1678) and his descendants*, (1917), 7.

in two distinct bodies, retaining a brotherly affection each to other, and endeavoring to promote the good of each other what you can, as many years you have done....[46]

Deane says that Rev. Baker "left here no memorable name for great powers of great success in his ministry, but records ... show his peaceful and godly influence."[47] Those "peaceful efforts" included the reconciliation between the two parishes. In one conciliatory gesture Baker wrote a letter to the Second Parish of Scituate in which he said, "We do willingly and gladly lay aside all former offenses taken up, or ancient disagreements and differences betwixt us; we desire God to forgive you and us whatsoever may have been displeasing to him."[48] He also returned First Parish to the practice of infant sprinkling, so abhorred by Rev. Chauncy and a cause of the creation of a second parish in Scituate. And so, the two congregations, while reconciled, never reunited.

Having been denied the re-union of the two parishes, the people of the First Parish voiced their objection to the Plymouth General Court for being taxed for the erection and maintenance of a church in which they did not worship. The General Court concurred and so the South Society built a new meetinghouse on the same site as the one it replaced and only the inhabitants of the south precinct paid for it.

In 1665 the town agreed to pay the two ministers, Rev. Baker of the North Parish (the First Church) and Rev. Witherell of the South Parish (the Second Church) by way of a yearly rating (taxes). In 1669 the raters (tax assessors) voted to raise one hundred pounds for the repair of the two meetinghouses, to be divided equally. In 1672 both Mr. Baker and Mr. Witherell were granted fifty acres of land but at the cost of a reduction in pay. In 1680 First Parish, wanting to

---

[46] Pratt, 73-74n.
[47] Deane, 181-182.
[48] Deane, 88.

build a new meetinghouse, proposed taxing all the town's inhabitants for that purpose. But, not surprisingly, the inhabitants of Second Parish, returning the earlier objection of First Parish, protested supporting a ministry outside their own. The General Court, being consistent, agreed and divided the town along the mill brook in Greenbush with the parishes on either side supporting their own ministry.[49]

Even though Deane dismisses Baker's ministry so casually, Baker was influential in bringing reason to a panic that roiled the Puritan colony to the north. Unlike the Massachusetts Bay Colony, the Plymouth Colony did not experience the frenzy of witchcraft accusations, trials and executions. Before the Salem witch trials of 1692, Scituate and Marshfield alone of all the towns in Plymouth Colony had incidents, fortunately isolated and without Salem's panic. Mary Ingram of Scituate was indicted in March, 1676 for causing Mehitable Woodworth "to fall into violent fits, causing greatest pain unto several parts of her body at several times, so as she…has been bereaved of her senses." Ingram was found innocent most likely because the court believed that the fits were brought about by Woodworth's own poor health.[50] Baker's calm presence may have limited the threat of witchcraft frenzy to this one case in Scituate.

Toward the end of his life, Rev. Baker's attention was given to another dramatic event. For fifty years relations between the Pilgrims and the Wampanoag were amicable, a relationship established by the Wampanoag leader, Massasoit, and the first Pilgrim settlers. By the 1670s tension increased because the growth of the European population and native tribal leaders grew distrustful. John Sassamon (born, Wassausmon) was a Native American Christian convert and early Harvard College graduate. He was a translator and adviser to Metacom (known by the English as King Philip and son of Massasoit). Sassamon told Plymouth Colony officials about Metacom's preparations for attacks on colonial settlements, but

---

[49] Waite, 21.
[50] Willison, 320.

before the officials could investigate, Sassamon was murdered, allegedly killed by a few of Metacom's Wampanoag men, angry at his betrayal. On the testimony of a Native American witness, the Plymouth Colony officials arrested three Wampanoag, including one of Metacom's counselors. A jury, which included Indian members, convicted the men of Sassamon's murder and they were hanged on June 8, 1675, in Plymouth. Some Wampanoag believed that both the trial and the court's sentence infringed on Wampanoag sovereignty. It was an insult to their people. On June 20, a band from the Pokanoket tribe attacked several isolated homesteads in the small settlement of Swansea and the devastating battles known as King Philip's War began.

Scituate was the site of a battle with the Wampanoag. In April 1676 the town was attacked by "a large body of Indians" coming from an earlier skirmish in Weymouth. According to later histories, the raid was "bravely repulsed by the inhabitants of Scituate."[51] A month later another attack on Scituate resulted in the deaths of some settlers and the burning of homes, barns and mills. Deane recounts the story of Sarah Ewell, who upon seeing the raiders, ran from her house on Walnut Tree Hill (near present-day Old Oaken Bucket Road) and down the hill toward the garrison. In her panic she left behind her infant grandchild, John Northey, sleeping in his crib. The attackers entered her house, stopped to take bread baking in the oven, and headed toward the garrison. While the fighting was going on Mrs. Ewell, remembering her grandchild, went back to her house and found her the baby boy sleeping in the crib, just as she had left him. The attack continued by the Stockbridge mill where both sides suffered many wounded and dead. The battle lasted until nightfall by which time "the whole force of the town" defended the mill. In payment for their service in the war some of Scituate's soldiers received their compensation in land [52] Many Scituate church members went off to war including militia leaders James Cudworth,

---

[51] Deane, 124.
[52] Deane, 126-129.

Isaac Buck and Isaac Chittenden, who lost his sons, Isaac, Jr. and Benjamin, in the war.

All these events, church-related or military, must have weighed heavily on Rev. Baker for he died on August 22, 1678 at seventy. Cotton Mather, in his *Magnalia Christi Americana*, offered this eulogy

> And into this catalogue I am content that there should be received (for the saints of this catalogue already departed have received him) honest Mr. Nicholas Baker of Scituate; who, though he had but a private education [sic], yet, being a pious and zealous man; or, as Dr. Arrowsmith expressed it, so good a logician, that he could offer up to God a reasonable service; so good an arithmetician that he could wisely number his days; and so good an orator that he persuaded himself to be a good Christian; and being also of good natural parts, especially of a strong memory, was chosen pastor of the church there; and in the pastoral charge of that church he continued about eighteen years, until that horror of mankind and reproach of medicine the stone (under which he preached patience by a very memorable example of it; never letting fall any word worse than this, which was an usual word with him, 'A mercy of God, it is no worse') put an end to his days.[53]

---

[53] Mather, 42.

Chapter Five

New Meetinghouses

After Rev. Baker's death the First (or North) Parish church was without a settled pastor for more than thirteen years. But First Parish persevered through the changes and growth the congregation and town experienced. The reasons for the thirteen-year hiatus between ministers are unknown because the church and town records from this period are lost. It was during this time that First Parish's second meetinghouse was built. The first was showing its age due to the elements and use. With the need of a new meetinghouse, the question arose as to its location. Second (or South Parish) also needed a new meetinghouse and with the old feud between the two churches resolved there was the hope that one meetinghouse, located in the Greenbush section of town, could serve the whole town. The North Parish, considering the reduction of costs for maintaining one ministry, agreed. However, as noted, the General Court in Plymouth opposed the effort and advised both parishes to retain "a brotherly affection each to other" as they kept to their own ways.[1] One of the reasons for the General Court's opposition was the consideration of distance. Since most churchgoers walked to the meetinghouse on Sundays and for other religious observances, as well as civic meetings, the cold New England winters and other inclement weather created a real hardship; thus, the Court's decision to maintain

---

[1] Waite, 23.

two parishes each with their own meetinghouse. So the original, deteriorating meetinghouse of First Parish was taken down and a nearly identical one was erected in the same location on Meetinghouse Lane. The new Second Parish church building was erected in 1680 near the present First Parish (Norwell) Cemetery.[2]

The first, second and third (built in 1708) meetinghouses of First Parish were located on a rise on Meetinghouse Lane up from the marshlands along the Driftway. By General Court law, new homes had to be built within a half mile of a meetinghouse but as the population grew, the law was ignored. The meetinghouses of First Parish, like most others in the colony, were built on a hill. It was a landmark and could be seen for miles around by travelers or ships coming into Scituate Harbor or the North River. The early meetinghouses did not have steeples; most were long squat buildings with thatched roofs.[3] Little more than a cabin made of rough-hewn timbers enclosed by simple palisades, "the meetinghouse could be distinguished from private houses only by virtue of its location at the village center.[4] Despite the breeze coming off the ocean, it must have been very hot in the Scituate meetinghouse in the summer because trees were cut down in a wide area around the building for the materials to construct the building and also out of fear that a forest fire would burn it to the ground.[5]

---

[2] Waite, 23.
[3] Alice Morse Earle. *The Sabbath in Puritan New England* (1902), 4-9.
[4] Stout, 14.
[5] Earle, *Sabbath*, 4-9.

A typical meetinghouse from the mid 1600's

The plain construction and interior of the meetinghouse conveyed the Pilgrim's insistence to evoke the "simplicity and purity" of the early Christian church, uncorrupted by the encrustation of "human," "arbitrary" and superstitious customs.[6] In the early years, the seats in the meetinghouse were likely to be hard, long and narrow benches made of wood from the surrounding trees. They had oiled paper in the shuttered windows, and when glass was used it was not set with putty but was nailed in. The outside of the meetinghouse was not painted or stained but was left to turn grey by the weather.[7]

The physical simplicity of the meetinghouses contradicted "the complex social relationships that existed within."[8] With the call to worship heard throughout the town on Sunday morning, people would assemble at the entrance and then, a few minutes before nine o'clock, men and women filed in separately through different doors and sat on opposite sides of the meetinghouse, as they also would during civic meetings. As years passed this practice changed and

---

[6] Stout, 14.
[7] Earle, Alice Morse, *Home and Child Life in Colonial Days* (r. 1969), 286.
[8] Daniels, Bruce, *Puritans at Play* (1995), 77.

117

caused some consternation when men and women were ordered to sit together "promiscuously."[9] The minister and his wife might enter before every one else or after. If after, the congregation would rise as he led his wife to her pew and then ascended a step to the pulpit. When the service ended, the minister and his wife would walk to the church entrance and greet the parishioners as they left. This would all be repeated at 2 o'clock when the afternoon service would begin.[10]

Children entered the meetinghouse after their parents. Girls sat beside their mothers or on footstools at their feet, or sometimes on the gallery stairs; a little enclosure held babies during the meeting. Boys did not sit with their families but were in groups by themselves where they were carefully watched by the "tithing-man."[11] He was also a town officer and usually had a number of families to watch over. He would visit houses and ask children to recite their catechism. He would ensure the family attended church and made certain no one tarried along the way to church. In the meetinghouse he would keep out dogs and wake those who slept. He would walk up and down the aisles with a stick which had a knob on one end and a foxtail on the other; the knob to keep the boys in order, the foxtail to awaken a sleeping parishioner.[12]

In colonial Massachusetts when people attended the meetinghouse, they were assigned specific places according to their standing in the community. People had the right to purchase seats and also to dispose of them if they departed from the settlement. By the 1660s the practice of arranging seats by status in the

---

[9] Earle, *Sabbath*, 47

[10] Daniels, 77.

[11] Earle, *Home and Child Life*, 289.

[12] Earle, *Child Life in Colonial America (r. 2009)*, 192.

*The "Old Sloop Church" pew chart (1859)
with names of owners or renters*

meetinghouse became quite customary.[13] There was a seating committee usually composed of selectman plus the elders and deacons of the church for seating in the meetinghouse was considered very serious business. In most cases, monetary worth and age still were the two most important considerations, though other factors such as high political

---

[13] Dinkin, 451.

119

office could also be influential.[14] The place of greatest importance, after the pulpit, was in the front, where the "seat of highest dignity," the "foreseat," was for the persons of utmost influence in the community. [15] Servants and slaves sat at the rear, or if there was one, the balcony. It was after the Revolutionary War that the majority of towns in Massachusetts abandoned the formal, status-based seating plan. But in order to raise money for their meetinghouses, a number of towns, like Scituate, began selling pews by auction rather than appointing them and, as before, wealthy persons sat in the most prominent locations, though people of lesser status were now able to purchase desirable pews, if they were willing to pay the price.[16]

The deacons sat in a "Deacons' Pew" just in front of the pulpit. In some churches there was a "Deaf Pew" in front for those who were hard of hearing. After choirs were established, the singers' seats were usually upstairs in the gallery. High up under the beams in the loft sat blacks, slave or free, and native people. If any person sat in a place not assigned to them, they had to pay a fine.[17]

Worship, by any standard, was an exercise in patience and self-discipline, as well as piety. Two or three hour sermons were customary and prayers were almost as long. "Do not pinch them with scant sermons," one minister advised a novice.[18] A short sermon would have been regarded as "irreligious and lacking in reverence." "In every New England town 'pious, plain-hearted Christians' spent weeks of their waking lives, year after year, seated in a pew, listening."[19] The meetinghouse doors were closed and watched and so that no one could leave even if tired or restless unless they had a

---

[14] Robert J. Dinkin. "Seating the Meeting House in Early Massachusetts" in *The New England Quarterly*, Vol.43, No. 3 (September, 1970), 453.

[15] Earle, *Sabbath*, 47.

[16] Dinkin, 452-453.

[17] Earle, *Home and Child Life*, 289.

[18] Earle, *Home and Child Life,* 291-2; Winslow, 91.

[19] Earle, *Sabbath*, 81; Winslow, 91.

good excuse. The singing of the psalms was tedious and unmusical. Singing was by ear since no musical instruments were allowed, as they were deemed frivolous. Many parishioners had no psalm books so the psalms were "lined" or "deaconed," that is, a line was read by the deacon and then sung by the congregation. Some psalms, when lined, took a half hour to sing during which the congregation stood.[20] People also stood during prayers since kneeling and bowing the head was a reminder of the Catholic liturgy and ritual. Sometimes the minister would pause to allow the elderly and infirmed to sit down during the prayer. The others would stand patiently until the end of the lengthy petition.[21] In the later colonial period, when the severity of worship was relaxed, bass viols, clarinets and flutes were played to help the singing. Contributions at first were not collected by the deacons, but the entire congregation, one after another, would walk up to the deacons' seat and place money, goods, wampum or promissory notes in a box. The service concluded with a prayer and a blessing.

The meetinghouses and churches were unheated from autumn to spring. Dogs were allowed inside so they would warm the feet of their owners. Women and children also carried foot stoves, which were small metal boxes that stood on wooden legs and held hot coals. During the noon intermission in winter, the chilled church attendants would go to a noon-house or a Sabbath Day house, a long low building near the meetinghouse, with horse stalls at one end and a chimney at the other.[22] Around the warm fire parishioners would eat their noon meal of cold pie, doughnuts, pork and peas, and brown bread that they had brought in their saddlebags. "The dining-place smelt to heaven of horses, for often at the further end of the noon-house were stabled the patient steeds…but this stable-odor did not hinder appetite, nor did the warm equine breaths that helped to temper the atmosphere of the noon-house offend the senses…."[23] As

---

[20] Earle, *Home and Child Life*, 291-2.
[21] Earle, *Sabbath*, 80.
[22] Earle, *Home and Child Life*, 290.
[23] Earle, *Sabbath*, 52.

a building where public meetings were also held, notices of varied content and importance were nailed to the door where all of the congregation would readily see them—notices of town meetings, of sales of cattle or farms, lists of town officers, notices of intended marriages.[24]

The Rev. Jeremiah Cushing was a highly regarded minister when the church elders asked him to come to preach in Scituate. They must have approved his sermons and demeanor because the congregation ordained him on May 27th of that year. Cushing was born in Hingham, Massachusetts on July 3, 1654 to Daniel and Lydia Cushing. Daniel was the Hingham town clerk and graduated from Harvard College. Jeremiah Cushing was Scituate's first native-born minister. He studied for the ministry under the Rev. John Norton of Hingham. Little is recorded of Rev. Cushing's ministry, though it lasted fourteen years. In addition to being the first Scituate minister born in the colonies, Cushing was the first graduate of Harvard College to serve First Parish. His salary was only sixty pounds but the Conihassett partners gave him twenty acres of land.[25] In January 1694, the parish voted to build a new parsonage for the minister. A portion of land that was given to Rev. Chauncy and his successors was sold to purchase fencing and the building of a barn on the new parsonage site. The church and society made it quite clear that Mr. Cushing was expected to keep the fences in good repair.[26] Unfortunately, Mr. Cushing was a man of poor health, and suffered from lengthy illnesses. He died in Scituate March 22, 1705 at age 51 after a lingering illness of several months during which he took leave from his ministry. He is buried in what was then the First Parish Cemetery (now known at the Men of Kent Cemetery) on Meetinghouse Lane in Scituate. Several months after his death his widow told the church that she expected to receive the salary it owed her husband. While not admitting any debt, the church and society

---

[24] Earle, *Home and Child Life*, 287.
[25] *Sibley's Harvard Graduates Vol. II* (1942), 499.
[26] FPS records.

gave her twenty-five pounds and allowed her and her children to stay in the parsonage so as not to be "turned out of doors."[27]

By the early 1700s, the second First Parish meetinghouse was in such disrepair that it was clear a new building had to be erected. On August 18, 1707, church records note that the church received £300 from the town to build the new church/meetinghouse. Once again, there was a dispute as to its location. In the twenty-five years since the second meetinghouse was built the town's population continued its westward movement. No longer could the brook at Greenbush serve as the dividing line between the two parishes. Although the two Scituate churches had reconciled, there continued to be tension between the two precincts of the Scituate parish, specifically about the boundary of the two societies. The church and society of First Parish voted to send its agents, Joseph Otis, David Jacob, and Lt. James Briggs to negotiate the boundary, or to make a settlement by levying a tax upon the whole town and dividing it equally between the two societies.[28] At first it was agreed that the building "should be set upon some part of the meeting house hill not to be further west then where the ways meet below Lt. Bucks shop (near the present intersection of First Parish and Stockbridge Roads). However, this proposal was promptly objected to by some so it was agreed that advice be sought from the General Court in Boston. (The Plymouth colony as a political entity ended in 1691 and was incorporated into the Massachusetts Bay colony.) A committee authorized by the Massachusetts Bay General Court came to Scituate and made the recommendation that a third meeting house be erected on the same sight as the previous two. This was done in 1708.

The members of First Parish had the foresight to construct the new church with galleries along three sides of the building. In 1714, pews were placed up in the galleries. Since there were more people seeking pews than available, a committee was formed to assign seating. The crowded church caused a lack of proper behavior,

---

[27] Waite, 24.
[28] FPS records.

123

so much so that the church had "to look after and inspect all disorders in the worship of God or in times of intermission on Sabbath days by boys, Negroes or indens (indentured servants)...."[29]

Arriving just before the building of the third meetinghouse was the Rev. Nathaniel Pitcher, the eighth minister of First Parish. Pitcher was born in nearby Milton, Massachusetts on November 30, 1685. His studies at Harvard College were cut short due to financial circumstances so he became a teacher of English and Latin in Sudbury, Massachusetts. After Harvard forgave him his "detriments" at the end of his freshman year, he returned to Harvard where he received his B.A. and then his M.A. in 1706.[30] Pitcher, only twenty-one and before he received his degrees, was asked to come to preach in Scituate during the illness of Mr. Cushing. This being the circumstance, Pitcher was not paid by the town or the church but rather received income through contributions "for his encouragement and his diet." Following Cushing's death the church voted and the society (the town) concurred in the calling of Rev. Pitcher. This was a departure from the earlier practice where the church alone chose and ordained a minister and it suggests the very early stages of the separation of church and state since this "concurrence" acknowledges the existence of the two entities, church and town.[31] This was the practice until disestablishment in the 1830s. Mr. Pitcher was ordained on September 24, 1707. At the time of his ordination there were sixty-three male and twenty-seven female members of the church. An additional eighty-one joined the church during his ministry.

Soon after he moved onto the land Rev. Chauncy once owned, Pitcher was involved in a suit regarding the property which took years to resolve. It seems that a parishioner had removed fences on the parsonage land; Pitcher sued and lost. He refused to enter into arbitration and appealed to a higher court where he was successful.

---

[29] Waite, p. 25.
[30] Silbey's Vol. 5, 234.
[31] Waite, 25-26.

124

Despite this matter with the parishioner, tradition says that Pitcher was noted for maintaining peace and unity among the people. He was described as "an unusually able preacher and had a charming personality." Stories of Rev. Pitcher's ministry recounted a time of "peace and union" within the congregation. It was during his ministry that the controversies over baptism and the treatment of Quakers had subsided as a moderate Calvinism grew in influence even in the midst of the "Great Awakening."[32] Pitcher was also known for his poetry, several written as a form of condolence for the loss of a parishioner's loved one.[33] Some poems have been preserved but, as Deane says, "more for the sake of antiquity, than for their merits."[34]

An example of Rev. Pitcher's poetry is the following, written as a eulogy for the Pilgrim's pastor the Rev. John Robinson's wife and daughter, who were lost at sea crossing the Atlantic on September 22, 1722:

In trembling airs perfume the sable Night;
Tread soft, while we relate the Tragedy,
Perform'd by Him who dwells and rules on High.
Let thundering billows in due concert meet,
And raging winds and waves each other greet,
And all th' obsequious Elements combine,
To pay Devotion to the Will Divine,
Of Him, whose Infinite and matchless sway,
The proudest of Created Powers obey.
Behold the ghastly visage of each face,
Besmear'd with Griefs, deep mourning in each place;
Not one without a tear upon the Hearse
Of the bright subjects of my Fainting verse.

---

[32] Deane, 185-186.
[33] Silbey's, Vol. 5, 236.
[34] Deane, 185.

REV. SIR,
Can Heart conceive, or Tongue express your grief?
Can any hand but Heaven's give relief?
Who wounds and heals, who kills and keeps alive?
And when depress'd, makes Grace to live and thrive.
Behold bright Sovereignty in clear Displays
Turning your Halcion into Gloomy days;
Your Nuptial Knot, the fatal Stroke unty'd,
By Heaven's Decree, on the Atlantick wide;
The Noisy Waters, on the Seas that move,
Which cannot quench the streams of Boundless love
Translated yours unto the Joys above,
Transported far beyond all Fears and Harms,
Guarded by Angels to their Saviour's Arms.
You could not close your Vertuous Lady's Eye;
You must not see your dearest Consort dye,
Nor her expiring, gasping agonies,
Nor listen to her fervent Farewell cries,
Bright Hannah's prayers for you are swiftly gone
On Eagle's Wings, up to the Sapphire Throne,
And you are left to grieve and pray alone.
One of the Gowned Tribe and Family,
Of bright descent and Worthy Pedigree;
A charming daughter in our Israel,
In vertuous acts and Deeds seem to excel:
As Mother, Mistress, Neighbor, Wife, most rare;
Should I exceed, to say beyond compare?
Call her the Phoenix, but you cannot lye,
Whether it be in Prose or Poetry.
For Meekness, Piety, and Patience;
Rare Modesty, Unwearied Diligence;
For Gracious Temper, Prudent Conduct too,
How few of the fair Sex could her out do?
Beloved of all while living, and now dead,
The female Hadadrimmon's lost their head.
Her precious Daughter bears her company,
Taking her flight up to the Joys on High

To dwell and feast with her eternally.
God's Will is done, 'Tis duty to resign
Yourself and all unto the Will Divine:
You often pray'd " God let thy Will be done! "
Still do so, now your dearest Ones are gone.
If your Great Sovereign takes but his own due,
You are obliged to Him, not He to you.
May God Almighty Sanctify this frown,
To the bereaved Family and Town:
May the tender brood, under your mateless wing,
When Clouds are passed over, chirp and sing.
May you Sir, fill the Consecrated Place,
With purest doctrines and displays of Grace,
Till you have run and finished your Race, I
That when your dust shaI1 unto dust go down,
You may receive the Bright and Massy Crown,
And with your dearest Ones enhappy'd be,
In light above, Throughout eternity.

By the time the Plymouth Colony merged with the Massachusetts Bay Colony in 1691, Scituate was the largest and wealthiest of the seven Plymouth Colony towns. Not surprisingly with rapid growth came conflict. Scituate was now a town of merchants and ship builders as well as farmers and tradesmen. No longer suffering the adversities of the earliest settlers three generations before, ministers lamented the fact that "New England had forsaken its original purpose and now ran idolatrous after new gods."[35] The new gods were the deities of materialism. Divergent theological viewpoints spoken or suppressed within the First Parish congregation caused such friction that it was agreed that the congregation needed to re-covenant with one another.

On March 12, 1710 a new covenant was presented to the congregation. After an introductory statement that "the covenant

---

[35] Bernard Bailyn, *The New England Merchants in the Seventeenth Century* (1955) 140.

wherein we have stood united is in such terms as is not agreeable to sundry persons among us who are of sober conversation and religiously disposed," there follows this pledge:

"We do give up ourselves to that God whose name alone Jehovah Father, Son & Holy Ghost, cleaving to God the Father as our chief and only good and unto our Lord Jesus Christ as our only Savior the prophet priest & king of our souls, and to the spirit of God as our only sanctifier and comforter. And we do give up ourselves one unto another in the Lord covenanting to walk together as a Church of Christ in all ways, of his own institution agreeable to ye prescriptions, of his Holy Word. Promising that with all tender and brotherly love we will faithfully watch over one another's soul and that we will freely yield ourselves to ye discipline and power of Christ in his church and attend those seals and censures and whatever ordinances Christ hath appointed, so far forth as the Lord by his word and spirit hath or shall reveal to us to be our duty; and wherein we fail and come short of duty, to wait upon him for pardon and remission, beseeching him to make our spirits steadfast in his covenant and to own us as his church and covenant people forever. Amen.

Forty-two members of the church signed the 1710 covenant and it was this covenant that was central to the dispute that led to the schism of 1825.

Rev. Pitcher was a member of the ordination council which gave its blessing to the arrival of the Rev. Ebenezer Gay at First Parish in Hingham in 1717. Gay's biographer describes Nathaniel Pitcher as a "quiet liberal" who fit in nicely with the other members of the council, all of whom were moderate Calvinists. The moderates tended to emphasize the importance of human ethical responsibility in the process of salvation, rather than God's grace which the more zealous Calvinists saw as the only means of salvation.[36] By the 1720s, sermons were getting shorter as ministers preached to appeal to both the hearts and minds of their congregation. The message was meant to be readily understood and to be consistent with personal experience. Sermons followed the familiar and comfortable structure: a biblical passage, explication of doctrine, proofs from Scripture and finally, application to one's life. The minister was expected to offer learned words but not be ostentatious; "neither flowery nor bombastic, but warm enough to stir emotions."[37]

Ministers and congregations often wrangled over salaries, though most ministers just kept on doing what they had to do to make ends meet. They farmed their own land and took as part of their pay, produce and firewood.[38] With times being hard and the colonial economy not strong, Mr. Pitcher's first regular salary was set at fifty-five pounds a year. Compensation was not his only worry, as Pitcher also suffered from poor health. Over the next ten years he suffered lengthy serious illnesses and the congregation responded. In 1717 his salary was set at £114 out of "consideration of great sickness and want and expensive circumstances he and his family have been laboring under."[39] Mr. Pitcher died at the age of 38 on September 27, 1723. His widow, the former Sarah Cushing (they were married in the Second Parish Church in 1710), was left with four small children to care for and she remained in the parsonage for over a year after which nothing is known of her or her four children.

The ninth minister of the Scituate congregation was the Reverend Shearjashub Bourn (or Bourne), a Harvard graduate, class of 1720. At Harvard, Bourn's only distinction appears to have been his leadership in a "general assault on the windows, an activity that once cost him the very considerable sum of 9 shillings."[40] Bourn was

[36] Wilson (1984), 40.
[37] Patricia Bonomi. *Under the Cope of Heaven* (1986), 68-69.
[38] Bonomi, 71.
[39] Waite, 26-27.
[40] Sibley's Harvard Graduates, Vol. 6, 371.

a member of a prominent Cape Cod family. His great grandfather, Richard Bourne (1609-1682), was a missionary to the Indians and was ordained as the pastor to an Indian church in Mashpee in 1670. Richard's son, named Shearjashub (1643-1718), grandfather of Scituate's minister, was a lawyer who procured from the Plymouth General Court a ratification of Indian land deeds so that no European could buy any of those lands without the Indians' consent.[41] Shearjashub's father, Melatiah (1674-1742), was a judge and a colonel in the colonial militia. The name, "Shearjashub," is taken from the Bible, the symbolic name of the prophet Isaiah's son, which means, "a remnant shall return." Rev. Bourn was married four times and widowed three. Of his first wife, Abigail Cotton, it was said that she was "a prudent, virtuous, diligent woman." Of his third wife, Deborah Barker, her newspaper obituary stated, "She was an ornament to Human Nature in her sprightly Genius and uncommon application to books. Being favored with a religious and polite education, she excelled in her strict devotion toward God, dutiful and affectionate deportment to her husband, tenderness to her domestic dependents, neatness and prudence in her economy, kindness to her relations and fidelity and kindness and gentleness to all around her. She opened her mouth with wisdom and in her tongue was the law of kindness."[42]

Among the ministers of the colony, Bourn is described as "obscure" and it is peculiar that Bourn is described as such for he was the longest serving minister (thirty-seven years) of the congregation up to that time. Still, there is no record that he took part in the intellectual revolution or religious controversies of his era. Nevertheless, his ministry is described as both "harmonious and prosperous"[43] and "a most acceptable one."[44] His salary in 1724 was one hundred pounds and two years later it was increased by ten

---

[41] William Allen. *An American Biographical and Historical Dictionary* (1832), 125.
[42] *Boston Evening Post*, March 1, 1756.
[43] Waite, 28.
[44] Damon, 425.

pounds, though the church refused to give him any more money for repairs to the parsonage and its fences. Nevertheless, the parish did vote in 1750 to give him three hundred and fifty pounds because the church had fallen behind in its payments to him.[45]

Church records indicate that during his ministry Bourn baptized one thousand one hundred-sixteen people, married two hundred seventy-four couples and admitted one hundred sixty-eight to the church. Among those baptized and admitted as members were free blacks as well as servants. On May 13, 1735, the church voted "that servant children may be baptized upon the faith of their master or overseer, they promising to bring them up in the nurture and admonition of the Lord."[46] One wonders if Rev. Bourn had conflicted feelings about baptizing free blacks or about his son, Shearjashub, Jr. who was an active slave trader out of Newport, Rhode Island. Rev. Bourn did not have any slaves or servants.

Scituate's population continued to grow and by 1729 there was need for a newer, larger, and more centrally located church, moving it to what is now Lawson Common near the Cudworth house, and a few hundred yards from the present location of the First Parish Church.[47] A year later, in February 1730, the parish accepted a piece of land from Nicholas Litchfield at the site where the church leaders wanted to put the meetinghouse. Agents for the church were appointed to remove and rebuild the old meetinghouse. But the people living to the east raised objections to the General Court. This group, led by David Jacob, believed the present location, on Meetinghouse Lane, was still suitable and that the existing building was "a very commodious house."[48] As the old meetinghouse continued to deteriorate, a committee of the General Court came to

---

[45] Waite, 28.
[46] *Document of the Pilgrim Conference Containing an Historical Sketch of the First Trinitarian Congregational Church of Christ in Scituate, Mass.* (1853), 33-34.
[47] Deane, 31.
[48] Pratt, 80.

Scituate in 1733 and, after hearing the contesting parties, voted against moving the church from Meetinghouse Lane. During the long delay from the time of the Litchfield gift to the General Court's decision, the agents hired by the church to oversee the removal and rebuilding of the meetinghouse proceeded and contracted with workman for construction and vendors for materials. With the Court's decision against moving the meetinghouse, the contractors sought damages for the broken contract and the town paid them £35. By 1737, a majority of the town voted in favor to move the meetinghouse to the new location (Lawson Common.) Unfortunately, that structure's usefulness lasted only thirty-seven years for the parish had outgrown it once again.[49]

The new, fourth meetinghouse had stone steps and sheds for horses and carriages. It was whitewashed and the interior was plastered. But within five years of use the meetinghouse became inadequate.[50] It was at first recommended that the pews be rearranged to make room for more. This never happened probably be cause a lack of funds. There is no further mention of any other renovation or enlargement of the building in the church records until twelve years later, in 1749, when it was voted to cut the meetinghouse in two. The increase in space would be accomplished by inserting a fifteen-foot section in the middle. This practice was not uncommon for the time.[51] The project was to be accomplished by volunteer labor who would also build the pews which the laborers would own for as long as the building was used.[52] But this plan fell through as well due to a lack of a sufficient number of volunteers, so the more modest plan of a dozen years earlier of rearranging the pews to provide more space was done and paid for by the selling of the new pews.[53]

---

[49] Deane, 31-32
[50] Waite, 37.
[51] Waite, 37.
[52] Waite, 37.
[53] Waite, 37.

Chapter Six

New Lights, Old Lights and Revolutions

The primary characteristics of the Pilgrims and Puritans were their introspection and self-analysis. Not only did these apply to their personal piety and behavior but it also defined the community's self-image. The idea we have of Puritan society is that of a community seeking great control over itself and the individuals in it, thus the pejorative, "puritanical." However, this introspection and self-analysis also led to a desire to improve society and the individual. There was no self-delusion in the Puritan community, but there was a great deal of self-criticism.

By the first quarter of the eighteenth century, many Puritan leaders saw a decline in faithfulness, even though the number of congregational churches was over four hundred in all of the colonies with the greatest concentration in New England. In 1720 a period of intense religious activity known as "The Great Awakening" began. Aroused religious passion brought to the fore the long simmering divisions within Puritanism. Two factions arose. One was known as the "New Lights," evangelicals who supported and participated in the revivals. They sought to restore strict Calvinistic theology and the "sense of immediacy of the Holy Spirit in the conversion of souls" that was so central to church membership a hundred years earlier. The other faction in the Great Awakening was the "Old Lights," rationalists who opposed the revival and call for a return to strict

Calvinism. One of the leaders of the Old Lights was the Rev. Charles Chauncy of the First Church of Boston, the namesake and grandson of the minister in Scituate. He, like the other Old Lights, was troubled by the "enthusiasm" of the revivalists.

Rationalism, born of the Enlightenment, was slowly influencing theology. Liberal Christians were believers of the Bible and liberal scholars and ministers read the Bible with a deep analytical discernment. Being students of the history of the Church as well, these "rationalists" believed that since some ancient texts made it into the Bible and others did not, the Bible was divinely inspired, rather than written by God Himself, and therefore not all Scripture was equally authoritative.[1]

Another irritant to the Old Lights were the itinerant ministers of the Great Awakening who would preach in communities where they weren't invited, upsetting the churches and ministers of the "Standing Order." One itinerant minister from New Jersey who toured New England wrote a pamphlet in which he suggested that the majority of New England clergy might not even be Christian! One consequence of this division was to end the Congregational hegemony in New England. Churches took sides and either became a New Light or an Old Light congregation. The former broke away from town control contending that they were the true keepers of the faith and many of these New Light churches became Baptist. It was this clash between the supporters and opponents of the Great Awakening that would also lead to the Unitarian Controversy and the schism of the churches of the Standing Order seventy-five years later.[2]

---

[1] Charles Forman. "Elected Now By Time," in Conrad Wright, ed., *A Stream of Light: A Sesquicentennial History of American Unitarianism* (1975), 15.
[2] Edwin Gaustad and Leigh Schmidt. *The Religious History of America* (2002), 6; Wright, xiii.

Conrad Wright, the preeminent historian of American Unitarianism, observed that the development of liberal Christianity was a consequence of the contentious and fierce debates between the Old and New Lights. There were some "continuities" between liberal Christianity and what the New Lights sought to restore. One such "continuity" was the belief in the duty to God and the obligation to one's fellow human beings. This "imposed on [them] the responsibility for constant self-scrutiny to be sure that [they were] doing what [they] ought." [3] This would lead to the long-standing Unitarian belief in "self-cultivation" and self-improvement; that a person's salvation depended as much on character and works as it did by way of God's grace. More importantly, there were disconnections on matters of doctrine. The New Lights saw God as sovereign and judge who condemned sinners while the liberals preferred to think of God as a loving father with benevolence toward humanity. The Old Lights believed that Scripture revealed a triune God, while the liberals were beginning to see the Trinity as both unscriptural and irrational. In responding to these doctrinal differences, the liberals were laying the foundation of their own beliefs

Cedric Cowing makes the interesting assertion that most of the churches from the Massachusetts Bay and Plymouth Colonies were resistant to the New Light ministers because their origin lay in the settlers and pastors from Southeastern England (including Kent). It was this part of England, closest to the Continent, that accepted the Reformation more readily than the rest of the country. [4] Because Puritanism relied more on the Bible than on tradition, and because it was intent on reducing the Catholic vestiges and encouraging the "Plain Style" in sermons, dress and art, it found a receptive audience in the growing mercantile class in and around London. People coming in from the rural and pastoral northwest of England were less receptive to the rationality of Puritanism and more open to the evangelical sects. [5] In Kent, the ancestral home of many of Scituate's

---

[3] Wright, *Stream of Light*, xiii.
[4] Cedric B. Cowing. *The Saving Remnant* (1995), 12.
[5] Cowing, 16.

early settlers, Methodists and evangelicals in the 1770s, found little fertile ground. A Methodist preacher described Kent as "a profane place. There was revelry in the pubs during Sunday services." John Wesley, the founder of Methodism, came to the conclusion that Methodists were "ploughing upon the sand" in Southeastern England.[6] And so it was along the coast of Massachusetts.

Rev. Ebenezer Gay in nearby Hingham and the Rev. Nathaniel Ells of South Scituate were the leaders of Congregational ministers south of Boston. Just prior to the Great Awakening, ministers on the South Shore were meeting as a group. They were continuing the tradition of the clerical association going back to the Cambridge Platform of 1648. During the height of the Great Awakening, Rev. Bourn, an Old Light, had no need to worry about theological competition from the evangelicals, for the Rev. David Barnes, another Old Light minister, received a unanimous call to be Rev. Ells' successor at Second Parish in Scituate.[7] In Scituate, the Great Awakening was "quite mild" and so it was "naturally unresponsive to evangelism." [8] According to Cowling, wherever immigrants from the southeast of England were dominant, from Rye, New Hampshire to Scituate, Massachusetts, the Old Lights dominated and became the "seedbed for Unitarianism after 1800." [9]

Rev. Bourn had a stroke in 1755 while in the pulpit. Although he recovered, he performed his pastoral and preaching duties with difficulty, so much so that the congregation became concerned, but not alarmed. Six years later, with compassion, the congregation convinced him to resign and he accepted a dismissal on August 6, 1761. The effects of the stroke added to Bourn's depressive state brought on over the years by the deaths of three wives and, more recently, the deaths of his three adult daughters in the space of

---

[6] Cowing, 157.
[7] Cowing, 260.
[8] Cowing, 260.
[9] Cowing, 263.

thirteen months. The pastor acknowledged his condition to the congregation in a letter,

> Whereas the Sovereign God in the way of his holy and righteous providence hath been pleased to exercise me with affections of various kinds, whereby I am...broken both in body and mind, and have been for more than twelve months...taken off from my ministerial labors and by reason of my growing bodily infirmities, I have no rational prospect of ever being so far restored to health again as to be any further serviceable to your souls.... [It] makes it necessary for me to ask of you a dismission from my pastoral office over you...

The church responded to Rev. Bourn's resignation in a letter:

> That we have enjoyed the benefit of your labors for so long a course of years testifying on your behalf that you have been a peaceful, prudent diligent and faithful minister of Jesus Christ and doubt not but that you have been instrumental of converting many souls in this place from the error of their ways for which you merit our thanks.

Upon his dismissal Bourn was given one hundred pounds and the use of the parsonage for eighteen months. He moved to Roxbury, Massachusetts and while his health was poor he survived another six years until he died on August 14, 1768. Upon his gravestone were written these words: "Cautious himself, he others ne'er deceived; Lived as he taught and as he taught, believed."[10]

At a meeting of February 8, 1762, the church called the Rev. Abiel Leonard of Plymouth to be minister beginning March 1, 1763. Apparently, Rev. Leonard was not sure about accepting the call to

---

[10] Silbey's, 371.

Scituate for, on April 19, 1762, the parish voted to allow Mr. Leonard more time to consider. Ultimately, either Rev. Leonard declined or the parish felt it could no longer delay in calling a minister. Leonard became the minister at Woodstock, Connecticut in 1763, where the Rev. David Barnes of South Scituate, Massachusetts gave the ordination sermon. Soon after the Revolutionary War began, Leonard became chaplain to Gen. George Washington. Sadly, Rev. Leonard took his own life on August 14, 1778. He shot himself after learning that Col. Benedict Arnold censured him for having overstayed his furlough to attend to his sick child.[11]

After the disappointment over Rev. Leonard, the church voted at a December 27, 1762 meeting, to call the Rev. Ebenezer Grosvenor. Born in Pomfret, Connecticut in 1738, Grosvenor is the only First Parish minister to graduate from Yale. Upon receiving the call to become minister of First Parish, Rev. Grosvenor wrote the following on January 31, 1763

Hon [ored] & Beloved

It is with gratitude to God & you that I would take notice of the kind reception which my humble and imperfect labors have found among you; and that he hath inclined your hearts, with so much unanimity (I wish I could say unanimously) to invite me to settle with you, in the work of the gospel ministry to take upon me the care & charge of your souls. Having taken the matter into serious consideration and asked counsel of others, especially of the wonderful councilor for Light and Direction in this great and important affairs of His Kingdom.

I do now with much fear and trembling under an awful sense of the greatness and difficulty attending the work I am about to engage in; and with a humble

---

[11] George Sears Greene. *The Greenes of Rhode Island, with historical records of English ancestry, 1534-1902 (1903)*, 243.

dependence on Divine Assistance, accept of your invitation, to settle with you, in the great work of the Gospel Ministry; and to take the Pastoral Care & Oversight of you, in the Lord: Trusting also that while I am faithfully ministering to you in the spiritual things for the good of your souls, you will readily minister to me of your temporal things as my necessities shall from time to time require and this I am the more encouraged to hope for, from the offers you have already made for my comfortable support, which I cheerfully accept.

And now my brethren & friends, let us strive together in our prayers, that the great head of the church and bishop [of] souls would smile upon [us] and bless in coming into the near relation of Pastor & People; and enable us aright to discharge the duties mutually incumbent upon us; that he would make me a faithful and successful minister of the New Testament and you a holy and happy people; that so when we shall have done worshipping together as a Church Militant here on earth, we all may be admitted to join the General Assembly of the Church triumphant in the heaven and having finished our course and kept the faith, there may henceforth laid up for us a Crown of Righteousness, which the Lord, the Righteous Judge shall give unto us and not only to us but to all those who love his appearing – and now may the God of Peace, who brought again from the dead, our Lord Jesus Christ, the great shepherd of the sheep, make you perfect, work in you that which is well pleasing in his sight; to whom be glory and honor for ever and ever Amen.

This from your unworthy Pastor-elect, Eben. Grosvenor

The Rev. Samuel Dunbar, Pastor of First Church in Stoughton, gave the ordination sermon in April 1763 at Rev. Grosvenor's installation. His text was 2 Corinthians 2:17, "For we are not, as so many, peddling the word of God; but as of sincerity, but as from God, we speak in the sight of God in Christ." The church records indicate that the ordination was carried on with "much order and decency." The First Parish moderator, Thomas Clapp, offered this prayer which was written into the church records,

> May Mr. Grosvenor prove a great blessing to this people, and be long continued a successful as well as faithful laborer in this part of his Lord's vineyard may he be an happy instrument of gathering in God's elect of saving many souls that he may hereafter be found among the wise that shall shine as the brightness of the firmament and among those that turn many to righteousness, who shall sparkle as the stars forever and ever.

The congregation did its best to welcome Rev. Grosvenor by improving the fences and the grounds of the parsonage but religious controversy between the orthodox and the developing liberal faction in the congregation was growing bitter. He was also a moderate Calvinist, more so than many of his parishioners. This was what Grosvenor referred to in his acceptance letter, regretting a non-unanimous call. In fact, seven members of the congregation voiced their objection to the ordaining council and were "disposed to give him trouble," because his theological approach was not the same as Rev. George Whitfield's, the most prominent preacher of the Great Awakening.[12] A few years after Grosvenor's arrival the more orthodox in the parish called for a vote as to whether the deacons should read Psalms publicly on Sunday "as it had been done before."
[13] The request was defeated indicating the growing liberal influence in

---

[12] Deane, 187.
[13] Waite, 33.

the Scituate church. In spite of his moderate views, and the division and conflict, Grosvenor's ministry lasted seventeen years.

On March 13, 1769 a proposal for a new meetinghouse was approved. The following month a plan for the new building was accepted. It was to be sixty-seven feet long and fifty feet wide with sixty pews on the lower floor. Its dimensions were later revised to be sixty-eight feet long and fifty feet wide. It was also voted that the church should have a steeple at the west end and a portico on the east end and stairs going up to a gallery. The congregation voted to sell the pews to procure money to build the meetinghouse and, if the dues did not produce enough income, it was voted that the precinct (parish) make it up by way of assessments (taxes). The idea of a new meetinghouse became contentious once more, mostly because of the location issue again, but also because of the growing theological divisions and so, its building was delayed. In March of 1771, two years after the initial decision to build, the design of the church was slightly altered. Now it was to have the dimensions of sixty-six feet long by forty-eight feet wide. Once again a decision as to the church's location was delayed so a committee headed by the Hon. John Cushing (superior court judge and father to future U.S. Supreme Court Justice William Cushing) was asked to return with a recommendation. At another meeting in May, the location was still not finalized but by the end of 1772, the dimensions were set with a ninety foot spire, whereupon it was finally agreed to build the new meetinghouse atop the hill in Mr. Daniel Jenkins's pasture two hundred yards to the west of where the church was then located. That site is the present location of the First Parish church. The building was completed and occupied in late 1774 and was painted a dark stone color; the doors were a chocolate color with white trim and the roof, red.[14]

Israel Litchfield, a Scituate tanner and member of First Parish, wrote in his diary on December 4, 1774, a "dull and cloudy" day, that work on the interior of the church was still underway as "the

---

[14] Waite, 41

carpenters have got all the pews sat up and some of the seats. The place for the singers was erected last week. The stairs in the westerly porch are not yet built."[15] A few days later, a day of thanksgiving was celebrated by proclamation of the Provincial Congress. Rev. Grosvenor used as his text Psalm 10: 1, "I will sing of mercy and judgment: unto thee, O Lord, will I sing." Litchfield was pleased with the sermon and noted that following the "public service" a collection was taken up for a church member, the widow Hayden and her family, all of whom were sick with a fever and, as a result, were "reduced to very needy circumstances." About forty pounds was contributed.[16]

Samuel Deane, writing in 1831, described the then fifty-seven year old First Parish church building in this manner: "It had a spire at the westerly end and a portico at the easterly end. It is a building of just proportions and respectable appearance, and with proper attention to repairs, promises to last at least another half century, and exhibit its ancient model to prosperity."[17] Deane, of course, had no way of knowing how accurate and dispiriting his prediction would be.

The new First Parish meetinghouse stood on a high tree-cleared hill, its steeple a prominent marker for ships seeking to enter Scituate Harbor, and thus, it earned the nickname, "The Old Sloop Church." Alongside the building there were ten sheds for horses and carriages. Although the parish owned the sheds, individuals who paid for them had their shed's use for life. Due to its exposed location or poor construction, the church required repairs and constant maintenance. Only twenty years after it was built the church galleries needed reinforcement for their support; the doors and windows needed repair, and the roof shingles needed refurbishing. In 1804 a cupola replaced the deteriorating spire but soon the cupola was in turn replaced with a newer and better-constructed steeple. Much of

---

[15] Johnson, Richard Brigham, ed., "The Diary of Israel Litchfield," *New England Historical and Genealogical Register* 129, 250 - 269.
[16] Litchfield diary
[17] Pratt, 82.

the wear and tear in the interior of the building came from frequent and rowdy public meetings. In the early nineteenth century people were prosecuted for defiling the meetinghouse when they threw grape skins, apple cores, or whortleberry husks on the church floor. During Sabbath worship, tobacco chewers were asked not to spit tobacco juice onto the church floor.[18] Stoves were not in the church because many feared they would causes headaches and drowsiness,[19] and so it wasn't until 1823 that a stove heated the meetinghouse. The Scituate church still has in its possession six communion cups or "beakers" used in the late 18th century and early 19th century.* In days long gone, the deacons of the church had custody of the beakers and they were used during the Lord's Supper. Whatever conflicts occurred about the details of the new meetinghouse and the behavior within it was minor compared to a conflict of greater import.

Israel Litchfield noted in his diary on January 1, 1775 the following,

> After public exercise was ended there was a contribution made for the use of the suffering industrious poor of Boston who are suffering on account of the cruel oppression of the Boston port bill or act of Parliament. [20]

These were the days leading up to the American Revolution and with the threat of war and public worry the meetinghouse took on a special role as the central location for news and action. Both Scituate parishes would often join together for services as men

---

[18] Waite, 41.
* Two additional beakers were sent to the Scituate Historical Society in September 2012 from a descendant of the Merritt family living in Washington State. They will be added to the collection if First Parish assures the Historical Society that the two beakers will never be sold.
[19] Waite, 38.
[20] Waite, 39.

gathered to train on the parade and training grounds. Israel Litchfield describes one day, January 11, 1775

> We went to the training field by the Rev. Mr. Barnes's meetinghouse [Second Parish]. The lower, middle and upper companies of the militia of this town met under arms in order to enlist minutemen. After we were embodied and marched some the three companies were marched into the meetinghouse for to hear a lecture. The Rev. Mr. Barnes went to prayer, then there was sang the two first stanzas of the 144th Psalm after which the Rev. Mr. Grosvenor preached a sermon, his text Second Chronicles [17:18: "And next to him was Jehozabad, and with him an hundred and eighty thousand ready prepared for the war."]
>
> Ready prepared for the war. It was generally concluded that he talked very well. After the sermon Mr. Grosvenor made a short prayer after which they sang two stanzas in the 101st Psalm. Then we were marched out of the meetinghouse and embodied again and they beat up for men to enlist as minutemen. There was about 66 men enlisted and I was one amongst them that enlisted. [21]

Litchfield was not only a soldier preparing for war, he was also a deacon of First Parish and church matters also needed his attention. He wrote in his diary about a meeting with lay leaders, just days before the battle of Lexington and Concord, which discussed the "facing and seating" in the church. It was voted that the singers in the new choir loft would face the minister when they sang. [22]

---

[21] Litchfield diary
[22] Litchfield diary, April 10, 1775

A month after the battles at Lexington and Concord (April 19, 1775), anxiety was clearly felt south of Boston for rumors were heard about Boston being on fire and there was also fear that British soldiers were landing in harbors along the Massachusetts coast with Scituate a target. Litchfield wrote in his diary on May 21

> This day being Sabbath day, the morning cool, I rode down to the meetinghouse. Just as I had got off from my colt and was putting on the halter I saw a couple of men come riding up to the meetinghouse...upon a full run. They and their horses were all of a sweat.... They told us that there were two ships at Hingham, landing regulars [British troops] as thick as grasshoppers. They told us that the Cohasset company had marched off for Hingham. Mr. Grosvenor had not begun his exercise when [the men] came to meetinghouse. The people all rushed out of the meetinghouse to hear the news. Thus being alarmed we all went home and got our guns. [23]

On July 20, 1775 there was a day of fasting and prayer throughout all the English Colonies in North America. On that day, Rev. Grosvenor preached from the text of Jonah 3:10 [And God saw their works, that they turned from their evil way; and God repented of the evil, that he had said that he would do unto them; and he did it not (KJV).][24]

> Litchfield's diary notes

> That morning [July 20, 1775] colonial soldiers from Nantasket set the lighthouse [Scituate or Minot] on fire. Residents of the island were rescued just as British tenders fired on them which lasted "very

---

[23] Litchfield diary, May 21, 1775
[24] Litchfield diary

145

furiously" for an hour though no British soldiers landed on shore.[25]

During the Revolution, Rev. Grosvenor frequently preached on the fight for liberty as a "cosmic drama pitting the New England Israel against the red-coated enemies of God."[26] In one sermon delivered in December 1776, Grosvenor spoke of the anxiety the military and political battles caused and the belief that God was on the side of liberty:

> Oh, my hearers, what a dark and difficult time it is with us! This is such a day as neither our fathers or we ever saw before. Where is there peace, where is there safety to be found? Our enemies encompass us on every side and unless the Lord appears for our help they will swallow us up quickly…The most effective of our men are gone and this house of praise which used to be thronged with men on this anniversary is now almost empty; behold their seats and pews left destitute; and whether ever they will all return to fill them again is quite uncertain….
>
> If we were but a humble, penitent, reformed and thankful and holy people I have no doubt but divine Providence would maintain our right and our cause, support and carry us through; but for the vices and wickedness that abound us God may see it necessary to continue our afflictions till we seek and serve him in sober earnest. [27]

While the American Revolution brought a growing acceptable of a liberal theology, it also produced great

---

[25] Litchfield diary
[26] Timothy D. Hall. "The American Revolution and the Religious Public Sphere," http://revolution.h-net.msu.edu/essays/hall.html
[27] Waite, 34-35

146

economic hardship for many and Rev. Grosvenor and his family were not exempt. Adding to their deprivation was Mrs. Grosvenor's growing displeasure with the vociferous opposition that caused Rev. Grosvenor to submit his resignation in early 1780. On October 15, 1778 the parish voted to make a grant of one hundred pounds to Mr. Grosvenor for his support in the work of the ministry. On April 5, 1779 the parish voted that one hundred pounds be raised by taxes to fulfill the earlier vote in October providing for Grosvenor's salary. Later, an additional two hundred pounds was granted to Mr. Grosvenor for "the encouragement in the work of the ministry…provided he continues in work among us."

Rev. and Mrs. Grosvenor believed that First Parish could not support them and their family. It was humiliating to the family to see the community pay Rev. Grosvenor in such a piecemeal manner while at the same time being subjected to the fierce criticism of the opposing faction. On January 17, 1780, Mr. Grosvenor wrote the following letter to his congregation:

My Brethren and Friends

It is with great reluctance I am constrained to write you again about salary matters being deeply [*indecipherable*], that the agitating these things between minister and people has a very unhappy tendency. But any present circumstance obliges me to it. I am far from desiring to make any interest in these deplorable times, but I have a plain right to expect a [*indecipherable*] comfortable support. I have therefore requested the meeting to desire you to pay me in the necessities of life instead of the money…. Because the addition granted in the year 1778 not being paid sooner is now become of very little value….

I therefore desire you to take these things into consideration and agree to let me have produce instead of the present currency; or at least to enable me to procure it.

And if you only keep in mind the Golden Rule of doing unto another as you would want done unto you I hope and believe you will meet with little or no difficulty, in this matter.

Even to the last, there was either conflict about or an inability to pay Rev. Grosvenor for his ministry and so in the spring of 1780, Ebenezer Grosvenor resigned as minister of First Parish. Following Grosvenor's resignation, five hundred-eighty pounds was raised for his support, more like severance pay. In June 1780 it was also voted to give Mr. Grosvenor one hundred-eighty bushels of good "merchantable" Indian corn that was to be considered as the whole of his pay for his work in the ministry since February 1, 1779 as well as full compensation for the money he paid for parsonage repairs.

When Samuel Deane wrote his history of Scituate in 1831 he noted that many older people in town remembered Rev. Grosvenor as a man of "middling stature but of noble and commanding presence." Some said his preaching was mediocre, "but as a man and a Christian" he was said, "to have excelled in the finest and gentlest traits."[28] Others claimed that Grosvenor was a good, even eloquent preacher and a benevolent, large-hearted gentleman. Another historian observed that the hardships and poverty of the Revolutionary War increased Grosvenor's misfortunes and added to his misery.[29] Grosvenor was a slave owner, who, while in Scituate, performed marriages of his servants to other servants in town.[30] After leaving Scituate, Grosvenor became minister in Harvard,

---

[28] Deane, 188
[29] Damon, 426
[30] *Vital Records of Scituate, Massachusetts: to Year 1850, V.2,* (1909), 343.

Massachusetts where he died in 1788 at the age of forty-nine. Upon his gravestone were imprinted these words:

> ... of such endowments as rendered him an ornament & blessing in the various relations which he sustained, he was a good steward in the house of God, and discharged the duties of his pastoral office with prudence & impartiality, care & fidelity. He was a man of polite address and peculiarly formed for social life a tender & loving husband, an affectionate & kind parent, an agreeable friend & pleasing companion, he was much beloved & respected in life, & in death greatly lamented and is we trust receiving the reward of his labours in the kingdom of his Lord, his bereaved & grateful people have erected this stone the monument of his virtues, & their affection . . .. Blessed are the dead that die in the Lord, for they rest from their labours & their works do follow them.[31]

Immediately following Grosvenor's departure, in May 1780, First Parish authorized a pulpit committee to hire itinerant preachers; to raise the money for their payment until a called minister could be chosen; and, to rent the parsonage until the following April, reserving for Mr. Grosvenor's "use and improvement," the parsonage house, barn and other buildings. It is not known to what extent he used the parsonage after his departure. The parish also voted to give Mr. Grosvenor "liberty to take off and appropriate to his own use a hog house," which he built on the parsonage land. It is most likely that Grosvenor dismantled the building and took it with him.

The Revolutionary War ended with the surrender of General Cornwallis to George Washington at Yorktown, Virginia on October 19, 1781. British troops began to leave in January 1782 with British loyalists fleeing in great numbers including some in Scituate.

---

[31] Jason David LaFountain. *Reflections on the Funerary Monuments and Burying Grounds of Early New England* (2004) thesis, 155.

Washington declared an end to the fighting on April 19, 1783, eight years to the day that the war began at Lexington and Concord. By September the Treaty of Paris was signed formally ending the War of Independence.

In Scituate, as in many other New England towns towards the end of the eighteenth century, the gathered church was no longer representative of the whole community. People of other Christian creeds were living in towns that were once solely Pilgrim or Puritan (the churches of the "Standing Order.") With the growing numbers of Baptists and Quakers as well as Anglicans, the homogeneity, and therefore the influence of the Standing Order, was weakened. Statutes passed by the General Court in the 1690s added to the growing confusion between church and state. Ministers of a church of the Standing Order were finding themselves pulled in two directions. On the one hand, the minister was the religious leader of the community with its own doctrines, ways of administering the sacraments and rules for disciplining the church's members. On the other hand, the minister was also the settled minister of the town and had the responsibility of communicating moral precepts that conveyed a civilizing element to all in the town.[32] This added to the increasing tension, in Scituate and elsewhere in New England, between Orthodox Calvinists and the growing number of "liberal" Christians.

For fifty years the Cambridge Platform of 1649 had governed church polity, including how ministers were called. Congregations would select a minister and an ecclesiastical council would give its approval. But with the passage of statutes in 1692 and 1693 all inhabitants of a town were taxed to pay for the maintenance of an "able learned orthodox minister." While providing the ministers a salary, the statutes changed the prevailing form of church polity. Taxpayers in the town, not necessarily members of the church, were added to the relationship between ministers and church members. The 1692 law gave to the town the exclusive right to choose its minister, thus limiting the power of church members. The law

---

[32] Conrad Wright. *Congregational Polity* (1997), 28.

required that the minister was to be elected "by the major part of the inhabitants...at a town meeting duly warned for that purpose," thus making him minister to all the inhabitants of the town. The 1692 caused such an uproar among the members of the Standing Order that a year later the law was amended in support of a compromise which would complicate matters years later. The revised law allowed for members of the church to call their minister and the town would endorse (or not) the church's decision. Why would church elders acquiesce and not oppose an infringement on their power? The answer was money. The church elders agreed to the statutes because they provided the churches with a source of money (taxes) and with so many churches in financial distress opposition was muted. "What they gained in fiscal support they forfeited in power."[33] This arrangement would have significant impact on the schism in Scituate in 1825.

The inability of First Parish to offer a steady and consistent income to Rev. Grosvenor was another indication of the deepening bitterness between the two orthodox and moderate Calvinist groups. Another symptom was the seven-year period following Grosvenor's ministry when First Parish had no settled minister. The congregation could not agree on who should be their spiritual and community leader. Potential ministers would be heard but would preach on a subject and in a manner that would estrange or outrage one or the other party. Liberal ministers would not preach a particular doctrine but would emphasize the role of public teacher. Orthodox ministers would preach Christian doctrine. Ministers who once were willing to exchange pulpits with colleagues stopped for fear that their congregation would be infected with words bordering on heresy, so church elders often led the worship service.[34] During this time guest or itinerant ministers were boarded at the houses of various parishioners while the parsonage was being rented out to non-clergy. Rent was often paid in corn, a commodity more valuable than currency during the Revolutionary War and early nationhood. Even

---

[33] Peter S. Field. *The Crisis of the Standing Order* (1998), 21.

[34] Wright, *Congregational Polity*, 35.

so, tenants found it difficult to pay the rent and the church frequently had to send a delegation to collect it.

First Parish church records recount how difficult it was for the congregation to agree upon a minister and for a minister who was willing to come to such a conflicted congregation. A number of ministers provided a makeshift solution, with Mr. Barnes of South Scituate, performing most pastoral duties including preaching and baptisms. On one particular fast day called to seek Divine guidance, the Rev. Martin Fuller preached. He must have impressed the congregation because in a later vote the precinct was asked if it would concur with the church to call Rev. Fuller. The vote was sixty-four in favor and thirty-six against, but Mr. Fuller declined probably because of the high negative vote.

On July 29, 1782, the congregation voted to ask the Rev. Bezaleel Howard of Bridgewater, Massachusetts to supply the pulpit for four days and, if he couldn't be hired, a committee was formed to ask Mr. Ebenezer James, a tutor at Harvard College to confer with the president of the college to recommend candidates. Even with this assistance, the committee struggled and sought to contact ministers that were the in Cambridge area. In 1783 the quarrelsome parish attempted a compromise by voting "that each party should be gratified in turn viz., if the whole of the committee shall have liberty to apply to one of their own choosing for an equal term of office." In September 1784 a Rev. Hazlet was asked to preach, but if he couldn't or wouldn't, the pulpit committee was directed to go to Cambridge again to seek advice. Since Hazlet was not called, a vote was taken on March 28, 1785 to "know the minds" of the town as to whether they would vote to concur with the church in calling Rev. Adoniram Judson of Malden, Massachusetts, to be minister. Apparently Rev. Judson was not acceptable to the town, for on May 26, 1785 the committee was directed to continue supplying the pulpit with itinerant preachers. On January 9, 1786 the church voted to ask the town to concur with the church to call Rev. Zechariah Howard of Bridgewater to be minister and it was passed. On March 15, 1786 the church voted to give Rev. Zechariah Howard eighty pounds in salary and the parsonage if he accepted the call. He did not. On March 26, 1787 the church formed another pulpit supply committee. On June 7, 1787 the congregation asked the Rev. Ebenezer Dawes to preach for four Sundays. Then, in the following month, on July 2 there was a vote to call Rev. Dawes, with fifty-nine yes, seven no and four proxies voting no, and the town concurred. Seven years of searching for a minister had come to an end.

In his letter of acceptance Rev. Dawes acknowledged the problems that awaited him,

> ...The anxiety of mind under which I must necessarily labor when viewing the state of this church and society you will readily conceive must fill the tender breast with painful sensations. But though there is not that happy unanimity and agreement in sentiments which are sincerely to be wished for, yet I trust I am not deceived when I flatter myself that it is only in some lesser speculative points while we all harmoniously agree in the great essentials of the gospel doctrines.... neither does this disagreement lessen my concern and care for the spiritual welfare and happiness of those who have discovered a disinclination to settle me as their minister. Each individual undoubtedly hath a light of private judgment in matters of religion, for to his own Master must we stand or fall.

Ebenezer Dawes became the tenth minister of First Parish on November 14, 1787. He was born in Bridgewater and graduated from Harvard in 1785. At Dawes' ordination, the Rev. William Shaw, pastor of the First Church in Marshfield, gave the sermon. In his remarks Mr. Shaw reminded Dawes that he was devoting himself to God in the "bonds of the Christian covenant and to the service of this church and congregation in the character of a gospel minister."[35] In further evidence of the growing "freedom of the pulpit" where ministers were allowed to interpret Scriptures free from any ecclesiastical council, Shaw said to Dawes, in front of his new congregation:

> You are a witness for me, sir, that I have not heretofore, nor do I now pretend magisterially to dictate to you what particular doctrine you should preach unto your people. The Bible is before you; and, from intimate acquaintance with you, I am verily persuaded that you will endeavor to explain and recommend its sacred contents in the best, the most instructive and edifying manner you are capable of.

Shaw pointed out to the congregation that,

> For a number of years, you have been as sheep without a shepherd. We rejoice that God is at length shining upon this sanctuary which has been so long desolate.... Receive this therefore as a precious gift of your ascended Savior. Do nothing to weaken his hands, to discourage his heart and obstruct his usefulness among you. Respect his person so far as he is found deserving of your esteem. Carefully guard against all prejudice and disaffection; for these things have the most unhappy tendency to prevent a minister's usefulness among his people. [36]

Even before Rev. Dawes' settlement there was vocal opposition to his call. An ecclesiastical council was convened on the day of Rev. Dawes' ordination, a process set forth by the Cambridge

---

[35] William Shaw. *A Sermon Preached November 14, 1787, at the Ordination of the Rev. Ebenezer Dawes to the Pastoral Care of the First Church in Scituate*, (1788), 21.

[36] Shaw, 23.

Platform synod of 1649, which, in most cases, would affirm a congregation's selection of its minister. In Rev. Dawes' case a letter of protest was written to the ecclesiastical council. The stated objection was that, "Instead of instructing into the great things of the gospel and leading us to see the distinguishing difference between righteous and the wicked it appears to us that Mr. Dawes' preaching is calculated to destroy all such difference and confound the character of saint and sinner."[37] It is likely that in his brief time of preaching at Scituate, he revealed a version of Calvinism that did not sit well with the conservative faction. Nevertheless, the council did vote to affirm the congregation's vote but Deane describes the state of affairs as "laborious and perplexing to Mr. Dawes beyond measure, and his office truly a crown of thorns, owing to the violence of the opposition.[38] Those antagonistic to Dawes sought to have him dismissed by calling another ecclesiastical council to hear their grievances. A letter was written to the council and read as follows:

> When the church in this place gave
> Mr. Dawes an invitation to settle, ten
> out of twenty-two of the brethren
> took an active part in opposition to
> this settlement and eleven only acted
> in favor of it and when the parish [the
> town] met to see whether they could
> concur with the proceedings of the
> church not more than one fourth out
> of those who according to long usage
> in the parish have been allowed to
> vote on such occasions concurred
> with the church's doings.

The council met at the home of Deacon David Jenkins on April 15, 1789. Dawes did not attend nor did he acknowledge the legality of the council hearing. The arguments of each party fell along

---

[37] Waite, 43.
[38] Deane, 189.

the familiar doctrinal positions. The council's letter reveals a problem that would cause great friction during the schism between the liberals and orthodox thirty-five years later and would also be the subject of an acrimonious debate fifty years later as to which church was the "true" First Parish gathered in 1634. The matter of voting status of parish members, that is, the citizens of the town, as distinct from church members, was another source of divergent opinion. The laws of 1692-93 did not provide for rules covering this situation which led to the dispute at First Parish. The letter to the ecclesiastical council added this

> Although it hath been the custom of this parish to admit all male inhabitants to vote in parish meetings yet when the parish met to vote concurrence with the church in the call of Mr. Dawes there was but a quarter of them voted a concurrence. Perhaps it may be said that a number of persons were at sea when the meeting took place.

In other words, the letter suggested that the town's vote was not truly representative; but, whose fault could it be, if not every citizen who could vote did not vote?

The council's unanimous report was that while Mr. Dawes was espousing principles "utterly subversive to the fundamental doctrines of the gospel" nevertheless he "has represented them as the sober sentiments of his heart."[39] In other words, what Rev. Dawes was preaching was wrong, but nonetheless, it was heartfelt. The council also recommended "to the aggrieved and others to be on their guard against such dangerous errors" and called on them to "attend the public and stated worship of God [and to] furnish their proportion of the pecuniary compensation which this parish have

---

[39] Waite, 44.

voted to Mr. Dawes for his temporary support, thereby submitting themselves to that ordinance of man for the Lord's sake that they make no schism in the church...and endeavor to reclaim those who are in error."[40] Despite the council's efforts there seems have been little desire for compromise on both sides. It also took its toll on Mr. Dawes, who was caught up in long-standing antagonisms not of his making; this, in spite of "having such manners such as might disarm enmity, and in all the gentleness and meekness that adorn the Christian character, he was nobly accomplished."[41]

Rev. Dawes died September 29, 1791 after ministering in Scituate for less than four years. Adding to ill health, the doctrinal turmoil probably caused his early demise at thirty-five. In the spirit of generosity and charity, a month after his death the parish voted to continue Dawes' salary for six months to aid his widow and two children even though his ministry was probably the most contentious since Charles Chauncy's. On October 8, 1792, a year after Dawes' death, the town voted to pay off his debts. Deane described Dawes as having a "pleasing" person." His death caused "poignant grief" among his ardent supporters. Such was the depth of grief for this man "in the ascendancy of his reputation" that the date of his death, according to Deane, "became an anniversary of sorrow" and for a long time, no mourner at the cemetery for a family member or friend, would fail to stop at Rev. Dawes' grave, sigh, and lament a life lost too soon.[42]

---

[40] Waite, 44.
[41] Deane, 189.
[42] Deane, 189.

Chapter Seven

"My Heart Trembleth"

Many in the Scituate congregation were still grieving the death of Rev. Dawes when the Rev. Nehemiah Thomas of Marshfield was called to be their minister on July 9, 1792. The vote was eighty-eight yes, thirteen no; and it was also voted that Thomas receive the annual sum of eighty pounds along with use of the parsonage "so long as he shall continue in the work of the ministry in this place." The minutes of the meeting convey that the gathering was held with a calm belying the turmoil growing about liberal Christianity within the congregation. The number of votes disapproving the call, however, hinted at trouble ahead. The meeting's minutes include the following:

> This church taken into consideration the grievous hand of providence upon them in the removal of their late worthy and beloved Pastor, the Rev. Ebenezer Dawes by death and humbly conceiving that it is their duty to seek for a speedy resettlement of the Gospel ministry and ordinances among them…and whereas Mr. Nehemiah Thomas of Marshfield hath merited our affection and given us full evidence of his qualifications for the work of the ministry. We do hereby vote and make choice of him to be our minister and to take upon him the pastoral

office over us in the Lord. Beseeching the God of the Spirits of all flesh to incline his heart to accept of this invitation and to make him a rich blessing to us and our posterity after us…. And if God shall incline his heart to accept of this call to settle in the work of the gospel ministry among us and shall be ordained over this church and congregation.

Rev. Thomas responded to the vote of the church with this letter, written September 21, 1792,

Christian Brethren, I have take into serious consideration the votes presented by your committee giving me an invitation to settle with you in the work of the gospel ministry. I have been earnestly looking up unto heaven for direction in this affair, and my prayer hath been, "Lord, what will thou have me to do." When I consider the importance of the work and how nearly the prosperity of the church is connected therewith, my heart trembleth and is moved out of its place, who is sufficient for these things…a tender concern for the Redeemer's Kingdom among you hath I hope had a suitable influence upon me and— and although the situation of things in this place has not at present so encouraging an aspect as could be defined, yet the advice of those who have the welfare of the church at heart a real wish both for your temporal and spiritual prosperity have at length prevailed on my inclinations to accept of your invitation and settle with you in the work of the Gospel ministry and while I express my gratitude for the honor done me by you invitation to this important office, I must at the same time request your prayers for me to the throne of grace that I may be [endowed] with wisdom and strength enabling me rightly to discharge the duties incumbent on it.

Brethren, it is my earnest desire that Supreme wisdom may guide all your transactions; that Christian charity and heavenly love may possess the hearts and be conspicuous in the lives of us all and that after we shall have faithfully served God and our generation there below we may all at length though faith in the merit of Christ the Redeemer be so happy as to join the Church triumphant above and unite under the great Captain of our Salvation, together spend and eternity of happiness and peace in the mansions of immortal glory.

I am yours affectionately, Nehemiah Thomas.

There was great anticipation for the arrival of Mr. Thomas among his supporters as elaborate plans were made for his ordination on November 14, 1792. The town voted funds for "the purpose of making the entertainment." Invitations were sent to other ministers in the area as well as to "scholars." The gallery of the church was reinforced and the meetinghouse doors repaired; plastering was restored and eight new pews were installed. At the ordination, the Rev. Zedekiah Sanger of Bridgewater, Massachusetts gave the sermon and used as his lesson, Matthew 13:52: "He said to them, "When, therefore, a teacher of the law has become a learner in the kingdom of Heaven, he is like a householder who can produce from his store both the new and the old." In the sermon Rev. Sanger spoke of how Jesus used parables and "extracted lessons of wisdom from the various employments of life."

Since the beginning of the Pilgrim churches the covenant among a congregation's members and the covenant between the congregation and its minister were critical to church life. It laid out a social contract within the church community and it also echoed the covenants that God had made with Noah and Abraham. Early in his ministry Rev. Thomas had new congregation members affirm the covenant written by him, which said

Now hold in the presence of Almighty God, before angels, this church of our Lord, Savior, Jesus Christ, solemnly as far as you know your own heart, sincerely recognize the Lord, Jehovah, to be your God…Now do also declare your acceptance of submission to Jesus Christ as the great prophet…king of the Church; the holy spirit as your enlightener…In this now, you do now give up yourself to this Church of Christ, promise by the help of Divine Grace you will attest on the word, sacrament and prayer, so long as God shall continue you in Church relations with us…. This you promise.

And the congregational response was

We, then, the Church of Christ in this place, do now receive you into our…fellowship, communion, promising that we will treat you with that Christian tenderness which your relation to us as a church member may require. May God almighty prolong your days on earth; may you be made a blessing to this church and may we be finally admitted to partake of the rewards of the faithful in Christ's kingdom of glory. Amen.

This new covenant planted the seeds of separation in the soil of discontent.

While tension continued to grow, practical matters at First Parish needed attending. On April 12, 1803, it was voted to sell some of the parsonage land and the interest from the proceeds was paid to Rev. Thomas for the length of his ministry. It appears from the church records that Mr. Thomas received a total salary of close to $6,000 over thirty-eight years; he began earning $266 annually, and by the time of his death, his salary was $500. On March 5, 1811, the town voted to purchase a bell weighing thirteen hundred pounds for the meetinghouse costing $400. That bell didn't last long and so a new bell with the same weight was purchased three years later. Once again, the church's bell proved unsatisfactory and the acquisition of yet another bell was authorized on December 9, 1822. Apparently, the problem was the weight of the bell because the third bell purchased was three hundred pounds lighter than the other two.

A new level of comfort came to Sunday morning worshippers when it was voted on April 14, 1823, to "admit" a stove in the meetinghouse. Two years later the church underwent extensive repairs. The east portico of the church was removed and sold to Asa Merritt who made it into a house on his land. A two-story cupola was placed on top of the bell tower garnished with a weathervane and lightning rod. The weathervane was gilded by Asa Merritt's brother, Shadrach, the same two who made the bass viol which was the first instrument to play music in the church and is presently on display in the church sanctuary. (The weathervane can be seen in Mary Ann Cole's painting of the "Old Sloop Church," done in 1840, which hangs in the Old Sloop Room in the present church building.[1]

The second and third decades of the nineteenth century were tumultuous for the church, the town of Scituate and the young United States at large. In addition to the theological controversy in the church, the country was again at war with England. The War of 1812 began in June 1812 due to the United States' opposition to trade restrictions brought on by England's war with Napoleonic France, as well as the impressment of American merchant seamen into the British Navy. In spite of these national affronts, New England still had mercantile interests with England and was ambivalent about the war. Many in Scituate saw the conflict as detrimental to their commercial enterprises; they would rather ignore English aggression than suffer the hardships of war. Shipbuilding along the North River came to a standstill. The prices of corn and flour and other necessities were exorbitant. Fear of invasion by British troops was high, increasing the anxiety of an already worried

---

[1] Margaret Bonney, "Wandering Weathervanes" (unpublished) in First Parish files

community.[2] In the summer of 1814, six months before the end of the war, the *Bulwark*, a 182-foot British warship with seventy-four guns, anchored near Scituate Harbor and stayed for several weeks. Provisions aboard the ship were depleted and the ship's commander demanded from the town fresh beef and produce. The citizens of Scituate refused. In response, the British sent two small boats to set fire to some fishing and other vessels moored in the harbor. Rev. Thomas, with "great resolve and courage," boarded the *Bulwark*, confronted the commander, and asked him how much more violence and destruction would befall Scituate. The commander responded by saying that no further harm would come to Scituate. He accomplished what he wanted, the destruction of tax revenue producing shipping. No further harm befell Scituate though a guard was kept on duty in the harbor for months just to make sure.[3]

The Old Sloop Church c.1830

---

[2] Damon, 419.
[3] Deane, 141-142.

It was during Rev. Thomas' ministry that the Unitarian Controversy broke out into the open in New England and Eastern Massachusetts, in particular. Jedidiah Morse, an orthodox clergyman (and father of the inventor of the telegraph, Samuel F. B. Morse), in 1812, printed a pamphlet containing correspondence between Theophilus Lindsey, an English Unitarian minister, and several liberal Boston ministers. Lindsey founded the first Unitarian chapel (by English law, it could not be called a church since it was not Anglican) in London in 1774. The pamphlet contained correspondence going back to 1787 and it produced a great theological dispute. The orthodox accused the liberals of hiding their true beliefs which the former believed were at odds with the "true faith" and therefore the liberal ministers should be excluded from Christian fellowship. The Rev. William Ellery Channing of the Federal Street Church in Boston (now, Arlington Street Church) responded to the criticism with a pamphlet of his own, an open letter to one of the critics. In it, Channing approached the main point of criticism head on. He said, "We preach precisely as if no such doctrine of the Trinity had ever been known.... We speak of the Father as the one true God, and of Jesus Christ, his son, who yet is distinct from him and subordinate to him."[4] In 1812, Channing and other liberal Christians had no desire to claim for themselves the name their opponents gave to them, "Unitarian," for they did not want to, nor saw the need for, separation from their orthodox brothers. By 1819, the reluctance to separate had disappeared. In an ordination sermon titled "Unitarian Christianity," given in Baltimore, Maryland, Channing offered a "powerful statement of principles" that united the liberals and distinguished them from the orthodox.[5] Taking on a name that was once a term of derision, liberal Christians began calling themselves Unitarian.

One indication of the growing theological split in the Scituate church is revealed in the minutes of a meeting in April 1823. The treasurer was directed to get an unpaid five-year old loan in the

---

[4] Forman, 18.
[5] Forman, 23.

amount of $50.70 against Deacon Israel Litchfield renewed with satisfactory security. Israel Litchfield was one of the leaders of the orthodox group in the church and most likely was withholding payment because of his dissatisfaction with Rev. Thomas, the majority in the congregation, or both.

It is a matter of curiosity and disappointment that there are no records of church meetings that discuss the division of the church in 1825 when the orthodox Calvinists left the First Parish Church, formed their own congregation and erected their own building the following year. The only available historical material concerning the rift is in the form of correspondence between the First Parish moderator during the 1840s, Mr. John B. Turner, Esq., and the Rev. Daniel Wight, the pastor of the First Trinitarian Congregational Church, which resumed the passions of the dispute twenty years earlier. The debate began with the printing of the *Church Manual of the First (Trinitarian Congregational) Church of Christ in Scituate, Massachusetts*, written by Rev. Wight in 1844. The parentheses in the church's name are significant because the Trinitarian church claimed to be the "true" First Church of Christ in Scituate, a name both sides would not yield to the other. Rev. Wight asserted in a brief historical introduction to the church manual that a "majority" of First Parish church members "feeling greatly dissatisfied with the present loose state of things in this church...." sought to change the situation.[6] This claim about "the loose state of things" raised the ire of many at the First Parish Church, including Mr. Turner. A key point of contention in the Turner-Wight debate, as it was in the schism two decades earlier, surrounded the desire of the orthodox faction to renew the covenant of 1710 that had, in the view of this faction, been "neglected" for many years by Rev. Thomas.[7] Another irritant in the manual was the

---

[6] Daniel Wight. *Church Manual: or the History, Standing Rules, Discipline, Articles of Faith, and Covenant, of the First (Trinitarian Congregational) Church of Christ in Scituate, Mass.* (1844), 2, 4.

[7] *A Second Series of Letters Concerning the History of the First Parish in Scituate* (1845), 1. This publication was printed along with some

statement of Rev. Wight that Samuel Deane's history of Scituate, specifically on the subject of the schism, made "false statements" on the matter.[8]

In early 1825 a few members of the congregation, displeased with Rev. Thomas' theology, asked to speak to him on several matters, mainly about re-affirming the covenant of 1710, which they believed was closer to the orthodox Calvinism they favored. Rev. Thomas refused to meet with them despite several invitations and so the group called for an ecclesiastical council of orthodox ministers to give the group (or as they saw it, the "church") advice on how to proceed. On April 27, 1825 the council met and declared that "the First Church in Scituate [that is, the orthodox faction] has just cause to be aggrieved" that the church had done everything it could to remove "difficulties and to restore harmony among them;" and that provided that a majority of the male members of the church shall, at a meeting, vote that they are "dissatisfied with the present administration of the word and ordinances…it is expedient and proper that the relation between said church and their present pastor, *be dissolved, they will be justified in so doing* (original emphasis)." Later that day the group, which included Deacon Israel Litchfield, met at the home of Rowland Litchfield and voted to accept the vote of the council. They created a committee of four to notify the entire congregation of a meeting on April 29, 1825 at the home of Jacob Vinal. The meeting, with twenty-three members of the church voting, decided by a vote of twelve to eleven – a one vote majority – that "it is expedient and proper that the *relations* subsisting between this church and their present pastor *be dissolved*, and that *the same is hereby dissolved*, a *majority* of the male members of this church concurring in this vote (original emphasis.) Apparently the women of the church had no vote in the matter. The fact that the orthodox did not include Rev. Thomas' vote (he was present) is also telling. Wight wrote in the First Trinitarian Church Manual years later that, "There was a *clear*

supplementary letters from and to John Turner with Turner's permission.
[8]*Letters*, 8.

166

majority in favor of the above action, as the pastor could have no vote when *his own case* was on trial."[9]

Rev. Wight, in his account of these events, was defensive in response to the accusation that in 1823 eleven people joined First Parish for the sole purpose of dividing the church. Mr. Turner noted in a letter written to Rev. Thomas' successor, Rev. Edmund Quincy Sewall, that Rev. Thomas, "a man without guile himself, and therefore not expecting it in others" welcomed these newcomers with "open arms." Some had doubted the motives of the new members but did not object to their fellowship, even though they believed that these Scituate residents were "instrumental in hurrying their beloved Dawes to his grave." "Nothing can be farther from the truth, as living witnesses will testify," wrote Wight. Most of the eleven had wanted to publicly accept Jesus as their savior but they were "not being satisfied with the character of the preaching they enjoyed by the First Church in Scituate" and so they did not join but attended "evangelical preaching" in surrounding towns. Nonetheless, believing it was their duty to join some church of Christ and that travelling ten to fifteen miles to other churches was a hardship; and, knowing that the Scituate church, "*the dear church of their Puritan fathers*, was originally evangelical, and still had a *church covenant, fully Trinitarian and evangelical*, on their church records (though for a time laid aside, on the responsibility of their pastor alone, with whose views it did not coincide)"; and, after advice and counsel from "experienced" ministers and other Christians, they decided to join First Parish. Their object, Wight stated, was not to bring about a separation – "this was the farthest from their thoughts" but rather to bring out a *reform in the church;* to 'strengthen the things that remained, and were ready to die;' and "to re-establish the old covenant and early faith of the fathers, and thus secure to themselves and posterity the *true faith and ordinances of the gospel* (original emphasis)." Despite all the votes and declarations, according to Wight, Rev. Thomas persisted in preaching without "the least regard" to the votes of the church and therefore, those members and others in the orthodox faction, were

---

[9] *Church Manual*, 10-12, 45.

167

"obliged" to leave "their" house of worship and find another. Later that spring a new society was gathered and first met in the home of Lot Vinal until a meetinghouse was built in 1826 where it stands today, around the corner from First Parish on Country Way. When the Baptist Church was built later at what is now the GAR Hall, that area of Scituate was called Church Hill or Christians Hill.[10]

John Turner, in challenging Rev. Wight's account of the events of the schism, stated that in order for Rev. Thomas to be dismissed it had to be so voted by members of the "Church and Society." Turner, a lawyer, contended that a certificate dated April 15, 1825, revealed that those who voted to dismiss Rev. Thomas declared themselves to have formed into "another Society;" that is, two weeks before the vote of April 29th, therefore making the dismissal of Rev. Thomas invalid, since they had formed another church. To further his argument, Turner added that even by Rev. Wight's admission, the 1710 covenant was "found," supporting Turner's argument that the covenant had not been used in many years and was supplanted by the newer covenant written by Rev. Thomas and affirmed by the congregation.

Turner also pointed to religious history to support his position. The Reformation brought about by Martin Luther and later, the Age of Enlightenment, advanced freedom of conscience and knowledge in matters of truth, "both civil and religious." Turner reminded Wight that the great Pilgrim leader, John Robinson, told his followers "not to stand still with Luther and Calvin, but to be ready to receive truth from other sources." "Since the settlement of this country," Turner wrote, "one superstition after another has fallen before the progress of truth, but there is still room for further progression." Turner went on to point out that "the liberal part of the church did not attend the church meetings" when Rev. Thomas' ministry was discussed. At first Thomas and others did attend some of the meetings until they believed that the orthodox group "wanted

---

[10] *Letters*, 66; *Church Manual*, 12-13.

168

more to control the opinions of others, than peaceably enjoy their own."[11]

Twenty years after the schism, Turner, in another letter written to Rev. Sewall in 1845, laid the blame for the revival of the controversy and the aversion between the two congregations squarely on Rev. Wight. "These difficulties, and feelings attendant, had mainly subsided previous to the time Mr. Wight was settled here," Turner wrote. "The members of the two societies had in great measure lost their former enmity.... Members of one society would frequent the meetings of the other." When the First Parish meetinghouse was being repaired the Trinitarian Church gave First Parish the use of its building for meetings. Turner believed the attack on the veracity of Rev. Deane's account of the separation in his *History of Scituate* was "altogether unwarrantable" and so began the correspondence in defense of Rev. Deane. "His [Wight's] condemning me [Turner] as an infidel, troubles me not. He has not the power of the holy inquisition, although I think he shows the spirit."[12]

Rev. Wight was a very influential minister but he had his detractors elsewhere in town. Wight was known for being "strict and obdurate" in his religious views and this extended into the civic area. A member of the Scituate school committee, Wight protested, at the 1856 town meeting, the hiring of a teacher he thought was unsuitable. The offended teacher proposed two resolutions to the meeting. First, "That in the opinion of the town any school committee inquiring into the religious opinion of candidates are out of its legitimate sphere"; and, second, "That in the opinion of this town occasional indulgences by teachers at their own or other residences in dancing or card-playing or other innocent recreations does not unfit them for the duties of teaching." Both resolutions passed handily, causing Rev. Wight to resign from the school committee.[13]

---

[11] *Letters,* 12ff.

[12] *Letters,* 67.

[13] *Letters,* 66-67; Waite, 61-62.

At the height of the schism crisis, the Rev. Samuel Deane, minister of the Second Parish in Scituate, exchanged pulpits with Rev. Thomas. Deane gave a sermon titled, *A Discourse on Christian Liberty*. In its printed form it was dedicated to Rev. Thomas. Deane spoke about freedom of thought and the attempts in the early church "to enslave the consciences of men" and "the corruption and tyranny of that church; her efforts to bind all Christians in her bonds, and their struggles to regain their liberty."[14] This, Deane said, was the meaning of the Protestant Reformation:

> What was the liberty recovered [from the Roman Church]? It was nothing worth having, if it consisted only in breaking away from the Pope, to fall into the power of another tyrant; or in changing one set of forms for another set of forms.... No, but all that was of any value in the Protestant Reformation consisted in this: in teaching men to look at the Scriptures for their rule of faith, and not to Popes, or churches, or councils; and that everyman is responsible for his own faith.... This was the substance of the Protestant Reformation. Its influence is still felt; for since that day, the liberty of Christians has never been wholly suppressed, although many attempts have been made to bring back again a yoke of bondage.

> I cannot forebear, however, to notice, even hear, repeated attempts to bring back the yoke of bondage. Had our fathers, who first peopled these shores, remembered well the parting words of their venerable pastor at Leiden [the Pilgrim, John Robinson], and his exhortations to Christian character, and his

---

[14] Deane (1825), 6.

prophetic suggestions, that their faith might be purified more, and 'further light might break forth from God's word', the darkest page of our little history might have never existed. But now it must go down to all ages with our history, that those who fled from persecution soon learned to persecute, when they found the power in their hands....

Deane then spoke about how the Puritans of the early colonies persecuted the Quakers and how Scituate people like Timothy Hatherly, James Cudworth and Rev. Henry Dunster spoke for tolerance, before returning to his main point and of current interest to the congregation:

What is Christian liberty in any church or society, where certain articles of faith, not expressed in scriptural language, but in some sectarian explanation of scripture language, are adopted, and where people of sober lives and conversation should be excluded from the benefit of religious ordinances, because they could not subscribe to all the articles, although they can freely declare their belief in Scriptures, and only claim the right to interpret then according to their own light.[15]

In the years since the schism and the emotions revived by the Wight/Turner correspondence, relations between First Parish and the First Trinitarian Congregational Church have had its ups and downs. As late as the 1930s the minutes of First Parish committee meetings refer to the "Orthodox" church and yet over the years the congregations have worshipped together on special occasions. Most recently, the Rev. Richard Stower accepted invitations to speak at the

---

[15] Samuel Deane. *A Discourse on Christian Liberty* (1825)

installations of Revs. Jerry Alan Smith and Michael Dunfee, ministers at the Trinitarian Church in Scituate.

Even in the midst and the aftermath of the turmoil of the momentous events of the mid-1820s First Parish dealt with more mundane issues. In April 1827 a committee was created to take care of the boys and girls who "make too much noise at the meetinghouse on the Sabbath;" and, to "prevent boys from sitting in the gallery, whose parents or guardians own pews below; and, that they keep those still who sit by the stove." Another committee was formed to encourage singing and instructed to look up some of the old singing books, and "if they can conveniently have some of the old hymns sung occasionally, it is presumed about by so doing, they would gratify the wishes and feelings of a large portion of the Parish."

Town meetings held in the meetinghouse became so rowdy the church voted on March 9, 1829 that "the condition on which the Town of Scituate shall hold the Town meetings in the meetinghouse of this parish be that the inhabitants of said town when assembled here in Town Meeting shall be required to take their seats and that they shall in no case be allowed to stand on the seats or on the railing of the pews when attending town meeting in the meetinghouse of this parish." Even with this admonishment the meetinghouse was still available to all. Located at the geographical center of town as well as the civil and the religious center First Parish, at a meeting in March 1830, voted to allow other societies to use its church bell to be tolled at deaths or funerals provided they pay the bell ringer for his time and trouble. Also voted as this meeting was approval of the use of the meetinghouse of the parish to the Baptist congregation in order to accommodate the ordination of their new minister.

Rev. Nehemiah Thomas portrait by Rufus Hathaway

Among the many weddings he celebrated, Rev. Thomas performed the marriage of Enoch Cole and Maria Curtis in 1827. The Coles occupied pew #23 in the "Old Sloop" church for the rest of their lives together. Frequently they would write notes to each other in their hymnal. Later, in 1881, when the newer church building was constructed, Enoch, then seventy-nine, instructed his son to bid on pew #23 to keep it in the family.[16]

---

[16] Margaret Cole Bonney. *Scituate's Sands of Time* (privately published n.d.), 53.

A few years after Rev. Thomas arrived in Scituate he sat for a portrait by Rufus Hathaway, a self-taught painter, who would gain some renown, not in his lifetime, but two centuries later. The Thomas portrait itself would provide an interesting episode in First Parish's twentieth century history. If the portrait was anything close to a true likeness, Rev. Thomas was not a handsome man. It shows him seated on a chair, wearing a wig, looking considerably older than his age at the time, thirty. Perhaps it was the wig. Had the portrait been done thirty years later one may wonder what Hathaway would have seen in Thomas' face for personal sorrows and afflictions added to Rev. Thomas' burden over the years. A son died soon after graduating from Harvard College; his wife (the daughter of Dr. James Otis of Scituate) also died; and his daughter's deteriorating mental health were serious shocks. Thomas himself suffered a stroke, the effects of which handicapped his activities for the last four years of his ministry.

An example of Thomas' warmth and compassion was when he took into his home a young man who showed "traits of genius" in his writings. With the approval of the boy's parents, a young Samuel Woodworth spent one winter in the Thomas household where Rev. Thomas tutored the boy in English and Latin grammar and classic literature. Believing in Woodworth's talent, Thomas sought to get a "liberal education" for the young man. Unable to fund the college expenses himself due to his meager salary, Thomas tried to raise funds from his wealthy parishioners. Unfortunately, no one came forward to fund Woodworth's formal education. Nevertheless, Woodworth became a journalist and ultimately a renowned poet whose best-known work, *The Old Oaken Bucket*, recalled his Scituate childhood. Woodworth would later write that he had the "greatest respect, esteem and gratitude" for Rev. Thomas and his "amiable" family. [17]

---

[17] Samuel Woodworth. *The Poems, Odes, Songs and Other Metrical Effusions (1818)*, v.

Scituate is blessed with several beaches with wide swathes of sand providing opportunities to seek refreshment on warm, sultry days. On such a day, August 10, 1831, Rev. Thomas sought relief in the cool waters on the Scituate shoreline as he waded into the ocean. There, Rev. Thomas suffered a fatal stroke.

"From the frequent tenor of his conversation [Thomas'] friends well know that he had no wish but to be resigned to the hand of divine Providence, whether he were to meet his fate in the society of his family and flock, or whether his frame were to sink in a moment upon the sea-beach as it did, and his spirit take its flight like the halcyons of the cliffs."[18] In appreciation of his thirty-nine years of service to First Parish and to Scituate, the congregation voted on September 5, 1831 to continue Rev. Thomas' salary through November 14th of that year for the support of his orphaned children.

At the time of his death Rev. Thomas was (and continues to be) the longest serving minister in the history of First Parish, thirty-nine years. An obituary in the *Christian* Register praised him for his faithfulness, "especially when we consider the character of the times in which his ministry has been exercised."

[He] healed divisions that existed at the time of his settlement, and continued to soothe theological animosities, until the 'fountains of the great deep' seemed to be 'broken up,' and division and separation were publicly urged and preached by some.... [He] was distinguished for an open heartedness and a guileless simplicity; for much freedom in expressing his own sentiments, and yet without that bluntness of manner which gives offence, and for much candor in accepting the same freedom from others.... In faith and affection, in character and proactive, he belonged to the class of liberal or Unitarian Christians; but while he resorted to no arts to conceal his own belief,

---

[18] *Christian Register*, August 27, 1831.

he was fired with no zeal to enforce the peculiarities of his faith upon others.... he aimed not at the doubtful reputation of attacking the faith of other men; the rights of conscience and of private judgment in matters of faith were sacred in his estimation.[19]

---

[19] *Christian Register,* August 27, 1831, Vol. 10 Issue 35, 159.

Chapter Eight

A Ministry of Pain:
"My eyes fill with tears, and my heart throbs with emotion."

Many in Scituate, not only church members, thought Rev. Thomas was irreplaceable but his successor, the Rev. Edmund Quincy Sewall, became just as prominent in town and was also influential in the growing Unitarian movement. He was among the most beloved ministers in the history of First Parish even though poor health afflicted him through his entire ministry. Rev. Sewall came from a long family line of letter writers and chroniclers. Family letters, journals, church documents and published writings offer a picture of Mr. Sewall that is the most complete of First Parish's ministers.

Soon after Rev. Thomas' death, First Parish voted to call Sewall as the new minister on November 21, 1831. The vote was sixty-eight, yes and five, no. Sewall was called with the following conditions: that he provide ministers to preach in his absence at his expense; and, that either party could dissolve the relationship by giving three months notice. This was the first time the church presented such conditions. If Rev. Sewall agreed his annual salary would be $700.

Rev. Sewall accepted the offer with this letter,

To the First Church and Parish in Scituate,
Christian Friends,

The invitation to become your Pastor and Minister I
hereby respectfully acknowledge, and in humble
reliance on the All wise and Benevolent God, whose I
am and whom I am bound to serve, do cordially
accept. Let future consequences prove to every
witness on earth and to the judge of all on high, that
your choice was made with a single eye and a pure
heart, having for its end your highest spiritual benefit
and the promotion of whatever is most important to
the Redeemer Kingdom. In due time I shall
consecrate myself to that solemn office to which you
have called me. Meanwhile, Brethren, pray for me!
Pray for yourselves and to one another! So may the
relation be formed between us, be begun as it ought,
and we may hope, may continue as it is begun,
increasing in tender interest and in happy effects until
the hour where God shall appoint its termination.
Shall I not venture to suggest to you how suitable and
how favorable is this period for such a review of your
past use of Christian privileges as shall lead you to
perceive what good you have arrived thence, and how
you might have made them more beneficial. Let
pleasing anticipations be accompanied with serious
musings on the days and means of grace now forever
gone. Pay to the honored dead the tribute due to their
worth and for the living determine that he shall not,
through your fault, labour less useful than they, but
by God's blessing, to far greater profit. So may it be!
Your servant and friend in the Gospel,
Edmund Q. Sewall, Newburyport,
November 28, 1831.

The First Parish and Society of Scituate invited an
ecclesiastical council to gather December 21st at the house of George

M. Allen. The council continued the tradition of a group of ministers formally agreeing to the worthiness of a congregation's called minister. The churches represented at this council were the Second Parish, Scituate; Pembroke, Duxbury, Kingston, all three parishes in Hingham; the First Parish Churches in Cohasset, Quincy, Concord, Danvers, Marshfield, and the Federal Street Church in Boston. The Rev. Morrill Allen of Pembroke was chosen moderator and Rev. Deane of South Scituate was the scribe. The council read Mr. Sewall's response to the church's invitation; and "having heard testimonials of his character and qualifications" from Sewall's former church in Amherst, New Hampshire, the council voted to proceed with an installation later that day.

At the installation service, the Rev. Charles Chauncy Sewall of Danvers, Edmund's younger brother, gave the opening prayer; the Rev. Ezra Stiles Gannett (William Ellery Channing's successor at the Federal Street Church) gave the sermon. The selection of Gannet by Edmund Sewall to give the sermon is telling and gives a clue as to Sewall's theological perspective. Gannett's views, though moderate, would soon place him in the group of Unitarian ministers who opposed the more radical transcendentalist movement within Unitarianism. Transcendentalism, personified by the former Unitarian minister, Ralph Waldo Emerson, had a more sweeping concept of an individual's relationship with the Divine that the traditional Unitarians. It was part of the larger Romantic Movement influencing art and music that favored emotion over reason.

Gannett summarized the key points of his theology this way: "Filial reverence for God, brotherly love for man, a grateful faith in Christ, receiving him as the revelation of divine and the model of human character; the reality of the spiritual world and regeneration, consisting in such a change of temper and way of life as may be wrought by ones' own will and effort."[20] Also at the service, the Rev. Brooke of Hingham gave a consecrating prayer; Mr. Allen of

---

[20] David Robinson. *The Unitarians and Universalists* (1985), 265-266.

Pembroke gave the charge to the minister, reminding Sewall of his pastoral responsibilities; Mr. Deane of Second Parish, Scituate

Rev. Edmund Quincy Sewall

offered the right hand of fellowship; the Rev. Flint of Cohasset gave the address to the people; and the Rev. Goodwin of Concord gave the benediction. Col. Newhall and Mr. Burrell of the congregation played music, likely the first time music was played for such an occasion at First Parish.

Born in Newburyport, Massachusetts, Rev. Sewall came from a notable Massachusetts family. His great-great grandfather, Judge Samuel Sewall, presided over the Salem witch trials in 1692 (and later publicly apologized for his role). His grandfather, Samuel Sewall, was married to John Hancock's sister-in-law. His father, Samuel, was a United States Congressman (1797-1801) and Chief Justice of the Massachusetts Supreme Judicial Court (1813-1814). His aunt Dorothy was the mother of the Rev. Samuel J. May, pastor of the South Scituate (formerly Second Parish) church and grandmother to Louisa May Alcott, the author. Although Sewall could have entered Harvard at fourteen his father did not think it was "expedient for him to enter at such a young age."[21] The elder Sewall died while Chief Justice and when Edmund was seventeen. Young Sewall studied for the ministry with his father's Harvard classmate and close friend, the well-regarded Rev. Ezra Ripley of Concord, Massachusetts. Edmund was physically frail and was in pain for all of his life. His wife, Caroline, was the daughter of Col. Joseph Ward, an aide-de-camp to George Washington and her sister and mother were boarders at the Concord home of the mother of John and Henry David Thoreau.

A few months after beginning his ministry, Sewall wrote a letter to his brother, Henry Devereux Sewall of Watertown, New York, recounting the "pains" he endured by moving from Amherst, New Hampshire to Scituate, some eighty miles in the midst of winter, without any help. With him were his wife, Caroline, daughter Ellen and Edmund, Jr. Another son, George, was born later in Scituate. In the letter to his brother Rev. Sewall continued:

> We have been for some time comfortably established in our new home. When I tell you that I have made seventy visits, chiefly as pastor, and not exchanged [a pulpit] but once, you will see that my time has been occupied fully. My parish is very widely scattered and contains 214 families. I have been on foot many miles

---

[21] R. M. Hodges. *The Ministry of Pain* (1866), 11.

to make my calls, and find it impossible to rely on that plan any longer. [Our home is] a mile from church. Some of my people live four miles from me, and almost all are two from the house of worship, and more than that from my house. There is no village around the church. At the harbour, 2 miles off, there are stores, post office, etc. The mackerel fishing is a staple here. My parish is called a rich one, and we have a fund of nearly 5,500 dollars. [B]ut not an educated (literally, I mean) man in the parish. No lawyer. The physicians [are] not college men. The degree of information is considerable however, not below mediocrity in the larger number. The schools are as usual in the country.... A Baptist, Methodist, Calvinistic Congregationalist Society, each composed out of the original parish, nearly coeval with mine, and Unitarian.... The Second Parish [of Scituate] is more refined and literary probably, but not as wealthy nor flourishing. Population and business have increased in mine largely in ten years....

The ocean is so near as to mingle its roar with the many-voiced winds that whistle around my house, and is in sight from the church. I occupy the dwelling of the last clergyman [Rev. Thomas]. It is pleasantly situated, has a wide unbroken prospect, a garden, front-yard, large lawn about the house on each side, has the sun from the rising till its setting, some fruit trees. On the whole it will be called by most people a beautiful spot.[22]

Sewall then went on to share with his brother his regrets, some financial, others professional. He expressed extreme disappointment in not being called to the First Parish Church in Cambridge, despite the support of William Ellery Channing of the Federal Street Church

---

[22] Sewall letter, February 3, 1832, in First Parish files.

in Boston. In Scituate he wanted to buy some land adjacent to the parsonage but his monetary situation wouldn't permit it and he feared it would be sold to someone else. "There is not a house or a part of one to be had within the limits of my parish. No one. The demand for them is so great that half the houses have two families." He laments, "Could I but have the means I would purchase this place at once. It is a part of the parish where land is at the lowest price.... I suppose the premises could be had for less than 1500 dollars. It is now that I feel the want of money. My employment...has pinched me blue. I have had my family subjected to wants that no one of my father's house ever knew." Still, he was thankful "for so favorable a turn to my affairs." The people of the parish

> tho' unrefined, are yet so apparently well disposed and so kind to me, that I anticipate nothing but comfort and am fast forgetting my disappointment at Cambridge, where my heart was but too strongly fixed. Had I gone there I had in view many literary pursuits now impossible, and access to works which I have pined for a sight of, which I can never hope now to get the privilege of reading.... It almost broke my heart to come so nigh obtaining what I so much longed to have. But the wisdom and goodness of God provided for me as I did not deserve and I am contented and happy.... We are all well. My health has not been so for a year as now. Last summer I was once very ill. My head is still troublesome sometimes. But on the whole I am a robust man compared with what I was in 1829....[23]

During most of Sewall's ministry the church suffered severe financial problems and it affected his salary. Sewall's salary was originally $700 and lowered to $500 in 1832. There was a modest increase to $520 in 1833, then down to $430 in 1834. In 1835 the salary was $500; from 1837-1841, it was $550; in 1842, $500; in 1843,

---

[23] Sewall letter, February 3, 1832.

$450; and its lowest in 1846, $300. The ups and downs of his salary affected Sewall's family life but not his devotion to the ministry and to his church.

The minutes of a meeting on March 18, 1834, recorded First Parish's gratitude to Rev. Sewall for his offer to relinquish a part of his salary for the coming year and its appreciation of the motives which prompted Mr. Sewall to make the generous offer.

Rev. Sewall's letter:

To the First Parish In Scituate: My Respected Parishioners:

The contract into which you entered with me more than two years ago, by an almost unanimous vote stipulated a certain sum to be annually paid for my support.

What you have offered so freely, I accepted with confidence, and in the strength of that confidence I removed my family from a distance hither. Nor have I had occasion for one moment seriously to regret the step, or to suppose my confidence in you misplaced.

But yet, I am told there are among you some who now think what you contracted to give me is too much for me to receive, or for you to pay. This arises, perhaps, from the late change in the Constitution of our state relative to public worship. Whatever be the cause, however, I can only say that when I came by your call to take upon me the responsible office I hold, my desire was to be a blessing and not a burden to you and your children. That desire is yet warm as ever in my heart. God forbid I should become chargeable above measure to any man, in the ministry of the Lord Jesus. I only seek to know what is best for you, all in order to do it, if I can. And, with the hope of meeting your present wishes and to remove all occasion for complaint. I do hereby propose to relinquish for *one year* (emphasis by Rev. Sewall), one hundred dollars of my annual salary. Provided, that in that case you shall raise the remainder due to me in the manner contemplated in the contract. This condition I am induced to add, not merely by my sense of duty to my family but because I believe your interest and independence, your prosperity and peace as a Parish will be so most effectively secured.

I am now as always, your affectionate friend and pastor, Edmund Q. Sewall.

The change in the Massachusetts constitution Rev. Sewall referred to was the adoption of the eleventh amendment which freed churches from government control but also from public financial support. The once pervasive "Standing Order" of churches had crumbled. By the 1830s growing numbers of Baptist, Episcopalians, Methodists and Universalists had changed the religious topography and culture of Massachusetts so thoroughly that the Congregational majority was reduced by thirty percent in a generation. Another compelling reason for the collapse of the Standing Order was the schism between the orthodox and liberal branches in the decade and a half before.[24] Under the new constitutional amendment and laws, towns no longer raised taxes for the support of the established church nor for the support for the ministry. Now, First Parish in Scituate, like all the other Standing Order churches in Massachusetts, had to raise money solely through members and friends. On March 23, 1835 it was voted that Mr. Sewall's salary be raised again to $500 but it also voted to have a committee consult with Mr. Sewall on the subject of his salary and to consider the feelings of the people of the parish.

---

[24] Field, 209.

Forced by law and the cost of the precariousness of his health, Rev. Sewall's generosity to the church was a hardship on his family. Ellen Sewall, the eldest child, at boarding school, knew the consequences of Rev. Sewall's reduced salary. In 1837, at the age of fourteen, Ellen wrote her grandmother, Prudence "Dency" Ward

> It does not seem possible to me that I have been here a year and seven weeks, but it is. Mr. Kent [the headmaster] says he shall be obliged to raise the board to three dollars next quarter and I do not think father can afford to keep me here much longer. I shall be contented to go home whenever they say so. I am sure I have enjoyed the privilege of coming to a good school so long that I think I ought to be perfectly contented to go home and assist my dear mother in her many cares and labours.[25]

A year earlier, Ellen's mother, Caroline Ward Sewall wrote to Dency about the family's need to purchase some things second-hand

> We have a new horse & chaise. That is the chaise is second hand—but good--ours was too old. Unsafe. Our "Rolla" [the horse] is a dear. Husband says he has about declared he had no love for a horse, but he cannot say so now. We had him of Mr. Allen [a member of First Parish], notorious for his honesty, so we cannot be cheated. I know he is thought a good horse by people congratulating us that we have him. He goes fast & is gentle. He has not such an appetite as Brownie, not having so big a body to fill.[26]

---

[25] Letter to Grandmother Prudence "Dency" Ward, [undated, 1837, quoted in "Transcendental Romance Meets the Ministry of Pain: The Thoreau Brothers, Ellen Sewall, and her Father" by Shawn Stewart in *The Concord Saunterer*, Vol. 14, 2006, 8

[26] Letter to Prudence Ward. November 4, 1836, Stewart, 9.

These laments about money must have caused some tension in the Sewall-Ward family, particularly when the Sewalls relied on Mrs. Ward for financial support.[27] However, the tension may have been minor and not long-lasting for Rev. Sewall sent a letter to his wife as she was taking care of her dying mother in Concord.

> It has been one of my best blessings to have had your excellent mother for my mother so long, and to have had her so often in our home. I feel I owe her a debt of love and gratitude more than words can express. Tell her I do thank her for all her goodness and all the patience and kindness she has manifested to us throughout our relation these many years. [28]

Despite financial worries, there were more often than not, times of great fun shared by the Sewall family in Scituate. According to Edmund Sewall, Jr.'s journal entry of September 7, 1837, there was a much-anticipated event, a Sunday School Celebration, held in the Alewin Grove. The young Sewall (nine years old at the time) recounted the event this way:

> The scholars all went before Mr. A[lewin]'s house where they were formed into a procession each under his own teacher. The children marched by twos and in the order of their classes. I being in the 1st class was in the first part of it. The way from the road to the grove was lined on both sides with people between who we marched up to the place where the ministers and two or three other people sat which was a raised platform with a bench on it with green pine branches driven into the ground all around. There were several hundred people present including the children who were in number above 300, and formed quite a long procession. Mr. Carter made an address. He said that

---

[27] Stewart, p. 9

[28] Letter to Caroline Ward. February 6, 1844, Stewart, 10.

kindness and obedience were the duties of children, and related this anecdote. 'A stage was entirely filled with gentlemen when a little girl wished to get in. She said, "If the people on the stage will be kind to me, I will be kind to them." After the exercises were finished, the procession marched to the table which was very long. When we arrived at it we divided and passed in single columns on each side of it. With the aid of the spectators we ate up every eatable on the table except a few apples. I had a <u>very</u> pleasant time though rather tired. [29]

Notes from the church and minister's ledgers mark the day-to-day concerns of the congregation. In the church records for 1832, there is mention of a loan made by the Trustees of the Fund of First Parish that was made for real estate investments in Boston and Braintree. There is also mention of a financial payment to the heirs of the Rev. Thomas in the amount of approximately $115. On March 19, 1832 the parish chose to hire a collector of taxes. The winning bid came from someone who offered a fee of one cent and eight mills on the dollar for his services. The meeting also named people to tend to the fire in the stove at meeting time and to clean it before winter. The following year the church hired a bell ringer and someone to take care of the meetinghouse repairs. Samuel Curtis, John B. Turner, Marshall Hatch, James and Paul Merritt were appointed to supervise unruly boys and girls during meeting time. The church meeting also voted that the time of the intermission between the morning and afternoon services be left to the discretion of Mr. Sewall. It was understood by the congregation that when the intermission was lengthened, the afternoon services would begin at one-thirty.

By January 1838 it became clear to the congregation that something had to be done with the church building as it was showing

---

[29] Edmund Q. Sewall, Jr. journal at the Thoreau Institute, Lincoln, Massachusetts

the wear of sixty years. The congregation voted to consider either building a new meetinghouse or repairing the present one and making new pews and such other alterations as necessary. Two months later, on March 12th, it was decided to build a new meetinghouse by a narrow vote of forty-two for and thirty-three against. Another indication that renovations were necessary was the decision in late December (Christmas Eve, in fact) to create a committee to consider enlarging the seating area for "all the singers of the church," no doubt in response to the desire of the choir.

Some members of the congregation were having second thoughts about a new church building, a year after the vote to build a new structure. The earlier vote was rescinded and a committee was charged with exploring the cost of a thorough renovation, as well as estimating the cost of a new meetinghouse. In May the committee reported that after consulting with experienced carpenters, a new meetinghouse, along the design of the South Parish meetinghouse, could not be built for less than $4,375. The present meetinghouse, the report said, could be repaired and renovated for $1,750, with the addition of Venetian blinds, the removal of the South and East porticos, the relocation of the galleries, pulpit and pews; and placing the choir loft over the new entrance. The committee recommended repairing and renovating. With this work the church would last another fifty years. At a meeting on December 23, 1839 it was agreed that church pews were to be sold, one-third of the amount was to be paid in cash the rest could be paid to the church within six or nine months with interest. If payment was defaulted, the pews would be re-sold to the highest bidder. The meeting also voted to give a "gratuity" of eight dollars each to the Methodist and the "Orthodox" (Congregationalist) societies for the use of their churches while First Parish was being repaired. The parish also offered to the two churches their old window shades and blinds.

Rev. Sewall was beloved not only in Scituate but was widely respected in the greater Boston Unitarian Community as well. He served as a trustee of the Derby Academy in Hingham. He was editor for a time of *The Christian Register*, which, according to historian George Willis Cooke,

> conformed to 'the mild and amiable spirit' in which it began its career, rarely being aroused to an aggressive attitude, and seldom undertaking to speak for Unitarianism as a distinct form of Christianity.... [I]t was mild and placid enough, given to expressing its friendly interest in every kind of reform, from the education of women to the emancipation of slaves, thoroughly humanitarian in its attitude, not doctrinal or controversial, but faithfully catholic and tolerant.[30]

In other words, the weekly newspaper was the voice of the Unitarian establishment and Sewall fit in nicely. As testament to his reputation within that group, Sewall was given the honor to present to his colleagues, in 1843, the Berry Street Essay, established by William Ellery Channing. His subject was "The Religious Aspects of the Community, and the Duty of Unitarian Clergymen in Regard to Them."

While most honored Sewall for his "liberality," others thought he was too timid. In 1838, the radical dreamer and Transcendentalist, Bronson Alcott, (father of Louisa May Alcott and brother-in-law to Sewell's cousin, Rev. Samuel J. May) visited Sewall in Scituate, while visiting May in South Scituate. Afterward Alcott wrote in his journal, "Had some conversation with [Sewall] on intellectual and moral topics. His mind is too conventional, his piety too feeble, owing to the predominance of ill health, and the necessary dependence to which he has been subjected, to give him sympathy with my own views. I fear that I gave him pain rather than pleasure by the utterance of them." An education reformer as well, Alcott also met with First Parish Sunday School teachers, "I believe these interviews were of service, by way of quickening thought on spiritual subjects. I also addressed the Sunday School in two instances, giving

---

[30] George Willis Cooke. *Unitarianism in America* (r. 2006), 99-101.

the children a talk, and a reading." [31]

In January 1840, while the church was being repaired there was a meeting of the First Parish Church at the "Calvinist" (First Trinitarian Congregationalist) meetinghouse. It met to write new by-laws regarding membership:

> Any person wishing to become a member of this parish shall make application in writing to the Parish clerk, in substance as follows: I, _____ of _____ consent to become a member of the First Parish in Scituate, Dated at _____this _____day of _____. And such person shall thereafter be considered a member, unless a majority of the Parish Committee which shall be annually chosen for admission of members, shall, within thirty days, make known to the said clerk in writing, that they refuse to permit such applicant to become a member of said parish.

> It shall be the duty of said clerk, to furnish the chairman of said committee with a list of all persons who may wish to become members within seven days, after application shall be made.

> And said clerk shall keep a list of all applicants and make report at the annual meeting of all new members; he shall also report the names of all persons who have been refused admission by the said committee.

> The Parish may, at their annual meeting, choose a committee consisting of three, five or seven for admission of members and in case of neglect or

---

[31] Larry A Carlson. "Bronson Alcott's Journal for 1838", Part Two, in *Studies in the American Renaissance*, (1994), 1310.

refusal to choose such a committee or in case no such committee shall exist, for any cause whatever, the assessors shall be a committee for that purpose. Provided however that any applicant may be admitted a member at any legal meeting of the Parish by a vote of a majority of the members present and voting thereon and provided moreover that no persons shall be permitted to vote in the same meeting at which he is made a member.

The membership process was quite different from what was required in colonial times. There is no reference to a public conversion statement. All that was required was that the applicant was agreeable to the congregation.

Rev. Sewall was happy in his ministry in Scituate. Still, financial security was very much on his mind as Rev. Sewall's health had been fragile for most of his life and made the future of his ministry uncertain. The members of First Parish and the town offered poignant compassion to Sewall when he was unable to perform his pastoral responsibilities. As an adult he was frequently debilitated by illness, particularly epileptic seizures. For over ten years Rev. Sewall was debilitated by a bone disease of the skull, which caused him to have, in addition to constant pain, frequent and violent convulsions, some lasting as long as two hours. He convulsed and lost consciousness two or three times while in the pulpit prompting medical treatment. Some parishioners were becoming inpatient with Rev. Sewall's frequent absences from the pulpit and sought to dismiss him at the December meeting. His daughter, Ellen, wrote to her Aunt Prudence that "Father was not dismissed.... The clause about dismissing him was passed over at the meeting.... All will turn out right at last, I daresay.[32] It was also voted that Mr. Sewall, if he chose, would be given a leave of absence "for a season" for reasons of health while work was being done on the Meetinghouse.

---

[32] Letter dated December 26, 1839, quoted in Stewart, 13.

Sewall sought out the best medical care. Dr. George Hayward of Massachusetts General Hospital in Boston examined Rev. Sewall and was convinced that the only relief was to remove a portion of the skull where bone pressed against his brain. A small button-sized piece of bone was removed and, although the pain during the operation was intense, Rev. Sewall did not complain. When the operation was over he said he was free of the pain that afflicted him for twelve years. A medical journal reporting on the operation was understated in calling it "a most interesting triumph of surgical skill."[33]

Caroline Sewall was with her husband for the entire length of his stay at the hospital and prior to the operation she wrote to her children trying to calm their fears by providing only the barest details.

> You must have become impatient to hear from us again. I have been waiting to know certainly what was to be done for your father. The Drs have been in every day, & have twice cupped him on his head--that is, taken blood from him. He is about as well as usual. We go out to walk every day. Dr. Hayward has been in this morning & decided to have a general consultation of all the physicians & surgeons of the hospital on Friday, & if they conclude [to?] operate, it will take place on Saturday. He is disposed to think they will conclude on the operation. [34]

An entry in Edmund Jr.'s journal on April 8, 1838 refers to his father's hospitalization in Boston

> Father had his head operated upon for the removal of his disease in his head. The thing was performed by Doctor Hayward. "It was found that the bone was depressed inwards and that a small point of bone adhered to the membrane which covers the

[33] "Epilepsy Cured by Trepanning," *The Boston Medical and Surgical Journal,* ed. Smith, J.V.C., (1838), Vol. XVIII, 144.
[34] Letter to Ellen Sewall, March 21, 1838, quoted in Stewart

brain." [The operation] was proposed by Dr. Thomas. He brought a book which contained an account of two cases similar to this in which relief had been obtained by an operation. Father was easily convinced for he said he would have the most painful operation rather than be plagued by this disease. He went and had it performed. (Original emphasis.)

Mother went with him as nurse. The operation took up 37 minutes. 3 doctors ran to tell mother as soon as it was over. He bore it without flinching. I knew he would.... How thankful we ought to be to God for His great mercy. [35]

When Rev. Sewall returned home some weeks later Edmund, Jr. wrote, "Father brought home the bone that has troubled him so long for us to see." [36]

Sewall preached a very personal sermon on May 29, 1838, which, he said, was "contrary to all my habits." His text was 1 John 4:16, "And we have known and believed the love that God hath to us; God is love; and he that dwelleth in love, dwelleth in God, and God in him." Sewall's purpose was to make people less fearful of hospitals for the treatment of their illnesses, whatever they may be. He recounted his experience at Massachusetts General Hospital. His purpose, he said, was to tell the congregation that he came back with "renovated strength and new hope" and that he appreciated "the healing balsam" of their "unremitting sympathy and care." The experience made him humble in the light of others' pain and made him "bear his own [pain] with more fortitude." [37]

---

[35] Edmund Q. Sewall, Jr., journal in First Parish files
[36] Sewall, Jr., journal
[37] Edmund Q. Sewall, "Sermon" May 29, 1838 (1838), 17.

Nevertheless, the operation and his persistent health problems did take a toll on Sewall's ministry. Before the operation, his seizures surely alarmed his parishioners. Sewall frequently was away from the pulpit. Other ministers preached to his parishioners. He couldn't make the pastoral calls that were expected of him. When he considered leaving the ministry he sought the advice of his older brother, the Rev. Samuel Sewall, a Congregational minister in Burlington, Massachusetts. His brother wrote back

> I cannot but think myself, in view of what you say in your letter, that it was an unadvised step. But you ask, how could you otherwise "appease the anxiety and satisfy the claims of (your) people, when all the time exposed to epileptic fits in the pulpit?" But will asking a dismission please them any better? You acknowledge that they "seem much grieved, and reluctant to let (you) go." Would they not then have been better satisfied to have let you remain at ease among them, though exposed to epilepsy continually, if they could have been made acquainted with Dr. H[ayward's] opinion, and should see it confirmed by the mitigation of each succeeding attack? [38]

Even years after his surgery, Rev. Sewall once more contemplated resigning his ministry, when the effects of his epilepsy returned. Sensing that his strength and health couldn't meet the demands of his work, he again sought counsel, this time from his cousin, the pastor of Second Parish, the Rev. Samuel J. May

> I received some particulars respecting your malady-- and a confirmation of the report that you have determined to relinquish your profession, or at any rate resign your present parochial charge. I grieve that you think it must be so, because I know how much

---

[38] Letter of Samuel Sewall to Rev. Edmund Quincy Sewall. August 23, 1839, quoted in Stewart, 7.

you have loved the duties of a minister, and how admirably you are qualified to discharge them.[39]

Rev. Sewall's anguish was quite clear when he wrote the following letter to the members of First Parish on June 22, 1846

My Christian Friends,

Esteemed and beloved parishioners. It having seemed good to Almighty God, our most merciful Father, to try me yet again by the return of that alarming illness which has, in former years, not just a few times broken the Sabbath quiet of this sacred place, I have been deeply concerned to know what was my next duty in relation to so afflictive an event.

Submissive still under the Holy and Gentle hand of God and not at all distrusting, His Infinite Goodness, yet have I been bowed down and very sorrowful when I look toward you, the long suffering partakers with me in the grief, the flock so justly endeared to me.

With feelings which refused to let you go I have supplicated strength to utter the request today, which must, when granted, separate you from me...

Brethren and sisters in the Lord! When I came here to be your minister, now more than fourteen years ago it was in my heart both to live and to die with you. Nor could any common cause prevail to withdraw me from your service. But, my dear friends, the Divine Providence speaketh for me! It

---

[39] Letter of Samuel May to Rev. Edmund Quincy Sewall, June 10, 1846, quoted in Stewart, 8

summons me away from the altar when my care can avail no more. For six months I have been unable to command that measure of efficiency requisite to the progress of the work given me to do. My strained and failing nature obeys not always the anxious spirit's call. I would, but oh! I cannot serve you as you ought to be served, and as the great interests of Religion demand of your minister.

Therefore, do I now, ask you to relinquish me, that I may seek the restoration of health in prolonged rest. I greatly desire to see you flourishing once more in the charge of some man of God to whom are granted the qualifications for such a ministry which are desired to one. Therefore, do I now lay down my pastoral office among you, agreeably to the teams of the covenant we have made together.

Pardon the errors and the deficiencies you may have noticed in my past course. Forgive me, if even a word or act of mine have given you pain. Accept what I have done faithfully for your soul's good and let it bring forth more fruit when I am gone.

Permit me to dwell in your own and your children's remembrance as one who wished and strove to do all he could to advance your and their highest happenings.

Many have been your trials, but only let them purify and make you better and they will change their nature and become blessings. There is no need to remind me how broken ties afflict. I know it all. But, dearly beloved, the bonds which unite you and me to Christ and through Him to one another cannot experience rupture or decay. If, in a letter while we may no more see each other face to face and time and absence should mar and dim the lineament of the outward for upon Memory's tablets, yet those Imperishable Afflictions which have bound these living hearts together shall, I hope, remain untouched and still the same. And when we have ascended to the Heavenly Mansions we may meet to be separated no more....

May He, who alone can reward you for your untiring fidelity and kindness to me and mine. Engraved indelibly upon my heart is all your goodness to me and my family in our troubles.

I remain your devoted friend and pastor,
Edmund Q. Sewall

In reaction to Sewall's letter a committee was formed and instructed to "request the Rev. Mr. Sewall to continue his services as minister of this parish, either by himself or by his substitute and if he declines, the committee is authorized and directed to supply the pulpit." Bowing to the desire of the congregation, Sewall did not resign but rather took a leave of absence. Six months later at another Parish meeting the congregation asked Rev. Sewall to resume his services as minister of the Parish. In his answer Rev. Sewall noted that:

Since my resignation of my pastoral charge until the present time with a prayerful consideration of the subject in all its bearings and after much time taken for reflection and counsel I have come to the conclusion to repeat my request for a dissolution of my ministerial commission and I do relinquish to the Committee the care of the Sacred Desk for which it has for so many years been my happy privilege to dispense religious instructions as I have fulfilled the condition of the contract of the settlement by giving three months notice of my desire to retire from my office.... Most painful act of my whole life.

The Divine Providence has withdrawn from me the power to rely upon my physical health as one must who has charge of a larger society.

Responding, John B. Turner notified Mr. Sewall that a meeting held to discuss his health decided, without a dissenting vote, to request Sewall to resume his services at First Parish. We must wonder about Sewall's deepest emotions when he wrote on December 31, 1846:

I must be allowed first of all to express my most grateful sense of the unabating and confiding attachment of my respected and beloved parishioners for which alone that request can have provided and since it is so that after my twice repeated resignation my people still have preferred to waive it and to ask me to return to them, there shall on my part be no longer any hesitation.... I now consent to resume my pastoral office, all the health and ability I may retain shall be given again to the labors.

But over a year later, Mr. Sewall again asked to resign. In January he had a seizure during the service and he gave the congregation three months notice. On March 1, 1848 Sewall wrote to the congregation, "You cannot but see how necessary the change is to me, however hard I find it, do not offer a word to withdraw me from my purpose."

The congregation responded on March 20, 1848

[A]t former times yielding to our entreaties and continuing in your office has perhaps been prejudicial to your health and happiness, we therefore with undiminished feelings of love and attachment to you thought we ought not again to plead for a change of purpose however much we might wish a continuation of ties between us, the Parish voted that pursuant to your request, your connections with them as pastor cease forthwith.

The thrice-given resignation, finally accepted by the congregation was accompanied by a gift of $100.

"It was pleasant to him from his sick chamber in his new home [with his daughter, Ellen in Cohasset]...to look...upon the peaceful dwellings of those whose religious interests had engaged the best thoughts of his mind and the holiest affections of his heart." [40] His friend, the Rev. R. M. Hodges of Bridgewater, Massachusetts, would later say of Sewall, "The patience with which he bore all, the fortitude that he showed, the resignation that he displayed, were lessons which were given to his friends to ponder and to study with wonder and with admiration." [41]

Edmund Quincy Sewall died September 15, 1866, eighteen years after his resignation from First Parish. Despite years of ill health he lived to be seventy. Sewall's funeral service had Rev. Hodges offering the main eulogy. "No mark of disgrace," he said, "in morals or conduct, ever attached itself to him during his college life. The mantle of purity that he brought with him at the beginning, he took away with him at the end." [42]

Sewall's last days were quite painful. Hodges remarked that the distinctiveness of Sewall's ministry was one of modeling great character in the face of pain. "The public services of our brother as a minister were always listened to and received with marked attention and respect. Not because his sermons were very profound, but

---

[40] Hodges, 13.
[41] Hodges, 13.
[42] Hodges, 12.

because they bore evidence that they were written under the influence of a spirit that cometh by prayer, and a sense of duty to the Master whose servant he was." [43] Hodges quoted from a letter Sewall sent to him shortly before his death

> If I had capacity to proclaim all that my experience has afforded me, in proof of Divine goodness and the riches of Christ's gospel, I would preach now as I never did before. Unspeakable mercy has followed and upheld me as I have trodden the path of a life of much suffering. The religion we both love is ever unfolding to my mind some new trait of glory and blessedness. I have been lately reading, the Greek Testament, the Gospels, Acts, and Epistles, just as a simple youth might do who had an honest heart, but no learning of the schools. My eyes fill with tears, and my heart throbs with emotion, as I go over the familiar pages, interpreting by my own experience and wants the great truths given us by Jesus Christ. Oh, that I could once more be allowed to communicate to others what I so love to dwell upon my lonely struggles, and my prostration under pain! I envy my brothers the privilege of preaching, as I envy nothing else the world contains. [44]

Rev. William S. Heywood, the present minister of First Parish and Rev. Ezra Stiles Gannett also eulogized Sewall. It was Gannett, who gave the sermon at Sewall's Scituate installation thirty-five years earlier. Now, at Sewall's funeral, Gannett described him as being self-deprecating, a scholar and one who had a delicate nature. Sewall's pain and suffering made him unmistakably a man of consolation, one who had a full understanding of the pain of others; and, the "bereaved, the afflicted, and the dying found in him a friend who

---

[43] Hodges, 14.
[44] Hodges, 17.

could enter into all their wants and give, with a delightful spirit, the relief they needed. He was in truth, a gifted man."[45]

---

[45] *The Christian Register*, September 29, 1866.

Chapter Nine

A Romantic Interlude:
The Sewalls and the Thoreaus

Edmund and Caroline Ward Sewall had three children, Ellen, Edmund, Jr., and George. Ellen was named after the heroine in Sir Walter Scott's poem, "The Lady of the Lake." (Ellen's daughter, Louise, wrote in 1962 that Rev. and Mrs. Sewall were "young and romantic.") [1] Ellen was playful with her father. Once when he was invited to speak at the ordination of a minister in Norton, Massachusetts, a role usually reserved for "old men," Ellen suggested to her father that he "cultivate" gray whiskers so as "to look venerable." [2] As a child, Ellen frequently visited her grandmother, Mrs. Prudence (Joseph) Ward and her favorite aunt, also named (Miss) Prudence Ward in Concord, Massachusetts. They were boarders in the house of Mrs. Cynthia Dunbar Thoreau, the mother of John and Henry David Thoreau. The Wards were originally Scituate natives.

On a warm summer day in July 1839 Ellen arrived by stagecoach for a two-week visit in Concord. It had been several years

---

[1] Louise Osgood Koopman. "The Thoreau Romance," *Massachusetts Review*, IV (1962)
[2] Edmund Quincy Sewall, Jr., letter April 20, 1841, First Parish Files.

since she visited her grandmother and aunt. Ellen was now an attractive young woman, full of humor, sensitivity and a deep intellectual curiosity. Her father had encouraged Ellen to study languages. She would frequently visit Concord because it "is a very pleasant [place]." [3] The relationship between the Sewalls and the Thoreaus began long before Ellen stepped off that stagecoach. Maria Thoreau, one of John and Henry's aunts, was an acquaintance of Mrs. Ward, who had moved from Scituate to Boston, following the death of her husband, Col. Ward, a distinguished veteran of the Revolutionary War. Maria Thoreau introduced Mrs. Ward's daughter, Caroline, to a ministerial student at Harvard. The young man came from a prominent family with a notable pedigree. He was Edmund Quincy Sewall. After a suitable courtship and engagement, Edmund and Caroline were married in 1820. In 1833 Mrs. Ward and her other daughter, Prudence, moved from Boston to Concord and became boarders in Cynthia Thoreau's house. Early on

Ellen Sewall

---

[3] Ellen Sewall quoted in Stewart

in her visits to Concord as a child, Ellen became friends with Sophia Thoreau, John and Henry David's sister. Ellen was a striking young woman who, in youth already showed a curiosity and an intelligence that would make her attractive to many men, particularly the Thoreau brothers. Ellen was also a good letter writer and diarist. Ellen's brother, Edmund or "Eddie" as the family called him, was also gifted in that way.

On June 17, 1839 a month before Ellen's trip, Edmund, Jr. travelled to Concord for a week's stay along with his mother to see his relatives. They travelled by stagecoach stopping off in Boston to spend the night with other relatives before heading to Concord. The precocious young boy immediately intrigued Henry Thoreau. During Eddie's visit Henry took him sailing on the Concord River and hiking along wooded trails.[4]   The sojourn caused Henry to write the following in his journal:

> I have within the last few days come into contact with a pure, uncompromising spirit, that is somewhere wandering in the atmosphere, but settles not positively anywhere. Some persons carry about them the air and conviction of virtue, though they themselves are unconscious of it, and are even backward to appreciate it in others. Such it is impossible not to love; still is their loveliness, as it were, independent of them, so that you seem not to lose it when they are absent, for when they are near it is like an invisible presence which attends you.
>
> That virtue we appreciate is as much ours as another's. We see so much only as we possess.[5]

After Eddie departed for Scituate, Henry wrote a poem, "Sympathy," about "a gentle boy, whose features all were cast in

---

[4] Walter Harding. *The Days of Henry Thoreau* (1982), 77.
[5] Harding, 77.

Virtue's mould." Some modern Thoreau scholars believe this poem reveals a latent homosexuality in Thoreau, but most scholars reject this interpretation and apparently the elder Sewalls weren't concerned. Though Eddie was embarrassed by the poem, it didn't stop the family from calling him the "gentle boy." [6] His brother, George, was envious and disappointed that he didn't have a poem of his own. The Sewalls wrote Henry about George's distress and he sent George a copy of a his poem, "Bluebirds," with the inscription, "To Master George W. Sewall. In consideration of his love of animated Nature, the following poem is humbly inscribed by the Author H. D. Thoreau." Another indication of the Sewall's comfort with Thoreau was that a year later the Sewalls enrolled Eddie into the Thoreau's revived Concord Academy. Surely they would not have sent him to the Concord school if they had any question about the relationship. Thoreau appreciated Eddie's intellect, curiosity and he certainly wrote well, as revealed by his diary entries.[7] But it wasn't long before Thoreau turned his attention to another member of the Sewall family.

The school Henry and John ran would today be called an "alternative" or "progressive" school. The traditional lessons were taught with John instructing in English and associated subjects along with mathematics while Henry taught Latin, Greek, French, physics, natural philosophy and history. But what made the school special was that at least once a week all the boys would take a walk in the woods or fields or along the banks of a river or the perimeter of a pond, perhaps even Walden Pond. Edmund noted in his journal that one day Henry amazed the boys by picking a small plant, which could have been easily overlooked, and using a magnifying glass, he showed them a tiny blossom.[8]

Concord in 1839 was a very sleepy village in the country. While it was the home of Emerson, Hawthorne and the Alcotts, it

---

[6] Koopman, 63.
[7] Harding, 79.
[8] Harding, 82.

was mostly a community of farmers, tradesmen and blacksmiths. John Thoreau, who had been living in Roxbury, a community adjacent to Boston, came back to Concord to teach with Henry. He described Concord as a "Sahara" for unmarried men "with nothing to offer but 'antiquated Spinsters.'" [9] Ellen Sewall's beauty, charm and intelligence transformed that vast wasteland, if only briefly.

John Thoreau   *Henry David Thoreau*

John and Henry had known Ellen from her visits to Concord as a child when she would play with their sister, Sophia. Now, the brothers were immediately taken by her as a woman. Both men wanted to spend as much time with her as they could. Sometimes as a threesome, but most times as a couple, Ellen and the brothers went rowing on Concord's rivers. On at least one excursion Aunt Prudence accompanied them. They walked through meadows, picked berries and searched for Indian arrowheads in the woods. They had picnics under shady trees and spent some evenings at parties. One evening they amused themselves by trying to read the bumps on each other's heads, phrenology being the rage then. When Henry announced, after feeling Ellen's scalp, that she didn't have any bumps on her head, everyone burst into laughter for Henry didn't realize that his observation meant that Ellen was either a genius or an idiot. [10]

---

[9] Harmon Smith. *My Friend, My Friend: The Story of Thoreau's Relationship With Emerson,*   (1999), 25.
[10] Koopman, 67.

Ellen wrote to her father about all these things with youthful exuberance, "I can not tell you half I have enjoyed here till I get home.... I have had so many delightful walks with Aunt...and the Mssrs. Thoreau that a full account of them all would fill half a dozen letters."[11] Certainly, she enjoyed Henry's taking her to see a camelopard (giraffe) that was on exhibit in Concord. For his part, Henry was inspired to write some poems with Ellen in mind and by the fifth day of her visit he was in love and wrote, "There is no remedy for love but to love more."[12] As the days passed, the young woman's attraction for the Thoreau brothers "grew stronger and stronger."[13]

Everyone was saddened when Ellen's visit ended. Leaving Concord, Ellen later admitted that she had cried as the town faded in the distance. Almost immediately upon returning to Scituate, Ellen wrote to her Aunt Prudence that her visit had been one of the happiest moments in her life and she asked her aunt convey an "affectionate remembrance" to the Thoreaus. [14] For their part, Henry and John felt that rain clouds dimmed the brightness of summer. Shortly after Ellen's leaving someone discovered that she had left behind the Indian arrowheads gathered during her walks. In their response to this situation the Thoreau brothers revealed a difference in their personalities. John, the more socially adept of the two, immediately sent the relics to Ellen with a note. Henry, the silent type, sat by quietly and watched events unfold. In his note, John mentioned that he and Henry would soon be leaving on a long-planned trip boating together on the Concord and Merrimack Rivers. It was this trip that Henry wrote about in his journal and later expanded into *A Week on the Concord and Merrimack Rivers*. One wonders what reveries about Ellen served as a filter through which Henry made his observations on the trip.

---

[11] Harding, 95; Ellen Sewall letter, July 31, 1836.
[12] Harding, 95.
[13] Smith, 26.
[14] Harding, 96.

John had more direct things to ponder. In September, upon returning from his trip with Henry, he at once packed clean clothes and hurried off to Scituate despite Aunt Prudence's protestations that it was not a proper visit since Rev. and Mrs. Sewall were away for two weeks at Niagara Falls (a trip to improve Rev. Sewall's health months after his brain surgery). Well, Eddie and Georgie were there at home with Ellen to provide "adequate chaperonage." Whether Ellen's brothers accompanied John and her on their walks is not known, but John did regale "Eddie" and "Georgie" with stories about "his recent trip with his brother, as well as tales about wild animals. The one sour note was that five-year old George continually called John, "Henry."[15]

Ellen wrote to her parents in Niagara Falls about how pleased the family was to hear of her father's improved health. Ellen added, "We have ourselves been preserved by our Heavenly Father from every evil, and continue happy and in good health, as when you left us." She mentioned a "very pleasant companion" and housekeeper, Miss Sarah Otis, but no reference at all of John.[16] Ellen was more open with Aunt Prudence in a letter written a few days after the one sent to her parents. John's visit gave Ellen "much pleasure." She told Prudence that Sarah Otis had come to the house to do chores while John was there but Ellen sent her away because she "thought it would be so much pleasanter not to have a stranger with us when he was here...."[17] We can only speculate on what Rev. Sewall's parishioners and other townspeople might have thought if they caught a glimpse of Ellen Sewall and John Thoreau, unattended, on one of their walks along the beach.

Henry must have thought John insufferable, upon his return home, when he reported the good time he had in Scituate. For much of the fall Henry wrote in his journals glum thoughts about maidens and love. In one entry he wrote, "But alas! To be actually separated from that parcel of heaven we call our friend, with the suspicion that

---

[15] Harding, 97.
[16] Ellen Sewall letter, September 26, 1839
[17] Ellen Sewall letter, September 29, 1839

we shall no more meet in nature, is source enough for all the elegies that ever were written."[18]

When John and Henry heard that Prudence Ward was going to spend Christmas in Scituate they were eager to join her for part of the holiday. While there, Henry wrote poetry during solitary walks on the beach and played his flute as Ellen polished the family "brasses." Henry's deferential and serious manner led Ellen to call him, "Dr. Thoreau." John, the more handsome of the two brothers and more casual and fun loving, was the "source of endless merriment.[19]

Soon after her Concord visitors returned home, Ellen wrote to her aunt a letter she must surely have known would have been read to the Thoreau household. "The house seems deserted since you left us; I never was so lonely in my life as the day you went away, and I have not quite recovered my spirits yet. You will say 'how foolish,' but I can't help it.... I have wished you and John and Henry here a thousand times this week."[20]

John and Henry couldn't get Ellen out of their thoughts either and the fraternal contest was on. Henry, knowing where the greatest Sewall family influence lay, sent Rev. Sewall a book of poems by the poet, Jones Very, which the whole family enjoyed. He also sent Ellen some of his own poetry. John, as always, being more direct, sent Ellen opals for her collection. Shrewdly, John also sent to Eddie some books and a long letter to George which ended, "I send you Sir nothing but a letter, and now if sister has read it through to you very carefully you may give her a kiss for me and wish her a Happy New Year!!"[21] An indication, though unintentional, of the ranking Ellen placed upon the brothers can be seen when Ellen expressed her gratitude for John's gifts but did not acknowledge Henry's. When Ellen was told of this oversight she immediately sent a letter, not to

---

[18] Harding, 97.
[19] Smith, 29-30.
[20] Harding, 98.
[21] Harding, 98.

Henry, but to Aunt Prudence apologizing and sincerely regretting it. "I wish you would give him to understand that we really were much please at receiving it."[22]

In March 1840 Eddie was again enrolled at the Concord Academy and in June Ellen arrived for a brief visit and Henry asserted himself. As the two of them went for another boat ride on the river, Henry might have dreamed about what life would be like with Ellen.[23] In his journal entry for June 19, 1840 he wrote, "The other day I rowed in my boat a free, even lovely young lady, and, as I plied the oars, she sat in the stern, and there was nothing but she between me and the sky. So might all our lives be picturesque if they were free enough."[24]

Fearing that he was losing the upper hand for the attention of Ellen, John a few days later, travelled with the Wards to Scituate on a mission. As Ellen and John walked along Pegotty Beach in Scituate, this time with Aunt Prudence chaperoning at a comfortable distance, John proposed. Ellen immediately accepted. And yet in the short distance from the beach to her home, she developed doubts and thought she made a mistake. Cleary, Ellen was "in love" with both Thoreaus but she realized that it was Henry, not John, that she preferred.[25] Ellen told her mother of the proposal and Mrs. Sewall expressed fear that Rev. Sewall would not be pleased. She was right. John paid his respects to Rev. Sewall, who objected to the proposal. This gave Ellen the opportunity to tell John she had changed her mind.[26] Later John would send Ellen a crystal as a token of their friendship making one last attempt to curry her favor, unaware of Rev. Sewall's opposition. When the disappointed John came home with the news Henry was ecstatic, in his understated way. He had not written in his journal for a couple of days but on July 19th he wrote,

---

[22] Harding, 99.
[23] Smith, 33.
[24] Harding, 9.
[25] Koopman, 63; Harding, 100.
[26] Koopman, 63.

"Night is spangled with fresh stars" and a few weeks later added, "A wave of happiness flows over us like sunshine over a field."[27] Dejected, John wrote in his diary, "Tonight I feel doleful, somewhat lachrymose, and desponding 'Bluey.' Not absolutely suicidal, but viewing the world at a discount, disposed to part with my lease of life for a very small 'bonus'."[28]

As the summer waned, Rev. and Mrs. Sewall, perhaps dreading another surprise visit by a Thoreau, sent Ellen off to visit family in Watertown, New York. A cousin there had been a classmate of Ellen's at a boarding school during their early teen years. If the elder Sewalls thought the exile would remove the Thoreau brothers from Ellen's thoughts they were wrong. One again, she relied on her Aunt Prudence to be her confidante and informant. Ellen wrote to her,

> I always think of you when I see any beautiful prospect [view], or such like, for we have seen so many together. You are not the only person in Mrs. Thoreau's family whom such scenes call to mind. What delightful walks we had together in Concord last summer, to the cliffs, etc. Oh, those were happy times…. What great work is Henry engaged in now? Will the school go on as usual this winter?[29]

Perhaps hearing of Ellen's inquiry about him, Henry wrote to Ellen in Watertown. The letter was destroyed, probably by Ellen, as were all her diary entries from this period. Ellen's daughter, Louise, would later write, "One would know more of this period if my dear mother had not cut out from her diary all mention of the Thoreau brothers. It pleases to me to know that my mother had such delicate

---

[27] Harding, 100.
[28] Stewart, 17.
[29] Harding, 101.

feelings, but one can't help wishing the she had kept those items in."[30]

Although Henry's letter no longer exists, one Thoreau scholar believes a journal entry of November 1, 1840 is a draft of a part of his letter to Ellen Sewall.

> I thought that the sun of our love should have risen as noiselessly as the sun out of the sea, and we sailors have found ourselves steering between the tropics as if the broad day had lasted forever. You know how the sun comes up from the sea when you stand on the cliff, and doesn't startle you, but everything, and you too are helping it.[31]

The letter contained a proposal of marriage. Once again Ellen was presented with a dilemma and again she sought counsel from her beloved father before she made her reply to Henry. Rev. Sewall instructed Ellen to return to Scituate immediately. On her way home Ellen wrote another letter to Aunt Prudence. It is clear that Ellen had made up her mind to decline Henry's proposal but she needed paternal and pastoral guidance as to the best manner with which to inform him.

> [Father] wished me to write immediately in a 'short, explicit and cold manner to Mr. T. He seemed very glad I was of the same opinion as himself with regard to the matter. I wrote to H.T. that evening. I never felt so badly at sending a letter in my life. I could not bear to think that both those friends whom I have enjoyed so much with would now no longer be able to have the free pleasant intercourse with us as formerly. My letter was very short indeed. But I hope it was the thing. It will not be best for

---

[30] Koopman, 63.
[31] Harding, 101.

213

either you or me to allude to this subject in our letters to each other. Your next letter may as well be to Mother perhaps, or Edmund. By that time the worst of this will be passed and we can write freely again. I do feel so sorry H. wrote to me. It was such a pity. Though I would rather have it so than to have him say the same things on the beach or anywhere else. If I had only been at home so that Father could have read the letter himself and have seen my answer, I should have liked it better. But it is all over now. We will say nothing of it till we meet.... Burn my last [letter].[32]

Henry probably anticipated Ellen's response but nevertheless he surely felt the pain of a lost love.

The romantic triangle put a strain on Henry and John's relationship though neither talked openly about it for fear of making each other uncomfortable. By February 1841 Henry felt he could no longer live in the Thoreau home with John and so he started looking for another place to live. He thought of renting a farm in Concord and even thought of joining Bronson Alcott's utopian community, Brook Farm, in Roxbury. The solitary Thoreau changed his mind and commented in his journal that he would "rather keep bachelor's hall in hell than go to board in heaven."[33] John's health in the later winter became poor, and by March Henry had decided to close the school, citing John's health.

Henry was now adrift. His friend of four years, Ralph Waldo Emerson, noticed the change in Henry's behavior, as he became even more withdrawn than normal. Emerson wondered why he was seeing so little of Henry and when he did, why Henry was so silent and sullen. No matter what the reason, Emerson became concerned; concerned enough to invite Henry, in April 1841, to live in his house,

---

[32] Harding, 101-102.
[33] Harding, 125.

where, in a small room, he could spend time writing. The agreement was that, in return for being Emerson's handyman, he could stay, rent free, for a year. Henry stayed three.[34]

On New Year's Day 1842 John cut his finger on a shaving razor and he soon developed tetanus. Henry became the "most untiring and watchful of nurses." On his last day, January 11, 1842, John asked Henry to talk "of nature and poetry." In his journal entry of that day, Henry wrote that John turned to him with "a transcendent smile full of Heaven," which Henry returned. That last exchange of smiles was the "last communication that passed between them." Henry held John in his arms as he died.[35]

The Thoreau and the Ward-Sewall families had known each other for over twenty years. Rev. and Caroline Sewall were introduced by a Thoreau aunt; Caroline's mother and sister boarded at the Thoreau home and were considered members of the family. The Wards and the Thoreau aunts were among the charter members of the Concord Female Anti-Slavery Society (and were very influential on Henry's abolitionist views.) Edmund, Jr. attended Henry and John's school. So what was wrong with Ellen marrying into the Thoreau family? Could it have been a matter of religion? The Thoreau aunts attended the Concord Trinitarian Church but Henry and John's mother attended the Unitarian Church. Once Henry refused Ellen's request to offer grace at the dinner table during that visit in the summer of 1839; Henry also declined Ellen's invitation to attend church with her in Concord or even in her father's church; and perhaps a most significant event, Henry resigned his membership with the First Parish Church in Concord in 1840.[36] Could it have been the growing Transcendentalist influence on Henry? But then Aunt Prudence subscribed to the *Dial*, the new Transcendentalist magazine that Emerson called, a "journal in a new spirit."[37] Perhaps it

---

[34] Smith, 36-37.
[35] Smith, 60-61.
[36] Stewart, 14.
[37] Philip F. Gura. *American Transcendentalism*, (2007), 129.

was economic. The Wards had more money than the Sewalls and there was little hope that Henry and John, as teachers, would sufficiently provide for Ellen and a family, particularly with Rev. Sewall's sensitivity to domestic finances.

As in all matters of love, there are no easy answers. As one writer has put it, "One cannot entirely regret [Henry] Thoreau's failure in love, at least so far as literature is concerned. His Spartan simplicity of life is essential to his character, and he could retain his contempt for poverty only if he remained a bachelor. Marriage might perhaps have been a very serious hindrance to his literary development, and it would certainly have modified the essential and unique qualities of his genius."[38]

Ellen's youngest daughter, Louise Osgood Koopman would write over a hundred years later (when Louise was ninety-eight), "I have never understood my grandfather's attitude.... He has always been depicted to me as a saint and yet the stupidest saint might realize that young people do fall in love.... My grandfather appears to have been busy during my mother's early youth in shooing away aspirants to her hand."[39]

Ellen, in the months following the end of the romantic triangle, still had second thoughts about her relationship with the Thoreaus. As discreet as ever, Ellen did not name which brother she was thinking of in these journal entries

> I sat and gazed at it [a sunset] and mother & the boys did too, but there were dear ones that could not look with me & exclaim "how glorious!" Poor father could not see it and another, too, was in my thoughts, though not by my side, to whom I would have loved to communicate my emotions. Alas, that

---

[38] T.M. Raysor. "The Love Story of Thoreau," *Studies in Philology,* XXIII (October, 1926), 463.
[39] Koopman, 64.

happiness will never be mine again. Never! And is it so? Yes, the word has passed…. [March 8, 1841]

Mother and I visited at Mr. Amhurst Call's. We walked around and the beautiful moon rose from the cliff just before we reached Kent Street. Mars, too, was in her train, and Venus shone most brilliantly to the west. Such a lovely evening we have not had for some time. I am sometimes sad on such evenings at the thought that one to whom I loved to communicate my feelings will always be separated from me by insurmountable barriers. [April 6, 1841] [40]

Ellen resumed what once was a casual relationship with the Rev. Joseph Osgood in 1842. Osgood had just been ordained as the minister of First Parish in neighboring Cohasset when he asked Ellen to marry him. Prior to the proposal Rev. Osgood asked Rev. Sewall for Ellen's hand as the two ministers drove in a carriage from Cohasset to Scituate for a scheduled afternoon service led by Rev. Osgood. Rev. Sewall gave his consent. Joseph and Ellen Osgood remained married for 48 years until her death in 1892. Louise Osgood Koopman wrote that her mother and father "lived happily ever after – truer in this case than in many. It was a lively, happy household and a busy one."[41]

One day, a few years before Ellen died, as her daughter Louise recounted, she and her mother had a conversation on a "gray, misty Sunday afternoon." Rev. Osgood was in his study reading or taking a nap after preaching earlier that day. Mother and daughter were all alone. Louise was writing letters and somehow the Thoreaus came up in the conversation. For once, Ellen was open to talk about something she never did. Ellen began by telling Louise about that wonderful summer of 1839, particularly about the delightful walks in

---

[40] Stewart, 16-17.
[41] Koopman, 65.

Concord. Then she talked about that fateful stroll with John in Scituate and the shame she felt afterwards. She also talked about Henry's proposal, but as Louise wrote later in her memoir, she deeply regretted that she could not remember much of that part of the conversation. "A walk on a beach, with an offer, at that time, was more romantic to me than a letter," Louise noted. Did Henry continue to care for her, Louise asked. Ellen replied that Sophia Thoreau told her that shortly before Henry died he told Sophia, "I have always loved her." Reflecting on the conversation she had with her mother Louise said that "it was Henry whom she at this time loved. But of course John's tragic death moved her deeply." A few days after Ellen died in 1892, "for the first and only time," Rev. Osgood referred to Ellen's "early love affair." Louise, the youngest of the Osgood children, and her father were alone and feeling sad, as they both missed Ellen. In speaking about that time, Rev. Osgood wondered out loud if Ellen had had a happier life with him. Louise assured him that she had, and as she said, "I meant it."[42]

---

[42] Koopman, 66-67.

Chapter Ten

Rumors of War

Edmund Quincy Sewall Sr.'s predecessor, Nehemiah Thomas, was an example of the liberal Christian minister who was caught up in the turbulent birth of Unitarianism. By education and experience Thomas saw orthodoxy as an impediment to the transformation of a person's character. Rev. Sewall was representative of a new kind of liberal Christian, now proudly called Unitarian. Sewall was influenced by William Ellery Channing, pastor of the Federal Street Church in Boston, who preached insistently on the importance of moral culture and a person's ability to transform for the good. Sewall and others took Channing's assertion and expanded it to apply to society at large. Thus, began the long history of Unitarian efforts at social reform. At first the emphasis was on temperance. Unitarians played a leading role in the effort to reduce, if not eliminate, the effects of alcohol on society. Over much of the nineteenth-century prominent Unitarians would lead other reform movements including the abolition of slavery, women's suffrage and public health. Nevertheless, the emphasis Unitarians put on the importance of individual opinion and personal liberty made them often reluctant to join societies that sought to promote temperance by restrictive and coercive measures. As a religious movement Unitarians at this time showed a greater inclination for the use of moral suasion than legislative power.[1] Rev. Sewall, for his part, was a local leader in the temperance cause. A newspaper account reported that at a series of meetings one week in the spring of 1833 a total of almost three hundred and fifty Scituate residents signed a pledge of abstinence from alcohol. As result of the temperance society's efforts one Scituate merchant stopped the sale of "ardent spirits" and another merchant promised to stop his sale of alcohol as soon as his stock was depleted.[2]

The first African slaves came to British colonial American in 1619. Eighty years later Quakers in Philadelphia started the first organized movement to abolish slavery. The rebellious Thomas Paine, in 1775, published the first colonial pamphlet calling for the abolition of the slave trade and the freeing of slaves in the colonies. By 1787 African slaves accounted for one-fifth of the new nation's population. That year, at the convention to form a new national government, there was an acrimonious debate between northern and southern delegates on whether to abolish the importation of slaves no earlier than 1808. Moreover, the Constitutional Convention took no action on the buying and selling of slaves within the United States. The response to this stalemate was the movement to organize the emigration of slaves back to Africa (Liberia, in western Africa, was colonized by some of these slaves in 1821) or Central America.

William Lloyd Garrison, who would become the most prominent abolitionist in America, initially supported the emigration of slaves back to Africa. By 1831 his stance changed and he began publishing his newspaper, *The Liberator,* which unwaveringly supported abolition. The following year Garrison founded the New England Anti-Slavery Society. Many prominent Boston Unitarian clergy and laity joined, but not all. A significant number of Unitarians did not endorse the methods of the abolitionists and numerous Boston Unitarian merchants relied on slavery for the cotton for their textiles. Others, like Rev. William Ellery Channing (and even

---

[1] Cooke, 273.
[2] *Christian Watchman*, May 10, 1833.

Garrison, who, though not a Unitarian, believed as one), saw themselves as "just, rational, and open-minded," were criticized for being too timid in the face of inhumanity.[3]

Rev. Samuel J. May, another ardent abolitionist, was among those Unitarian clergy who criticized their colleagues and co-religionists for their timidity. "The Unitarians as a body," he said, dealt with the question of slavery in anything but an impartial, courageous and Christian way.... [W]e had the right to expect from the Unitarians a steadfast and unqualified protest against so unjust, tyrannical, and cruel a system as that of American slavery" [4] On the other hand, the statement by historian George Cooke that, "In proportion to its numbers no religious body in the country did so much to promote the anti-slavery reform as the Unitarian" while extravagant, is plausible.[5] Unitarians believed in the innate goodness of humanity in contrast to the orthodox belief in humanity's depravity; and thus, people had the capacity to progress towards a higher moral life. This ideal, professing individual liberty and self-culture, incarnated into religious practice, meant that actions in this world were important. It was the obligation of liberal Christians to balance individual liberty with social reform by giving support to whatever furthered the cause of social justice.

Among those present in Boston in October 1830 when William Lloyd Garrison first presented his views in favor of immediate emancipation were Samuel J. May, Samuel E. Sewall, and Bronson Alcott. Samuel was a cousin to Edmund Q. Sewall; May and Alcott were in-laws. It is quite likely that Scituate's Rev. Sewall was with them. These men immediately became close associates of Garrison. Another Sewall cousin, Edmund Quincy was, for many years, editor of Garrison's *The Liberator.*

---

[3] Cooke, 276.
[4] Cooke, 278.
[5] Cooke, 276.

The American Anti-Slavery Society began flooding Congress in 1834 with petitions to abolish slavery. Southern members of Congress responded by passing a resolution that tabled all petitions regarding slavery without giving them a hearing. Over 130,000 petitions were received between 1837 and 1838. Former president John Quincy Adams was Scituate's congressman then and had strong abolitionist support in the town. In Congress, Adams repeatedly sought to bring those petitions to the floor of the House for a debate.[6] Time after time he was voted down and was even censured in February 1837 by the House of Representatives for trying to introduce a petition by slaves, thereby showing "gross contempt of this House."[7]

Reacting to this series of incidents, a crowded meeting in Scituate on May 1, 1837 passed the following resolution "with great unanimity."

> Resolved, That we view with serious apprehension, the encroachments made by the Representatives of the United States, upon the Sacred Right of Petition - a right which we deem inherent in man – absolute and inalienable – a right vital to the free institutions of our Country – a right, which by the Constitution of the Republic, Congress is peremptorily forbidden in any way to abridge.

> Resolved, That we do cordially approve the conduct of those Representatives and Senators, who have resisted these daring assaults upon our liberties.

---

[6] "Struggles Over Slavery,"
http://www.archives.gov/exhibits/treasures_of_congress/text/page10_text.html
[7] "Gag Rule Controversy,"
http://www.archives.gov/exhibits/treasures_of_congress/text/page10_text.html

Resolved, That we tender our grateful acknowledgments especially to our own Representative – the Hon. John Quincy Adams, who has so highly distinguished himself in the advocacy and defence of the Right of Petition, and the Constitution of our country.

Resolved, That Dr. Cushing Otis, Ebenezer T. Fogg, Esq., Rev. Edmund Q. Sewall, Rev. Samuel J. May and Rev. Mr. Holbrook be a committee to present to Mr. Adams a copy of the resolutions and to express to him our high respect and confidence."[8]

Rev. Sewall's wife, Caroline, and her mother and sister, Mrs. Ward and Prudence Ward, surely influenced his participation in the abolitionist effort. Sewall's in-laws were radical abolitionists and charter members of the Boston Female Anti-Slavery Society. The Society was remarkable because it was led by women and was independent of any other national anti-slavery group and, most importantly, it was interracial. In their correspondence, (along with a running dialogue about neighbors, politics, and personal matters) Prudence Ward, her niece Ellen Sewall, and Maria Thoreau, routinely chatted about shopping at, sewing for, and staffing the tables of anti-slavery bazaars.[9]

In October 1845, another meeting of Boston area Unitarian ministers was held to "discuss their duties in relation to American slavery."[10] At a later meeting the Unitarian ministers, by a vote of forty-seven to seven, declared "that we consider slavery to be utterly opposed to the principles and spirit of Christianity, and that, as

---

[8] *The Liberator*, May 12, 1837.
[9] Sandra Harbert Petrulionis. "Swelling That Great Tide of Humanity": The Concord, Massachusetts, Female Anti-Slavery Society, *The New England Quarterly* Vol. 74, No. 3 (Sep., 2001), 385-418.
[10] Cooke, 280.

ministers of the gospel, we feel it our duty to protest against it, in the name of Christ, and to do all we may to create a public opinion to secure the overthrow of the institution." It was also decided to appoint a committee to draw up, secure signatures to, and publish "a protest against the institution of American slavery, as unchristian and inhuman."[11]

The protest letter was written by Rev. James Freeman Clarke of Boston and was signed by one hundred and seventy-three ministers, almost two-thirds of the entire Unitarian ministry. Rev. Sewall of Scituate was among the signers. "This protest," said the editor of *The Christian Register*, in presenting it to the public, "is written with great clearness of expression and moderation of spirit. It exhibits unequivocally and distinctly the sentiments of the numerous and most enlightened body of clergy whose names are attached to it...."[12] The letter, reprinted in *The Liberator* said, in part,

> Especially do we feel that the denomination which takes for its motto Liberty, Holiness and Love should be foremost in opposing this system. More than others we have contended for three great principles,-- individual liberty, perfect righteousness, and human brotherhood. All of these are grossly violated by the system of slavery. We contend for mental freedom; shall we not denounce the system which fetters both mind and body?

> We implore all Christians and Christian preachers to unite in unceasing prayer to God for aid against this system, to leave no opportunity of speaking the truth and spreading the light on this subject, in faith that the truth is strong enough to break every yoke.

---

[11] Cooke, 281.
[12] *The Christian Register, October 4, 1845*

> And we do hereby pledge ourselves, before God and
> our brethren, never to be weary of laboring in the
> cause of human rights and freedom until slavery be
> abolished and every slave made free.[13]

Rev. Sewall's resignation from First Parish in March 1848 was a relief for both him, and the congregation. Both had deep sadness with their parting, yet his dedication to the ministry, even with his doubts about his stamina, was a source of pride to his family and inspiration to his congregation. Now First Parish had to proceed with finding a new minister to follow the beloved Rev. Sewall. The man they chose did not have the drama and romance that surrounded Sewall and his family, but he, too, was a man of deep conviction and courage.

Ephraim Nute, Jr. was born in Boston in 1819, the son of a Universalist merchant. As a child he attended the Bullfinch Street church (originally Universalist, later Unitarian). Universalism began in the United States in the 1790s and was concentrated in New England and the Middle Atlantic states. Universalism's central tenet, hence its name, came from the belief that *all* human beings will ultimately be restored to a right relationship with God, (universal salvation) because God is Love.

Nute enrolled at Harvard Divinity School on scholarship and among his classmates was the future Unitarian hymnist Samuel Longfellow, brother of Henry Wadsworth Longfellow, and Thomas Wentworth Higginson, the great Unitarian abolitionist. Nute was described as "upright to a fault," "stiff with New England Unitarianism," and "pious."[14]

---

[13] *The Liberator, October 10, 1845*

[14] Barbara Groth. "Ephraim Nute,"
http://www25.uua.org/uuhs/duub/articles/ephraimnute.html

On May 15, 1848 a vote of First Parish was taken to call Rev. Nute as minister with a salary of $500 per year and the benefit of two Sundays off. This was the first time the Scituate congregation called a minister for a specific term with renewals, if the congregation so decided. Before Nute it was expected that a minister would be with a congregation for life, unless there were unusual circumstances for leaving, such as Rev. Sewall's poor health. Rev. Nute responded to the offer in a letter dated May 25, 1848

> Dear Friends and Brethren, I am happy to signify my acceptance.... I am influenced to choose this course...which was suggested.... I now entertain that the difficulties now in the way to my making a permanent home with you of which [we] then spoke will in some way be obviated in the course of a year.

Nute arrived at First Parish to a changing Scituate. Like most of the Northeast, industrialization and transportation were transforming Scituate. On January 1, 1849 the South Shore Railroad line began service. Though originally chartered to provide service from Braintree to Duxbury with service to Scituate along the way, the line ended at Cohasset. The train would not come to Scituate until the late 1870s. Still, a train coming to neighboring Cohasset allowed Scituate farmers to bring their produce to Boston; businessmen could better conduct their trade in the city; and, residents of Scituate would have a more comfortable ride to Boston and enjoy its cultural attractions.

There was another dramatic change to Scituate. For two hundred years, ever since William Vassall successfully petitioned the Plymouth Colony General Court, Scituate was divided into two parishes. For many years town meeting alternated it's site between the First and Second Parish meetinghouses. By the 1840s it was clear that the Second Parish of the town had different needs than those who lived closer to the shore; consequently, in 1849, the Massachusetts legislature once again divided the town, but this time

Second Parish became incorporated as its own town, South Scituate. Later, in 1888, it was reincorporated as the town of Norwell.

Rev. Ephraim Nute, Jr.

Like his predecessor Rev. Sewall, Rev. Nute was an ardent abolitionist but more a man of action than the thoughtful Sewall. Still, Nute had to minister to his congregation. Like Sewall, he supported the local temperance society that held lectures at the church. A fiery but compassionate preacher, Nute had to contend with a sometimes unruly or disrespectful congregation. At one meeting, in 1851, the congregation once again had to vote "to post up in large letters that it be recommended to all persons to refrain from defiling the meetinghouse with tobacco spittle, apple cores, grape skins...or other filth of any description." Later that year a committee was formed to control the decorum in the church during worship. There was the problem of "boys and girls who make too much noise at the meetinghouse on the Sabbath." The committee also was called upon to respond to complaints about the newer hymns. It was instructed to look at the old singing books so that some of the old and familiar hymns could be sung, thus satisfying "the wishes and feelings of a large portion of the Parish."[15]

Rev. Nute became active in Scituate civic affairs, serving on the Scituate School Committee. Still, he bigger issues. Soon after he arrived in Scituate, Nute wrote an essay that was published in the abolitionist journal, *The Liberty Bell*. In it Nute said,

> Why do we cherish this hope [of ending slavery], so widely accounted as the dream of enthusiasm? Why grows it stronger in our hearts day by day in the face of all opposition, notwithstanding every triumph of oppression? Is it not because we believe in the power of that truth by which all tyranny of man over his brother stands condemned?; because we believe in the spirit of Love which must, in its certain conquest, break all chains and abolish all oppression?; because we believe in Liberty for which we contend as, under God, the inalienable birthright of every human being....[16]

Echoing the social reforming strain of Unitarianism at the time, Nute spoke of the cultivation of character. "Our work then is to manifest that truth for the conviction of every mind; to cultivate

---

[15] First Parish Records

[16] Ephraim Nute. *"The Leaven of Liberty,"* in *The Liberty Bell*, (1851), 86. (Written October, 1849.)

and impart that spirit to all hearts within the sphere of our influence."[17]

After a three-year ministry, Ephraim Nute was becoming restless for reasons related to First Parish and beyond. In July 1850, with permission from the congregation, Nute and his wife travelled west visiting many Unitarian churches, gathering information "relative to the moral and religious condition of the people" in that part of the country. When he spoke in Cannelton, Indiana, a town along the Ohio River, "he was heard with marked attention by a well-filled house."[18] The trip, to what was even then considered the far west, instilled in him a desire to do something more than get an awareness about the depth of religion and moral behavior in Indiana, Kentucky, and other places.

A year later, on July 14, 1851 Rev. Nute wrote the following to the congregation:

Dear Friends,

After long and careful deliberation and with great reluctance, I feel myself compelled to the discharge of a duty, the most painful of all that have grown out of our connection as pastor and people.

I must ask you to release me from my present pastoral charge.

To most of you this cannot be an unexpected announcement. To those who are aquatinted with the circumstances of my settlement it must rather have been an occasion of surprise that it was not made long before this.

---

[17] Nute, *"The Leaven of Liberty,"* in *The Liberty Bell*, 87-88.
[18] *Christian Register*, July 13, 1850.

Nute apparently believed and expected that he would have a long-term commitment from the congregation and that he would be able to live somewhere near the center of the Scituate parish before the close of his first year as minister. That expectation was based upon the encouragement received from individuals in the congregation about the prospect of living in a parsonage, thus relieving the Nutes of the financial burden of renting a home. From time to time this support was renewed but often ended in disappointment.

> At last I am forced to the conclusion that I have waited long enough; that the prospect with which commenced my labors among you are never to be realized, and with great sorrow I must relinquish the hope which I have so long and so fondly cherished of spending my days among you, in the work of the Gospel.
>
> I am anxious that you should understand that the cause of this separation is not with me, a matter of mere personal convenience. It is a matter of duty and necessity and concerns most deeply your religious prosperity.

Nute was concerned from the beginning of his Scituate ministry that his health and strength would not be sufficient to carry out his ministerial responsibilities if he had to live a good distance from the church.

> Of these difficulties I would remind you, not in the spirit of complaint, but for the future prosperity of your society, and the better success of him whom you may call to fill my place.
>
> I would not leave you with any complaint or the least feeling of unkindness, and cannot close this communication without adding the assurance of my

grateful sense of the great kindness which you have ever-manifested toward me.

In the sadness of this separation I am comforted by the hope that a friendly connection—a spiritual union has been formed between us, that shall never be dissolved...

In its response to Mr. Nute it is clear that the minister and the Parish parted on good terms, "They [the congregation] regret that there should have been circumstances to induce you to take this step for they believe that it could have been agreeable to you to have remained. The kindness and good wishes manifested in your letter is duly appreciated and will be held in grateful remembrance. For your future prosperity and usefulness, the Committee has to say that it would be a source of pleasure to hear of your successes." [*September 23, 1851*][19] The brief ministry of Rev. Nute set a pattern of short ministries that lasted over one hundred years until the ministry of the Rev. Carl H. Whittier in 1960. The issues of salary and living quarters were to vex the congregation over that time.

Personal interests were important to Rev. Nute but so were larger issues. After leaving Scituate, Nute served a four-year ministry in Chicopee, Massachusetts, but even there Nute has his mind out West. For most of his time in Chicopee, Nute sought a commission from the American Unitarian Association in Boston to spread the Unitarian gospel. The history of Orthodox missionary work had been to convert the "heathen" but Nute and his liberal Christian colleagues went west to prevent the pioneers from losing interest in religion. He finally succeeded in getting the commission in 1855. His instructions were to bring Unitarianism to the West and to Lawrence, Kansas in particular. He built the Unitarian Church of Lawrence, the first church in the state and the city's first schools.[20] Still, that wasn't

---

[19] First Parish Records
[20] Groth, http://www25.uua.org/uuhs/duub/articles/ephraimnute.html

Nute's only goal. He also joined the fight to make Kansas a free state. By planting Unitarianism in Kansas, the American Unitarian Association and its anti-slavery allies, such as the New England Emigrant Aid Society, sought to increase the number of abolitionists in Kansas, thus improving the chances that Kansas would enter the United States as a free (non-slaveholding) state. Immediately upon his arrival Nute started preaching the liberal Christian message of Unitarianism. A Lawrence, Kansas paper, *The Herald of Freedom*, welcomed Rev. Nute and noted that his first sermon took place outside Lawrence on Mount Oread, "For the want of a smaller edifice, Mr. Nute chooses for the present to worship in the sunset dome which nature has erected."[21] It was said of Rev. Nute that "he was a good fighter when the fight was on," and, "he never hesitated to say his say in plain and unmistakable terms." Nute's sense of humor was "keen," and he was "aggressive and had an abundance of self-assurance, qualities which were needed in the tumultuous days and chaotic condition of Kansas".[22]

Nute arrived in Kansas as the violence between anti-slavery Free-Staters and pro-slavery "Border Ruffians," crossing in from Missouri (a slave-holding state), escalated, and he soon found himself in the thick of it. Nute had some relationship with the abolitionist John Brown who also was in Kansas at that time. In May 1856 Lawrence was attacked by a band of ruffians led by the pro-slavery county sheriff. Buildings were burned and the presses of the anti-slavery paper, *The Herald of Freedom*, were destroyed, as were the presses of another anti-slavery paper, *The Free State*. Nute's feelings against the Border Ruffians became personal when his brother-in-law was ambushed by a pro-slavery band, murdered, and scalped. While trying to help his sister-in-law recover her husband's body, Rev. Nute was captured and for a short time held prisoner by the ruffians.[23] When the Civil War began in 1861 he enlisted as a chaplain in the

---

[21] Samuel Atkins Eliot. *Heralds of a Liberal Faith, Vol. 3* (1910), 272.
[22] Eliot, 275-276.
[23] Groth,
http://www25.uua.org/uuhs/duub/articles/ephraimnute.html

First Regiment of Kansas Volunteers but it was reported that he was "more a fighter than a chaplain." [24] Following the war his theology turned even more liberal and, while he had a short pastorate in Petersham, Massachusetts, for the rest of his life he was an itinerant preacher and was an editor and writer for several newspapers and magazines. He died in January 1897 from injuries in a horse-riding accident.

Back in Scituate in 1852, life was quieter though the church was trying to find a minister to succeed Rev. Nute. On February 9, 1852 the congregation voted to call Rev. Samuel F. Clarke as minister but there was an immediate vote to reconsider and the vote was withdrawn. No reason for the change of mind was given in the meeting's minutes. Then, in September, a vote was taken to call Rev. Fisk Barrett offering him a salary of $700 and three Sundays off a year. A month later, the parish met to increase Mr. Barrett's salary to $800. Though the motion was defeated, Barrett agreed to serve.

Rev. Barrett's ministry was marked by hard financial times. By 1857 the church was in such financial straits that it petitioned the Massachusetts legislature to authorize First Parish to assess a portion of the town's taxes for the repair of the meetinghouse; this was an odd request in light of the change in the Commonwealth's constitution twenty-five years earlier abolishing public support to churches through taxes. Not surprisingly, the petition was not granted.

By the mid-nineteenth century, fast days and days of humiliation and prayer were no longer as common as they were during colonial times. However, disgust at the thought of the expansion of slavery in the West so infuriated many of the Massachusetts clergy that Thursday April 6, 1854 was declared a Fast Day for prayer and reflection on the issue of slavery. In his sermon that day, Rev. Barrett used as his text, Matthew 16:3, "Can ye not

---

[24] Eliot, 276.

discern the sign of the times?" He began by criticizing those Barrett viewed as hypocrites, slavery apologists and "Johnny-come-latelies." He denounced the Compromise of 1850, a collection of Congressional legislation which, among other provisions, enacted the Fugitive Slave Act and allowed the New Mexico and Utah territories to determine if they wanted to become slave states. One positive provision was the admittance to the Union of California as a free state, due in large part to the efforts of the Universalist and Unitarian minister, the Rev. Thomas Starr King.

Barrett, in his sermon, said:

> Pulpits, all over the State, which, for years, have either been dumb with respect to slavery, or its cringing apologists, will today speak out, and call it infamous. Methinks I hear them. Men, who, three years ago, today, denounced all agitation on the subject [referring to the debate on the Compromise of 1850], and all its agitators; defended the Compromise of the previous year, and the Fugitive Slave Bill, that quintessence of villainy and inhumanity, a bill which turned the whole North into a slave hunting ground.... [M]ethinks I hear these preachers now, sounding the tocsin [alarm], calling upon their people to bestir themselves, to rise in their might, and oppose the fearful aggressions of slavery. Hear them! How eloquent they are! How fearless and brave!.... How anti-slavery they all are, just now!

> To my view, "the signs of the times' are dark and portentous.... [I]n every conflict between Slavery and Liberty, the former has triumphed. By browbeating, by bribes and threats, by getting up the cry, "The Union is in danger!" the South has invariably gained her point.

My hearers, I would raise no false alarm, nor make any exaggerated statements here today. The simple truth, the most palpable "signs of the times," are quite enough to sadden and fill with dark forebodings every New England heart. We see slavery fast becoming the controlling principle of the nation.... We see our Government and its hirelings pledge to do any thing and every thing for the perpetuity and extension of slavery....

No mortal eye can penetrate the future, nor tell with certainty the fate of this nation. That she is approaching a fearful crisis is too evident. That her fairest honors and her dearest interests are threatened with an ignominious betrayal and overthrow, cannot be denied or winked out of sight. We have been warming and nourishing a deadly viper in our political bosom, which now turns upon us, and would sting us to death. Whatever may be the result of all the plans and measures now in operation for the aggrandizement of the institution of slavery.... should you, as you visit the metropolis of your state, hear the hoarse voice of the auctioneer offering to the highest bidder men, women and children; remember then who have been instrumental in bringing all this shame, wretchedness and wrong upon us. Remember that such are only the legitimate consequences of compromises, especially of the Compromise of 1850, which our pulpits so vigorously defended. Remember then, too, how that those who had the honesty and independence to protest against that enormity were distrusted and denounced.

This sermon was published a month later in *The Liberator*, which described Barrett's words as "able and valuable." [25]

---

[25] "The Signs of the Times," *The Liberator*, May 1854

It was during this time that the church, failing to get financial support from the legislature, sought to insure that members were contributing to the church all they were assessed. Once again a church member was chosen by bid to collect the assessment of members for the church. For a few years in the mid-1850s Turner Litchfield outbid all others by offering to collect the assessments for a fee of one mill (.0001 cents) on the dollar. The church was suffering financially and voted to include a provision in the new bylaws of 1857 that if members were in arrears for two years they would be barred from voting on church matters. To encourage prompt payment by parishioners of the church's "taxes" the church allowed for a sliding scale of discounts beginning with five percent off their assessment if the money was paid before a certain date.

In the midst of this financial crisis a parish vote in January 1858 accepted Rev. Barrett's voluntary salary reduction of one hundred dollars for one year to help with the church's debt. People were not paying their assessments; some had not paid for over a year; others withheld them, perhaps because of some dissatisfaction with Mr. Barrett. One explanation for this may lie in the establishment of a committee at the end of 1858 to "investigate the cause of the misunderstanding among the singers and try to heal the difficulties," although further details were not recorded.

In the middle of all this, Rev. Barrett resigned writing in a letter in March 1859, "It is enough to assure you that having weighed the subject with much deliberation and feeling myself prompted alike by choice and a sense of duty to yield to your wishes so unanimously expressed, it is now my solemn determination with the aid of Heaven to devote myself to the promotion of your religious and moral interests…." The Parish Committee accepted the resignation and a loan was taken out to pay the remainder of Barrett's salary. The pulpit supply committee was charged with finding a minister for two Sundays a month, if the church could raise enough money. The soliciting committee reported in May 1859 they had done nothing and asked to be discharged. They were, and a new committee was assigned the difficult task of raising money. For a year, until a new minister was called, many Sunday services were lay-led because the church could not afford to pay a preacher.

In the late fall of 1855 Caleb Prouty, Clerk of First Parish, met with Rev. Wight of the First Trinitarian Congregational Church to discuss the possibility of conducting a union service of public worship to mark the Thanksgiving observance. There is no known record of what was the tenor of the meeting, though it must have been very polite but still downright cold, for in a letter to Mr. Prouty, dated November 26, 1855, Rev. Wight and four men identified as the "Committee of the First (Trinitarian Congregational) Church, Scituate" (note again the use of the parentheses to indicate their belief that they were the *true* First Church in Scituate) wrote the following

Hon. C. W. Prouty;

Dear Sir:
In view of the recent conference held with yourself as a member of the committee, chosen to confer with the Pastor, or Committee of the First (Trinitarian Congregational) Church of Christ in Scituate, inviting us to review our decision in regard to a union with the Unitarian and other churches in town, in Public Worship, on Thanksgiving Days:

We, the undersigned, a committee of said church, after further deliberation and prayer, and after some delay, expecting a more formal interview with your whole committee, would respectfully reply:

That it would be exceedingly pleasant to us, could the whole town come together for Public Worship, were it only on Thanksgiving days, and cordially unite in the worshipping the God of our Fathers, as he was worshipped by them for some two hundred years till nearly all our religious, civil, educational and benevolent institutions were happily established. But we exceedingly regret, that in later years, unhappy divisions have arisen, diverting many from the venerated Faith of our Fathers, and one branch of this proposed Union to such an extent, that little or no sympathy can exist between us, relative to the most vital doctrines of our holy religion – doctrines so fundamental and precious to us, that we cannot conscientiously or with propriety, unite with them in regular exercises of Public Worship.

On other occasions, we would cheerfully continue to unite as fellow citizens, in promoting the great reforms of our day, as Temperance and Freedom, or in elevating the Standard of Education and good morals in our midst, but we are here free to say, as our fathers already said, that we cannot conscientiously "compromise" the great principles of Christianity, in so solemn an act as Public Worship. For these, and other reasons which we refrain to mention, we would respectfully say, we must still decline joining the proposed union on Thanksgiving days.

Please transmit, Dear Sir, these are our unanimous sentiments, as expressed in a Special Church Meeting, to our fellow citizens, who may assemble with you on Thanksgiving Day.[26]

So the two congregations held separate services.

At the August 20, 1860 meeting, First Parish voted to invite the Rev. William Gustavus Babcock to be its next minister. The committee charged with extending the offer to Mr. Babcock, wrote the following letter:

---

[26] Letter, November 26, 1855 in First Parish files

Dear Sir,

The undersigned, a Committee of First Parish, a religious society in Scituate, in behalf of said society and Parish, present you the resolution which was offered by the Hon. Caleb W. Prouty at the parish meeting…and adopted by a vote of twenty two in the affirmative and three in the negative…annual salary of $700 to be paid quarterly…. The committee begs leave to add their kind regards to yourself and family and earnestly hope you will give a favorable response to the above vote and commence your ministerial labors with us as soon as you conveniently can.

Rev. Babcock responded on August 23rd,

Gentlemen committee,

After due deliberation I accept your kind invitation to become the minister of the First Parish in Scituate on the terms specified…. Your confidence in me notwithstanding my unworthiness in many respects to be a light and guide, a comforter and example to my fellow men.

Having had some experience in ministerial labors, I cannot personally expect nor desire unmixed prosperity in time to come; but I never felt a stronger desire to devote what little strength, wisdom and zeal I may possess to the work of a religious teacher and pastor. That we may long continue to be successful co-workers in the application of religion to all private and social relations is the sincere prayer of yours most truly….

Rev. Babcock was born in Milton, Massachusetts on June 1, 1820. He graduated from Harvard in 1841 and the Divinity School in

1844. He also served churches in Providence Rhode Island; and, Lunenburg and South Natick, Massachusetts. He died July 30, 1911.

The installation of Rev. Babcock as minister of First Parish took place on September 16, 1860. The service featured remarks by Seth Webb, Jr., who spoke of First Parish's long history and the present congregation which would be under his care and education. Webb also spoke of the "free pulpit" in which a minister in a liberal Christian congregation was expected to speak his own mind, free from the shackles of orthodox Biblical interpretation. The congregation in Scituate expected their minister to be bold and forthright in his sermons, even though parishioners would often disagree.

Rev. William Gustavus Babcock

Welcoming Rev. Babcock to First Parish and to Scituate, the estimable Mr. Webb made these remarks:

> Mr. Babcock, I take leave to present to you a book [The New Testament] and a list of names.... I need not say to you that this book is to be the chief bond of union between you and those who have invited you among them....
>
> The list of names which I...put into your hands is made up of the little group of families and persons who are to form your future flock, and with whom you have just entered into a close and intimate relationship of preacher and pastor....
>
> To have the willing ear of any people, fifty-two times a year, on themes of vital import to all, is of itself a vast source of influence; and this is rendered all the more interesting where the words fall, not on merely passive recipients, but are subjected, as in every New England congregation, to the crucible of keen though friendly examination and of enlightened consciences.... [T]his pulpit should continue what I believe it always has been, a free pulpit. Let the torch of absolute Truth burn forever on these time-worn altars. Whatever your honest, conscientious and natural convictions prompt you to speak, that we shall be glad to hear, even though it may sometimes differ from our own conclusions.
>
> You are also to become our pastor. And here, even in this secluded village, is a field wide enough to satisfy the noblest ambition and the warmest heart....
>
> Here, as elsewhere, are sickness and pain and want, loneliness and strife and death, the aching and the

breaking heart. Between these calamities and their victims you will often be called to stand....

And, if you have imposed on yourself duties so numerous and varied towards us, we trust not to forget that we also have duties towards you. In every good word and work, I hope that you will receive the hearty cooperation of your parishioner and if, in the vicissitudes of life, you, in your turn, should be called to taste the cup of sorrow, sickness, or bereavement, I am sure that these who sit around us will not let you stagger on alone, but will be found promptly and actively at your side.

It may not be amiss to remind each other today, that, as this religious society is among the simplest in its rites and forms, so also it is one of the very oldest now in existence in New England. In a new country like America, [it is] now and then refreshing to look on any institution, however humble, which has withstood the shocks for centuries, and to which the moss of ages clings.

It has witnessed the beginning and the end of the three great social convulsions of the modern world, the English Revolution [1688], the American Revolution, and the French Revolution [1789].... These reminiscences indicate, that, if your society has a future, it has also a past. If it has hopes, it has also memories and prejudices, and old and dear traditions.

You notice, sir, that this bare hill looks out upon the open ocean; and the weather-beaten spire above us is one of the surest and most welcome landmarks of the sailor.

And now, sire, in the name of this congregation, I publicly recognize you as its minister; and we cordially and cheerfully receive and greet you as our pastor and friend.[27]

Mr. Webb's eloquence at the installation of Rev. Babcock came naturally to him. One of the most notable members of First Parish, Webb was from a prominent Scituate family. His father Seth Webb, Sr. was a merchant sea captain and co-owner of several clipper ships. Seth, Jr. went to Phillips Exeter Academy in Exeter, New Hampshire and he, too, set sail, mostly along the coast of South America. The junior Webb was a fervent abolitionist. He was active during the 1850s in the Free Soil Party whose main purpose was to make sure the western territories did not permit slavery. It was one of the political parties that later came together to form the Republican Party. In 1860 Seth Webb was a delegate to the Republican Party convention in Chicago that nominated Abraham Lincoln.

Webb was involved in one of the most notorious events in Boston prior to the Civil War. In 1854 Congress passed the Kansas-Nebraska Act which allowed settlers in those territories to decide whether they would allow slavery. This further enraged many New Englanders already upset with the passage of the Fugitive Slave Act of 1850, which required, by law, the return of runaway slaves to their masters. A slave, Anthony Burns, who had been hired out to a series of temporary masters by his owner, Charles F. Suttle, escaped from Virginia and arrived in Boston as a stowaway on a boat. He worked at several jobs and was employed at a clothing store at the time of his capture. Burns wrote to his brother in Richmond, who was also a slave, telling him that he was working in Boston. Unfortunately the letter to his brother was delivered to his master, Suttle, who discovered Burns' Boston whereabouts.[28] On May 24, 1854 Burns

---

[27] Seth Webb, Jr. in *The Monthly Journal of the American Unitarian Association*, November 1860, 509ff.

[28] *New York Times*, May 29, 1854

was arrested under the Fugitive Slave Law and was taken to a holding cell at the Boston Court House. By the next day news of Burns' arrest spread. The hearing was delayed so that Burns' lawyers could prepare their case, thus giving time for the Vigilance Committee of abolitionists to plan resistance to the rendition. Some on the committee supported an assault on the courthouse. A meeting at Faneuil Hall on the evening of May 26th attended by several thousand people heard fiery speeches from Wendell Phillips and the Unitarian minister, Theodore Parker. Parker called for a gathering at the courthouse the next morning but the crowd, already agitated, left en masse for the courthouse. In the throng were Seth Webb, Rev. Thomas Wentworth Higginson and Lewis Hayden, also an escaped slave, who once was owned by Sen. Henry Clay of Kentucky. (Hayden went on to become a Boston businessman and served a term in the Massachusetts legislature in the early 1870s.) Webb, Higginson and Hayden ran from Faneuil Hall to the courthouse to find an attack already underway. The door to the courthouse was well guarded but it was knocked down and a number of people got inside, including Webb, Higginson and Hayden, now joined by Bronson Alcott. Shots were fired and a guard was stabbed and mortally wounded in the melee; the crowd retreated and the attempt to rescue Burns failed.[29]

---

[29] Horace Howard Furness, Jr. ed. *The Letters of Horace Howard Furness,* (1922), 32n; Sarah Ebert. *Louisa May Alcott on Race, Sex and Slavery* (1997), xxi; Earl M. Malz.*Fugitive Slave on Trial,* (2010), 60-63

Anthony Burns

Seth Webb, Jr.

Rev. Thomas Wentworth Higginson

Amos Bronson Alcott

The day after the assault on the courthouse to free Burns, Webb sued Charles Suttle, Anthony Burns' purported owner, along with another man for conspiring to have Burns, "a free citizen of Massachusetts," arrested as a slave; and, to prevent Burns from being returned to Alexandria, Virginia. Webb also sued the United States marshal for the release of Burns. A couple of days later, Burns appeared in court for a hearing on whether to return him to Virginia. The judge ruled that under the Fugitive Slave Act Burns must be returned to his owner. When the word of this reached New

Hampshire church bells in Manchester tolled for an hour in honor of Burns.

When the day came for Burns' return Boston under martial law as he was placed on a ship in the harbor. Hundreds of troops lined the streets from the courthouse to the ship to keep the tens of thousands of people along the way in order. Signs of mourning hung from houses and office windows, as did a coffin with the word, "Liberty," painted on it. Below, Burns walked along the street surrounded by soldiers no doubt hearing cries of "Shame" and "Bloodhounds" from the crowd lining the way. He wore a black suit given to him by friends and "presented a very respectable appearance." At Court and State Streets, from the same window which held up the black coffin someone threw paper packets containing cayenne pepper which landed all over the police, "handkerchiefs were instantly in demand and the police and deputy marshals were seized with irrepressible fits of sneezing."[30]

The Burns case increased anti-slavery feelings across the North as the abolitionists in Boston sought to raise $1,200 to buy Burns from Charles Suttle, but he obstinately refused to sell Burns knowing that it would bring about Burns' freedom. Eventually though, Suttle did sell Burns to a cotton planter in North Carolina who, in turn, sold him to an abolitionist. Burns returned to Boston a free man, where he wrote his autobiography that provided funds for his education at Oberlin College in Ohio. He became a Baptist preacher and died from tuberculosis in Canada at the age of 28.[31]

William Gustavus Babcock had graduated from Harvard two years before Seth Webb, Jr. and was a classmate of Thomas Wentworth Higginson, Webb's partner in the courthouse assault. Babcock himself was actively involved in social reform. When he served a church in South Natick, Massachusetts he was involved with workers in the Great Shoemaker's Strike in 1860 which affected

---

[30] *New York Times,* June 5, 1854; Furness, 35.

[31] http://www.masshist.org/longroad/01slavery/burns.htm

South Natick's and surrounding towns. Most of the unfinished leather goods to be made into shoes were sent to Massachusetts tanneries from the South. The shoes went back south to be used by slaves. As an active member of the Massachusetts abolitionist movement, Rev. Babcock felt the complicity of the shoe factories in slavery was morally offensive. He began a boycott of the factories and encouraged work stoppages. On at least one occasion, he tried to disrupt the delivery of leather at a train depot. Mr. Babcock and others were attempting to convince the factory owners to buy leather from free states. When this met with some success, the southern leather suppliers raised their prices to exorbitant levels. This forced tannery owners who got their leather from southern states to cut the wages of shoemakers who were already making very low wages. "While the intent of the abolitionists was laudable, the effect on the workers was detrimental."[32]

According to a news report in February 1860, an orderly procession of hundreds of people marched in the main streets of Natick to protest the workers' low wages. They gathered at Schoolhouse Hall to hear speakers supporting their cause. Among the speakers was Rev. Babcock.[33] It is generally agreed that the abrupt dismissal of the Rev. Babcock from the South Natick church was due to his active support of the strike. Babcock addressed the strikers at several other meetings, and on one notable occasion was shut out of his Natick church and forced to use a piece of wire to pick the lock in order to let the strikers in.[34]

Abraham Lincoln's election in 1860 as President (and the Unitarian Hannibal Hamlin of Maine as Vice-President) made civil war almost inevitable; the firing on Fort Sumter in Charleston, South Carolina's harbor in April 1861 made it certain. The war brought an inflationary economy to New England and once again First Parish

---

[32] Paul Ouimet, personal correspondence to author, August 5, 2002.
[33] "The Strike of the Massachusetts Shoe-workers," *The New York Times*, February 24, 1860.
[34] *Natick Bulletin*, August 20, 1975.

was in a financial bind. There was real fear that the two hundred thirty year-old congregation would dissolve. To prevent that, Rev. Babcock agreed to waive his salary and depend on whatever the church could raise by subscriptions. Not until the fifth year of his ministry, the year he resigned, did the congregation vote him a salary again. During this period, the Parish constantly voted to "tax" the pews at $200 and the ones in the gallery at $20. It was at this time that the Ladies Sewing Circle of First Parish was formed. The women, as they socialized, made quilts and other items to be sold at various church fairs to raise money. These gatherings were held twice a month, not only in the church but also at the Town Hall, the town armory and Jenkins Hall, now the Grand Army of the Republic (G.A.R.) Hall, but most often in the homes of the Ladies Sewing Circle members. In addition to making items to raise funds for the church, the women also made bandages and other items for the Union soldiers. After the war, and for many years following, the Sewing Circle held an Oyster Supper in February and a Strawberry Fair in June, also to raise funds for the church.

A month before the end of the Civil War, Rev. Babcock sent a letter to the Parish Committee submitting his resignation signing it "Your Minister and Friend,"

> Gentlemen of the Parish Committee, I most respectfully offer through you to the First Parish in Scituate my resignation as their pastor, to take effect, according to contracts, within 3 months after date. I also ask that what I might have claimed once a year during the last four years but have not taken, a vacation of one month, the pulpit to be supplied at the expense of the parish or closed at their option.

At the March 27th Parish Meeting the resignation was accepted. Knowing that Rev. Babcock resigned because of an insufficient salary, First Parish, for the first time, required a monetary contribution as a condition of membership, "Resolved that all persons without distinction of sex ... paying to the amount of two dollars and upwards per year, for the support of Liberal Christianity to be preached from our pulpit, shall be considered as full member of the Parish."

After leaving Scituate Babcock became the minister at the Warren Street Chapel. The chapel was founded by the Reverend Charles Francis Bernard in 1835. Bernard was an associate of Joseph Tuckerman, the minister called by the Unitarian ministers of Boston to aid the poor. The chapel was also known as "The Children's Church," for its activities included Sunday School classes in the morning and afternoon; also, lessons in reading, writing, arithmetic and industrial arts. Day care was provided for the young children of working mothers. William Ware Locke, who would later become superintendent of the Brooklyn, N.Y. school system and minister at First Parish of Scituate, served twice as minister of the Warren Street Chapel from 1886-1893 and again 1917-1918.[35]

In October, First Parish voted to invite the Rev. William Sweetser Heywood to serve as its minister. A Rev. Hatch was also considered, but the vote favored Rev. Heywood. Because of the expense involved it was voted not to have any installation celebration for Mr. Heywood.

---

[35] Peter Richardson. *The Boston Religion*, (2003), 80.

Chapter Eleven

The Age of Reformers

William Sweetser Heywood was born in Westminster, Massachusetts on August 24, 1824. At age twenty-four he became part of the Hopedale (Massachusetts) Community, a utopian society founded in 1842 by the Universalist minister, Adin Ballou. Heywood studied theology under Rev. Ballou and was ordained into the ministry by the Hopedale Community in 1849. In 1851 he married Ballou's daughter, Abigail, and they became co-principals at the Hopedale Home School. Later Heywood became the Hopedale community's president, but by 1856 the community was bankrupt. Though the utopian dream ended, Heywood and Abigail continued to run their progressive school which educated the children of William Lloyd Garrison. Soon after being ordained as a Unitarian minister, Rev. Heywood and his family left Hopedale and prepared for his first ministry in Scituate.

For a generation First Parish struggled to adequately pay its ministers resulting in a series of calls and resignations, calls and resignations. Another cause of this instability was the absence of a parsonage. Ministers simply could not live on their salary while also paying rent for their lodging. In November 1866, in an effort to keep ministers for a longer period, the congregation voted to explore the idea of building a parsonage on what was referred to as the "Old

Meetinghouse Lot." It is not clear from the meeting minutes if the lot was on the present Lawson Common or Meetinghouse Lane near the Men of Kent Cemetery, but it is probably the former, which was closer to the site of the church.

In January 1867 the idea of building a parsonage was abandoned and a committee was appointed to meet with Mr. Heywood about renting for his family a house for a year or more but the troubles around lodging proved untenable for the Heywood family and on September 23, 1867 the Parish accepted the resignation of Mr. Heywood, who agreed to stay until the first of November. The lack of a parsonage was a significant issue because a new committee was appointed to "take into consideration what can be done to promote the best welfare of the Parish with regard to buying or building a dwelling house to be used as a parsonage..."[1]

Rev. William Sweetser Heywood

---

[1] First Parish Records

For several months following the departure of Rev. Heywood the church did not call a minister because of its continuing financial struggles. The Rev. William H. Fish, pastor of the South Scituate church, provided worship services in the afternoon after his South Scituate church duties. During this time and for several years after, the church appointed a member to call on "all delinquent" members and "insist upon the payment of their taxes [pew fees] and subscriptions." Despite these difficulties, on April 19, 1868 the congregation voted to have two services each Sunday. Presumably, lay members led most of the services when an itinerant minister could not be found.

Then, in March 1869, the church hired H(enry) L(orenzo) Cargill. When he came to Scituate, Rev. Cargill was a recent graduate of the Boston School for the Ministry, a short-lived seminary, and Scituate was his first call. His ministry in Scituate was also brief. Rev. Cargill was invited to serve Scituate, like Heywood, for one year "provided the money can be obtained." The following March the contract was renewed for one year at the same salary but eight months later, in November 1870, the church coffers ran dry. The congregation needed to paint the building and pay for insuring it, among other expenses, and that left the congregation with little money to pay for its minister beyond December. The Parish Committee took the responsibility to supply the pulpit "when they think it proper;" and so, from December 1870 until August 1872, First Parish did not have a minister to call its own. Rev. Hatch, who was passed over by the congregation in favor of Rev. Heywood in 1865, preached on numerous occasions during this period. For his part, Rev. Cargill went on to serve churches in Troy, New York and Omaha, Nebraska.

The continuing financial crisis constrained the congregation so that it once again called a minister fresh out of seminary, presumably because he would demand a lesser salary. First Parish called the Rev. Nicolas Paine Gilman in August 1872. Gilman was from Quincy, Illinois and graduated from Harvard Divinity School in 1871. He was offered one thousand dollars per year and even with a troubled budget, the congregation wanted to celebrate his arrival, so it paid for an ordination ceremony, the first in many decades.

One of the most significant decisions First Parish made during Rev. Gilman's ministry was the creation of a "Bond of Union" (December 1873) with his help and encouragement. Since their beginning, New England congregational churches gathered under a covenant with each other. After being accepted into membership a new parishioner was required to state and accept the church's covenant. For almost two hundred years most churches based their covenant on Biblical scripture or Christian creed. Some Protestants moved away from strict Calvinism, as the Unitarians and the Universalists did, and their covenants evolved as well. Since the term "covenant" had always been associated with the gathering of a church, liberal churches were broadening the view of what "church" meant, thus the Scituate Bond of Union welcomed all who desired to cooperate in the advancement the Kingdom of God, no matter the "private judgment" or "individual conviction." This appears to be the first covenant in many years that the members ascribed to and was certainly of a different character than the covenant new members affirmed in 1831. At the same meeting that adopted the Bond of Union, Mr. Gilman was voted in as a member of the Parish, an indication that he planned a lengthy ministry.

> We, whose names are hereto subscribed associate ourselves together as a Christian Church for the purpose of moral and spiritual improvement and of promoting truth and righteousness in the world through the study, practice and diffusion of pure religion as taught and lived by Jesus of Nazareth: "Love to God and love to man."

> Recognizing the right of private judgment and the sacredness of individual conviction, we require no assent to any other doctrinal statement as a basis of Christian Fellowship but we welcome all who desire

to cooperate with us in advancing the Kingdom of God.

As the United States was becoming more industrialized and large corporations and monopolies were forming, a growing managerial class was developing more efficient methods of organizing tasks. Church administration was no exception. In the months following the adoption of the Bond of Union there was discussion about writing articles of organization or by-laws. When new by-laws were adopted on December 14, 1873 a group was commissioned to nominate people to the new committees. Three weeks later another parish meeting recommitted the by-laws to the committee that wrote them with instructions to submit a report at the next annual meeting. Apparently there was dissatisfaction with the new structure though there is no record as to the nature of the complaints. Still, a month later the Parish met again to vote. Included in the reconsidered by-laws was a new name and mission for the church: "The Church and Society of the First Parish in Scituate." The "object of this association shall be united thought and action in the study and practice of Christianity." Also incorporated into the bylaws was the Bond of Union passed the month earlier.

First Parish was hereafter to be organized and run by various committees. A Pastoral Committee was created to make sure the pulpit was filled; to welcome strangers and visitors; to aid the pastor in his ministry; and, to have general supervision of the religious and other interests of the Parish. There was a Committee on the Young, responsible for the Sunday School directed by a Superintendent. A Committee on Social Life provided for social entertainment to promote the social life of the church. A Committee on Music directed the music in the Sunday services and was to do "all in its power to increase the usefulness of this part of the worship." A Board of Assessors and the Parish Committee took charge of the business affairs for the Parish and its property. The expenses of the parish were to be met from the income from taxes on the pews and by annual subscriptions. The clerk and treasurer, a collector and soliciting committee, were to request subscriptions from members for the purposes of the Parish. Monies collected in the church and society were to be recorded on the books of the treasurer. The annual meeting was to be held in April or May, weather-wise a better choice than March. Membership was open to anyone at least fifteen years of age and those desiring to become a member had to communicate with the Pastoral Committee or to the clerk, who would submit their names at the next meeting of the church. The adoption of any motion at a meeting was by a majority vote and members could withdraw at any time by notifying the clerk in writing. The minister was ex-officio to the several committees. Significantly, the by-laws provided that women could serve as church officers and committee heads for the first time. One other significant by-law was Article 16: "The Lord's Supper shall be administered to all who desire to partake thereof at such times as the Church and Society shall determine." Communion might not have been celebrated every Sunday at First Parish, but when it was, it was open to all who walked through the door.

The national economy was affected by the Panic of 1873. Immediately after the Civil War the economy boomed but railroad speculation and other investments soon went bust, affected by political and economic events in Europe following the Franco-Prussian War. Scituate was, of course, affected and once again, the church's already precarious finances resulted in the resignation of its minister. In May of 1874, a committee was formed to meet with Rev. Gilman to discuss the "condition of the church, financially and otherwise." A week later at another parish meeting a communication from Mr. Gilman was read: "Being informed that the subscription for the support of the First Parish for the ensuing year is not sufficient to enable it to fulfill its pecuniary engagements, I hereby tender to you my resignation as Minster of the Parish to take effect…[September 1, 1874]."

Rev. Gilman's ministerial career was brief. He served only three churches but he had cordial relations in all. He probably was best suited for academia and writing books about economic and social reform. "His books have to do largely with social betterment, with the spirit of restlessness and misunderstanding between employer and employee, with American labor problems, and with the reaction of the American spirit upon Socialist and Utopian schemes of government. They are permeated with a warm sense of human brotherhood and with a confident belief in the efficacy of applied Christianity.[2] Those who knew him or read his books or heard his lectures regarded Rev. Gilman as a first-class intellect who often showed flashes of wit.[3]

Rev. Nicholas Paine Gilman

After resigning from Scituate, Gilman departed for the Unitarian church in Bolton, Massachusetts. From there he went to Antioch College for three years as a professor of ethics and English

---

[2] Frank C. Lockwood. "Professor Gilman's Literary Activities," *Meadville Theological School Quarterly Bulletin*, April 1912, 8.
[3] Lockwood, 9.

literature. He returned to parish ministry serving First Parish in Wayland, Massachusetts, but only for two years. Then he went on to be editor of the *Literary World*, a journal devoted to critical reviews of current literature; and, *The New World*, a quarterly review of religion, ethics and theology. He also wrote several books on socialism, profit sharing and employee rights. Some of the titles are *Socialism and the American Spirit* (1893), *Profit Sharing between Employer and the Employee (1899), and Methods of Industrial Peace* (1904). For the last seventeen years of his life (he died at sixty), he was a professor of Sociology and Ethics at Meadville Theological School in Meadville, Pennsylvania.

Rev. Gilman was particularly attentive to the social consequences of capitalism. He was among the liberal Protestant clergy of the day who applied what was called "practical Christianity" and Christian ethics to the growing social problems caused by industrialization and the concentration of wealth. He also advocated for "Christian Socialism." Such concerns among Protestant clergy led to the Social Gospel movement. Christian principals, adherent argued, should guide individuals and society at large in dealing with urban slums, sanitary conditions, racism, child labor, crime, education and the right of workers to form unions.

When he was a professor at Meadville Theological School, Gilman was given the honor, as was Scituate's Rev. Sewall before him, of addressing the Berry Street Conference in Boston organized by Rev. William Ellery Channing in 1820. It was a forum where liberal Christian ministers could meet and exchange practical ideas for strengthening their ministries. In his address titled, "Socialism" Gilman began by saying

> Socialism is an appropriate subject…to bring before an audience like this. It is a great scheme for social improvement. Where can one find a body of men more likely to be rationally interested in such a matter than the clergy of the Unitarian church? From the beginnings of our gospel in this country it has been a

gospel of man, a gospel for the actual world, based on reason, respecting human nature and all nature.[4]

Gilman authored many articles about the nature of Unitarianism. In one he wrote:

We [Unitarians] are the Protestants of the Protestants. We carry the doctrine of personal independence and private judgment to the limit.... [I]f we hold up the highest personal ideal, however imperfectly it may be illustrated by us, we may rest assured that the eternal forces of God's universe which work on the side of character will never desert us. Day after day, in the severe laboratory of life, the pure gold of personal substance will make itself known....

The righteousness of our Unitarian body has always...had a healthy color. We have believed that there is enough for us here to learn, to know, to turn into life, while we are here.

It is not a mere coincidence that Massachusetts, the State of education, philanthropy, and reform, is the focus of Unitarianism. Take our faith, its principles, its apostles, its insistence upon the practical righteousness of civilization, out of Massachusetts, and you have left, may I say? – Connecticut.[5]

Scituate in the mid-1870s was a quiet town, even with the railroad was close by. There were two hundred forty-one farms and the economy was based upon agriculture, fishing, shipping and mossing. There were three gristmills in town along with two sawmills

---

[4] Nicholas P. Gilman. "Socialism," *Meadville Theological School Quarterly* Bulletin, April, 1912.

[5] Nicholas P. Gilman. "The Personal Ideal of the Unitarian Faith," *The Unitarian Review and Religious Magazine*, February 1878.

and a small amount of shoe manufacturing. By then, Scituate had four churches, First Parish (Unitarian), First Trinitarian (Calvinist), First Baptist and the Methodist Church.[6] Not everyone was happy about the influence of First Parish and other Unitarian churches in the area. In 1877, a Mr. Sankey from Cohasset wrote to *The Methodist Recorder* that "this rocky coast [of Scituate and Cohasset] has been burned over by Unitarianism, and that it would be impossible to do any Orthodox thing here."[7]

On July 4, 1875, the Parish Committee was authorized, by the vote of the congregation, to confer with the Rev. Sheldon C. Clark to determine if he was interested in coming to Scituate as minister for one year for the salary of one thousand dollars. Two weeks later Rev. Clark agreed and was paid twenty dollars per Sunday and three dollars a week for board. The congregation seemed pleased with Rev. Clark as they asked him to stay for another year through the first Sunday of May 1877, but at a reduced salary. In his acceptance of the extension Rev. Clark acknowledged the "general depression of business and the present unhappy state of the finances in the parish" and agreed to the "diminished salary of $900." Clark continued, "...in the hope of restoring this old parish to something of its former prosperity, and of making this church the religious home of the large number of liberal persons living within the bounds of the parish who at present attend no public worship, I accept the charge to which this church invites and entrusts me...."

During this period the church moderator was Captain John Manson, a well-respected merchant seaman and ship owner. He was born in Scituate, married Abigail Turner Ford and had five children, one named Edmund Sewall Manson, in honor of First Parish's minister. He sailed to the West Indies and Brazil for coffee but most often to the Mediterranean. He retired from merchant shipping in 1861 because of the Civil War. Mr. Manson presided over parish meetings that were continually dominated by financial issues.

---

[6] Elias Nason. *A Gazetteer for the State of Massachusetts*, (1874), 453.
[7] *The Independent*, July 19, 1877.

259

Committees were constantly repopulated with different people who were charged with encouraging members to pay their subscriptions to the church. Others were elected as assessors to determine the value of the church pews and charge rental fees for the use of a particular pew. The congregation was straining under the by-laws that were passed in February 1874 due to the committee structure that the by-laws created which proved too burdensome for the small congregation. So, at the April 22, 1876 meeting, it was voted to repeal the by-laws with the exception of Article 3, the Bond of Union. No alternative was proposed. The Ladies Sewing Circle proposed to have the names of former ministers painted on the wall panels at the front of the church, but the parish as a whole voted against it because of the cost. The meeting also voted not to renew the insurance on the church building because of the cost, a decision that would have distressing consequences a few years later.

Rev. Clark's ministry in Scituate was unremarkable, yet he was anything but. Born in 1846 in Smithfield, Pennsylvania, near Morgantown, West Virginia (then, Virginia), he enlisted as a private in the Minnesota Infantry when he was eighteen. Why Minnesota is not known, although it is possible that his family had moved there from Pennsylvania. He was discharged from the army following the end of the Civil War and in 1873 Clark graduated from the Meadville Theological School. In May, 1877 at the end of Mr. Clark's contract as minister, it was noted in the minutes of the May 6th meeting that the "Parish Clerk be instructed to insert a resolution in the *Christian Register*, the Unitarian newspaper, expressive of the good will of the Parish to Rev. S. C. Clark."

Rev. Clark is one of the most intriguing yet enigmatic ministers to have served First Parish. Clark's wife, Martha Strickland Clark, is of greater renown than her husband. She had a notable life years before she married Rev. Clark. The daughter of a progressive thinking lawyer and a one-term Michigan Congressman, Strickland also became a lawyer and was the first woman lawyer to argue before the Michigan Supreme Court. Martha began her legal career after graduating from the University of Michigan Law School as an assistant county prosecutor. It was highly unusual for a woman to practice criminal law then, but her mentor and friend, John Fedewa was eager to give her the responsibility.[8] She later became a well-known writer and lecturer on woman's rights. In addition to her statewide fame as one of Michigan's few female attorneys, Martha Strickland achieved national celebrity of a scandalous nature in Victorian America.

Leo Miller, born in Massachusetts, was a "charismatic" and "provocative" believer in radical causes. A lawyer, Miller was an advocate for opposite ends of controversial issues at various times in his life. Once he was outspoken against the Spiritualist movement then gaining popularity. The distinctive feature of Spiritualism was the belief that spirits of the dead could be contacted, either by individuals or "mediums," who provided information about the afterlife. One evening, however, after giving a "forceful attack" on spiritualism he fell into a trance and then became an ardent supporter of Spiritualism.[9] Another turnabout involved Martha Strickland. By the 1870s Miller was an outspoken and well-known advocate of "free love" and, as a fellow lecturer on the subject, it is likely that Miller and Strickland met each other on the circuit. On November 2, 1875 they entered into a contractual arrangement for a "civil and conjugal union" outside a legally sanctioned marriage. Soon they moved to a conservative area of Minnesota for the express purpose of challenging the state's anti-cohabitation laws.

In June 1876, following a disturbance at a lecture in Waterford, Minnesota, Miller were indicted on the charge of "lewdly and lasciviously cohabitating and associating together" and distributing obscene literature. A newspaper account reported that as

---

[8] Carolyn Jacobs. "Friends & Allies Paper: Martha Strickland Clark: Reformers and Liberal Thinkers: The Men in Strickland's Life," 2006 (unpublished), 4, http://womenslegalhistory.stanford.edu/papers05/StricklandM-Jacobs05.pdf
[9] Jacobs, 12.

Miller spoke at the lecture, "his hearers…rotten-egged him from their midst." The newspaper stated that Miller and Strickland entered into a "co-partnership…to carry on the business of man and wife without any of the restraints which the marriage law imposes…." Miller openly admitted to cohabiting with Strickland without being married and stipulated "that said cohabitation and association between said parties is a conscientious belief of each of them, and they claim the right thus to associate and cohabit under the Constitution of the United States and the State of Minnesota, which guarantees liberty of conscience to every citizen." The trial and appeal to the Minnesota Supreme Court made news across the country. Miller was found guilty but Strickland was not brought to trial because of her health. She was pregnant. In September 1876 she gave birth to a boy who was given the name, Elwin Miller-Strickland.[10]

By 1879, the Strickland-Miller relationship was strained, primarily due to Miller's drinking (years earlier he had spoken on behalf of the temperance movement.)[11] Strickland left for Boston for reasons unclear and Miller either went with her or joined her later. It is possible that it was during this time that Strickland first met Rev. Clark. In April 1885, Strickland and Miller dissolved their "civil and conjugal union" and Miller did it in a very public way. Miller, who once described marriage as "slavery" and "legalized prostitution," now declared marriage "a divine institution" and placed public notices in various newspapers, among them, *The New York Sun* and *The New York Times*.[12]

> Believing that personal experiences involving the welfare of society are rightfully the property of the whole species, the undersigned feels it incumbent upon

---

[10] Jacobs, Carolyn, "Biographical Essay 2: Martha Strickland Clark" 2006, p. 2 (http://womenslegalhistory.stanford.edu/papers05/StricklandM-Jacobs05.pdf); *The New York Times*, July 5, 1876

[11] Jacobs, Biographical essay, 2.

[12] Jacobs, Friends, 14.

himself to make known the conclusion of a social event which has caused no little public interest and comment. Nine and a half years ago Martha (Mattie) Strickland of St. John's, Mich., and myself formed a civil and conjugal union without the customary sanction of law and published to the world our declaration and contract. This step was taken with the conscientious conviction that the proceeding was, under the circumstances, right and justifiable, and through all those years we have continued to live together in endearing relations, virtual husband and wife, notwithstanding repeated assertions of the press that we had separated. Years of reflection and experience have brought with them the conviction that the step we took was ill-advised and wrong; that it would have been wiser, nobler, to have sacrificed our own personal happiness and what we deemed to be our natural rights than to have made this revolutionary assault upon the marriage institution. These facts and considerations have become more and more deeply impressed upon the mind, compelling at least a frank confession that the marital alliance contracted between Miss Strickland and myself, in disregard of custom and law, was a grave mistake through which we have unwittingly done society an injury. Honor and duty alike require that the only reparation now possible in the case should be made, viz., public renunciation of the self-instituted marriage. It is done. The union, civil and conjugal, formed by myself and Martha Strickland on the 2d day of November 1875. Is by mutual consent dissolved.

[signed]

LEO MILLER.[13]

---

[13] *The New York Times*, April 24, 1885

263

Sheldon Clark may have been a quieter companion to Martha Strickland, if not a more stable one. When they first met in 1875 or 1876, most likely while Clark was minister in Scituate, he fell immediately in love with Strickland but she had just fallen in with Miller. With regret, she later wrote to a friend, "I now think I should have loved him as naturally as a flower turns to the sun had my heart and mind not been filled with Leo."[14] Still, the friendship remained over many years with Clark's love of Strickland undiminished. During Strickland's Boston stay, while Miller continued his heavy drinking, she considered Clark her "devoted tender and respectful friend."[15]

When, in the early 1890s, Clark went to Detroit he was back into Strickland's life. By this time it appears that he had left the ministry some years before. Strickland told a friend that he had "become too radical for the ministry" and that he favored "state-socialism." Seeing Clark again made Strickland realize that she loved him and that he had never stopped loving her. Their financial situation may have delayed their marriage, which took place on January 1, 1897 in Cripple Creek, Colorado, where the last big gold rush was taking place.[16]

Clark by then was involved in "very large mining interests" that took him from Colorado to Texas to Sonora, Mexico. He was listed as president of the Ben Travato Gold Mining Company of Denver.[17] By 1900 the couple were living in El Paso, Texas, where, according to census records, Clark gave his occupation, not as a miner, but as a "newspaper solicitor." A year or two later, the Clarks were living in Los Angeles where Strickland taught and lectured on parliamentary law. It is not known how Clark was employed, if at all. [18] It was during their days in Los Angeles that the relationship

---

[14] Jacobs, Friends, 15.
[15] Jacobs, Friends, 16.
[16] Jacobs, Friends, 16.
[17] *Cripple Creek: A Standard Handbook of the Mines and Mining Companies,* (1901), 14.
[18] Jacobs, Friends, 18.

between the two becomes mystifying. Clark seems to have remained in the Los Angeles area as Strickland traveled around the country giving lectures. She moved to Chicago where she became friends with the noted trial attorney, Clarence Darrow, and for a time, boarded at the Darrow house.[19] There are no known records of a divorce and by 1933, Strickland was back in Michigan living with a niece. She died in June 1935 at the age of 82.[20]

Sheldon Clark, for his part, did keep dabbling in mining. In 1918, still living in Los Angeles, he applied for a passport for a trip to Baja California, Mexico noting that he was a mining engineer and he was travelling there for business. By 1920, at the age of seventy-four, Clark was a resident of the National Military Home in Malibu, California. Census records indicate that he was married at the time. The records from the United States Homes for Disabled Veterans show that he suffered from "chronic bronchitis and neurasthenia" (depression). The records also show that when he first was a resident of the home from 1907 to 1910, his next of kin was listed as his wife, Martha Strickland Clark of Rockford, Illinois. However, at the time of his death on June 20, 1928 his remains were given to Anna R. Clark of Brentwood, California, identified as his wife.

There was another odd incident involving Rev. Clark that adds more color to his character. Clark was a member of the Masons, first joining a lodge in Iowa. When he came to Scituate, Clark expressed a strong desire to advance up the Masonic order. He served as the Scituate lodge chaplain. By January 1, 1878 he was behind in his dues of five dollars to the Satuit Lodge. He was then charged with "unmasonic conduct" for the "intent to defraud" the Lodge by "falsely" pretending that he could not give his support to the "Institution of Freemasonry, because said Institution is narrow in its brotherhood, antiquated in its religious principles, and barren of moral results in the world...." The "fraud" charged was that Rev. Clark "falsely and fraudulently pretended to renounce the principles

---

[19] Jacobs, Friends, 10.
[20] Jacobs, Biographical essay, 5.

of Masonry, [so as] to evade the performance of one of its most simple duties, the payment of Lodge dues." From the beginning, according to a report presented to the Masonic Commissioners of Trials, Clark conversed "frankly and openly" with lodge officers and members about Masonry and its principles. Never, the report states, was he heard to speak negatively about Masonry, except when he responded to the lodge's dunning letters. The findings led the Trial Commissioners to suspend Rev. Clark "indefinitely from the rights and privileges of Masonry."[21]

Since Rev. Clark was "hired" with two one-year contracts, the church records show no communication regarding a resignation. It was simply a matter of not renewing Rev. Clark's relationship with the church. Perhaps he had worn out his welcome among the Masons in the congregation, although First Parish expressed its goodwill toward Rev. Clark upon his departure. No doubt the insufficiency of the salary was an issue.

Now, in the late 1870s, with the absence of a minister, First Parish frequently relied upon the Rev. Allan Gay Jennings, the pastor of the South Parish (now Second Parish) in Hingham, to preach and solicit subscriptions from parishioners. As always, money was a problem. Again, the insurance payment for the building was put off as options were considered to find a minister at an affordable salary. At the Meeting of May 4, 1879 a vote was taken to confer with the church in neighboring East Marshfield about the prospect of sharing a preacher. For most of 1879 and into 1880 members of the congregation led services. Episcopalian priest G. Munroe Royce preached during this period. Other ministers were invited and were paid ten dollars a Sunday, half of what Rev. Clark was paid five years earlier and so, First Parish was without a called minister until 1882.

---

[21] *Proceedings of the Grand Lodge of the Most Ancient and Honorable Fraternity of Free and Accepted Masons of the Commonwealth of Massachusetts* (1878), 39-44.

Chapter Twelve

"To our memory sound, dear old Bell"

First Parish faced its greatest catastrophe in the summer of 1879. A simple, direct sentence in the church records, dated July 4, 1879, states, "The Old Church was burned to the ground today." In 1958, Edith Dunbar Webb Bonney recalled the fire seventy-nine years earlier.

This I remember. Father, Mother and I were on the piazza of our cottage on Hyland Street (now Greenfield Lane) when we saw smoke on the horizon. "Let's go!" No, a long way off, as far as the Centre! More smoke, right in the range of the Church. Then flames. It was the Church, our beautiful Church at the Centre! The Church of Christ. Why should that burn! We watched the flames die away. All of us very much awed and saddened.

Henry came home later. He was one of the group of boys who discovered the fire as they were returning from a celebration at No. Scituate.

As the fire started near the door little could be saved. The pulpit, sofa, and [a] big table were taken through the windows. Also some of the pew cushions.

I remember very vaguely of going to morning services there but I was only eight or nine....[1]

A newspaper account of the fire noted that the "Old Sloop Church" was located on a high hill commanding an excellent view of the surrounding area. There was little hope of saving the church since there was no fire truck within several miles. It was impossible to save the organ, "the finest in Scituate," the newspaper reported. The tower, which contained the bell, stood until one wall of the church had fallen, and the interior of the tower was burned before the weight of the steeple proved too much for the charred beams, and brought the rest of the building to the ground.[2]

Following the fire, a poem was published in *The Boston Transcript*. The author is identified only as "E.A.O."

The Knell of the Old Church

Tolling its knell, swung the old church bell,
As the steeple swayed in the smoky air,
And the merciless fire crept higher and higher,
With stealthy tread on a viewless stair!
Tolling! tolling! tolling!
Moaning its last hour away,
While from many an eye is rolling
The tear no hand would stay;
For we loved it well, time-hallowed bell,
Silver-toned herald of holy day.

---

[1] First Parish files
[2] First Parish files

What says its tongue, as 'tis airily swung,
Inspiring awe in the gaping crowd?
"Behold the wraith of the fathers' faith
Vanishing here in a fiery cloud!"
Tolling! tolling! tolling!
Moaning its last hour away,
While from many an eye is rolling
The tear no heart would stay;
And we, agonized, stare on the rafters bare
Of the grand old house 'neath the fire-fiend's sway.

"Oh! for our town, with this landmark down!"
And we join the old bell in its moan -
"O'er the country far, a guiding star
To the home of the Pilgrims it shone"; -
And we sigh at the tolling,
And breathlessly gaze,
While around it is rolling
The horrible blaze,
And picture with sorrow the dreadful to-morrow-
The old meetinghouse not in its place!

Oh! for the rover, the treacherous deep over,
Returning to port with light heart;
No more with gay whoop may he hail "the old sloop,"
Ere aught else from the mist stands apart.
Now, feebly, 'tis tolling,
And sadly we toss
Where broad ocean is rolling
A thought to the loss
From the mariner's night of the soul-cheering
sight,
It has been the wide sea far across.

It bound us so fast to the dim distant past,
Naught so loth from our village we'd spare,
From the mist of the ages it shone o'er the pages

Our land's history aye must hold fair.
Now list the last stroke
Of the low-moaning bell,
As these fond ties are broke
By the enemy, fell! -
O, long with but pain will that dying refrain
To our memory sound, dear old Bell.

On July 16th the members of First Parish met at the Scituate
Town Hall, across the street from the destroyed church, and voted to
hold services at the Town Hall temporarily. Now, concern about the
church's fragile finances was even more urgent. The destroyed
building was uninsured and the church's cash savings were nearly
depleted because of poor fiscal management. This left the
congregation scrambling to raise money for a new building. There
was a strong desire to rebuild a church on the spot where the old
church stood with the same external appearance as the old one.
There was an equally strong desire to raise money. Members were
"willing to make sacrifices" to "continue their organization, and
rebuild their church." By the end of 1879 the church's subscription
committee reported that a total of $3,337 had been raised for the new
building from members, friends and other Unitarian churches in the
area. When the fundraising and construction were done the church
was in debt only three hundred dollars.[3]

*Piece of the bell and the key to the Old Sloop Church
destroyed in the July 4, 1879 fire*

---

[3] *South Scituate Herald*, May 20, 1881

In September, two months after the fire, church members were shown a plan for a new building similar in design to the Old Sloop Church. Thomas Silloway of Boston, a former Universalist minister and the designer of the Vermont State House in Montpelier, did the architectural drawings. The congregation approved the cost of $6,000 and construction was to start as soon as $5,000 was raised. Rev. Jennings assisted the First Parish soliciting committee and was paid extra for his work. By December the building funds had grown to $4,247. To lower costs some thought was given to building the church without pews which would also allow construction to begin sooner. Eager to begin building, the congregation voted to overturn the earlier vote to wait until the $5,000 was raised, but in January 1880 the Silloway plan was cancelled and a new one was adopted, which is the present building. Six hundred pounds of metal from the old bell were transformed into one hundred small bells which were sold to raise building funds. The rest of the metal was taken by Charles Jenkins, Esq. of Boston, who in turn, presented the church with a new bell weighing one thousand pounds. William Blake & Co. of Boston cast the bell. Edwin Young, a church member, was the painter.

The cornerstone of the new church was laid on May 10, 1880 with ceremonies featuring music by the North Scituate Brass Band; a prayer by the Rev. H.B. Hibben of the Scituate Methodist Church; and an address by Rev. Jennings. Church president, Andrew J. Waterman, laid the cornerstone. A reception was held at Jenkins Hall. Stone for the foundation, "the best Rockport granite," was a gift from Everett Torrey, Esq.[4] It was used alongside the original stone foundation of the Old Sloop Church. Mr. Torrey, a Scituate native and son-in-law of Captain Seth Webb, owned a wholesale marble and granite business. That summer a train stopped at the old Egypt Station with three flat bed cars delivering timbers, freshly cut from Maine, for the new church. While the building was being erected services continued at the Town Hall. The congregation agreed to

---

[4] *South Scituate Herald*, May 20, 1881

raise funds to pay for preacher; and once again, Rev. Jennings was hired to preach during July and August 1880.

A year after the cornerstone was laid, on May 18, 1881, the dedication celebration of the new church (the present building) was reported in *The South Shore Herald*. The day was "stormy and gloomy" but within the new church building all was "cheerful and pleasant." Every window was filled with beautiful flowers. The newspaper account described the church as measuring forty-one by seventy feet on the outside. The steeple on the southeast corner stood ninety feet high (five feet less than the old steeple) with a weathervane and compass points on the top. There were two double door entrances on the south and west sides. The interior of the church had an "auditorium" forty by fifty feet; a vestibule, sixteen by ten feet; two halls on the west end, the "upper" one was eighteen by thirty-six feet and the "lower" one measured eighteen by twenty feet. The lower hall was planned for a library. The upper room was to be used for a collation room with a capacity for three hundred. The cushioned pews were made of brown ash, "making them very comfortable." The pulpit was two feet above the floor with an "elegant black walnut desk, the gift of Scituate native and merchant ship owner, Thomas L. Manson of East Boston. The walls were plain with only sconces on them but there were plans to have frescoes painted on them. A central chandelier also was to be installed later. The carpeting was "the Lowell super," a bronze geranium pattern. The church's building committee made up of Henry Merritt, George C. Lee, Job Otis and George O. Allen supervised the work of the construction.

The dedication celebration featured several former ministers as well as town officials. A letter from Massachusetts Governor John D. Long was read. The Rev. William H. Fish of South Scituate, who preached at the First Parish Church for several months in 1868, read from the Bible. Rev. Edmund Quincy Sewall Osgood of Plymouth, grandson of the beloved Rev. Sewall offered the prayer. Rev. Babcock returned and spoke to his former parishioners as reported by the *South Shore Herald*:

He [Rev. Babcock] felt that we were dedicating ourselves on this occasion to the service of Almighty God as well as a temple. "This church," he said, "is a resurrection. It is not like the old church; but I suppose our bodies in the resurrection will not be like the present one." He alluded to his pastorate of five years and although he had been away sixteen years, he had not forgotten how he was welcomed during his stay in Scituate by every family.

Rev. William P. Tilden of Boston preached the sermon. In it, Tilden asked and answered the question, "What does Unitarianism stand for?" First, he noted that Unitarianism "never stands for a fixed dogmatic statement, but for a *movement* to a purer and higher life." He noted how the Unitarianism of his day was different from William Ellery Channing's, though "we stand for God, Christ, and the Bible; for the Kingdom of God, and immoral life, doctrines held in common with all Christian believers. We stand for character by religions. But before ordinances, creeds and rituals, we put life and character.... We stand for *liberty* in religion; we are not afraid of free thought.... We stand for progress in religion.... We stand for progress, not by discarding the past, but for growth out of it.... We stand for confidence in human nature." The newspaper reported that Rev. Tilden was "impressive and eloquent" in his fifty minute sermon.

Rev. Courtland Y. De Normandie of Kingston also spoke and he called upon the congregation "to dedicate yourselves anew to the service, and to come to this house from Sabbath to Sabbath with such humble and teachable hearts that you will be better fitted to bear all the ills and sorrows that may come to you and your homes." Andrew J. Waterman, chair of the Parish Committee, followed the sermon with some remarks and introduced Rev. Joseph Osgood of Cohasset (Ellen Sewall's husband). Henry Merritt of the Building Committee then handed over the keys of the church to Mr. Waterman and with one final hymn the dedication service concluded.

Following the service a collation was held with so many people in attendance that there were two sittings. "The edibles seemed to increase rather than diminish, in quality and quantity."[5]

By the fall of 1881 the congregation was settling into its new building and finally, after many months of sporadic discussions, it agreed to "unite" with the East Marshfield church as soon as they could agree on a minister. In November both congregations hired the Rev. Edward Bartlett Maglathlin to preach for six months. Rev. Maglathlin was also in charge of a school in Duxbury, Massachusetts but it soon became clear that the three posts were too much for him and so, on Christmas Day, 1881, his letter of resignation was read to the congregation. Two weeks later, the Scituate Parish Committee asked the Rev. Nathanael Seaver, Jr. of Melrose, Massachusetts to preach in both Scituate and East Marshfield for one thousand four hundred dollars with Scituate contributing eight hundred dollars. By February Rev. Seaver was preaching in both parishes.

Rev. Seaver was born in Boston, April 21, 1836. Before coming to Scituate, he served several months with the United States Sanitary Commission at Winchester, Virginia. The United States Sanitary Commission was a private agency, created with the blessing of the Secretary of War, William Seward and the approval of President Lincoln in June 1861. Its purpose was to coordinate the volunteer efforts of women who wanted to contribute to the Union cause. They went to Union Army camps to observe the sanitary conditions (or lack of). Its only president was the Rev. Henry Whitney Bellows, a Unitarian minister who served a church in New York City. Other prominent Unitarians that were active in the Commission included Samuel Gridley Howe, who was a director of the Commission and was the husband of Julia Ward Howe, the author of "The Battle Hymn of the Republic;" the landscape architect, Frederick Law Olmstead; and Louisa May Alcott. Seaver retired from ministry in 1904 and returned to live in Scituate until two years before his death in 1919.

---

[5] *South Shore Herald*, May 20, 1881

Rev. Nathanael Seaver, Jr.

In 1882 the location of the First Parish church caused another controversy. The conflict arose this time among the women of the Ladies Sewing Circle. The meetings were often held at the new church but many of the members thought the location was not convenient for most who lived in the harbor area and the meetings seemed to be more sociable when gathered in a member's home parlor. When a vote decided that the meetings were to be held at the church, rather than in homes, the newly elected president of the Ladies Sewing Circle immediately resigned in protest.[6]

The year-old church building hosted a significant "first" in Scituate. Mr. S. A. Snow, principal of Scituate High School, wanted to

---

[6] Margaret Bonney papers

do something never done before in town, a high school graduation ceremony. At the time the high school was located in the town hall, across the street from the church, and there wasn't a room large enough to accommodate students, teachers, parents and dignitaries. Mr. Snow made a request to the Parish Committee to hold the graduation in May 1882 at First Parish. The church leaders responded with pleasure, permitting its use for several years. Later, in October, the Ladies Sewing Circle held one of its fairs at the church and raised $100 and with that money the first electric lights were installed. At the same time, kerosene lamps (a chandelier and twelve wall lamps which were later electrified in 1917) were installed in the sanctuary. More kerosene lamps were placed in other rooms of the church.

The Ladies Sewing Circle voted to change their name to The Ladies Aid Society in June 1883. The preamble to the society's newly adopted constitution read: "We, the undersigned, hereby unite for the promotion of the religious, social and philanthropic activities of the Parish." Due to the continuing financial pressures on the church, the Ladies Aid Society's primary focus was to raise funds so the church could carry on its "religious, social and philanthropic" presence in the community. The society organized parties, dances and entertainments that were enjoyed by all church members and friends. "Sociability for profit" became their slogan.[7] For many years the ladies' enjoyment preparing for and participating in these events was tempered by the fact that the church had no running water. Whether water was needed for cooking, refreshment or cleaning, the ladies found that they had to rely on a male volunteer to carry water to the church from elsewhere. Finding this burdensome, the Ladies Aid Society began holding their meetings and entertainments at the Satuit Library (later named the Allen Library) at the end of the nineteenth century. For a fee of three dollars the ladies had the use of the library hall for a year plus all the apples they could harvest from the trees on the library's front lawn.[8]

---

[7] Margaret Bonney papers.
[8] Margaret Bonney papers.

First Parish was challenged by a difficult post-Civil War era that lasted until the end of the century. Ministers came and went with alarming regularity and church finances got worse. When the church agreed to build a new shed for thirty-four dollars it also agreed to put up for auction the excess wood and the wood from the razed shed. Money from subscriptions for preaching and building costs was hard to come by. When the church granted Rev. Seaver four weeks vacation in April 1884, it was done with the understanding that in his absence the pulpit would be filled voluntarily (that is, without a fee). Income raised by pew rentals decreased from $618.25 in 1882 to $488.00 in 1884 while the number of pews rented was thirty-two out of the forty-four pews. In 1885 the number of pews rented declined to twenty-eight, bringing in just $430. The Parish Fund (endowment) was $9,697.24 as of April 1886. In 1884 a call went out for contributions to buy a pipe organ to replace the one that had been lost in the fire. The Universalist Church in Wakefield, Massachusetts offered an organ for sale, similar to the one destroyed in the fire, and it was purchased for $250.

Mr. Seaver had been ministering at First Parish with a year-to-year contract and he wanted a longer-term commitment, but the church could not agree. In 1886 he resigned. Parish records note that Seaver's "brief pastorate was harmonious and that he retired with the most affectionate regard for his people…. His duty to his growing family, however, demanded that he should make better provisions for the educational and financial interests than seemed possible in Scituate." Seaver's resignation gave a more direct explanation. He told the congregation he was "disappointed because the question of settlement is annually reopened and discussed. It is also unjust to a pastor because he is conscious at all times that his engagement is precarious and can be terminated by a majority vote at the annual meeting without further ceremony or previous notice." Nevertheless, Rev. Seaver enjoyed living in Scituate because after retiring from the ministry he returned to live in the town and was active in the First Parish congregation for many years.

In November 1886, the Parish voted to explore with the congregation in South Scituate (soon to be re-incorporated as the Town of Norwell in 1888) about a minister to serve both churches. In the meantime, pending the outcome of those discussions First Parish closed. It reopened in April 1887 with Rev. John Tunis of South Scituate preaching. Eager to have a preacher again, albeit in conjunction with the South Scituate parish, the congregation thought it might raise more money for preaching by abandoning the decades old policy of renting pews and starting a "free pew" system. There was to be no auction, no rental; instead a collection was taken every Sunday. A notice announcing the free pew policy and the collection was published in the local newspaper in an effort to increase attendance (and income.) Church leaders asked Rev. Mr. Tunis to come regularly to First Parish for ten dollars per Sunday and preach in the afternoon after his preaching in South Scituate but he declined. Once again a new search for a minister began and there were no services held until late November.

Chapter Thirteen

Laboring in the Vineyard

First Parish had something to celebrate on January 1, 1888. After the morning Sunday service, the Rev. Henry A. Whitman was hired to fill the pulpit for one year. His salary was $800. In December 1888, Mr. Whitman's contract was extended for another five months at fifteen dollars a Sunday ($780 a year.) In an effort to keep Rev. Whitman the Parish Committee sought to join with the neighboring Second Society of Marshfield Hills in employing him.

Rev. H. A. Whitman

When that didn't happen, the congregation again offered Rev. Whitman fifteen dollars per Sunday salary but he refused to accept the offer and countered with a proposal for an annual salary of $1,000. The Parish agreed to his request, yet Rev. Whitman was gone by the end of 1889. Once again the church closed for the cold, harsh winter months. When the Parish Committee held a meeting in April 1890 it sought once more to join with the Marshfield Hills church in hiring a minister, but by June the congregation decided to share a minister with First Parish in Norwell instead.

The minister called by both the Scituate and Norwell congregations on June 15, 1890 was the Rev. William Henry Spencer. He preached in Scituate for six months of the year in the morning and in the afternoon he preached in Norwell. After six months the schedule was to be reversed. Rev. Spencer was described as a man "of energetic type and modern thought"[1] He was a frequent contributor to *The Index*, a radical religious paper published in Boston. The paper proclaimed as its purpose "to present the best thoughts of the day on all subjects relating to human welfare. It is the foe of superstition and the advocate of the religion of Reason and Humanity." His frequent essays supporting agnosticism got him into trouble with several congregations though he did get a number of letters from readers who approved of his ideas.

Spencer wrote a history of his family and in it he states that his father was one of the pioneers of Wisconsin. Henry Gould Spencer began as a farmer and soon became a prominent landholder and businessman. The family was comfortable financially but experienced periodic setbacks. William, or "Willie," as he was called in his family, was born in Johnstown, Wisconsin in 1840. He served as a private in a Wisconsin regiment during the Civil War. Following the war, he attended Harvard Divinity School and graduated in 1869.

In his family's memoir, Spencer reflected on his childhood and the changes that came to Johnstown after he left. The train, he

---

[1] http://www.firstparishnorwell.org/history.htm

wrote, now stopped exactly where he had driven the cattle to pasture. "The city had come, I suppose, but, oh! how would I like to have again the old things as they were; to hear in the morning the cheery notes of the martins and in the evening to watch the night hawks as they wheeled in their flight and the fireflies flashing their little lights; and hear that dear mother's voice once more calling, 'Willie, Willie, come, it is time to come in!'" Spencer described his parents as religious liberals. They were Spiritualists who believed, he said, in communion with departed spirits, in a very literal sense, and found joy and comfort in the faith. His father contributed to the "maintenance of Unitarian services" in the town; and, was a solid Republican, though he occasionally bolted the ticket in a "spirit of wholesome independence."[2]

Rev. William Henry Spencer

Like Rev. Sheldon Clark, Rev. Spencer's wife, Anna Garlin, was better known. They married on August 15, 1878. Anna was a

---

[2] William Henry Spencer. Spencer Family Record in the Anna Garlin Spencer Papers, Swarthmore College Peace Collection.

journalist for the *Providence (Rhode Island) Journal.* She left journalism to accompany her husband as he served several churches in Massachusetts. She became close friends with the Rev. Jenkin Lloyd Jones, the Unitarian missionary to the Mid-West, and at a time when Rev. Spencer was having difficulty finding a church to serve, his wife and Jones corresponded about their mutual concern. In a letter to Jones, Anna wrote

> You say in your note that you are sorry my husband's voice is lost from the pulpit. So am I. I shall never be reconciled to his working in any but lines of ideal effort. For all the deeper currents of his nature set that way. But the difficulty of satisfactory placement is with him unusually great, and he was haunted with the dread of growing old without a permanent abiding place. Had it not been for my home entanglements we might have gone to the Pacific Coast, where I think there would be a much more congenial field for him than in the east. But as it is, he is quite determined not to take a parish again, although I think he will most gladly do service in the liberal pulpit from Sunday to Sunday if the way opens. Will you bear that in mind, and if there is any place sufficiently near Waupaca [Wisconsin] for my husband to be able to reach it conveniently, which is hungering for the gospel of good hope, call upon him to give occasional ministrations? His duties in his office are too severe to give him time to look up such opportunities, and he is never one to push his way.... But he never preached so well as in the last three years, and for his sake as well as for the cause of liberal religion, I want his gifts utilized if possible, even if he never does regular ministerial service again.[3]

---

[3] Anna Garlin Spencer Papers, Swarthmore College Peace Collection.

Rev. Spencer and his wife just about gave up on his ministry when the Scituate and Norwell churches employed him in 1880. As Anna was developing her own liberal view of religion, James Eddy, a wealthy art collector who wrote about religion and philosophy and who had built a chapel for "religious and moral purposes," died in 1888. He bequeathed the Bell Street Chapel in Providence to his executors who asked Anna, because of her reputation as an advocate for social reform, to establish the Religious Society of Bell Street Chapel where she became the first woman ordained into the ministry in Rhode Island.[4] Working at the Society kept her in Providence for extended stays but she once preached in Scituate, most likely the first woman to do so.

Less than a year after arriving in Scituate, Rev. Spencer was gone. His departure was due, in some measure, to the increased loss of hearing in his left ear.[5] Spencer left Scituate and Norwell to join his wife in Providence. Soon thereafter, he retired from the ministry. He helped run the Health Institute in Providence and established the Old Colony Co-operative Bank. In 1907, he and his wife moved to New York City where he was Chief of the Parole Department of the Prison Association of New York, an organization founded to "give humane attention to prisoners" and to provide services after their release.[6] He eventually became deaf and was an invalid for most of his later years. Anna became well known in woman's suffrage and peace-making circles. She was a prominent speaker at the World Parliament of Religions in Chicago in 1893. In New York she was the associate leader with Dr. Felix Adler, the founder and leader of the Society for Ethical Culture. The Ethical Culture movement was built on the idea that living by ethical principles was central to living a meaningful life and creating a world of peace and goodwill. Though ordained a Unitarian minister, Anna, like her husband Henry, saw

---

[4] Dorothy May Emerson, ed. *Standing Before Us: Unitarian Universalist Women and Social Reform, 1776-1936* (2000), 114.

[5] William Henry Spencer Journal, July 16, 1890 in Anna Garlin Spencer Papers

[6] *The New York Times*, June 3, 1870

religion in terms unlimited by denominational creeds or structure, and Ethical Culture was compatible with the growing humanist movement in Unitarianism[7]

For the eighth time since the end of the Civil War thirty-five years earlier, First Parish was once again in search of a minister. An offer was made to the Rev. Thomas Thompson. At first he begged off giving an answer, and when he did, he told the Scituate Parish Committee that he chose to become the minister in Norwell. As a result First Parish, yet again, voted in November 1891 to close the church until April 1892. Even without services the church needed attention; among many things, it needed painting. A contractor was hired and the Ladies Aid Society, not the congregation, paid for the work. In September 1892 the parish voted to offer a Rev. Porter $800 to preach at First Parish in connection with the Second Society in Marshfield Hills, but Porter declined.

Rev. Watson Weed of Ware, Massachusetts, who had preached in Scituate before, agreed to preach one year beginning in December 1892 for an $800 salary. Rev. Weed was installed as minister to both First Parish in Scituate and the Second Society of Marshfield Hills on February 1, 1893. He was a graduate of the Cazenovia (New York) Seminary and was credentialed as both a Unitarian and Universalist minister. An obituary described him as a "man of keen ethical feeling and strong moral judgments. He was fearless in utterance and uncompromising in practice. He was an earnest student of social and religious deeds, and always identified himself in an intimate way with the high life of the community in which he lived. With a spiritual nature alive to every inspiration, he converted these into moral commandments for himself and others."[8]

During his ministry at First Parish Rev. Weed composed a new Bond of Union replacing the one adopted in 1873. It reflected the continuing evolution of Unitarianism.

---

[7] Garlin Spencer papers.
[8] Minister's file at Andover-Harvard Library, Harvard Divinity School

We, whose names are here appended, feeling that in union there is strength and that social service is a help to individual righteousness, agree to unite in the spirit of Jesus Christ for the worship of God and the service of Man. [9]

Rev. Watson Weed

Under Weed's leadership the church became even more a place of culture and service in the town. The Unity Club of men and women was formed with Rev. Weed as the president. Numbering about thirty at its formation, the club was created for educational purposes. The magazine, *The Unitarian*, noted that the club, also known as the Browning Club, after the English poet, Robert Browning, studied his poetry along with the works of Henry Wadsworth Longfellow and William Shakespeare.[10] The club dissolved a few years later but was later reborn on October 6, 1935 when seven women including Kay Withington, wife of Rev. Robert Withington, met to re-establish the club as a woman's group. Its stated purpose was to "spin off" from the Alliance in order to

---

[9] First Parish files

[10] *The Unitarian: A Monthly Magazine of Liberal Christianity*, Vol. IX (1894), 133.

provide a means for working women and mothers of young children to meet in the evening.

The Ladies Aid Society, a group of about eight women, met at members' homes to sew aprons and quilts to be sold to raise money for the church. They also put on Strawberry Fairs and Ice Cream socials during the summer months, and began the tradition of the "Harvest Supper and Vegetable Auction." The menu featured a variety of cold cuts, hot vegetables, baked beans, hot brown and white bread, home baked Indian pudding, various pies, doughnuts and coffee. The admission price was fifteen cents and enough money was made for the women to sew new kitchen dishtowels. From these events the Ladies Aid Society gave to the church the considerable amount of money of $600 in a three-year period, a generous practice of the women's groups that continues to this day.

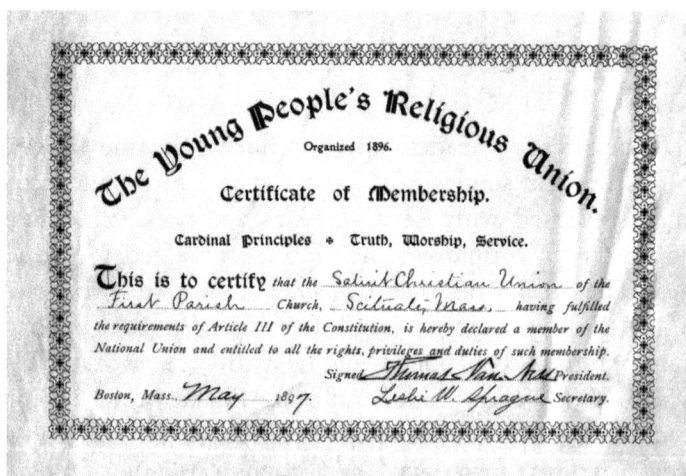

Acceptance of Scituate's YPRU Chapter
into National Organization, 1897

The Scituate Christian Union of the Young Peoples Religious Union was formed in February 1896. Its mission was "to foster the

286

religious life among the young people of our town, to bring its members into closer relation with our Church, the First Parish of Scituate, and with other churches of our faith, and to give them greater interest in the national missionary organizations of the Unitarian denomination." Membership was open to, "Any person…who is in sympathy with its purposes and who is willing to engage heartily in its work." The membership fee was
twenty-five cents a year. Members were expected to study Unitarian religious literature and disseminate that information; to engage in study towards the furtherance of religious truth; and to promote the feeling of religious devotion by attending the Union's meetings and the church's worship services. It was the Union's belief that "as salvation is found through service, every member promised to take part in some activity looking to the betterment of his fellows, or else to bring to the Sunday Service someone unfamiliar with Unitarian thought and life. May Prouty was the group's first president. After the business part of the weekly meeting concluded, there was a discussion led by Rev. Weed on the subject of "amusements," likely a cautionary conversation. Other topics also encouraged living a virtuous life. The entire Weed family was involved with the group. Mrs. Weed once lectured on "Duty" and Miss Ruth Weed, their daughter, talked about "The New Year." On another occasion Miss Cora Wilburn spoke on the topic, "The Place and Influence of Jewish Women in the Home." Dues were collected and then donated to the church for such things as piano tuning. Once, there was a joint meeting with the Norwell Christian Union with one hundred young people attending. The weekly meetings ended with a service, usually led by one of the members. The journal of the Satuit Christian Union ends with the meeting of April 14, 1901. It is not clear how long the Union lasted.[11]

Improvements to the church building were made during Weed's ministry including the installation of the first toilet, though it was located in one of the outdoor sheds. Indoor plumbing came to

---

[11] Satuit Christian Union book, First Parish Records.

the church in 1930 but that toilet was a chemical one. A flush toilet wouldn't be installed until 1949.

The social and educational life of First Parish was very much appreciated by its members. However, the relationship between the congregation and Rev. Weed, which began with great expectations, deteriorated. On September 21, 1895, Rev. Weed offered his resignation, writing to the Parish Committee, "Inasmuch as it seems that certain members of this church are dissatisfied with certain things that I have said and done, I deem it best to resign my office as Pastor of this church. I therefore now do so: said resignation to take effect on the last day of December 1895." Apparently, his "fearless utterances" exasperated some members. But a congregational meeting on September 24[th,] asked Mr. Weed to withdraw his resignation by a seventeen in favor and three against tally. Mr. Weed did withdraw the resignation only to submit it again in October 1896 after a parish meeting on July 12, 1896 voted to give Rev. Weed a three-month notice of dismissal. This time Weed's resignation was accepted. Lacking a minister and funds to pay for one, the meeting voted once again to close the church, this time from November 1 until the April 1897 annual meeting.

The First Parish Pulpit Committee invited Rev. Fred Henry Gile on May 16, 1897 to preach for a period of one year at a salary of $800 and he accepted. The son of an Alfred, Maine cranberry grower and state legislator, Gile was a Renaissance man. He graduated from Bowdoin College in Maine and from the University of Michigan Law School in 1882. He also earned a MD degree. After the ministry he practiced law at 6 Beacon Street in Boston. He was an inventor and the president of the Gile Engine Corporation which had a manufacturing plant in Michigan. He and Mrs. Gile were the parents of three sons and two daughters.[12]

---

[12] Edwin M. Bacon. *The Book of Boston: Fifty Years' Recollections of the New England Metropolis*, Boston, 1916, 447.

Rev. Fred H. Gile

A year later, in April 1898, First Parish considered rehiring Rev. Gile for another year beginning July 1, 1898, but even a generous donation of $700 from George O. Allen was not enough to alleviate the congregation's financial concerns. The vote to rehire was six yes, thirteen, no; however, a month later, the vote was reversed and Rev. Gile was rehired. Church records do not offer a clue as to why the vote was changed. The recorded votes regarding Rev. Gile's tenure indicate a small First Parish membership, or else an indifferent one.

Twelve months later, on April 2, 1899, Rev. Gile wrote the following letter:

Dear Brethren of the Parish,

As your Annual Meeting is at hand I beg leave to inform you that I shall not be a candidate for reelection as your minister.

The insufficiency of the salary drove me to so much outside work as to undermine my health and seriously hinder my pastoral work.

I am therefore compelled to seek a field where the salary will enable me to give up all work beside that belonging to the pastoral office.

With kindest wishes I remain as ever yours very sincerely,

FH Gile

Rev. Gile's future legal and business interests ultimately provided him a comfortable living but he still had a sense of duty to those who were down and out. By 1911 Gile was involved with an organization, The Society for the Promotion of Criminal Anthropology, which received "thousands of applications" from men who were out of work, whose health was poor or who "have made a failure of life." An article in *The New York Times*, described Gile's plan to establish several farms, "The Co-operative Farm Colony Chain," within a thirty to forty mile radius of Boston where the unemployed would work the farms. The supervisors were men with agricultural experience but who also had become unemployed. The purpose of the Society was not to be a charitable effort but a business enterprise. Still, Gile declared, "The reclaiming of men and women is good citizenship and a respected and self-respecting place in the world is a business investment. It brings idle energy into productivity, and lessens the burden laid upon the community of supporting people who would otherwise have to be supported either in hospitals, jails, or poorhouses." Shares in the enterprise were sold to investors for five dollars.[13] Unfortunately, we do not know if this enterprise succeeded.

---

[13] *New York Times*, November 5, 1911.

On July 9, 1899 the Rev. William Branigan of Dorchester was hired to preach until November 1. In late November the Parish closed again due to the lack of money. Then with the meager savings the church had accrued during its six-month closure, the congregation voted to hire the Rev. Joseph Cady Allen of Salem, Massachusetts from mid-June, 1900 until the first Sunday in December 1900.

Rev. Joseph Cady Allen

Rev. Allen was born in Rochester, NY on January 30, 1869. Raised as a Presbyterian, he was "marked in his early youth by his precision with words, by his inquiring mind and his criticism for old usages." After reading a series of sermons on evolution, he became convinced of the oppressiveness of Christian orthodoxy and its irrelevance to the celebration and practice of pure religion. He graduated from Meadville Theological School in 1893 and attended Harvard Divinity School. Prior to coming to Scituate, Allen served churches in Winona, Minnesota and Redlands, California. Curiously, he later had a "short, unhappy adventure" as a troubadour and Shakespearean actor in Britain in 1920. Though he served only small Unitarian churches, he was "proof against all backbiting [and] envy…. Throughout his long life he honored his profession with dignity." He died July 22, 1955.[14]

The congregation enjoyed Rev. Allen and in December the church extended his contract until April 1901; and, in April 1901 he was given another year's extension. However, seven months later, Allen resigned.

Dear Friends

Having received a call to become minister to another church where I think I can work more effectively for the cause that you and I have in common, I request that you kindly release me from my duties here allowing our relations to end at an early date. In offering my resignation, I am not forgetful of your interests dear friends, nor unmindful of the fact of my obligation to you is at present paramount.

I think however that it would be as well for our ways to separate now as to some later time. With thanks to our great Father for a brief but pleasant season with earnest hope that his love may be more and more a sustaining reality to you and that his providence with and through your efforts may advance this church in all spiritual things making it an increasing power for righteousness in this community I confidently commend all to his care.

In fellowship of the Gospel of Christ, yours,

Joseph Cady Allen

---

[14] from an obituary written by the Rev. Waitsell H. Sharp (in minister's file at the Andover Harvard Library).

The Parish asked Rev. Allen to reconsider his resignation, but he refused and left for his new ministry in Yarmouth, Maine.

Following Allen's departure, the church hired Rev. Stanley Mercer Hunter to preach two Sundays in December and then to finish Mr. Allen's term which ended in April 1902. At the April annual meeting he was hired for the next year at $800 and in April 1903, his contract was extended for another year, still at the $800 salary. Rev. Hunter was born in Manchester, England and he graduated from the Meadville Theological School in 1894. He previously served as one of the first ministers of the Unitarian church in Salt Lake City, Utah and he came to Scituate from St. John, New Brunswick, Canada. He was known as an "eloquent champion of liberalism."[15] He believed in phrenology, the study of bumps on the skull. Like other phrenologists, Hunter believed that "a competent phrenologist" could know a person's character by feeling their head. "We have," he wrote, "sciences of astronomy, botany, geology, chemistry, and indeed of almost everything with which we are acquainted. But there are comparatively few who are willing to admit that we have a *science of character* (original emphasis.)"[16]

Life at First Parish went on with a variety of activities and no doubt the minister's "head hunting" enriched parlor discussions. The Ladies' Alliance held a Valentine's Day party at Rev. Hunter's home and two weeks later the church held its worship service at the high school because the church's chimney was damaged during a fierce late winter storm. By April the chimney had been rebuilt and the Alliance had a whist party to celebrate. The women who scored the highest number of points chose their prizes which included a bushel of potatoes, a berry dish and a pincushion. In May a special Sunday service featured Rev. Charles E. St. John, the national secretary of the American Unitarian Association, who spoke about his recent visits to Unitarian churches on the Pacific coast. At an evening social in June,

---

[15] *Morning Oregonian*, September 29, 1895, 12.
[16] Stanley Mercer Hunter. "Is There a Science of Character?", *The Phrenological Journal of Science and Health*, September 1895.

an excerpt from Mark Twain's *Innocent Abroad* was read, while a gramophone, "a very enjoyable feature," provided musical entertainment. At a Sunday service later that month, Rev. Ida C. Hutton, a nationally known feminist preached the sermon.[17]

Rev. Hutton had spoken eight years earlier, at the 1895 convention of the National Council of Women. One session reported by *The New York Times* discussed the issue of "Dress." A report by the Committee on Dress stated that the committee, "in seeking an improvement in woman's dress which will give her the free and healthful use of the organs of her body when working or taking exercise, condemns not only the corset, but the long skirt, as a serious hindrance to freedom of movement." To prove the point, Rev. Hutton spoke on the "ethics of dress" to the gathering in her clerical garment. The newspaper account said that Hutton was so "exceedingly eloquent and forceful" and the applause was so long and loud that the president of the council commented, "that times had certainly changed when a woman who talked on dress reform could be applauded as loudly as an opera singer." In a delightful coincidence, another speaker at the conference was Martha Strickland, four years before her marriage to Sheldon Clark. Strickland's lecture topic was "Dress as an art." She presented herself in attire that modeled "dress reform." She spoke "against the dress of the fashion plates" which was "contrary to nature's dictates." Dressmakers, she argued, were artists who were restrained from "creating gowns embodying beauty, grace and comfort" by the demands of their customers.[18]

Sadly, like so many of his predecessors, Rev. Hunter left Scituate after a brief stay. On October 21, 1903, he submitted his resignation.

---

[17] *Scituate Mariner*, March 27, 2003.
[18] *The New York Times*, February 28, 1895

Dear Friends, This is a formal statement tendering my resignation (of which you have already had some intimation) as pastor of your church.

Believe me, it has been a source of good to me to have been connected with you and with the tradition and aspiration for which the church stands. My regret is that those changes which come more or less to all of us in our work of this world, lead me to take this step. My relations with you have always been genial; and, I trust, as helpful to you as to me.

It has been with a sense of loss that I have spoken the parting word for those who have passed to the Life Beyond. Nevertheless, it has been a comfort to me to know that I was delivering to those that remained, the Message of Modern Religion and Modern Faith. The Faith that enables us to live well, will enable us to die well. This Faith will grow more and more and will, I believe, strengthen you and our Cause in the community. May it be the privilege of each of you, long to maintain with a noble progressiveness and kindness, the traditions of the First Parish in Scituate.

I shall keep each of you in remembrance (for, having been one of you once, I shall always be one of you) and, though separated by distance, I shall be with you in spirit often.

Faithfully yours,

Stanley M. Hunter

The sentiments expressed in this letter suggest that Rev. Hunter was well liked and that he thought highly of the people of First Parish. With Rev. Hunter's leaving, the church voted to close its doors for five and a half months until April 1904. Hunter went on to join the faculty of the Pacific School of Osteopathy in Pasadena,

California. Despite Hunter's leaving, the life of the congregation was improving. Membership was up and much was happening.

First Parish hired Rev. George Adelbert Hathaway, fresh from Harvard Divinity School in May 1904, for one year for $800. He was re-hired annually for the next four years. Hathaway was ordained and installed as minister of First Parish and of the Second Congregational Society of Marshfield Hills on August 15, 1904. Prior to the installation, in the manner of earlier years, a meeting of ministers and delegates for the Plymouth and Massachusetts Bay conferences and others held council. A letter from the clerk of Mr. Hathaway's home church, the First Congregational Church of Berkeley, Massachusetts, was read advising that Mr. Hathaway was a minister in "good and regular standing" and, at his request, he was being dismissed as its minister. The council then formally voted to proceed with the ordination and installation. The afternoon service included choral music, a sermon by the Rev. Thomas Van Ness of Boston, and a hymn written by former minister, Rev. Nathanael Seaver, who was living in retirement in Scituate. Mr. Seaver also offered a charge to the people.

The congregation thrived during Rev. Hathaway's ministry. A Sunday School was organized in October 1904 and twenty-two children enrolled. By 1906 the enrollment grew to thirty-eight. Between October 16th, 1904 and April 5, 1905 there were twenty-one Sunday classes held (four were cancelled because of storm and cold.) The largest attendance was on December 4th with forty students present. The average attendance for that first year was twenty-seven. A highlight of the Sunday School Christmas celebration that year was when a Christmas tree was brought into the church on Christmas Eve with seventy adults and children attending. Hot cocoa and cake were served afterward the service. The following year ninety people attended a Christmas Day party and enjoyed ice cream, cake and coffee. The day was spent playing games and every child in the Sunday school received a box of candy.

Beginning in 1906, and for many years thereafter, the women of First Parish hosted what became known as the "Town Meeting Dinner." Town meetings were all-day events held across the street from the church, in the Town Hall, where the Gates School addition is now. The women, in that first year, served up a meal of cold meats, baked beans, rolls and butter, pies, pudding and coffee, charging twenty-five cents. The dinner was so successful, and the women earned a reputation for being the best cooks in town, that they began catering many meetings and events. Over the years, they provided dinners for the Scituate Historical Society, the Scituate Women's Club and the Scituate High School alumni reunions. Once it was learned that the ladies of the Harbor Methodist Church were planning a roast lamb dinner for fifty cents while the First Parish Alliance was planning to serve the same meal for seventy-five cents. The First Parish women decided not to lower the price because, after all, they were "the best cooks in town."[19]

The auditorium, as the worship space was called, was painted in a pale green in 1907. The funds were raised with the help of Rev. Hathaway. Pews and woodwork were stained a light oak; the pew cushions were stuffed with straw and covered in beige damask, as were the drapes. The floor was covered with a red carpet and the pulpit and chairs were covered in red velvet. The first furnace (wood and coal burning) was installed, a gift of the Ladies Sewing Circle. It would be another forty years before the furnace was fueled by gas. In 1956 the furnace was converted to oil, a gift of members, Arthur and Gail Anderson of the Anderson Fuel Company in Scituate.

Mr. George O. Allen, Parish President, gave an organ to the church in 1907 in memory of his wife, Deborah N. Allen, who had died the year before. Rev. Hathaway was the first person to play it. It was originally pumped by hand and then, in 1928, an electric blower was installed in the church cellar. The organ that was replaced by Mr. Allen's gift came from the Congregational Church in South Reading (now, Wakefield), Massachusetts. Before that, it was in the Episcopal

---

[19] Margaret Bonney papers.

Church in Cambridge in Harvard Square. What made the wooden pipes interesting were the inscriptions written on them. One said, "Put up by Gilbert & Woodbridge Organders to his Honor," indicating that the organ was built for the private chapel of a British nobleman. An older inscription says, "This pipe was made by Snetzer in London and has been made to sound by [George Frederic] Handel [1685-1759] and was heard by George Washington when commander of the American Army at Cambridge." This would suggest that the pipe was made in the 1730s and the great composer, Handel, might have played on an instrument that included this pipe. A third inscription states, "Put up in South Reading, April 1832." As the Allen organ was being installed in Scituate, the old organ with its notable pipes traveled to Palo Alto, California where the inscriptions were discovered. When the Palo Alto church dissolved, the organ became the property of the American Unitarian Association, and then it was installed at the First Unitarian Church of Stockton, California where the pipe still resides.

In April 1908 the congregation voted to rehire Rev. Hathaway for another year by a vote of seventeen to two. The church was now debt free and confident of the future under the well-regarded Mr. Hathaway. But the good fortune was interrupted. On August 17, 1908 Mr. Hathaway resigned. The congregation voted seventeen to two not to accept his resignation, but acknowledged the reality that Mr. Hathaway had been called to be minister of the First Unitarian Church in Great Falls, Montana. In his letter to the church Hathaway wrote, "I have given full weight to the future welfare of the First Parish in Scituate and conscientiously believe that I have done all that is at present possible for the benefit of your Society. I commend you to the love of God in His Spirit."[20] And so, another period of instability began. In November the parish considered three candidates and chose Rev. William C. Adams; but he declined. The rapid turnover the church had experienced since the Civil War increased, as First Parish would have five ministers over the next six years.

---

[20] Hathaway letter in First Parish files

In May 1909 Rev. Hilary Bygrave was invited to be First Parish's next minister, for a salary of $1,000. In his acceptance, Rev. Bygrave wrote

Thank you for the honor you have done me in asking me to become your Pastor. I am quite disposed to cast in my lot with you and I see no reason why such a relationship should not prove to our mutual advantage.

But two difficulties seem to stand in the way and it is for you, rather than for myself to decide whether they can be surmounted.

The one difficulty lies in the way I am placed myself and the other lies in the situation here at Scituate. I have a home in Belmont [Massachusetts] which I would rather live in or dispose of. I am willing to sell it, to let it, if I can find a purchaser but I cannot afford to turn out and leave it to a possible purchaser or tenant, and to secure rather might take two months, or even six.

The situation here is, that at present there seems to be no fitting house, in the right place, for Mrs. Bygrave and myself to live in. I am under the impression that we might better live somewhere in the region of the Church, as near as may be at the Center of the town, so that I might the more easily get to your homes and you to ours. Towards the end of September perhaps a suitable home might be secured.

Therefore it is for you to decide whether I am to accept your call to the Pastorate here on the distinct understanding that it may be six months before I could be living amongst you. I do not wish to over influence you in making a decision when I say that during that time I should not only come to you on Sundays, but once a week I would come down to see you, make calls and get into personal touch with the families that make up the Parish.

If you think such a line of action would be detrimental to the interests of the Parish we shall part the best of friends, but if you should decide that I am to become your Pastor on this basis, I shall use my best endeavors to see that it does not work to your disadvantage.

I understand the salary to be one thousand dollars per year to be paid in monthly installation. The proposed arrangement need not begin until the 1st of May.

Rev. Hilary Bygrave

Rev. Bygrave, like Rev. Stanley Hunter, was born in England in 1847 where he was educated and ordained as a Congregationalist minister. His daughter was the wife of the Rev. Loren B. Macdonald of First Parish in Concord, Massachusetts and a son, also named Hilary, was a prominent attorney in Boston. He retained a certain quality of speech and manner "gained in the land of his birth;" had a "fervent spirit in his preaching of the gospel," a genuine love of humankind, a warm sympathy for the sorrowing and a rare gift of poetic experience."[21] Bygrave was known to fervently annotate the first official Unitarian Hymn and Tune book with marginal notes, crossing out hymns, verses and words he did not like.[22]

The annual meeting in April 1910, heard a report from Rev. Bygrave who, like Rev. Hathaway, served as Superintendent of the Sunday School informing the congregation that the Sunday School had an average attendance of twenty-one for the year with thirty enrolled. Rev. Bygrave and Rev. Nathanael Seaver, the retired former pastor of the church, led the class of older boys. The meeting voted to continue Mr. Bygrave for another year at $1,000. He accepted, but noted that while he was pleased to serve another year, he was agreeing "with the understanding that if circumstances shall continue to prevent" his residing in Scituate, the relationship with him and the church could be terminated by mutual consent, if the "success of the parish shall be thought to be dependent upon a resident minister." At the next annual meeting on April 8, 1911, the congregation voted not to re-hire Mr. Bygrave under the "existing conditions." The congregation preferred a pastor who lived in town. Thus, Rev. Bygrave ended his Scituate pastorate in June.

In October 1911, the parish voted to call the Rev. Bertram D. Boivin as minister. At first, Mr. Boivin accepted but then later declined. On November 19, 1911 there was a unanimous vote in favor of uniting with Marshfield. It is not known from the church

[21] in Minister's file at Andover-Harvard Library.

[22] David Johnson. *Tidings, The newsletter of the Unitarian Church of Marlborough and Hudson [Massachusetts]*, http://www.ucmh.org/minister%E2%80%99s-column/

records whether this meant a union of fellowship or the continuation of sharing a minister. With that vote an invitation to the Rev. Charles Ames to become pastor was offered. Upon consideration, Rev. Ames also declined.

On February 4, 1912 a vote was taken to offer Rev. Robert P. Doremus $1,000 to come to Scituate with the Second Congregational Society of Marshfield Hill paying an additional amount for Rev. Doremus' preaching there. Doremus accepted on February 10, 1912

> On Sunday last you honored me by extending to me an invitation to become your minister. After thoughtful consideration of what is to you and to me an important matter, not lightly decided, I now accept your call, and look forward to coming among you as the minister of this Parish.
>
> It is a high and serious relation that we are assuming as Minister and people, in which we are to work together for the best interests of this church and community. May we be gifted with patience and sympathy and mutual understanding; may we be true comrades in our worship, in our aspirations, in the work we have to do together, loyal each to the truth and the right as he sees it, yet with respect and consideration each of us for the truth and the right as others see it.
>
> May these come to us out of the relation which we are about to enter upon together, a widening vision, a deeper reverence, a profounder spirit of good will and service to our fellow-men, a more complete consecration, a firmer loyalty.

Faithfully yours,

Robert P. Doremus

Rev. Robert Proudfit Doremus

Doremus was born in Wisconsin in 1879, the son of a minister and was both a Unitarian and Universalist minister. In a ceremony on May 8th, 1912 he was installed as the minister of the First Parish Church and of the Second Congregational Society, in Marshfield Hills. Participating in the service were ministers from the Baptist and Congregational churches in Scituate. Unitarian ministers, the Rev. Sidney S. Robins of Kingston gave the sermon and former minister and First Parish member, the Rev. Nathanael Seaver, gave the charge to the minister. However, a year and a half later, in December 1913, Rev. Doremus resigned to accept a call to become minister of the First Unitarian Society of Farmington, Maine. Once again, the parish voted to close the church, from mid-December until the annual meeting in April 1914. At the same time, the congregation received a letter from the Massachusetts Federation of Churches suggesting the union of churches in communities that appeared to be "over churched." Perhaps the letter was an attempt to "cull" struggling churches in order to make the successful churches, of whatever denomination, larger and more prosperous.

Chapter Fourteen

"A small congregation of plain men and women"

The doors of First Parish re-opened on May 3, 1914 after being shut for nearly five months. Several ministers, sent to Scituate by the American Unitarian Association's Committee on Ministerial Supplies, were paid ten dollars per Sunday to preach. One of them, the Rev. Henry W. Pinkham, was well received, and he was asked to be the First Parish minister beginning September 6th.

Henry Winn Pinkham was one of the most controversial Unitarian ministers of his time. In Scituate, though, he was well liked even though his ministry was among the briefest in the congregation's history. Pinkham was born in 1864 in Newton, Massachusetts, the son of a Baptist minister. His mother died when he was two. He graduated from Brown University and was ordained a Baptist minister in 1891. In 1909 he was admitted to Unitarian fellowship, after he and his congregation at the Bethany Baptist Church in Denver, Colorado were excluded from the Rocky Mountain Association of Baptists Churches for their liberal theology. Pinkham found Unitarianism appealing because of its trust in reason and its ideas about social justice. His point of view was so compelling that his Baptist congregation joined him in becoming a Unitarian fellowship.[1] He would later describe himself as a humanist.[2]

Henry Pinkham was a Socialist who ran in 1910 as the party's candidate for governor of Colorado, receiving 3.4% of the vote.[3] Pinkham said he became a Socialist by "the logic of the principles of democracy as laid down by Jefferson and Lincoln" and because…"I was a Christian and I saw that the private ownership and control for private profit of nature's resources and of the indispensable machinery of production on which all depend, flatly deny the basic Christian doctrines of the Fatherhood of God and the brotherhood of man."[4]

Rev. Henry Winn Pinkham

---

[1] Minister's file at Andover-Harvard Library.
[2] Pinkham letter, July 15, 1919.
[3] State of Colorado Roster of Elected Officers (1911), 76.
[4] Pinkham letter, July 15, 1919.

Moreover, Rev. Pinkham was an ardent pacifist, a calling that he followed for his entire adult life. The start of the Great War in Europe stoked that calling and affected his ministerial career (but not in Scituate.) Prior to arriving at First Parish and during his Scituate ministry, Pinkham spent time along the piers of Boston Harbor at St. Mary's House for Sailors run by the Episcopal City Mission. On Christmas Eve, 1914, four months after the start of the war, Rev. Pinkham arranged a dinner where English and German sailors ate together.

> I had asked the English sailors if they would be displeased by the presence of German [sailors]. "Oh no," they said, "they are not to blame for the war." The mediation of American Christmas turkey proved acceptable to both nationalities. In the concert that followed the dinner, a German sang a song with great spirit. I could not understand it, but judged it a sufficient expression of the German point of view to warrant me in calling for "Tipperary" which the Englishmen sang with a will. Finally [the] three national anthems were sung.[5]

Some might say Pinkham's pacifism was extraordinarily naïve, or worse, wrong-headed. He called the American Revolution a "deplorable mistake" in printed remarks to the Scituate congregation. He favored the Missouri Compromise of 1850 over the fighting of the Civil War, even though it included odious provisions such as the Fugitive Slave Act.[6] These positions must have upset some in the church because a number of the congregation's members had ancestors who fought in the Revolutionary and Civil Wars. Yet, overriding any objections to Pinkham's positions on those historical

---

[5] Henry Winn Pinkham. "English and German Sailors Dine Together," from the Henry Winn Pinkham Collection at the University of Denver (Colorado) Penrose Library
[6] One Hundred Years of Peace," sermon, First Parish files

issues was the present unease of many concerning their fear that the United States would enter the war in Europe.

In Scituate he was also persuasive. On Sunday, November 22, 1914, Mr. Pinkham presented to the congregation a petition for its consideration addressed to Woodrow Wilson, the President of the United States.

To the President of the United States:

As a small congregation of plain men and women, we feel our utter powerlessness in the presence of the appalling calamity in which the present war is involving mankind. But we are conscious of belonging to a great nation whose influence in world affairs is mighty. To you, as the head of this nation, various appeals have come from the warring countries themselves. Any word that you, as representing the people of the United States, may send to them, will be received with the utmost respect. We therefore earnestly petition you, as spokesman for this neutral nation, to appeal to the peoples now at war for an immediate cessation of hostilities in order that the international conference, by means of which existing controversies must eventually be settled, may begin at once.

We believe that four months of a war participated in by nations in the vanguard of civilization amply suffice for the teaching of whatever lessons for mankind such a war may contain. It is our conviction that the establishment of a durable peace, founded on international justice and good will, will be rendered vastly more difficult if this war shall be fought to a finish. The governments and the peoples of the countries not at war know what war means as they did not four months ago. All are chastened, but as yet neither side is elated by victory or humiliated by defeat. The ambition of the victor to dominate forever, and the longing of the vanquished for revenge, do not now exist as obstacles to permanent peace as they will if the war be prolonged to a decisive issue. Whichever side might win, humanity as a whole would lose by the sacrifice of lives through which humanity might have been enriched and ennobled.

These are reasons why our country should take a strong initiative in favor of immediate peace, nor wait to be formally asked to mediate. The time to act like reasonable, civilized human beings is also now. Postponement is never advantageous, never necessary. And an appeal to reason is always in order. If our country's influence is in favor of prolonging the war, how can we escape responsibility for its inevitable cruelties, its irreparable destruction?

Furthermore, it is not simply in the interest of civilization and of humanity as a whole that our nation has a right and a duty to speak in the present crisis. We ourselves are suffering and shall suffer from this war. Our accumulation of wealth, which ought to finance a conquering war against disease, ignorance, poverty, vice, and crime in our country, must be heavily drawn upon to repair war's ravages in Europe. Worse by far than our financial loss is the moral deterioration which is unmistakably manifesting itself among us as the natural consequence of this war. Our overtaxed sympathies are becoming blunted to its horrors, and we seem to be beginning to regard it as a intensely exciting spectacle, a football game on a colossal scale in which we are eager to see points scored before time is called! Various business interests are clutching with greedy joy opportunities afforded by the distress of foreign rivals. And insidiously the deadly evil of militarism, whose natural outcome is war, is fastening upon us.

Moved by these and other weighty considerations, and remembering that the time draws near the birth of Christ with is powerful suggestion of peace and good will, we implore you, Mr. President, to disregard precedents in an unprecedented situation, and speak to the warring peoples, through their governments, your strongest possible word for common sense, for civilization, for humanity, for the Christmas spirit of all-embracing love.

The petition was unanimously adopted by the congregation that same Sunday morning and sent on to President Wilson.

Two months later, after worship on February 21, 1915 Mr. Pinkham announced at an informal meeting of the parish that he had accepted a call to the Unitarian church in Melrose, Massachusetts and would preach only one more Sunday in Scituate. The decision to go to Melrose was one he would regret. Pinkham told the congregation that Rev. J.A. Hayes had expressed willingness to come to Scituate as a regular supply preacher and so it was voted to approach Rev. Hayes. At the April annual meeting, an invitation from Rev. Pinkham was read which "extended a cordial invitation to the Scituate Parish" to his ordination in Melrose. The congregation voted in return to convey congratulations to Mr. Pinkham for he was highly regarded in Scituate and, in light of the unanimous vote on the petition to President Wilson, well supported.

Sadly, Pinkham's ministry in Melrose was a brief one. He was forced to resign in June 1917 because of his outspoken opposition to American involvement in the Great War. The month before the Melrose church passed a resolution of support which stated that when Pinkham "said that, 'in choosing war our country had officially repudiated Christianity and crucified the Son of God afresh,' he was speaking from his conscience "and his patriotism to the community and country was unquestioned."[7]   However, his position at the church became untenable and, in his letter of resignation he said, "I wish to join with you, in a pledge of loyalty to our church, to the fellowship of free churches to which we belong, to our common country, to the President and our Government insofar as they stand for universal justice and brotherhood – above all, to humanity, the dwelling place of God. Cordially, your minister...."[8]

Rev. Pinkham was unable to obtain another pastorate, so he devoted himself to the pacifist movement. He was involved in the Fellowship of Reconciliation, an international peace organization, and was secretary of the Association to Abolish War for several years following the war. The organization of nearly three hundred members distributed free printed materials against war and held public meetings in the Boston area. Its platform included unilateral disarmament and argued that a plebiscite should be held before a declaration of war. Pinkham paid a price for his principles, finding preaching opportunities, even as a substitute, difficult. Income was also hard to come by. His work as secretary of the American War Resisters was voluntary. After 1927, he concentrated his energies on writing letters to the editor and articles, which were published in religious journals such as *Unity*, *The Christian Leader*, and *The Christian Register*, and in many major newspapers.

Pinkham's wife was a fervent advocate in her own right. Wenona Osborne Pinkham was a campaigner for women's suffrage in Massachusetts and one of the state's "most prominent women civic leaders."[9] This was because she was from Colorado where women had the right to vote in state elections since 1893. When she was refused the right to vote in Massachusetts she served as an officer of the Massachusetts Woman Suffrage Association and was executive secretary of the Boston League of Women Voters. At the time of her death from a stroke in January 1930 when she was forty-

[7] *Boston Daily Globe*, May 2, 1917.
[8] *Boston Daily Globe*, June 11, 1917.
[9] *New York Times*, May 9, 1930.

seven, she was one of Massachusetts's most prominent women civic leaders. Mrs. Pinkham was a moralist who, in a speech shortly before her death, spoke against Boston nightclubs, drunkenness and "drug distribution at Cape Cod summer resorts." She also pressed the Massachusetts legislature to enact a "padlock" law that would close bars and taverns, which frequently violated the law, as well as advocating for a law that provided "compensation" for prisoners.[10] Rev. and Mrs. Pinkham's passion for peace and social justice was passed on to their daughter, Louisa, who became a Radcliffe and Harvard educated sociologist and psychotherapist. She testified in the early stages of the *Brown v. Topeka Board of Education* suit that racial segregation was psychologically harmful to children. Ultimately, the United States Supreme Court agreed when it ruled that segregation was unconstitutional.

In 1936 Rev. Pinkham received some satisfaction from the American Unitarian Association when its annual meeting passed a resolution of "repentance" for the Association's "acts against pacifist ministers during the World War.... An ovation was accorded the Rev. Henry W. Pinkham, a pacifist driven from his pulpit. For eighteen years he has been urging the Unitarians to pass [the] resolution.... His resolution had been greeted derisively in previous conventions."[11] Following the American entry into the Second World War, Pinkham was often a solitary picketer, walking Boston streets with a sandwich board sign protesting involvement in the war and, later, following the war, he opposed the continuing imprisonment of conscientious objectors. Pinkham's vehemence and single-mindedness in his opposition to war also led to the rejection of articles he submitted to magazines such as the *Atlantic Monthly* and the ongoing displeasure of many in the leadership of the Unitarian Church. At the 1942 annual meeting of the American Unitarian Association (AUA), six months after the attack on Pearl Harbor, Pinkham rose to offer a resolution condemning war as a human activity. To his great embarrassment and humiliation, the motion was

---

[10] Obituary, *The New York Times*, January 9, 1930.
[11] *New York Times*, May 20, 1036.

not even seconded by any of the thousand in attendance. "There was not one who was willing, either out of devotion to free speech and fair play, or in sheer pity for my embarrassment to second my motion. I was flabbergasted."[12]

Pinkham denounced war as "collective homicide" that was contrary to human nature, and served no useful end. To Pinkham, there was no such thing as a defensive war, and peace would never be obtained through the use of violence. He urged religious leaders to recognize that their support of war was hypocritical and recommended methods of opposition for pacifists. At the age of 80, the Unitarian Pacifist Fellowship honored him at a testimonial dinner. Towards the end of his life Pinkham wrote poignant letters to the American Unitarian Association asking for an advance from the Society for Ministerial Relief to pay for his life insurance from which he already had taken a loan. "I can't let the occasion of a note to you pass without expressing afresh my appreciation of the benefit I enjoy, a retired impecunious old minister, by the grace of the Society, and its Directors," Pinkham wrote, "What could I do without it? I do not know."[13]

Rev. Pinkham continued to write until his death in Dorchester, Massachusetts, on January 5, 1947. An eloquent obituary written by fellow Unitarian pacifist, the Rev. John Haynes Holmes, described Pinkham as "among the purest and bravest of men." Haynes said Pinkham

> gave the untiring and dauntless service of a lifetime to an ideal untouched by selfish motive.... [He] was a frequent source of irritation, since he scorned amenities, compromises, even good tactics.... To his friends and supporters he was an inspiration.

---

[12] Pinkham letter, August 1942 in Minister's file at Andover-Harvard Library.
[13] Pinkham Letter, May 15, 1942 in Minister's file at Andover-Harvard Library.

His one enemy was war, his one consuming passion, peace.... He must make men see what he saw — a world perishing in violence and hate — and to this end must lose not a moment and miss no occasion! So, without thought of self, at bitter cost, he gave himself to his great cause and fought without hope of victory. But his victory will come! The heroes and the martyrs live not in vain.[14]

The *Unitarian Pacifist Fellowship Newsletter* devoted a memorial issue to Rev. Pinkham in May 1947, which included several testimonials to Pinkham's "courage" and "committed spirit." A Henry W. Pinkham Fund was proposed to aide fellow pacifists in the United States and Europe.[15]

Rev. George W. H. Troop

---

[14] Holmes obituary of Pinkham in Minister's file at Andover-Harvard Library.
[15] "Unitarian Pacifist Fellowship Newsletter" (May, 1947).

When Rev. Pinkham announced his resignation from Scituate he recommended that Rev. J. A. Hayes occupy the pulpit; however, the AUA's Committee on Ministerial Supplies sent other ministers. From June 2nd until September 5th, the Rev. George William Hill Troop, Canadian and Episcopalian by birth, (his father was a priest in Montreal) served the parish and resided in Scituate during the latter part of the period. Rev. Troop graduated from Harvard Divinity School and began ministry as an Episcopalian priest. At one time he was acting rector at the chapel of the Arlington National Cemetery in Virginia. According to a news report, he was not allowed to resign from the Episcopal Church but was "virtually defrocked" because he began his duties as a Unitarian minister before the Episcopal Church could take any action.[16] After a couple of decades in the Unitarian ministry it was harshly noted, "Mr. Troop is a thoroughly good, well-intentioned man. As you may know, he was at one time the minister of Roslindale [1912-1914]. It was not a successful pastorate. Troop appears to be peculiarly unfitted for American life, or perhaps any life…. He has no push – no punch"[17]

Rev. Troop ended his brief relationship with First Parish on September 8, 1915. He gave his final sermon at a rare union service at the Congregational church. The Rev. Louis Cornish, the General Secretary of the AUA, preached two Sundays after Troop's departure and he recommended, as Troop's successor, the Rev. William Ware Locke who was then serving the Civic Service House of Boston. The organization, founded in 1901, was the first vocational guidance center in the United States. It helped immigrants with citizenship as well as education, legal assistance and employment.

On October 31, 1915 Rev. William Ware Locke was invited to assume the pastoral duties of the Parish for the ensuing year—"or longer," for a salary of thirty-five dollars for each Sunday. In a letter

---

[16] Minister's file at Andover-Harvard Library.
[17] Rev. Kenneth C. Walker letter, March 19, 1930, Troop file, Andover-Harvard Library.

dated November 3, 1915 to the Parish Clerk, Mrs. Edith Bonney, Rev. Locke accepted the call

> Your communication from the Parish Committee is at hand and I take pleasure in accepting the call to be pastor of the Scituate Church for the ensuing year. I realize that there is much that a minister and his wife can do in addition to the Sunday services and we shall both enjoy entering as much as possible into the life of the community.
>
> I appreciate the kindly courtesies already received, and the intelligent hearing that has been given and look forward for co-operation in building up all the interests of the church. I hope that all the members of the Parish, whether they attend Church or not, will call upon me freely for such personal services as it may be in my power to give. My efforts will be to make the Church a live centre for loving service and high endeavor, which shall have its influence for good in the whole community.
>
> Yours most sincerely,
> Wm. W. Locke

The ministry of Rev. Locke was to be the most successful and positive ministry since Rev. Sewall's, seventy years earlier.

William Ware Locke was born in 1858 in West Dedham (now Westwood), Massachusetts. He came from a distinguished line of Unitarians whose scholarly instincts and social sympathies he shared and carried on. His father was a minister and teacher in West Dedham. Locke had "an almost childlike sweetness and simplicity of spirit [which] accompanied the insistent strength of his sterling character."[18] He graduated from Worcester Polytechnic Institute with a degree in Mechanical Engineering, which proved useful in his work at the Civic Service House, and in 1885 he graduated from Harvard Divinity School. A poet as well, Locke published two volumes of inspirational poetry.

Locke became active immediately in the Scituate community. He first lived on Union Street and later in the Manson House on Stockbridge Road. To celebrate the tercentennial anniversary of the founding of the Southwark Church by the Rev. Henry Jacob, he participated in a service at the Congregational Church. Soon, Locke was teaching English at Scituate High School and became a leader in the new Boy Scout movement. He was also quick to show his social side. At the annual Christmas Party held at the Allen Memorial Library on December 30' 1915 (postponed because of a severe storm the week before), Rev. Locke played the piano and proved himself to be "a very successful entertainer" to the forty attendees, who also enjoyed story telling, dancing, ice cream and cake.[19]

The annual meeting of April, 1916 voted that the Parish Committee would, in the future, meet monthly and the whole parish would gather quarterly for supper and conduct church business afterwards. Three of the quarterly suppers were to be served by the "ladies" and one by the "gentlemen." For the first time subscription cards were distributed among the members in an effort to establish a more reliable method of persuading members to donate to the church and, thus placing the church finances on a firmer basis.

The Alliance reported that it continued to send clothes to Miss Emma Wilson's school in Mayesville, South Carolina. The school, whose official name was the Mayesville Educational and Industrial Institute, was established to teach the children of former slaves. It started out with ten students in an old cotton gin house, taking chicken and eggs in payment for tuition. Eventually a new

---

[18] *Christian Register*, August 1945, 319.
[19] First Parish Records

building was constructed that served five hundred students and cared for fifty orphans. Perhaps the most famous graduate of Miss Emma's school was the American educator and civil rights leader, Mary McLeod Bethune.[20]

For a number of years there had been two women's organizations at First Parish: the Alliance and the Ladies Sewing Circle. The two groups worked closely together but the Alliance focused on religious and philanthropic activities while the Sewing Circle was more social. According to an early constitution, the mission of the Alliance was, "the promotion of the religious, social and philanthropic activities of this Parish, and to bring the Women of the denomination into closer acquaintance, cooperation and fellowship. And to devise ways and means for more efficient usefulness."[21] When, in 1916, Mrs. Rena Cole was both president-elect of one group and secretary-elect of the other due to the scarcity of members, it was clear that the two groups should unite, and they did. The consolidated group became the Alliance and was the only women's group at First Parish until 1935 when the Unity Club was re-formed.[22] Lagging far behind the well-established women's group at the church, a Men's Club was formed in 1919 as one of the first chapters of the National Unitarian Laymen's League.

Adapting to the ever-changing popular culture, the social activities that the women enjoyed ranged from "socials" and whist parties at the beginning of the century, to mahjong parties in the 1920s to Auction Bridge in the 1930s. Besides providing wonderful entertainment, these events also raised money for the church.[23] One anecdote from 1919 reveals just how dedicated the ladies of the church were in the caring and maintenance of the building. One of

---

[20] Gerda Lerner. *The Majority Finds Its Past: Placing Women in History*, (2005), 67.
[21] Alliance Secretary's Book, May 7, 1902 – May 6, 1909 #4 in First Parish files.
[22] Margaret Bonney papers.
[23] Margaret Bonney papers.

the sheds that survived the 1879 fire housed the church's toilet. When it was found to be leaking some men of the church volunteered to do the repairs. In appreciation, the women cooked meals for them on two different days but so few men showed up that the women wound up hiring a carpenter to do the work.[24]

The church building was now over thirty years old. In addition to periodic painting, maintenance and repair, the church added improvements, most notably its first electric lights, a gift from Charles Waterman. A chandelier hung from the ceiling of the sanctuary along with four wall sconces that are still in place, though the chandelier was removed in the 1960s. The old lamps were donated to the Mount Hope Improvement Association in Scituate's West End. From the time they were built, individual parishioners owned the carriage sheds along the northwestern edge of the property. Even though they were not destroyed in the 1879 fire, by 1918 the sheds had fallen into such poor condition and the titleholders were asked to relinquish their ownership to the church so the congregation could repair them. The Alliance offered to pay for the repair of two sheds, three members paid to repair another three and the parish voted to repair one shed for fire wood storage. The other sheds were torn down. Twenty-five years later the sheds were again in poor shape. Three were torn down in 1943 and the remaining sheds were repaired. In 1952 the sheds were once again in disrepair. On a Saturday in June 1952, forty men, some of them members of the Men's Club, worked on the sheds with donated funds and building materials. No doubt the large number of men were enticed by the lobster and clambake prepared by Parish Committee chair, Andrews Wyman.[25]

A well-attended Community Memorial Day Service was held at the church. Mr. Locke gave the sermon with a member of the Methodist church also participating. The Congregational and Baptist churches omitted their morning service in order for their members to

---

[24] Margaret Bonney papers.
[25] First Parish files.

attend. The order of service contained this note: "Recognizing that the soldiers of this Nation, irrespective of race or creed, gave their lives for the preservation of this Union, the Baptist, Congregational, Methodist and Unitarian Churches have joined in a Memorial Service, and welcome as special guests the George W. Perry Post 31, G.A.R., the C. E. Bates Camp 88, Sons of Veterans, and the George W. Perry W.R.C. [Women's Relief Corps] Post 121."

In the fall of 1916, a member of the Chief Justice Cushing chapter of the Daughters of the American Revolution attended a Parish Committee meeting to make arrangements for a special evening service in which the Daughters would present a portrait of the Rev. Nehemiah Thomas and place it in the custody of First Parish. The history the painting is an interesting one and it is a saga that lasts almost two hundred years.

Rufus Hathaway, who was Rev. Thomas' nephew by marriage, painted the 1794 portrait. Hathaway was born in Freetown, Massachusetts to a large Quaker family, and trained in the family business of carpentry and shipbuilding. He was an itinerant artist in the nearby Taunton area and by 1792 he made Duxbury his permanent home. There he painted portraits of both family members and prominent community people, works for which he is best known. The Thomas portrait stayed in the family after Rev. Thomas's death in 1831. For a time it hung in the home of Dr. Cushing Otis, the brother of Rev. Thomas's wife, Hannah. Somewhere along the way it came into the possession of the Chief Justice Cushing chapter of the Daughters of the American Revolution. It is not clear when the DAR became the legal owners of the portrait, maybe as late as 1916. Soon after acquiring the painting, the DAR paid twenty-five dollars to restore and re-frame it. In a letter written to the church, dated September 23, 1916, the DAR chapter secretary wrote

> It is the wish of the members of this Chapter that it [the portrait] be placed in the present Unitarian Meeting House of Scituate – for such a time as it may

be desired by the Parish Committee of said church – or – the members of this chapter may wish to place it in some more secure place – for such antiques are growing more and more valuable.

At present, at least, it seems the most appropriate place for it to be hung, as "Parson Thomas," as he was called, served as pastor from 1792 to 1831 and was settled there for life.

If you and the other officers are willing to hold it in your keeping under these terms it will forthwith be presented to you with an appropriate service as such an occasion warrants – to go back in mind a hundred years – and mark the time and its changes.

[Signed] Nellie L. Sparrell, Sec.[26]

Mrs. Bonney responded on behalf of the Parish Committee

Your letter concerning the portrait of the Rev. Nehemiah Thomas was duly received, and presented to the Parish Committee of the Unitarian Church of Scituate for consideration. Acting for the Parish, they desire to express their appreciation of the kindness of the Chief Justice Cushing Chapter, and feel quite willing to act as custodian of the portrait in accordance with the wishes made known in your letter. They hope a Vesper Service may be held, perhaps on October 8th and will very gladly cooperate in any plans the Chapter may arrange or suggest.

Yours truly,

Edith D. Bonney, Clerk of the First Parish Unitarian

---

[26] Margaret Bonney, *"My Scituate"* (privately published, n.d.), 49.

On the afternoon of Sunday October 8, 1916, a service was held with the DAR officers and members. Mr. William Waterman accepted the painting on behalf of the congregation which was then unveiled by Margaret Cole (later, Bonney). Miss Mary A. Ford and Rev. Locke spoke.

In an unsigned narrative written in 1970 by a DAR member, it was noted that no member of the DAR, save one, was aware at the time of the existence of the Thomas portrait. That one person was Dorothy Brown Wood whose mother had been a member of the DAR and whose father had been president of the Parish Committee and the Scituate Historical Society. According to the narrative, Dorothy Wood said the portrait was lent to the Scituate Historical Society around 1916. This may not be the case since much was made of the commemoration service at First Parish when the portrait was unveiled. It must be assumed that the portrait hung in the church a few years, possibly until 1919,[27] before it was removed and given to the Scituate Historical Society where it was placed, possibly by Dorothy Wood's father, Wilmot Brown, in the Cudworth House, an historic property owned by the society. It stayed there for many years until it was returned to the church. Why this was done is not known.

In the spring of 1970 a member of First Parish, who was an artist, suggested that the portrait be cleaned. Before that was done another church member took the portrait to Vose Galleries in Boston where it was appraised at $10,000. When the Parish Committee learned of this, it "panicked" when they learned that the church did not own the valuable portrait.[28] The first thought was to keep it safe in the local Rockland Trust bank vault but the bank refused believing the vault was too damp for such a valuable painting and so the painting was packed away in a church closet.[29] The next step was to

---

[27] Author unknown. "The Rufus Hathaway Portrait [of Rev. Nehemiah Thomas]."
c. 1970.
[28] Bonney, *"My Scituate"*, 48.
[29] *"My Scituate"*, 48; Bonney papers, "Hathaway Portrait."

insure the painting, which was done for an annual premium of seventy dollars. When the church asked the DAR chapter to reimburse it for the premium, it was the first that most members of the DAR chapter knew that they owned the portrait. A search of their records gave no indication as who gave the chapter the portrait and under what circumstances. After receiving the church's request an unpleasant exchange of words took place in telephone conversations and correspondence. The DAR refused to reimburse the church for the insurance stating that obtaining the policy was done without their authorization. At the same time, the DAR wanted to reprint a book, *Old Scituate*, that it had first published in 1920 but they lacked the funds to undertake the project. When the chapter learned of its ownership of the Thomas portrait and its value, it decided to sell the painting to finance the reprinting of *Old Scituate*.

Just before the portrait was returned to the DAR, the Rev. Carl Whittier, minister of First Parish, wrote to the Parish Committee chair that he was disappointed by the return of the portrait, especially since it was going to be sold. Rev. Whittier noted the curiousness of Mr. Vose's appraisals. Vose initially valued the Thomas portrait at $10,000. He then priced it at $7,500 and sold it for $6,000. It was sold to Winsor White of Duxbury and a descendent of Rufus Hathaway's wife. In a letter dated, August 18, 1970, Mr. White wrote that he "acquired [the portrait] through a close friend."[30] This friend was, in all likelihood, Mr. Vose, who may have sold the painting to White well below market value.

According to records of the Philadelphia Museum of Art, where the portrait of Rev. Thomas presently resides, Mr. White sold it for an undisclosed amount to Edgar and Bernice (Chrysler) Garbisch, well-know collectors of early American art.[31] Mr. Garbisch was a retired colonel in the United States Army, a graduate of West

---

[30] Winsor White letter, First Parish files.
[31] E-mail correspondence to author.
* Efforts by the author to return the portrait to Scituate have been unsuccessful.

Point, and an All-American football player who was elected to the College Football Hall of Fame. He was married to Bernice Chrysler, the daughter of the founder of the Chrysler Corporation, the automobile manufacturing company. In 1972, Col. and Mrs. Garbisch gave the portrait to the Philadelphia Museum of Art.[*]

A few weeks after the unveiling of the Thomas portrait, a Parish Supper and meeting was held on November 25, 1916. The parish journal notes that the dining room was "attractively decorated" and a "bountiful" dinner was served to thirty-three people. After the dinner children went elsewhere to be entertained with music and games while adults "attended to the more serious matters'" of the parish. Rev. Locke announced, to the surprise of some, that he had been called to the Barnard Memorial (also known as the Warren Street Chapel) in Boston. Because this new work would require more of his time, Locke said he would not be able to do as much for First Parish as he would like and it seemed to him that the parish must again find a new leader. This caused considerable discussion at the meeting without any decisions other than a vote that Rev. Locke be responsible for arranging preachers for December while he continued his work as Scituate's pastor. The name of the Rev. William Ichabod Nichols of Cambridge was mentioned at the meeting as a possible successor. Nichols recently had purchased a home in Hingham and was expected to move into it in the spring. Hope was expressed that it would be possible to invite Rev. Nichols to come to First Parish and he was contacted to determine the level of his interest in coming to Scituate. Upon instruction from the parish, Mr. H. Cole met Rev. Nichols and he reported back to the parish in December that Scituate and "its problems" interested Nichols, and that it might be possible to bring Nichols to Scituate for eighty-three dollars a month. The meeting thought the amount of $1,000 for the year was reasonable and so a call was made to Rev. Nichols.

On the evening of Monday, January 8, 1917, the fourth quarterly Parish Supper featured an excellent oyster stew with rolls, coffee, doughnuts and fruit. It was served by the men of the church and gave great pleasure and satisfaction to the thirty-five people in attendance. After the supper, young and old alike, engaged in the "full enjoyment of games and music" late into the night. The Sunday School contributed to the success of the party by providing ice cream and cake, that was served at nine o'clock.

Rev. Nichols began his ministry April 1, 1917 but it was cut short after only two weeks by an unspecified "serious illness" that ended his life nine months later. To discuss this unexpected event the church held a special meeting on April 15. Mrs. Rena Cole was elected chairman of the meeting, the first woman so elected in the church. Later in 1917 the parish committee contacted Rev. Locke about returning to First Parish. Mr. Locke agreed to come to preach as often as possible and to supply preachers on Sundays when he was not available. He also agreed to be accessible for pastoral calls. Rev. Pinkham, recently dismissed from the Unitarian Church in Melrose also offered his preaching services.

On December 8, 1917, a meeting was called to consider a course of action in response to the bequest of the recently deceased, Cornelia M. Allen. Her gift of $3,000 was the most generous given to the church up to that time. Miss Allen gave the money for the "support and maintenance of gospel worship of the Unitarian faith." In the event that First Parish Church ceased to exist (which the gift was meant to prevent), the money was to go to the AUA. The Parish decided, upon Rev. Locke's motion (Mr. Locke remained a member of the church while attending to business at Warren Street Chapel) that the money be turned over to the AUA in trust and the church would receive whatever income was generated. The church to this day gets a modest amount of income from the Cornelia Allen Fund.

When the United States entered the war in Europe on April 6, 1917, no reference to the momentous decision was mentioned in church records, but activities to aid the war effort were recorded. The Sunday collections taken in May were given for war relief work. Rev. Locke visited arriving soldiers billeted at the Scituate Proving Grounds and offered the church's assistance to them. The servicemen were invited to come to the Harvest Supper in

November. Miss Marian Cole offered a motion at a special meeting regarding "the Unitarian boys" who were in the military. To acknowledge the church's servicemen a service flag and honor roll hung in the church. On May 5th, a special service was held to dedicate a flag, which hung over the pulpit, that had fifteen stars on it signifying fifteen members of First Parish who were in the service. A news account of the service said the Rev. Locke "delivered a very inspiring patriotic sermon." Guests of honor were the G.A.R., the Woman's Relief Corps, the Sons of Veterans and the Boy Scouts.[32] Money was donated to the Red Cross War Fund. As occurred frequently during the war years, a union memorial service was held later that month at the First Baptist Church with Rev. Locke offering the opening prayer and a scriptural reading.

During the war years, both the Unitarian and Congregational churches in Scituate faced difficulties. First Parish voted to close the church from January 1, 1918 until March 1, 1918 mainly due to the war-related increase in heating fuel, however it held a meeting on April 13th in the smaller Allen Library to discuss ministerial leadership. The Parish Committee asked Rev. Locke what arrangements could be made with him for the future. Later, Louis Cole reported that Mr. Locke agreed to come back to Scituate for six months for a salary of seventy-five dollars a month.

In May 1918 the new Congregational minister resigned to take the pulpit in a Framingham, Massachusetts church. Upon hearing of the departure, Rev. Locke suggested that the two struggling churches unite in worship during the month of August, which took place. As the old sibling rivalry was easing the Congregational church's parish committee chair sought Rev. Locke's advice about the availability and affordability of ministers. Locke told him that it would be "almost impossible" to hire a young minister for less that nine hundred dollars for the year.[33] After the Congregational

---

[32] *Scituate Herald*, May 10, 1918.
[33] Waite, 85.

church hired another minister, arrangements were made for the two churches to hold union services on the last Sundays in September and October 1918, but one of them had to be cancelled because of the influenza pandemic. * From these combined church worship services came the idea for all Protestant churches in Scituate to join in a Thanksgiving service the Sunday before the holiday with the soldiers at the Proving Ground attending.

First Parish in the 1920s

Rev. Locke's ministry was very much appreciated by First Parish and it was clear that even when Locke was on leave as minister he was very active in church affairs as a member. He was often called upon to be chairman of the annual meeting or other parish meetings.

---

*The influenza outbreak was worldwide. Estimated global deaths range from fifty to one hundred million people. In the United States, the second wave began in Boston in 1918.

The December 16, 1918 meeting voted to extend Mr. Locke's contract through the church's fiscal year (to May 1919.) Services were to be held through the winter in the church except when union services were held with the Congregationalists on the last Sunday of every month.

A Wayside Pulpit was constructed on the church lawn at the suggestion of Mrs. Locke at a Woman's Alliance meeting. First introduced to North American churches in 1919 by Henry Hallam Saunderson, minister of the First Parish Church (Unitarian) of Brighton, Massachusetts, and also secretary of the American Unitarian Association's publicity department, the roadside bulletin board became a familiar sight in front of Unitarian churches in New England. Saunderson noticed "many bulletin boards in front of churches were ineffectual because they were either kept empty or held notices which had outlived their usefulness." Inspired by the local wayside shrines he had seen in Europe, he decided to create "wayside sermons," liberal messages that would make people stop, read, and search their conscience. Saunderson started by posting brief quotations each Sunday night on the bulletin board outside his church. When hundreds of people stopped to read the messages, he decided the idea might have a wider audience. After Saunderson polled various clergy in the Boston area, one hundred ministers agreed to subscribe to his wayside sermons.[34]

Rev. Locke brought to First Parish a sense of purpose and commitment. He suggested a new method of raising subscriptions from members, starting with a canvass committee that talked with members in an effort to increase their financial contribution. Locke also established a membership committee to increase the number of members of the church. The issue of membership and who was a member of First Parish came up at a special meeting on August 24, 1921. Mr. W. T. Clapp raised the subject and wondered what the privileges of membership in First Parish were. A "very free" discussion followed and it was clear that the current by-laws and

---

[34] http://www.uua.org/worshipweb/wayside/index.html

other church policies were contradictory, and on the whole, inadequate to a majority of those present. Rev. Locke, reporting as chair of the membership committee, suggested a review of the membership list and a slight change to the wording of the Bond of Union adopted during Rev. Weed's ministry in 1873. Locke offered the following change

"We, whose names are here appended, feeling that in union is strength, and that social service is a help to individual righteousness, agree to unite in the love of truth, and in the Spirit of Jesus Christ, for the worship of God, and the service of man."

The revision with the addition of "the love of truth" was approved unanimously.

At the next annual meeting in April 1922, with twenty-one members present, new by-laws were proposed and accepted. The church was to be known as The First Parish Unitarian Church of Scituate and the stated objective of the church was "to maintain a House of Worship, freely open to all residents and visitors of Scituate who desire to attend religious services, and open as a meetinghouse for promoting public welfare through civic, social, educational and philanthropic activities." The covenant read "Without discrimination against other covenants or creeds as test of membership in a church of Christ, we approve the following statement for those who desire to unite with us in spirit and in truth:

Our Faith - We believe in the Fatherhood of God, the Brotherhood of Man, the Leadership of Jesus, Salvation by Character, the Progress of Mankind onward and upward forever.

Our Covenant - In the love of Truth and the spirit of Jesus Christ, we unite for the worship of God, and the Service of Man.

It was the Rev. James Freeman Clarke, pastor of Boston's radical Church of the Disciples, who wrote the "Our Faith" section of the First Parish covenant. Clarke was also a nineteenth century social reformer and a Transcendentalist. In 1886 he wrote a collection of essays, *Vexed Questions in Theology*, in which he took the five central tenets of Calvinism which were based upon the belief in God's divine grace and transformed them into a Unitarian statement that believed in salvation by character and an optimistic vision of human endeavors. Many Unitarian churches adopted this statement as their own.

Membership in the church was open to all who signed the covenant, after being accepted at the Parish meeting and who contributed annually to the support of the church. The officers of the church provided for in the by–laws were the five trustees whose responsibility was the administration of the Permanent Fund (endowment); the seven members of the Parish Committee: chairman, clerk, treasurer, and four others; and, the minister (ex-officio.) The Parish Committee was to look after the general welfare of the church by working through special standing committees made up of members appointed annually. Other committees were Funds and Contributions, Grounds and Buildings, the Sunday School, Music and Religious Services, Membership and Hospitality and Community Activities. The new by-laws also required that the minister be called by a parish meeting on the recommendation of the Parish Committee. The invested funds were to support the minister, the maintenance of the buildings and the regular activities of the church; annual contributions were to be received from members; and special contributions were solicited for community activities promoting the public welfare. These by-laws didn't last long as they were superseded two years later in 1924 under the leadership of a new minister.

In March 1923 Rev. Locke wrote to the Rev. Louis Cornish, president of the AUA, telling him "it would be well for the church and myself to make a change." Locke still needed to supplement his income teaching literature and history at the high school and he believed his yearly salary (one thousand twenty dollars) was inadequate, plus there was no Scituate parsonage. Locke was aware, and told Cornish, that such conditions would make it difficult to find a successor. Still, he cited the strength of the Woman's Alliance, the Layman's League and the Sunday School as reasons to be optimistic about First Parish's future.[35]

On April 5, 1923, the Rev. Locke sent to the Parish Committee a letter his admirers feared

Dear Friends,

For the five years [seven years, total] that I have been the minister of the First Parish Church, I have enjoyed the pleasant relations that have been maintained and feel that they have grown stronger and more comprehensive as the time has passed, but my energies have been too much engaged in civic and educational interests for the church to have received the attention that is has deserved, and I feel that some change would be of mutual benefit. I would like to concentrate more definitely on civic or educational or religious work, and the church would gain by securing a young man who was devoting himself strictly to religious services. The church is fortunate in such a prosperous and growing condition, receiving such strong support from the Woman's Alliance, the Layman's League and the Sunday School, that it will not be difficult to make a confident step forward at this time.

Special support will be continued for our interesting summer program, and the new Theological School at Cambridge, combining Unitarian and Trinitarian

---

[35] Locke letter, March 1923, First Parish files.

foundations, is offering a project at this time which is full of promise for the advancement of the work. *

I therefore offer with some regret and much appreciation and good will, my resignation to take effect September 1, freely continuing certain pastoral services that may be desired during student services or pending the appointment of a settled minister.

Yours most sincerely,

Wm. W. Locke

The members of First Parish wanted Rev. Locke to stay as minister in view of all he had done for the church. An initial vote at the April 16th meeting granted Locke a year's leave of absence. However, the motion was tabled until Rev. Locke's arrival at the meeting. In his presence the discussion of the resignation resumed. He told those assembled that the AUA had asked him to become minister in Lawrence, Massachusetts and because the challenge interested him he had accepted the call. Once again, the Parish Committee was asked to find preachers, a task they did not welcome. On April 29, 1923, the vote of two weeks earlier which granted Locke a year's leave of absence beginning May 1 was reaffirmed. Clearly, the congregation hoped that whatever Locke wanted to do, or was needed to do in Lawrence, would be done in a year and he would then return to Scituate.

In July 1923 a letter came from Samuel A. Eliot, the President of the AUA, who had heard from Rev. Harold L. Pickett that he had been offered a salary of twenty-five dollars a week to be a supply preacher in Scituate. Mr. Eliot expressed concern about the effect on First Parish's budget and advised the congregation that the AUA

---

* Locke is referring to the move of the Andover Theological Seminary to the Harvard Divinity School Campus. While sharing facilities the two schools never formally merged and the Andover Seminary moved to Newton, Massachusetts and merged with the Newton Theological Institution in 1931.

would contribute five dollars a Sunday toward the costs of Rev. Pickett's preaching during the summer.

While the church struggled to find a replacement for Rev. Locke, the forty-year old building needed renovations, and so the church voted to use the gift of one thousand dollars from Mr. George O. Allen. However, the repairs were estimated to cost an additional thirteen to fifteen hundred dollars. There was confidence that the money could be raised and a letter went out to the membership "and any other people" willing to contribute, reminding them that the church had "stood as a sentinel" in the center of Scituate for generations. The church had "weathered many a gale and storm" and now needed repairs. The fundraising was successful enough for the old mahogany pulpit, saved from the 1879 fire, to be restored and brought back to the church and the walls were painted apple green with fresco panels added. The worn red carpeting was replaced with a green and beige design. A new sink and an electric stove were installed in the kitchen; the cabinets were stained and the floor oiled. The sanctuary windows were repaired with new cords and weights and the exterior was given two coats of paint. As the Committee on Church Repairs noted, "While we could have spent less, much that has been done is in the nature of permanent improvements. We lack funds to complete paying our bills, but still hope for sufficient contributions to cover our needs." Confidence in the church's finances was such that it also voted to raise the salary of the minister to $1,020 to $1,250 with the understanding that the AUA would add $250, resulting in a salary of $1,500 which would take effect upon the call of a full-time minister. There was also a discussion about providing a parsonage as an incentive for a minister to come to Scituate but no decision was made.

One of Rev. Locke's many accomplishments at First Parish was getting the congregation to consider the benefits of a long-term ministry. For many years the congregation had hired a minister, mostly with extended one-year agreements. At last the congregation heeded the admonition of Rev. Seaver, almost forty years earlier, when he said an annual contract was inconsistent with the best

333

interests of the parish. So, in recognition of the spiritual nature of ministry First Parish returned to the formal practice of blessing a minister and his ministry with an open-ended call.

The September 30, 1923 parish meeting rescinded its April vote granting Rev. Locke a leave of absence and the congregation invited Rev. Cornelus Heijn (also known as Cornelius Heyn) to become the half-time minister of the church, beginning October 1st for a salary of $1,500. Following Rev. Locke's departure, Heijn had served as a supply minister and impressed the congregation.

Rev. Heijn was born in Ilpendam, The Netherlands, on the outskirts of Amsterdam, in 1891. At a young age he helped his shopkeeper father and was a barber's apprentice. At thirteen he left school but over the years he was tutored in French and bookkeeping. He also attended an art school at night. In 1908 his family left Holland and settled in Minnesota where the family rented a farm. Heijn stayed in Minnesota when his parents and sisters returned to Holland, but just before World War I broke out he returned to Holland and worked for a grocery company. A year later, he returned to the United States, working briefly as a cashier and bookkeeper in New York and then he entered Meadville Theological School, graduating in 1919. In an autobiographical statement, Heijn said his seminary education was interrupted while serving as a private in the U.S. Army. "It might be fair to explain that where before I had been a pacifist, when the United States entered the war I could see no other way for me but to go and help make the world 'safe for democracy.'"[36] On October 3, 1923, Mr. Heijn accepted the call of First Parish

I have received your letter of September 30 acquainting me with the decision reached at the Special Meeting of your church on that date and thus inviting me to become the minister of your church

---

[36] Cornelis Heijn's file at Andover-Harvard Library

beginning October first, under the conditions outlined in your letter.

It is with feelings of gratitude and expectation that I accept the invitation. Since the last time I preached for you as a supply I have been glad to come here from the first. I have admired the fine spirit of true fellowship and the love for higher things I found among you.

I can make no promises in regard to my work in connection with your Church. I can only say that I shall try to walk in the footsteps and to follow the example of the worthy ministers who have served the First Parish of Scituate in the past; to interpret and bring more fully to fruition the aspirations of us all to "know the truth," to "do the will of God," and to enter into God's beauty and peace; to work with you and for you in the desire to make this community and through it our country and our world a better place in which to live.

Allow me to thank you all for your confidence in me.

When the church called Rev. Heijn he was working in Boston at his business restoring and photographing paintings. He was also an art critic for the *Christian Science Monitor*. The church allowed him to spend half a week in Boston but he soon decided that in order to properly minister to the church he had to give it his full time and attention. Later at an October meeting, Mr. Heijn said that three and a half days a week was not sufficient for him to accomplish what he hoped to do for the Scituate church. It was his intention, he told church members, to live in town and give himself wholly and heartily to the tasks of the church. Church records note that Heijn found the new "hymn and tune" books "incomplete" because they did not contain liturgical elements or responsive readings. Upon his suggestion, a modest sum was raised on the spot to arrange for an exchange of the more complete "hymn and tune" books which arrived a week later and were placed in the pews. The hymn board, where the hymn numbers are posted for the Sunday service, and still used in the church today, was a gift of Mr. E. Stoddard Cook, and it was formally hung in the church on November 25, 1923.

Revitalized by a new minister the Parish Committee began a review of the constitution adopted in 1921. There was a belief that the document was incomplete since it did not have any by-laws and since much of the constitution has "by-law language" it was felt that the best thing to do was to rescind the 1921 constitution and write a more complete one. A new constitution with by-laws was presented and the congregation was asked to review it and vote on the committee's recommendation at the next annual meeting in April 1924, which it did, approving the new constitution and by-laws. The new official name of the church was "The First Parish (Unitarian) Church of Scituate." The object (mission) of the church was "In the love of Truth and the spirit of Jesus we unite for the worship of God and the service of man." It is noteworthy that "Christ" was omitted from the same statement of the 1921 constitution. Membership was open to "Any person in sympathy with the purposes and methods of this Church, who shall be approved by the Parish Committee, may become a member by signing the Bond of Union; but the right to vote at business meetings shall be reserved for members who are annual subscribers to the maintenance of Worship." Officers remained: a chairman, clerk and treasurer. The Parish Committee was now made up of the officers, the minister (ex-officio) and four others; and, five trustees who were responsible for the administration of the Permanent Fund.

Rev. Heijn gave his first minister's report at the annual meeting in April 1925. He noted that the church was doing "as well as possible under the circumstances," referring to the ever struggling finances and the change of ministers. The average attendance since Heijn began the previous October was thirty-five adults and eight children; for every nine women there was one man. The highest attended Sunday that church year was on the December 9, 1924 for

336

the Laymen's League Sunday and the men surely had to come out for that! Mr. Heijn noted that more men had been attending Sunday services and that the ratio was now one to four, with an average attendance of fifty-seven (children were not counted). By the end of the church year there were thirty-two pupils enrolled in the Sunday School with five classes. Church membership totaled ninety-one. At another parish meeting the next month there was a discussion about an outstanding bill of three hundred dollars from the man who painted the church the previous year. There seemed to be some embarrassment on account of the delay in raising money to pay the bill. Since only fifty dollars had been raised it was voted that the remaining amount should be borrowed and paid back in six months. At that meeting the treasurer stated that the church had funds to meet expenses only for the next month or two.

The Annual Report of the Parish Committee noted that following Mr. Locke's resignation there were six months of uncertainty with supply ministers and candidates but "happily ended" with Mr. Heijn's acceptance of the church's call. The Woman's Alliance reported a very busy year with twelve gatherings having an average attendance of twenty-three; and the group's membership was fifty-four. The Alliance continued their financial support for the church building and the minister's salary. One of the highlights of the Alliance calendar was the Summer Fair, featuring a large outdoor wooden dance floor and booths which looked like log cabins.[37] One day that year, the ladies of the Alliance gathered at the church and removed the torn and faded seventeen-year-old carpeting. It took them all day and the next day the men removed the carpet tacks and washed and varnished the floorboards.[38]

For a number of years both the Woman's Alliance and the Laymen's League (the Lothrop Chapter), in order to increase

---

[37] Bonney papers.

[38] Bonney papers.

* Star Island, part of the Isles of Shoals off the coast of New Hampshire, has been a conference site since 1915.

attendance and membership, paid the Front Street Transportation Company and its successors to pick up people around town and bring them to the Sunday service.

In June 1925 former minister, Rev. George Troop returned to preach and in August, the Rev. Alden Cook preached twice. Rev. Cook and his wife, Agnes, also a Unitarian minister, were members of First Parish. There were also pulpit exchanges during the year between Rev. Heijn and Rev. Alan Creelman of the First Baptist Church in Scituate and Rev. Raines of the Methodist church in town.

The First Parish chapter of Young People's Religious Union (YPRU) was organized in 1924, finally joining the organization that began in 1896 (its name was changed in the 1960's to Liberal Religious Youth, the name of the national youth organization). The first Star Island* fund was created that year. One hundred dollars was raised to reward young girls in the church for their "most faithful and untiring devotion to the Sunday School. The first girls to go were Evelyn Merritt, Grace Waterman, Adella and Hilda Stenbeck and Margaret Cole. Thus began a constant stream of First Parish pilgrims to the Isles of Shoals that continues to this day. In 2000, parishioner Bessie Tufts Dooley gave the church twenty-one thousand dollars to endow a fund which granted scholarships for the young people of the church to go to Star Island after school ended in June.

The First Parish Sunday School Committee reported that for the 1924-1925 church year there was an enrollment of twenty with five teachers and five classes. The school had a Halloween Party, a Christmas Party at the Allen library and a Valentine's Day Party at the church. Money raised by the Sunday School was sent to the Children's Mission, the Floating Hospital and to the children of Germany, who were suffering after the war. The Sunday School received one hundred dollars from the Barnard Memorial Chapel in Boston, where Rev. Locke served before and during his Scituate pastorate. The money was used to hire a Sunday School teacher from the Tuckerman School, a place where Unitarians (mostly women) learned teaching skills required for religious education. Also during the year, a Visiting Committee was formed with the hope that it would "stimulate and strengthen" the life of the Church by calling on new people in town as well as on those already known and allied with the Church. Shut-in and homes of Sunday School children were also visited.

Rev. Cornelis Heijn

Rev. Heijn was favored by many in the congregation, so much so that they increased his salary ($1,800) to the highest ever given to a First Parish minster. This was due, in part, to the $250 subsidy from the AUA. The subsidy was well timed since the church had to pay attention to building maintenance. The furnace was showing its age, but it was still efficient and only minor repairs were needed. Some suggested that in anticipation of very cold Sunday mornings, the furnace should be started up on Saturday morning. There was also a suggestion from the Committee on Church Improvements that more space be created for a dining hall and kitchen, "both roomy and convenient," installed to take the place of the rooms that were no longer adequate. The plan included a system that would heat the entire church, but the cautious committee noted that this idea needed long and careful consideration (meaning, money issues).

It was clear that the church was flourishing under Rev. Heijn's ministry. The church school was growing so much it required a significant expansion of the building. Three options were placed before the congregation: First, excavate the dirt cellar; second, build a separate building to the east of the church, a two story Parish House with an auditorium and stage; or third, build a wing onto the existing building. It would have been a great benefit to future generations had the separate building been erected. Sadly, it wasn't, due to inadequate financial reserves. The unanimous choice was building an extension at the north end. The cost was $6,500, paid for by parishioners whose donations were added to their regular pledge. In September 1925 a special meeting was held to discuss additional church repairs and renovations. There was a leak in the steeple and copper roofing was needed. $123 from an Alliance whist party at the Old Oaken Bucket Homestead was used towards the repairs to the balky furnace. As part of church renovations, a coat closet was built, also paid for by the Woman's Alliance. It originally was a storage closet for sewing machines and cloth material for the Sewing Circle. When smaller, more portable sewing machines came into use there was no longer any need to store the materials in the closet and it became the present coatroom.

An important real estate matter was also discussed at the annual meeting. The town and First Parish co-owned a narrow strip of land at the east side of the church between what was then called

Central Street (now, First Parish Road) and the Thomas Lawson Estate. The trustees of the Lawson estate offered the church two lots for $1,250 or one lot for $250 and a deed to the strip of land in front of the second lot. The Parish Committee, the church's trustees and several individuals mulled over the offer for several months and sought guidance from the meeting. The church's endowment trustees were unanimous in their decision to recommend purchasing the one lot for $250. There was no such unanimity on the Parish Committee but a majority also favored the purchase of the single lot. Complicating the issue was an old tomb lot belonging to the heirs of the Hammond family.

The tomb lot was bounded by the Lawson property and the church property. The tomb was in poor condition and was an "objectionable feature." The boundaries of the church lot and the road had never been established and the minutes of the meeting note that "in accordance with the old customs, the Parish and Town still hold the church lot jointly." It was felt that it would be best for the church to ask the town to release the church from any interest it might have in the church lot. This would necessitate an article at Town Meeting to first, have the town relinquish its interest in the church lot; and second, to establish the boundary of the church lot and the road. The article would be needed whether or not the church wanted the additional land. The Parish Committee was also directed to see what could be done about the Hammond Tomb lot. A later parish meeting voted to approve the purchase of the single lot from the Lawson estate and a deed to the Lawson estate for the strip of land in front of the second lot.

The Hammond Tomb remains a mystery to this day. In an undated and unidentified newspaper article in the files of the Scituate Historical Society, written by Willard de Lue III, a story is recounted about the tomb. It was said that soon after Thomas W. Lawson built his Scituate estate, "Dreamwold," his gardeners kept their tools in the tomb adjacent to the church. Before the Lawson estate and the high school were built along Central Park Drive; and even before the road itself was laid out, there had been an open field. There was nothing beyond the western end of the common and First Parish, nothing except the home of Mr. and Mrs. Herbert Cole and the Hammond Tomb. Mr. de Lue asked Mrs. Cole if she knew who owned the tomb and she replied that it belonged to the Hammond heirs. Years before, the Hammonds lived down the slope on Branch Street and Lawson's property was next to their house. By the time Lawson's estate was built the Hammonds no longer owned their house which was then owned by the widow of William L. Day, who bought the house from William and Adelaide Hammond in 1887, when they moved to another part of Scituate. Mrs. Cole said there were stories around town that some boys from the high school were seen walking around town with old bones from the tomb. No one, not Mrs. Cole, not even Wilmot Brown of First Parish and the Scituate Historical Society ever recalled seeing a door to the tomb and both wondered if it ever was a tomb for the Hammonds. By the 1930s the tomb was a mound overgrown with blackberry and raspberry vines and other plants. Mr. de Luce commented in his article, "The Coles and the church people probably would like to see a bulldozer end its history." Harold Cole, moderator of the church's 1926 Annual Meeting, made the formal announcement (known to all that attended the Town Meeting the previous month) that the town voted to relinquish any right, title or interest it might have in the church lot. The land was to be surveyed, property lines established and the deeds and money exchanged for the Lawson lot. The matter of the Hammond Tomb lot came up again and a committee was formed to resolve the matter with the Hammond heirs. Soon thereafter, the committee informed the church that the tomb collapsed, had been filled and then later cemented over, doing away with the eyesore. To this day, the Hammond Tomb remains a curiosity.

Mr. Heijn told the meeting that he had been appointed trustee of the Julia A. Neely Fund. With about nine hundred dollars in the Fund, it was to be used for the care and relief of aged women of Scituate or for the education of young women who were preparing to become teachers in Scituate. Heijn also told the meeting that he was donating ten dollars to the Parsonage Lot fund established to find land and build a parsonage. The church granted Rev. Heijn some vacation time and in January 1927, a surprise sendoff party was given to Rev. Heijn as he prepared to travel to Europe. It is noted in the church records that one hundred and ten people attended with musical entertainment provided by an orchestra. The Revs. Agnes and Alden Cook preached during Mr. Heijn's absence. Samuel A. Eliot, President of the AUA also preached at the church that summer.

During the years following the Great War, the country prospered. The "Roaring 20's" embodied the good economic times and along with the country's good fortune the finances of the church also improved. Subscriptions (pledged donations) increased from $328 in the year ending 1917 to nearly three times that amount as reported at the annual meeting of April 1927. Average Sunday attendance rose to seventy-five. Seemingly flush with money, increased membership and favorable mortgage rates, the congregation began a discussion about building a Parish House and money was put aside. A committee was appointed with the charge to make a preliminary report in three months. Money from the treasury was sent to help the victims of a devastating Mississippi River flood. The April flood caused four hundred million dollars in damage and killed two hundred and forty six people in seven states

Adding to the church's good times was the much-anticipated dedication of First Parish's stained glass window that took place on July 18, 1926. The George W. Spence Company on Canal Street in Boston crafted the window. Spence was one of Boston's best known stained glass studios and was described by Charles Connick in 1933 as a "veteran glass man" who combined "traditions of art glass and stained glass from the craft's first days in Boston and whose work had "steadily developed into a more direct realization that stained glass is the handmaid of architecture."[39] The Waterman family donated the window in memory of Andrew and Lucia D. Waterman

---

[39] Charles Connick. " Boston Stained Glass Craftsmen," *Stained Glass*, Summer 1933, 92.

who were active members of First Parish. It depicts a three-mast sailing vessel of the type built in the

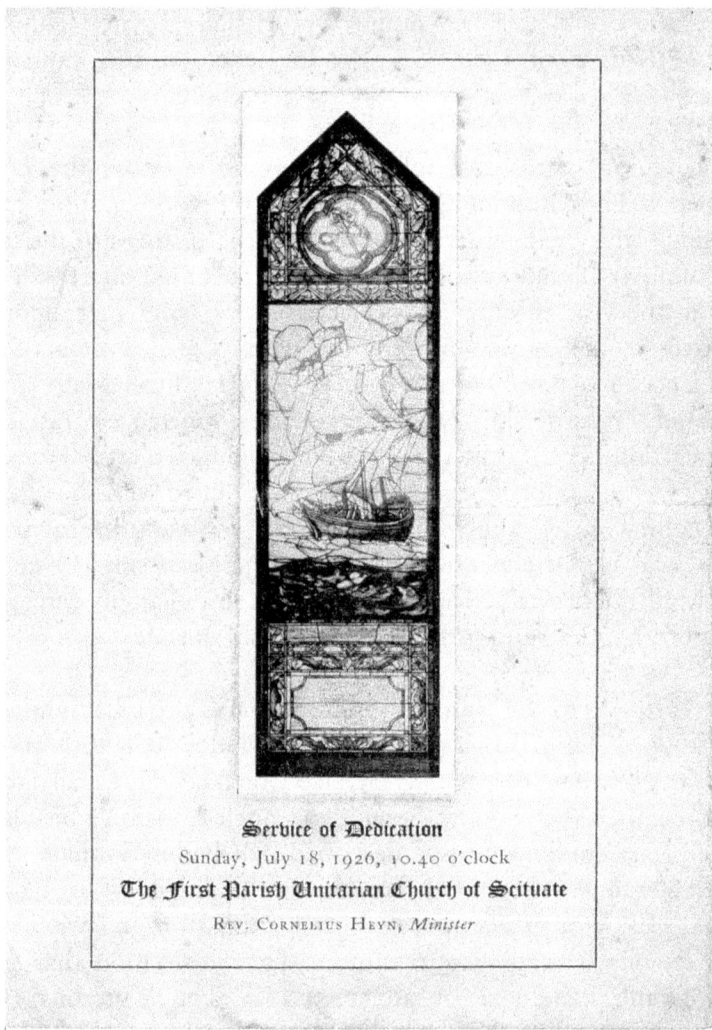

Service of Dedication
Sunday, July 18, 1926, 10.40 o'clock
The First Parish Unitarian Church of Scituate
Rev. Cornelius Heyn, Minister

*Program Cover for the Service of
Dedication of the Waterman Window*

shipyards of the nearby North River during the nineteenth century. The Watermans and other families in the church had been shipbuilders and merchant shippers. The window displays the verse from Psalm 107, "They that go down to the sea in ships that do business in great waters: these see the works of the Lord and his wonders in the deep." It was unusual for a Unitarian church, particularly one founded by Pilgrims, to have such a dramatically decorative piece in the sanctuary. It would have horrified Rev. Lothrop and the first members of the church. However, time has softened any opposition to the window. Now, the Waterman window is a treasure First Parish truly values.

By June 1927 the church had reached a steadiness it hadn't experienced in years. The budget was balanced and there was no deficit. The next month a special meeting with forty people attending heard a report from the Parish House Committee. Plans for a "most attractive and commodious" parish house next to the church were presented by Mr. DeGrange, the architect. The drawings showed a two-story building of three thousand two hundred square feet with a first floor that included a dining room, kitchen, minister's room, an Alliance Room, water closets and heating plant. The second floor was to hold a large auditorium and stage. The cost of the building adjacent to the church was estimated to cost thirty to thirty-five thousand dollars. After the architect's presentation, those assembled offered their opinions which were "numerous and diverse." Almost everyone agreed about the need for more space for the Sunday School and adequate working space for the minister, but some thought it was too grand a project for the church. Others wanted to raise money with an eye toward erecting the building in the future; some inquired about an addition to the church rather than a separate parish house; and still others felt that with $1,500 already raised the expansion project should proceed. In the end, the only course of action agreed upon was to form another committee to see what could be done to raise additional funds and have it report back to the parish in December.

At the December meeting, with fifty members present, reports from various committees were made regarding the Parish House. The Finance Committee informed the gathering that and additional $750 had been raised in just a few weeks. Two construction plans were presented. One called for an addition to the church, extending the building about sixteen feet to the west with two stories and a basement conforming to the existing lines of the church. Included in this plan was a new heating plant, lavatories, a minister's study and, in general, enlarged facilities. The cost was about $19,000. The second plan showed a separate one-story building of twenty-one hundred square feet. This building contained a stage, anterooms, a kitchen and a hall seating about two hundred people. The estimated cost for this building was $17,000. A third plan was offered from the floor which called for an addition of thirty-two feet on the west side of the church. That addition would have two stories with a stage on the lower floor. There would also be enough room for lavatories and a minister's office. The estimated cost for this plan was $13,500. A fourth plan was offered that would have built a balcony across the back of the sanctuary. Rev. Heijn offered his thoughts on the material needs of the church: more room for the Sunday School, a room for the minister, lavatories and larger kitchen and dining room. He believed that the improvements could be completed without incurring a large debt and that $6,000 could be raised in a few months.

Following these presentations and reports, parishioners reviewed the competing plans. It became clear that between $10,000 and $20,000 was required for any of the projects. It was then moved and voted that no more than $12,000 should be spent on whichever plan was eventually chosen. This would seem to have favored the two-story thirty-two foot extension on the west side. However, after further discussion and a number of motions that indicated most people favored some kind of expansion, no definitive action was taken except to dissolve the Finance Committee and form a new Ways and Means Committee.

Sixteen months later, at the annual meeting of April 8, 1929, the question of a parish house or a church addition was revisited. An informal vote was taken which reaffirmed the feeling that additional space was needed. The meeting was informed that the AUA would grant an interest free loan in the amount of five or six thousand dollars. Subsequent events suggest that the AUA's offer was not accepted, the reasons not known. The meeting decided that when $4,000 was raised, construction on an addition, not a separate parish house should begin. That November another special meeting was called to decide on the addition. Thirty-one people were present. The $4,000 had been raised and so the addition was open for discussion. The proposed addition would add just over eleven hundred square feet. While no central heating system was included in the plan, a minister's room, lavatories, a large room and a kitchen were included. The meeting approved and charged the Building Committee not to expend more that $6,500.

On April 14, 1929, the Rev. Cornelius Heijn married Florence Lamont of Waban, Massachusetts. A reception for the newlyweds was held at First Parish three weeks later with one hundred seventy-five people in attendance and the congregation presented the couple with a check for $175. As part of the festivities the Scituate Community Orchestra played.

In late 1929 the Parish Committee had a number of discussions regarding an invitation by other Protestant churches in town to join the World Friendship League, a peace organization, which sought understanding among nations, but the Parish Committee was reluctant to accept without fully understanding the purpose of the League's meetings. Furthermore, it appeared to church leaders that Unitarians had been disparaged in some of the League's publications and there were no retractions. Therefore, Rev. Heijn was instructed to respond to the invitation and explain First Parish's position and its offer of alternate constructive suggestions. Apparently Rev. Heijn's letter was not well received as no further references to the organization can be found in the church records.

East Side of Church with New Addition (1930s)

First Parish has a long tradition of opening its doors to many groups. In the early 1920s a group of Spiritualists asked to use the church and the Parish Committee approved, as long as the group paid the cost of lighting, heating and the janitor. Through the years, up to the present, First Parish has hosted Alcoholics Anonymous groups, union organizing meetings, support groups, the Girl and Boy Scouts, the Scituate Town Charter Commission, Scituate High School Peer Leadership training, and a community-wide diversity and tolerance training program.

The Great Depression hit Scituate hard, like the rest of the United States. Church membership declined and so, therefore, did pledged donations. In his minister's report of 1930, Rev. Heijn acknowledged the difficult times, but was hopeful. However, the church could no longer afford to pay for the transportation service from North Scituate. However, the Depression was not the only difficulty Mr. Heijn faced. His relations with some members of the church had deteriorated because his sermons about socialism and other matters were increasingly criticized. The congregation's political leanings and views of social reform had changed since the ministry of Rev. Gilman. The Depression caused great economic, political and social turmoil, and unease. The rise of communism, in the form of the Soviet Union, terrified many. Economic depravation increased fears about communism and together they overwhelmed any talk of Christian Socialism. Furthermore, Scituate was emerging as a bedroom community to Boston and many of the men of the church, in the face of the Depression, were executives and business owners who sought to preserve capitalism.

Heijn may also have alienated some of the women of the church. In one sermon titled, "Our Precious Heritage," Heijn talked about freedom, "the leaven of our religious life" and how precious it is to the Unitarian faith. "Freedom," he said, "chained to any particular cause or movement ceases to be freedom, for the cause becomes, in turn conservative, or the movement grows antiquated, and the spirit of freedom flees and leaves behind only its skeleton. For freedom refuses to be shackled..." Most in the congregation who heard these words could agree with them. What got Rev. Heijn into trouble with many was when he said, "We have all heard representatives of the Daughters of the American Revolution and other patriotic organizations mouthing phrases about the glorious freedom inherited from our forefathers, while in the next breath they spouted venom against the so-called radicals in general who, according to them, were trying to overthrow the Constitution and so rob us of our inheritance."[40] Of course, a good number of the women of the church were members of the DAR.

When Heijn asked the Parish Committee for a month's vacation in the summer, the 1930 annual meeting voted, on a motion made three prominent members, which voiced a preference for the vacation to be taken at some other time of the year. This did not sit

---

[40] Heijn, "Our Precious Heritage," in Andover-Harvard Library files.

well with Rev. Heijn. In June when the annual meeting reconvened, he offered to submit his resignation as of September 1 if the Parish wished it, as he thought it was necessary. One member responded that what was needed was not a new minister but a better understanding, "steady enthusiasm" and hard work by both minister and the congregation. One prominent member, who held Rev. Heijn in low regard, wrote a letter to her daughter saying, "I believe some people (men) rather be ministers and teacher because it isn't hard work. Mr. Heijn certainly has a snap – compared with our men. He gets up late and goes to bed late, invited out to dinners and sits and reads – by the hour. All the really manual labor he does is take care of the furnace Sunday P.M."[41]

The congregational meeting took no action on Rev. Heijn's offer. But later at a special meeting in September, with twenty-one people present, a formal letter of resignation from Heijn was read. George Brooks, the chairman of the Parish Committee, spoke of the seriousness of the occasion and reminded people that it was only by a vote of the entire parish that a minister could be dismissed. He told the meeting that Rev. Heijn had become unhappy and did not believe he was capable of continuing his ministry. Brooks then asked for a "full and clear expression" of opinions. All who were present spoke. When the discussion had run its course a motion was made not to accept the resignation and it was agreed to unanimously. Brooks ended the meeting urging everyone to work for a united parish, but to no avail. The next month at another special meeting, the earlier vote not to accept Heijn's resignation was rescinded, and the resignation was accepted, effective December 1st. A committee to find another candidate was formed immediately and it was agreed that the new minister's salary should be reduced to $1,500 from the $2,350 Rev. Heijn was receiving.

Evaluating his ministry in Scituate Heijn wrote that, "The church has done well since I came." He spent the first years in

---

[41] Letter to Grace Day Waterman Vines from Lottie Scott Torrey Waterman, January 1, 1930.

Scituate "calling and more calling, organizing, re-arousing the interest of some of the older families and bringing in new ones, one by one." Attendance was "satisfactory." The Alliance had grown and flourished. The Laymen's League, while small, "has done some fine, constructive work." The Church School had doubled in size to thirty-five students, so much so that the church built the addition to meet the needs of the growing Sunday School. Heijn saw himself as "neither a brilliant speaker nor a great organizer, but just a rather persistent plugger with an ability to make friends of people."[42] With Rev. Heijn's departure in 1930 a fifteen-year period of growth, prosperity and steady ministerial leadership came to an end. It would be thirty years before First Parish would have a minister for longer than five years.

Heijn left to serve the North Church in Hingham but eventually retired in Scituate. In the 1950s, he and his three sons built a controversially styled house on the corner of Hazel Avenue and Allen Street. Retirement was not easy for Rev. Heijn. In his sixties, his pension was only $900 a year, barely covering his mortgage and telephone bill. Mrs. Heijn was virtually blind and his own health was poor. Two of his sons wanted to attend medical school. The minister of First Parish at the time, the Rev. Charles C. Donelson, Jr., wrote to the director of the Department of Ministry at the AUA seeking help for "this fine old gentleman" from the old school, who "has been an idealist all of his life" with "no care for his personal welfare." Now, this "faithful servant" was "down and out," and needed help.[43] His son, Cornelis Heijn, Jr., did go to medical school and became a highly regarded psychiatrist and professor at Harvard Medical School. He recalled his father as one who tried to live the life of Christ in its purist form, whose desire to help people left him with little money. Heijn was very much a Socialist, once having the prominent Socialist and presidential candidate, Norman Thomas, stay at his home. "He was active in the real world," his son said.[44] When Rev. Heijn died in

---

[42] Heijn files at Andover-Harvard Library.
[43] First Parish files
[44] Author interview with Cornelis Heijn, Jr.

1968, a simple arrangement of flowers adorned the First Parish communion table in his memory.

Chapter Fifteen

"A world which will test your capacities"

The Rev. Robert Lewis Weis, thirty-eight years old and a descendent of Rev. John Lothrop, was a year out of the Pacific Unitarian School for the Ministry in Berkeley, California, when First Parish called him. It was his first settlement and it began on March 1, 1931. At that time it was common for Unitarian congregations to hear several candidates and choose a minister from among those they heard preach. Several candidates were considered and a vote was taken; Rev. Weis received the most votes. Earl Morse Wilbur, president of the Pacific Unitarian School, described Rev. Weis as a "man of irreproachable character, Puritan in habit and Puritanic in judgment of others. He has good mental ability, and great earnestness of purpose, totally sincere.... His theological position is pretty conservative; but I believe he will make a serviceable good old-fashioned minister who will be much beloved in proportion as people come to know him."[1]

For his part, Rev. Weis was "very happy" to be called to Scituate "because I have felt all along that the Scituate parish was particularly well adapted for me. The people there are most

---

[1] Letter from Earl Morse Wilbur to Dr. Patterson of the AUA, May 9, 1931, First Parish files.

democratic and exceedingly friendly...."[2] While Dr. Wilbur saw Rev. Weis' qualities as positive and Rev. Weis' happiness was real, Weis' ministry in Scituate was brief and ultimately, contentious. Salary was an issue from the beginning. Weis had expected his salary to be supplemented by the Sustenance Fund at the AUA, but the supplement was delayed. For its part, the parish by December 1931 had voted to increase Rev. Weis' annual salary to $1,800, retroactive to March 1. Weis was appreciative but was concerned that since there was no parsonage and no hope that there ever would be, too much of his salary was spent on high Scituate rent. But his $1,800 salary also left little money in the church treasury. The budget had been reduced seventeen percent since 1929 and in 1931 the minister's salary represented seventy percent of the church's expenditures. So, when the church provided Weis with a vacation in September, the church closed for the month, lacking funds to pay substitute ministers while Weis was away.

Rev. Robert Louis Weis
(after he became an Episcopal priest)

---

[2] Weis letter to Dr. Lewis Cornish, President of the AUA, February 10, 1931, First Parish files.

As Dr. Wilbur described, Rev Weis was more conservative in style, theology, liturgy and politics than Rev. Heijn. It is interesting to ponder whether the selection of Rev. Weis was in reaction to the displeasure many had come to feel towards Heijn at the end of his ministry in Scituate. Nevertheless, Rev. Weis' conservatism soon rankled First Parish members as well. Weis sought to resume the rite of communion to the congregation, a practice that had not been done for many years. At the annual meeting in April 1932, it was decided to leave it to the minister to decide when communion would be offered. The minutes of the meeting contain the enigmatic words: "... and that the symbolic form be not used." In November 1932, Rev. Weis conducted a communion service, the first since the Old Sloop Church was destroyed in 1879. A newspaper article describing the occasion cited First Parish lore that held that the man who kept the First Parish silver communion cups at his home after the fire said that "never again would the communion service be observed in [the] church." Years later when an old house in the West End of Scituate was demolished some of the old communion cups were found but other cups, which had been a part of that set, were never found. Rev. Weis invited the ministers of the First Parish Church in Norwell and the First Trinitarian Congregational Church of Scituate to participate in the service, which they did. Regarding the participation of the Congregational minister and parishioners, the newspaper noted that "Some 25 years ago this could not have been said as the old battle fanned to a white heat by the arguments which finally appeared in printed form [with] the Rev. Daniel Wight, pastor of the [Congregational] church in the middle of the 19th century, on the one side and John B. Turner, able lawyer, on the other."[3]

In December 1932 a special meeting was held to discuss the difficult financial situation of the church. Despite a tightening of budgeted expenses, more money than was allocated was spent on special music; the insurance premium was due; building costs were over budget and in the midst of the Depression collections were

---

[3] *South Shore Herald*, November 1932.

down, running about $200 short. To help offset some of the budget overruns the Christmas collection was reserved for the special music account; and, the organist's fee was cut two dollars per Sunday. Most importantly, Rev. Weis was informed that his salary might be reduced the following fiscal year and he was asked to consider a voluntary reduction in his salary for the current year. There is no record of Rev. Weis's response to the request though budget reports indicate there was a reduction of sixty-five dollars from the fiscal year ending March 1932 to that of March 1933.

Rev. Weis might not have made any comments about the vote at the special meeting but he was quite candid in a letter to Louis Cornish, the President of the AUA. Weis began by noting that the "relations between minister and people have been most cordial," but he was very worried about "trying to stretch my modest salary," particularly in light of medical expenses for Mrs. Weis, following surgery. He understood that the parish could not pay more and was aware that Rev. Locke had to supplement his income by teaching in "expensive" Scituate. "The fact is," he said, "I have been altogether uncomfortable and unhappy trying to support my family" on $2,100 a year. He remarked that the Scituate church had struggled financially for many years, noting the debt for the new addition. Still, Weis was grateful to some of the members and friends of the church who, despite the Depression, kept up their pledges. Moving on to other things, Weis informed Cornish "it is a fact that things have proceeded smoothly here, and I have not had an unpleasant word with a soul since living in Scituate." Yet, he felt that the time had come to move on. Assessing his Scituate ministry of nearly two years, Weis felt "a certain amount of satisfaction," even though he believed Scituate to be a "tough" and "difficult" parish.

The peculiar conservativeness of the people which causes them to prefer to remain in a lethargic state instead of working hard for their church; the limited resources; and above all, the tradition of short pastorates in recent years (which the people heartily approve of) all go to show that the pastor ministering to the Scituate Unitarians has no sinecure. My predecessor, Mr. Heijn, had the longest pastorate in over <u>eighty years</u> [original emphasis]. It is a sad story to read the parish records during that time. The church was closed time and time again for lack of funds or interest. It is a fact that with one exception the most liberal contributors to the church today are recent comers to Scituate. The native people, except in rare instances, cannot or will not do their share. [4]

Despite his earlier protestation about not having "an unpleasant word" with anyone in Scituate, Weis does cite a problem he was having with Mrs. Edith Bonney. Weis believed she so favored Mr. Heijn that "she has had no desire to see Mr. Heijn's follower a success here," and "has quietly but steadily blocked me whenever she could." In noting his desire to seek another pastorate, Weis said to Cornish, "the Scituate people have always resented their ministers candidating while they are still connected with the parish. In some instances they have been most unreasonable, and the fact is, practically all of the pastors of this church (in modern times) have had to end their relations with the society rather abruptly."[5]

By April 1933, five months after his letter to President Cornish, and just a little more than two years after he came to Scituate, matters had reached a crisis point between the church and Rev. Weis. While he insisted that he was unaware that anything was amiss, there certainly were strong undercurrents in the congregation. At the annual meeting on April 10th the crisis came to a decision point. The meeting began in its usual fashion, though Rev. Weis was not yet in attendance. Committee reports were read and officers elected. There was a motion, in anticipation of the end of prohibition, to support a petition circulated by Scituate resident

---

[4] Weis letter to Louis Cornish, November 9, 1932, First Parish files.
[5] Weis letter, November 9, 1932. First Parish files.

Henry Turner Bailey asking the Scituate selectmen to refuse to grant liquor licenses to town businesses but the meeting voted that the church should not take any action. A year later, Rev. Weis's successor asked the Parish Committee to empower him to take whatever action that he saw fit, in concert with the other ministers in town, to control the number of liquor licenses in town.

Then the meeting came the matter of Rev. Weis, who was "discharged" as minister, effective July 1st. The total number of people voting was quite small, sixteen, with eleven people voting to dismiss Rev. Weis and five voting to retain him. Weis, in another letter to Cornish, expressed his belief that a small group within the church prearranged the vote. Though the vote was at the church's Annual Meeting, the attendance was small due to two factors, according to Weis. The annual Parish Supper, usually held in conjunction with the annual meeting to attract a large number of participants, was not held. The second factor was that at an earlier meeting in December it was announced that the minister's salary would most likely be reduced $300 at the April annual meeting. Weis suspected that most church members did not want to be present for such a painful act.[6] Nevertheless, the vote to dismiss Weis was distressing for members of the Parish Committee, some of whom resigned from the committee.

Rev. Weiss, in his letter to Louis Cornish, wrote that he was clearly taken by surprise at the vote to discharge him. "There were no criticisms made of the minister at the meeting, the explanation of why his discharge was made was that it was due to financial reasons." But Weis doubted that finances were the real reason since his salary had been paid to date and, despite the December warning of a salary reduction no such vote was even proposed; another proposal to send out pledge cards earlier than scheduled was defeated. Clearly, there appeared to be an organized effort to get rid of the minister. Weis pointed his finger at one man "who alone is responsible for this piece of work." The unnamed individual Weis cited, among the wealthiest

---

[6] Weis letter, April 18, 1933, First Parish files.

contributors, was not involved in the calling of Mr. Weis as he was spending the winter in Florida. Weis believed that this person resented the fact that he had not been consulted in the calling of Weis and, through intimidation, got a better than two to one vote against the minister. Three of the votes to dismiss were from Weis's adversary and his family. Others were so upset that they refused to vote and two prominent men of the congregation, Walter Brooks and Frank Nason, made a "spirited defense" on behalf of Rev. Weis. Nason was one of those who resigned from the Parish Committee. "A wave of indignation rose against the ones" that Weis said might have been behind the plot. The fallout was immediate and became the talk of the town."[7]

As is often the case in such matters, there likely were several reasons for the deteriorating relationship between the congregation and Rev. Weis. Certainly finances, always a burden for the church, played a pivotal role. Undoubtedly the personal financial pressure Mr. Weis felt was also a factor. Perhaps Earl Morse Wilbur hinted at another concern in the letter of May 1931 to the AUA when he described Weis' theology as pretty conservative. Considering the liberal *theological* positions of his predecessors, it is apparent Mr. Weis and the members of First Parish were not right for each other, even though their conservative *political* views were better aligned. But Weis disagreed

> ...it seemed strange that a person who has been as tactful as I have been in the past two years or more; one who is conservative in theology and politics in a conservative town; with no trouble with anybody since coming else; whose sermons are apparently generally well received; and whose pastoral work has been most faithful; who in short is, like themselves, a Yankee, should have to leave. It is hard to exaggerate

---

[7] Weis letter to Cornish, April 18, 1933, First Parish files.

how much upset the decent people of the church and community are against the perpetrators of the act.[8]

A letter written by the president of First Parish's Woman's Alliance to the Second Universalist Church in Salem, Massachusetts, where Weis moved on to, is evidence of how much the church was divided over Rev. Weis' dismissal.

> As President of the Alliance of the First Parish Unitarian Church of Scituate, Mass. It gives me great pleasure to tell you how Mr. Weis has endeared himself into the hearts of many in our town. He is truly a cultured Christian gentleman, and we have all be greatly benefited and inspired by his sermons, and Mr. Weis has been a great spiritual help in this community. I cannot speak too highly of him as a sincere Christian leader.
>
> Very cordially yours,
> Sarah I. MacAlpine,
> President, Scituate Alliance

Following his leaving Scituate, Rev. Weis served several other Unitarian churches in New England. By 1947 he left the Unitarian ministry and was ordained to the priesthood of the Episcopal Church on June 4th at St. Thomas' Church, Providence, after which he served Episcopal churches in Rhode Island for many years.

First Parish was once again adrift. It's treasury, never full, was depleted; it's membership divided on the matter of Rev. Weis. The future and the identity of First Parish were uncertain. After Weis left, the leaders of First Parish and the Methodist Church in Scituate met to consider joining the two congregations without any formal contract. The Methodists proposed the arrangement for one year

---

[8] Weis letter, April 18, 1933, First Parish files.

with services held six months in each church. According to Parish Committee minutes, it was perceived that the Methodists' proposal was a means to save their church and would be more or less charity on the part of First Parish. No further mention of this arrangement was noted in the minutes of any subsequent special or annual meeting of the parish.

There was also a mutually respectful relationship with Scituate's First Baptist Church resulting in a number of combined services on special days like Memorial Day or Washington's Birthday. Although an invitation to worship with the "orthodox" (Congregational) church was declined with thanks, it is noteworthy that over a hundred years after the division of First Parish, the old nomenclature still remained. Soon the cool, but respectful relations between the two congregations would improve.

The Rev. Robert Withington, twenty-nine years old, was called to the ministry of First Parish by a vote of a special parish meeting on October 8, 1933. On January 7, 1934, he was installed as minister. Participating in the service were First Parish members, the Revs. Agnes and Alden Cook. Writing years later about coming to Scituate, Rev. Withington recalled meeting Wilmot Brown for the first time and Brown's first words were, "You can come [to Scituate] if you want to. If you don't, we will close up." Still, Rev. Withington came with a promised $1,500 annual salary. Without a parsonage, Rev. Withington and his wife lived with Edith Bonney.

Withington was born in New York City and was orphaned as a child. He came to Cambridge, Massachusetts with a loving guardian, a single woman, Miss Edith Bradford. Withington, in an autobiographical essay, later recalled his experience as a student in a grade school in Cambridge. The principal of the Agassiz School was a "Negress," Miss Maria Baldwin, and "no one ran a finer school than she." Withington wrote that he was "certain that many unrealized lessons I learned from this experience have had a life-long effect upon my race relation feelings and beliefs."[9] But for her race, Withington believed that Miss Baldwin would have been Superintendent of the Cambridge schools. Baldwin organized the first parent-teacher group in Cambridge and she introduced new methods of teaching mathematics. Another of her students was the poet, e.e. cummings, the son of a Boston Unitarian minister. In his book, *Six Nonlectures*, cummings wrote of Baldwin: "Miss Baldwin, the dark lady mentioned in my first nonlecture (and a lady if ever a lady existed) was blessed with a delicious voice, charming manners, and a deep understanding of children. Never did any semidevine dictator more gracefully and easily rule a more unruly and less graceful populace. Her very presence emanated an honour and a glory.... From her I marvellingly learned that the truest power is gentleness."[10] Rev. Withington believed the same.

In 1934, at a community Maundy Thursday service, communion was served at First Parish, overseen by Rev. Mr. Withington. First Trinitarian's minister, the Rev. Karl Bach, preached the sermon. The next day, Rev. Withington participated in the Good Friday service at Harbor Methodist Church. In spite of the harsh exchanges between the First Parish and First Trinitarian churches back at the time of the separation, there were a number of occasions, continuing to the present, of First Parish and First Trinitarian ministers exchanging pulpits or preaching at special services. There were other ecumenical and civic efforts promoted by Rev. Withington. One was an attempt "to raise the standard of motion pictures" shown to children. Churches, parents, and civic organizations like the Garden Club and the Grange, circulated petitions expressing the discomfort many in the community felt about movies that were being shown to children at Saturday matinees at the Satuit Theatre in the harbor and other theaters in the area.

---

[9] Letter to Margaret Cole Bonney, October 25, 1991, First Parish files.
[10] http://www.cpsd.us/BAL/history_baldwin.cfm

Rev. Robert Withington

Mrs. Withington almost immediately upon her arrival began serving as the Superintendent of the Sunday School, and Rev. Withington articulated the objectives of the First Parish Church School in an open letter to all Scituate residents

1. To train children for adaptability in religious thinking. We teach no set creed but encourage them to formulate their own beliefs as they grow to maturity.
2. To study the unfolding of religious beliefs and standards of conduct from ancient to modern times based on the Bible and other religious writings.
3. To stimulate and direct children in the every day practice of the moral ideals at their command. "Conduct should be voluntary to be moral."

4. To encourage reverence for the higher values of life and tolerance for those of different views.

On Sunday, July 15, 1934, a hot but clear day, Tercentenary Sunday was celebrated. The local newspaper, the *Scituate Herald*, described the occasion as a "memorable day" and "a fine spirit prevailed" upon the three-hundredth anniversary celebration of First Parish. The morning service was notable because of the attendance of several guest ministers. The Rev. Alfred J. Wilson of First Parish, Norwell and the Rev. Karl Bach of the Trinitarian Congregational Church participated in the service, their two churches having originated from First Parish. Rev. Withington was the host and preached on the subject, "Our Common Birthright." His sermon asked the congregation to build upon the noble heritage that was theirs. He reminded the worshippers that the history of the church had been one where their "little band had never been great in numbers, strong in wealth, or powerful in influence." "It would have been easier," he said, "to quit, to abandon effort, but successive small groups have ever struggled with the problems of the church.... We must dedicate ourselves anew to make the work of the church more effective and its influence wider. Our birthright is ours to spoil or to increase, the question being what we are going to do with our great gift."

Following the morning service an afternoon pageant was performed at the Colonial Inn near the site of the first and second meetinghouses and the Men of Kent Cemetery. More than three hundred people gathered in the open field just off Meetinghouse Lane. The pageant, written by First Parish member, Rev. Alden S. Cook, portrayed the early days of Scituate and the gathering of the church. A replica of the first meetinghouse with a stockade fence surrounding it gave the scene an added realism. Men, women and children, about thirty-five in all, from both the Unitarian and Trinitarian churches, sitting on plain benches, wore period costumes with the men wearing the familiar Pilgrim hats. A simple pulpit was built for the occasion.[11] Rev. Withington played the role of Rev. John Lothrop, Scituate's first minister. Rev. Bach was "masterful" in leading the people in the old style of "lining out" hymns.[12] What was most compelling for those in attendance was the fact that descendants of some of the original members of the congregation took part in the drama including Massachusetts State Representative Nathaniel Tilden.

Celebrating the 300th *Anniversary of the Founding of First Parish, July 15, 1934*

---

[11] *Christian Register*, September 6, 1934.
[12] First Parish files.

After the pageant, people gathered at First Parish where the Woman's Alliance served supper. Descendants of Humphrey and Lydia Turner, founding members of the church, played the Lawson Tower bells. Representing Barnstable, the town Rev. Lothrop and some members of the Scituate Church founded, were Revs. Anita T. Pickett of the Unitarian Church, and John A. Douglas of the West Parish Church. They offered greetings from First Parish's two other "daughter" churches. Additional greetings from the town of Scituate, from Harvard University and from the American Unitarian Association were conveyed. The Rev. Dr. Adelbert Lathrop Hudson of Dorchester, a descendent of Rev. John Lothrop, read a paper about his ancestor.[13]

Throughout his ministry in Scituate, Rev. Withington had a beneficial relationship with Rev. Bach of the First Trinitarian Congregational Church. The two pastors muted whatever theological battles the two congregations went through a hundred years earlier. Often they exchanged pulpits and spoke before the other church's women's and youth groups. During the summer, union services were hosted by one church in July; the other, in August.

On October 6, 1935 a group of seven women gathered at the Withington home to establish an organization for women who could not attend the daytime Woman's Alliance meetings either because they were employed or had young children. In addition to Kay Withington the other women were Beatrice Forbush, Dorothy Stenbeck, Margaret Cole Bonney, Eleanor Brown, Hilda Harris Stenbeck and Evelyn Merritt. Bea Forbush was elected the first president. The group's purpose was to meet for "sociability and to work for the church." The name Unity Club was chosen at the suggestion of Margaret Cole Bonney. Dues for the monthly gathering were five cents a meeting. When the club was formed the women agreed that when they turned forty, they would drop out of the Unity Club and join the Woman's Alliance, but this plan never worked out, because as Margaret Cole Bonney recalled, "Who would admit to

---

[13] First Parish files.

being forty, and who wanted to give up friends of long standing?" The Unity Club worked together with the Woman's Alliance to help with the latter's money-making projects, as well as working on their own projects to help the church. The Unity Club women served at the Alliance suppers or helped at other Alliance events. Years later, Bonney recalled how preoccupied she was in preparing for an event one Sunday afternoon. There was a rehearsal for a pageant for prospective brides which the Alliance and the Unity Club had organized. As she entered the church, a woman came up to her and said, "Isn't it awful!" Mrs. Bonney didn't understand the significance of the remark until she got home. It was December 7, 1941, the day Japan attacked Pearl Harbor.[14]

When the town of Scituate celebrated the three-hundredth anniversary of its incorporation in 1936, Rev. Withington delivered the sermon at the Union Service which began the weeklong festivities. Joining him were other local clergy: the Revs. Karl Bach of the First Trinitarian Congregational Church, Thomas Quinlin of St. Mary of the Nativity, Alan D. Creelman of First Baptist Church, and Manfred A. Carter of Harbor Methodist Church. In his sermon Withington said that he wanted to

> Think of this week as a celebration of a great faith and our renewal at the fountain of the Faith.... We celebrate a faith which we have as a heritage from the forefathers of our town that there is a virtue in certain values, that to them who will make these virtues theirs, praise shall be theirs. We come to the well of the faith and seek to drink deep of its waters. For as [the apostle] Paul sought those things that were first true, then honorable, just, pure, lovely and of good report, so, to the leaders of that colony which came across the waters these things were worthy of being values around which progress of the more lasting

---

[14] Bonney papers.

nature was built. The more we understand why these men and women left the comforts of England and came to the barren uninviting, rocky shores of New England, we see idealism in its highest form being one of the primary reasons. They were men and women whose beliefs were so important that hardships were bearable.

It is a good thing to remind ourselves today of this idealism. For we are very apt to look with scorn on all idealism today. We are in danger of replacing it with a cynicism and pessimism entirely out of keeping with the spirit symbolic of the history of Scituate and Plymouth County. In the rapidity of change we have witnessed during this 20th century we are losing sight of that which because it is more lasting is not so prominent or easy to achieve. Idealism is without flash or show, but discernible only in the range of time. It deals not with what we wear on our outer coats, but with that which we carry deep within to govern our whole trend of life. In a day where there is so much corruption in high places, so much indifference by the general run of those with whom we live, so much selfishness and the resultant carelessness of the thoughts and feelings of others, idealism has indeed a hard path to travel....

... there are signs everywhere that we are losing interest as a whole in these things [that] were so important to the men of yesteryear. We need a week as awaits us to reach out and awaken us again to some of those things which governed the lives of these men we would honor.

They believed in life. They believed earnestly that there were some things which they called virtues. They believed that though truth might change its cloak, whatsoever was true was worth discovering. That which they conceived to be true may have today been replaced or even proven by time to be other than truth. This fact does not permit us today to neglect our concept of Truth, to deny that the search for Truth is still a virtue.

Just as one generation succeeds another so Truth, Justice, Purity, Honor have their offspring in each age which carry to higher levels the usefulness of these virtues. Unless we discover their modern uses, they will vanish. [15]

The following year, in June 1937, Rev. Withington preached at the Baccalaureate Service for the graduating class of Scituate High School. The service was held at First Parish and the title of his talk was, "Whither Bound?" Before a large gathering and assisted by Revs. Alan Creelman of the Baptist Church and Rev. Manfred Carter of the Methodist Church, Rev. Withington called the attention of the senior class to the world that lay before them. There would be the need for more trained and skilled workers because of the technological advances being made. He spoke of the grave international political situation and urged the young people "to support every peace-making movement to the utmost." He urged the students "to use reason instead of passion and emotion" to solve the world's problems and he called upon the graduates to become an active part in the religious life of the nation. There was work ahead, he said, to help restore religion to the place it once held in the community. Ending his sermon, Rev. Withington said,

To such a world I bid you welcome, and Godspeed on your way. It may not be the best kind of a world.... But all the more credit to you, all the more honor to you, if through wisdom and reason and strength and service you make of this world a better

---

[15] *Scituate Herald*, September 4, 1936.

place than it now is, so that in later years as you welcome the next generation you can give them the kind of a world you wish for yourselves today. It is a world which will test your capacities, will prove your intelligence, will honor your resourcefulness. We join hands with you as you go forth with us to win where we have failed, to achieve what has thus far escaped our grasp. I charge you to so live and work and think that this world will be a better place because you were here, that men may be more kindly affectionate one to other because they have known you and that each of you may have a feeling of worth and value in all you do. Into this world take a high faith and an unquenchable courage and with these you can sweep away the dark clouds which hover over us.[16]

A few days after the Baccalaureate Service a special church meeting was held, with nineteen present, to deal with a delicate situation. In his four years in Scituate Withington built up the congregation and increased activity in the church school. The atmosphere in the church was more positive than it had been in the years before Withington's ministry, but he was discreetly, he thought, looking for another church. A resolution had been passed at the Parish Committee meeting held two weeks earlier which read,

> At a meeting of the Parish Committee on June 6 it was resolved that in their opinion, our minister, Mr. Withington, due to his action in candidating for a new position, has neglected the welfare of his church and therefore the committee recommend[s] to the Parish that a special Parish meeting be called prior to July 1 to consider the desirability for a change in our pastorate, and also to consider the financial condition of the church.

---

[16] "Good Advice for Scituate Seniors," First Parish files.

The Parish Committee was instructed to meet with Rev. Withington to express the "dissatisfaction" of some members of the parish regarding his actions in candidating and his neglect of church duties. It was also voted that Rev. Withington be instructed to occupy the pulpit every Sunday during July providing " he is still our minister." Rev. Withington tendered his resignation July 1, 1937, to be effective not later than September 1, in order for him to accept a call to the First Parish Church in Hudson, Massachusetts.

Despite what must have been hard feelings all around, Margaret Cole Bonney, the clerk of the church, wrote the following letter to the departed pastor

My dear Mr. Withington:

It is with deep regret that the Parish accepts your resignation. We feel very grateful that we have had as many years of your very fine leadership. We know your vacancy will be very hard to fill and we shall miss tremendously those excellent sermons to which you accustomed us.

We wish you to take with you to your new position the sincere good wishes of all the Parish and hope that you may find it convenient to visit us any time.

We wish you to express to Mrs. Withington our thanks for her generous co-operation in our many activities and convey to her our good wishes for a happy future.

Even though the church and Rev. Withington did not part on the best of terms, the affection for him was apparently strong. This was affirmed when he was invited back to Scituate to participate in the installation of his successor.

Soon after Rev. Withington's resignation, George F. Patterson of the AUA's Department of Ministry, wrote to Mr. Fred Waterman of First Parish with a recommendation for a new minister, the Rev. Clara Cook Helvie, most recently the minister of the Unitarian church in Middleborough, Massachusetts. Patterson noted that "she is a good preacher, an indefatigable parish worker, and I think will give a good account of herself wherever she may be called. I realize that there is some prejudice against a woman minister but I hope you will give Mrs. Helvie a hearing." Apparently Mr. Waterman did offer Rev. Helvie and another female minister invitations to preach in Scituate but he soon withdrew the invitations telling Dr. Patterson that though he was willing to give the women a hearing, the pulpit committee felt the church "must" have a man. In a letter to Mr. Waterman, dated September 27, 1937, Rev. Helvie did not hide her feelings about the dis-invitation.

> I cannot refrain from saying that my idealism has received a shock. As I inferred in my first letter to you, I have in the past cherished a sentimental regard for the Scituate Church and it hurt to receive from it the most discourteous treatment accorded by any Unitarian Church. It would have done no harm to let me preach one Sunday, after the invitation had been tendered, instead of closing the door of the church to me.

Paying Rev. Helvie's rebuke little mind, a special meeting of First Parish unanimously called Lewis Welton Sanford to be the new minister on December 19, 1937. He began his ministry the following Sunday and his installation was held on March 23, 1938. It was, according to church records, a "very impressive and inspiring ceremony," attended by AUA President Samuel May Elliot who gave the sermon. According to a newspaper report of Sanford's selection, "The parish feels that it is very fortunate in securing the services of

Mr. Sanford, and believed that under his guidance the church will go on to new life and activity."[17] Alas, this was not to be.

Born in Nova Scotia, Rev. Sanford was fifty-nine when called to Scituate. He was raised a Baptist but after serving two Baptist churches in Vermont he entered into the Unitarian fellowship. His obituary described him as one who "aroused the warm loyalty of his parishioners by his own friendly and helpful service to them." Henry Wilder Foote of the Harvard Divinity School also described him as having a "gentle, rather dreamy spirit." During the First World War Sanford served as an Army chaplain and later worked in the same capacity for the Civilian Conservation Corps (CCC) immediately prior to coming to Scituate. He came to First Parish directly from Eastport, Maine for a salary of $1,350. Prior to Eastport he served the Marshfield Hills, Massachusetts church in the mid-1920s, so he was familiar with Scituate.

Since 1737 the three church buildings of First Parish had been located in Scituate Center. With Lawson Tower, Scituate High School and the Town Hall all within a few hundred yards of each other it truly was the town center. This lead to a problem that still exists today. The location resulted in people parking their cars on the church lawn for public events. In the 1930s it got so bad that the chief of police was asked halt the practice. Even the Scituate Band had their bandstand on church property.[18]

In September 1938 Scituate was struck by what is known as the Great New England Hurricane. Most of the coastal damage was from storm surge and wind. The Blue Hills Observatory in Milton, Massachusetts recorded wind gusts over 180 miles an hour. Thousands of coastal homes were damaged or destroyed with six hundred people killed in New England. In Scituate, First Parish's steeple was not damaged, however the weathervane was blown away and the front and side doors of the church were wrenched from their

---

[17] *Marshfield Mail*, December 24, 1937.
[18] Parish Committee Minutes, First Parish files.

hinges. Church members managed to scrape some money together to make the repairs.

On December 24, 1939, there was peace at home, if not in Europe or Asia, as First Parish held its Christmas Pageant and Candlelight service. The pageant had five acts and the cast included the minister's daughter; Jean Cole (later, Strzelecki) as Mary and Elizabeth Damon (later, Libby Burbank) as one of the archangels.

The financial picture at First Parish was as bleak as it had been at any time during the past ten years. Collections had fallen off considerably. What should have been an average of six dollars collected each Sunday had, during the winter, dropped to as low as seventy-five cents. The Alliance cut their pledge and the Men's and Unity Clubs couldn't make any pledge at all. The Parish Committee discussed selling the Hammond Tomb lot to raise funds with $500 considered a reasonable sale price. By March 1939 the Parish Committee was asking the janitor, organist and violinist if they would agree to a twenty-five percent pay cut. As for Rev. Sanford's salary, the AUA helped with a one hundred dollar contribution. In April 1940 Rev. Sanford asked for two months vacation in order for him to increase his income by renting out his house, so the annual meeting voted to close the church in July and August thus avoiding the cost of guest preachers. The Parish Committee asked the AUA for some relief from a loan payment by reducing it from seventy-five dollars to fifty dollars a year. The AUA agreed to this but only if the church was unable to pay the full amount at the time the payment was due. Attendance at the church was dropping and it was thought that resuming bus service from the harbor and the West End was needed to encourage more people to come to church but the bus service was suspended after two months service in January 1941 due to lack of funds.

In 1941 Rev. Sanford informed the AUA's Department of Ministry that he wanted to leave Scituate to serve the New North Church in Hingham because the salary was higher. Nothing came of that, but clearly Sanford's mind was no longer focused on the

Scituate parish and it showed. By the annual meeting in April 1942 there was such growing dissatisfaction with church affairs that the Parish Committee agreed to bring the matters before the annual meeting for discussion. At the meeting Rev. Sanford gave his report orally and he announced his intention to resign effective August 1, 1942. He then abruptly left the meeting after handing the president of the Parish his formal resignation letter. A motion that the Parish not accept Rev. Sanford's resignation was made and the vote was fourteen not to accept the resignation; ten in favor of accepting; and three blank ballots. It was also voted to give Rev. Sanford the month of July as vacation and that the church close during that month. The tenor and substance of the meeting distressed many and church records state that "the general feeling seemed to be that we should still make every effort to keep the Church open at all costs and that every one, no matter what his personal feeling[s] were, would put them aside and work only for the Church." However, at a special June meeting with twenty-two members present it was voted, unanimously, to accept Rev. Sanfords's resignation, effective September 1. Wilmot Brown also offered his resignation as treasurer but it was not accepted by a unanimous vote of the meeting. Indeed, the meeting expressed its thanks and gratitude to Mr. Brown for his "splendid work and untiring interest." No such expression was given to Rev. Sanford.

A few days before Rev. Sanford left the Scituate parish, Wilmot Brown met with George Davis of the AUA in Boston. They discussed the ministerial situation and the prospects of getting a new pastor. Davis characterized the parish's hope of getting a new minister in the fall as "very slim" because of how little remuneration First Parish offered a minister. In the meantime several names were suggested for "guest preaching," including Cornelis Heijn, Scituate's former minister, who at the time, was summering in Scituate. In a memo to Dan Fenn, the Director of Ministry, Davis summarized his meeting with Wilmot Brown and reported Brown saying that since Heijn's ministry Scituate had "extremely unfortunate experiences and poor ministerial leadership." Rev. Weis came to a large congregation but it had dwindled down to such a point that the congregation

375

"almost vanished." Rev. Withington had revived the congregation but as a minister Brown described him as "still a kid" (he was twenty-nine when called to Scituate) and "gave the appearance of taking nothing seriously." Still, the attendance at that time was good and the Church School had a large enrollment. But, as of August 1942, Sunday attendance was down to nine and the Church School had a reduced enrollment of thirty. As for Rev. Sanford, Mr. Brown had a harsh assessment. According to him, Rev. Sanford showed little interest in the work of the parish. When asked if he was interested in improving the financial situation of the church, Rev. Sanford had told Mr. Brown that he wasn't interested because the situation was hopeless. According to Brown, as conveyed by Davis, Sanford told him that he had accepted the call to come to Scituate only "because he could find nothing better and did not expect to stay there any longer than he had to." Describing the three hundred year-old congregation, Davis wrote that the church had one hundred voting members with a constituency (adding children and friends of the church) of nearly two hundred. He noted that the church building was well kept and in good condition. The pew cushions and pulpit furniture had been re-upholstered in a green fabric and a velvet reredos was placed behind the pulpit, funded by donations and gifts. There was no parsonage though a member had been renting a home to the minister for twenty dollars a month. The annual income from the endowment was just under $450. The minister had been paid $1,440 a year, which from a budget of $2,400 left little anything else. Brown said that a new minister could get a much larger salary but he would have to "earn" it. Finally, Davis made the observation that at the present time, the town of Scituate was "over churched." There were five churches in a town of four thousand people. While Catholics had long lived in Scituate, the parish of St. Mary of the Nativity, was created in 1921 and soon became the largest congregation in town; First Baptist was the most populous of the Protestant churches, including First Parish The tone of Wilmot Brown's assessment of First Parish over the previous twenty years makes him the likely unnamed subject of Rev. Weis' unflattering comments about who was responsible for instigating his removal.[19]

Interim minister, Rev. Walter Reid Hunt, who also served as Field Secretary at the AUA, came to Scituate in the fall of 1942 and reported to the congregation at its annual meeting in April 1943 that he was disappointed he was not able to build up church attendance and finances during his time in Scituate. The minutes note that "he assured us that we must man the church as well as the boys are manning the guns." The congregation wanted to hear prospective ministerial candidates and Rena Cole volunteered to meet with Dan Fenn in Boston to inquire about available ministers. Invited to Scituate by Mrs. Cole, Fenn, head of the AUA's Department of Ministry, gave advice to the congregation at a special meeting in September 1942 about how to search for a minister and offered the names of some who were available, some fresh from seminary and others who had a good deal of experience.

One of the names offered by Rev. Fenn was the Rev. Alfred Schenkman. When asked, Rev. Schenkman accepted the offer from First Parish to be its minister. Schenkman began on September 1, 1943 and was ordained in Scituate in October 13th. Schenkman was born in New Jersey in 1919. He was home schooled, first by his parents and after they both died, his older brother took on the responsibility. His formal education began when he entered Rutgers University, where he graduated with a Bachelor of Science degree in biology. He received a Master of Science degree in zoology and public health from the University of Minnesota. While in Minnesota, he attended the First Unitarian Society in Minneapolis and decided to enter the Unitarian ministry. In 1943 he was granted a Bachelor of Divinity degree from the University of Chicago Divinity School. Scituate was his first and only parish.

---

[19] George G. Davis memo to Dan H. Fenn, August 25, 1942 in Sanford file at Andover-Harvard Library.

In commenting on Mr. Schenkman's qualifications as a minister, several references gave mixed opinions. His minister in Minneapolis, Rev. Raymond Bragg, wrote that Schenkman was "of a high order of intelligence.... [H]e has about him a certain quality of irresponsibility. This is both attractive and mildly alarming. He presses his own views with ardor but certainly without dogma. He is sincere and a man of good character. "[20] His professor of zoology at Rutgers described Schenkman as having "great zeal," and being "self-assertive;" not likely to listen to differing opinions, yet he had "many lovable qualities."

One of Rev. Schenkman's great contributions to First Parish and Scituate's civic life was his establishing the South Shore Community Forum in 1944 which brought prominent speakers to town to discuss a variety of subjects, including anti-fascism, race relations and what a post-war world would look like. He recruited speakers from Harvard, MIT and the American Civil Liberties Union. One speaker was the economist, educator, writer, political activist and purported communist, Scott Nearing. Scituate police were stationed on First Parish Road to note who was going into the church to hear Nearing speak.

Unlike his predecessor Rev. Sanford, Rev. Schenkman took the lead in the church's budgeting and fundraising. The results of the all-member canvass were noticeably encouraging, though the April 1944 annual meeting voted to close the church following the last Sunday in June and to reopen the Sunday after Labor Day. In an experiment to see if attendance would increase, a different worship time, in the evening, was voted. Three weeks later the vote was rescinded. During the winter of 1943-44 there was concern about the cost of fuel. In the midst of the war effort the church, like everyone else, had to get its fuel by ration. There was a stove in the building; both coal and wood were used. There was also a discussion about moving the services into the Old Sloop Room to save fuel but the idea was rejected. In addition to fuel rationing, another part of the

---

[20] Bragg letter, First Parish files.

war effort was price controls and it affected even the First Parish women's groups. The Office of Price Administration (OPA), created

Rev. Alfred Schenkman

to control prices during the war, approved the 1943 summer sale run by the Alliance and Unity Club even though prices of the items could not exceed the OPA's limit.

The First Parish Bond of Union, revised over the years, once again evolved during the Schenkman ministry. Reflecting the growing influence of humanism in Unitarian churches, the Bond was rephrased so that there was no mention of a divinity at all and it emphasized that one's highest calling was service to humanity.

> We join together, pledging ourselves to help one another in all good things. Our union is based upon no creedal test. We welcome all who wish to establish Truth and Righteousness and Love in the World. Human service is our aim in religion. We are the children of the mysterious and challenging universe, in which we live and move and have our being. But in the face of this eternal mystery we recognize and would affirm that our highest religious duty is to love and serve all mankind.

In January 1945, Mr. Schenkman informed the Parish Committee of his intention to enter the United States Army as a chaplain, perhaps as early as the following month. The War Department gave the congregation an award in recognition of Rev. Schenkman serving as a chaplain. It was framed and hung in the foyer of the church for many years. After his discharge as army chaplain Schenkman left the ministry to teach chemistry at the University of Illinois. He later returned to the Boston area and started a book publishing company in Cambridge.

Rev. Schenkman was the first to produce the church's weekly newsletter. Schenkman did the writing, editing and the printing on a mimeograph machine. When he left Scituate the task was taken over by the Unity Club. A contest was held to name the publication and the winner was "Our Church and Yours." In the winter the newsletter was produced at the home of Wilmot Brown because the church's heating system was rarely adequate. In the summer the newsletter was frequently published at Starr Island, where a boat would bring it to Portsmouth, New Hampshire for mailing. Members of the Unity Club, particularly Fran Ahern, Dorothy Brown Wood and Jeannette Muller did the work. The Unity Club paid all the costs of the newsletter, but the club later gave up responsibility for the newsletter; and the name, "Our Church and Yours," was dropped.

Schenkman also added to the church's letterhead the words "The Liberal Church, Unitarian."

One of Rev. Schenkman's suggestions for his replacement was the Rev. Raymond Johnson, minister of the First Parish in Hingham (Old Ship Church.) A message was sent to Rev. Johnson who said he would be "happy" to split his time with the Hingham church and serve Scituate once Rev. Schenkman left.[21] A special Parish meeting was held and a call to Rev. Johnson was voted, as was a change in the worship time from 11:00 am to 4:00 pm to accommodate Rev. Johnson's duties at First Parish in Hingham.

The end of the World War II was noted with a service on August 15, 1945.

---

[21] Parish Committee Meeting Minutes, First Parish files.

C. C. PRATT
PHOTO BY BACHRACH

HENRY J. CADBURY
PHOTO BY BACHRACH

ALVIN H. HANSEN
PHOTO BY BACHRACH

F. O. MATTHIESSEN

South Shore Community Forum

The Lectures and Discussions to be held at the First Parish Church in Scituate
every Tuesday Evening, January 4 to May 30, 1944, at 7:45 P. M.

		Current Events	Anti-Facist Weapons	Crisis In Minority-Group Relations	Post-War World
Jan. 4	Karl W. Deutsch, **Instructor in History, Massachusetts Institute of Technology.**	*			
11	Zechariah Chafee, Jr., **Langdell Professor of Law, Harvard, and Syndic of the University Press.**				"International Utopias"
18	J. L. McCorison, Jr., **Regional Director, The National Conference of Christians and Jews.**			"America's Biggest Battle"	
25	Hans F. Abraham, **formerly of the Court of Appeals, Berlin; Research Associate, Harvard; Lecturer at Boston University.**		Ideas		
Feb. 1	Dirk Struik, **Professor of Mathematics, Massachusetts Institute of Technology.**		Science		
8	Karl Deutsch	*			
15	Stephen H. Fritchman, **Editor, the Christian Register; Executive Director, American Unitarian Youth.**			"Anti-Semitism"	"World War, and World After War"
22	Scott Nearing, **Noted Economist and Lecturer.**				
29	Roger F. Clapp, **Relocation Officer in Boston, The War Relocation Authority.**			Americans of Japanese Ancestry	
Mar. 7	Sidney S. Grant, **Legislative Agent, The Congress of Industrial Organizations.**		Labor		
14	John S. R. Bourne, **Boston Attorney; Member, The Executive Committee, Civil Liberties Union.**			The Negro Problem	
21	E. Merrick Dodd, **Professor of Law, Harvard; Member, Executive Committee, C. L. U. of Massachusetts.**				"Our Peace Aims In the Pacific"
28	F. O. Matthiessen, **Professor of History and Literature and Tutor in History and Literature, Harvard.**		Literature		
Apr. 4	Karl Deutsch	*			
11	Henry J. Cadbury, **Hollis Professor of Divinity, Harvard, and Director of the Andover Theological Library.**			"The Problems of the Pacifist"	
18	Kirtley F. Mather, **Chairman of the Department of Geology, Harvard, and Dean of the Summer School.**		Civil Liberties		
25	Albert E. Navez, **Belgian Consul in Boston.**				"Western Europe In Post-War Period"
	C. C. Pratt, **Chairman of the Department of Psychology, Rutgers University; Personnel Director 1943-4, Harvard.** {				
May 2	Alfred Schenkman, **Director of the South Shore Community Forum, and Minister of the First Parish Church (Unitarian) in Scituate.**		Education		
9	Clarence R. Skinner, **Dean, the Tufts College School of Religion.**			"Putting an End to Prejudice"	
16	Alvin H. Hansen, **Lucius N. Littauer Professor of Political Economy, Harvard.**				"What We Will Face After the War"
23	To be arranged.		Religion		
30	Karl Deutsch	*			

*On each of these dates Dr. Deutsch will give
a talk on Current Events

*Schedule for the 1944 South Shore Community Forum established by Rev.
Schenkman*

382

Chapter Sixteen

" A better place of fellowship and learning for children of all ages "

Rev. Raymond B. Johnson was in the pulpit the Sunday after Rev. Schenkman's last service. He did his best to galvanize First Parish even though he split his time with the Hingham church. He earned a salary of $30 a Sunday while the church was open and his work in such difficult times was very much appreciated by the congregation. Because of Rev. Johnson's schedule, the Scituate Parish Committee decided that services would be held at four o'clock in the afternoon. Sunday School was held at its usual time in the morning making Sunday a full church day. In the fall of 1946 First Parish, along with the Congregationalist and Methodist churches, shared the cost of renting a school bus to collect children for their respective Sunday schools. Another ecumenical activity of the Scituate Protestant churches was the annual united service on Memorial Day. That May, Rev. Johnson could not participate due to his duties at First Parish, Hingham, so instead of canceling the Sunday afternoon service, First Parish worshipped that morning with the Methodists at their church.

The years immediately following the World War II were difficult for First Parish. Finances were once again in bad shape. The furnace needed repair and a special call went out to members. One member gave fifty dollars with the proviso that at least ten members give five dollars towards the furnace fund. Money that had been put aside for Star Island trips was diverted into a furnace fund. The church soloist donated her services. A member who won fifty dollars in a raffle at the summer fair turned it back to the church. The church had lost members, with some going to the Methodist Church,[1] but during Rev. Johnson's ministry the situation stabilized and slowly improved.

Social gatherings were a vibrant feature of church life, even in the darkest times. When the church had no minister or when there were no Sunday services, the strong sense of community helped the congregation survive. Better times were now ahead. In the post-war era, the church grew and so did the number of parish suppers. The annual Summer Fair Supper, in June, served hot turkey dinners to as many as 350 people. The Fall Harvest Supper, first held in 1896, was revived. Vegetables grown in parishioners' gardens were auctioned off after dinner. Attendees were also invited to guess the weight of a large pumpkin for a cash prize. In April, the Annual Meeting Supper, which often featured a simple meal of chowder (at no cost), was an enticement for people to participate in the governance of the church. The men again put on an Easter Breakfast, a tradition going back to the 1920s. The breakfast was so renowned it was written up in the *Boston Globe* and the *Boston Herald*. The Church School Suppers provided occasions for the children of the church to bring a parent as their guest. Suppers for adults were so well attended that tables and chairs had to be placed upstairs for the overflow. In 1954 over 150 people came to the dinner. (In the early 1970s, the minister, Rev. John Fuller, suggested a monthly supper that became the "Third Saturday Suppers." That dinner, like the others, was for fun and fellowship. It started out small with eighteen people attending the first year and as many people as seventy came at subsequent suppers.

---

[1] Parish Committee Meeting Minutes, First Parish files.

Rev. Raymond B. Johnson

In early 1947 the Parish Committee voted to present to the Scituate Historical Society the bass viol made by brothers Asa and Shadrach Merritt in 1823. This presents a mystery because church folklore has it that someone in the church in the early 1950s found the bass viol deposited at the town dump, rescued it and it has been displayed in the church ever since in a case crafted by a local artisan for the Woman's Alliance. It is possible that the Historical Society declined the church's offer or, at some point, they decided to dispose of the bass.

The Alliance, always generous to the church, was particularly so in the months following the end of the war. With thirty-eight members, the Alliance gave fifteen dollars a month to the church treasury for expenses. It bought new hymnals along with the Unity Club; gave money for the church Christmas party and it paid for the resurfacing of the driveway. The Unity Club also supplied flowers for the church on Sundays and sponsored the Halloween and Valentine parties for the Sunday School, which, during the 1945-1946 school year, had an enrollment of eighteen. By February 1949 attendance at Sunday morning services was improving which provided "excellent morale building for the old faithful and the minister."[2] From 1947 through the annual meeting of 1948 the church gained twenty-six members. The national post-war spiritual renewal was underway.

Many years had passed since the church owned or provided a parsonage for the minister, not since the time of Rev. Thomas. From the experience of both the congregation and its ministers it was clear that a parsonage would help make the Scituate pulpit more attractive in securing the services of a minister who would stay at First Parish for more than three years, which was the average length of a ministry for the first half of the twentieth century. In December 1947, after years of discussion, postponement and abandonment of the idea, the congregation voted unanimously, upon the recommendations of the Parish Committee, the Pulpit Supply Committee, the Board of Trustees, and the AUA, to raise funds for the purpose of building a parsonage. The argument made more than once at the meeting was that it was futile to look for a "permanent" minister until a parsonage was built.[3] When the parsonage and the new parking lot were finished it was obvious that something needed to be done about grounds in front of the church. It was actually a hay field, a "rough" one at that. It took many truckloads of loam to prepare the new lawn which ran in front of the church and parsonage and around to the back where the old sheds were. The strip of land on the east side of the church between the parking area and the Cole house was also landscaped.[4]

Following Rev. Johnson's departure in 1948 someone suggested that the congregation ask First Parish, Norwell if it was willing to share its new minister, Rev. Herman Geertz. In the end, though, the church chose to call e Rev. Leon Converse Fay. Other

---

[2] Parish Committee Meeting Minutes, First Parish files
[3] First Parish files
[4] First Parish files

ministers had been candidates, but Fay was selected, in part, because of the recommendation by Rev. Johnson. At the time, a sitting minister could recommend his successor. Today, the Unitarian Universalist Ministers Association's code of conduct prohibits a minister from being involved in the selection of another minister.

Quincy Patriot Ledger, Wednesday, August 11, 1948

A NEW PARSONAGE for the First Parish church rises in the shadow of the familiar Lawson tower in Scituate Center. The parsonage, one of the many new buildings under construction in the Scituate area, is not apt to be a victim of any further increases in labor costs since the parishioners themselves are doing most of the labor involved. (Ghiorse photo)

The New Parsonage, 1948

Rev. Fay began his ministry December 1, 1948, starting with a salary of $3,000. He was offered the free use of the new parsonage, which he accepted, and he thus became the first minister in one hundred and fifty years to live in the church's parsonage. His first service was December 5, 1948 when church services returned to Sunday morning. Another immediate change was that the Parish Committee started meeting regularly at the church rather than in committee members' homes, as had been the practice for many years.

The First Parish women's groups continued to be a source of strength and commitment. In 1949 the First Parish Wayside Pulpit was re-built with money donated by the Alliance. Floodlights illuminated the Wayside Pulpit facing First Parish Road and electrical outlets at its base provided power for the church's summer fairs. As the First Parish Unity Club grew it also was able to purchase many items for the church. For most of the early years, the Unity Club met in the homes of its members. As it described itself, the group was not meant to be a "serious or intellectual group" but rather it was a few women who worked on church projects and had fun together. A minister's wife once tried to "reform" the group by scheduling speakers at formal programs, but the group preferred its "own brand of informality and good fellowship."[5]

At the April 1950 annual meeting, Rev. Fay gave a cautiously optimistic report saying that the church was slowly being "re-established." Still, he offered his fear that the church would "slacken" and "begin to mark time." On the positive side, Rev. Fay cited his effort to build a sense of "churchmanship" which he described as a personal loyalty one feels towards their church, "an individual concern for the welfare of the church as a whole, a desire to be of service in some phase of the church work, and a daily life in keeping with the religious idealism of the church both in and away from it." Keeping that in mind Rev. Fay believed First Parish should not have any concerns about the stability and growth of the church. Acknowledging the challenges of a liberal church in post-war America, Fay told the congregation, "[The liberal church's] ideals of a reasonableness in religion, an honest pursuit of truth, its spirit of freedom and its demands of making religion actually operative in daily life are not of the interest or even within the reach of everyone in the community. Yet it is the very pursuit of these ideals, the adventure of truth-seeking, the joy of freedom and the broad interests afforded through the use of our minds in our religion that make our liberal fellowship perhaps the happiest, most zestful, active

---

[5] Bonney papers.

388

and alive of any church in the community, and perhaps the warmest in its friendships and comradeship."

Rev. Leon C. Fay

With Fay's guidance the congregation crafted an addition to the church by-laws that expressed a new-found purpose which was "the maintenance of a place of worship, freely open to all residents and visitors of Scituate who desire to attend religious services; and open as a meetinghouse for promoting public welfare through civic, social, educational and philanthropic activities." This new purpose and vision began to produce dividends. At the 1951 annual meeting Rev. Fay reported the good news that since the building of the parsonage and the calling of a full-time minister the congregation had added thirty-plus new members and the church school enrollment was about seventy-five. The operating budget had doubled, reflecting the church's growth.

First Parish celebrated Arbor Day in 1951 with a special service. The congregation gathered around recently planted trees, flowers and shrubs given to the church in memory of former members and other loved ones, and were appropriately dedicated and accepted by the church. The *Quincy Patriot Ledger* reported the following words spoken at the service, "Our descendants will take pleasure and interest in our present efforts to beautify and perpetuate the original pioneer work."[6]

With First Parish enjoying growth, it came as a surprise when Rev. Fay submitted his resignation in December 1951 in order to accept a call to the Nashua, New Hampshire Unitarian church. First Parish agreed to the resignation with great regret.

Rev. Henry George Cooper soon became First Parish's next minister. Cooper was born in Detroit on June 26, 1919, the youngest of seven children. He began his Scituate ministry on April 1, 1952, after serving the Littleton, New Hampshire Unitarian Church; and, he was formally installed on May 27th. Participating in the service was the Rev. John C. Fuller, then of All Souls Church in New London, Connecticut, who would later become minister in Scituate. In an obituary written by the Rev. Carl Scovel, Cooper was described as a pacifist who, during World War II, volunteered for the American Friends (Quaker) Service Committee driving ambulances in North Africa until September 1943 when he became a medic. After the war, he got a degree in mental health and counseling at the University of Michigan. He then entered Meadville-Lombard Theological School in Chicago.

At an eventful April 1952 annual meeting the parish discussed whether the church should sell its rights to the old cemetery (the Men of Kent Cemetery) to the town for one dollar and so it was voted. The meeting also voted to name the room outside the sanctuary "The Old Sloop Room," in memory of the fire-destroyed church that had been known by that name. In another decision, the congregation

---

[6] *Quincy Patriot Ledger, May 1951.*

390

voted to restore the old bass viol crafted by the Merritt brothers and, if church folklore is accurate, recently rescued from the town dump. The old carriage sheds, seen in the painting of the Old Sloop Church and built in 1774, had once again fallen victim to the ravages of time. Several years earlier all but one of the carriage and horse stalls and two storage rooms were torn down and the remaining shed was used as a garage for the minister's car. Because of sentimental reasons and budget considerations it was decided not to totally dismantle and rebuild the sheds but rather to refurbish the existing sheds and storage rooms. The meeting further voted to repair the church steeple and while that was being done, the church was given, through the generosity of the parishioners, a new weathervane to replace the one blown away in the Great New England Hurricane of 1938. It was made in the shape of a sloop in full sail and fashioned of stainless steel at the Fore River Shipyard in Quincy, Massachusetts. It, too, became the victim of a hurricane, Carol, in 1954. Though not blown away like its predecessors, it was badly damaged and after another storm in 1961 it listed in the wind for several years.[7]

Rev. Henry George Cooper

---

[7] Bonney papers.

The early and mid-1950s continued a period of growth and confidence at First Parish. To build on that confidence the congregation gave its approval to a master plan which set far-reaching goals: raising money by way of pledges and gifts for operating expenses; the completion of the building plan (begun in 1954); developing a comprehensive building maintenance plan; substantially increasing committee budgets; increasing the salary and allowances for the minister; including line items in the budget for denominational affairs; eliminating the fees for church organizations to use the church for social or other purposes; hiring a church secretary; and expanding the church's service to its children and young people. As part of the Master Plan, a building fund, with a goal to raise $30,000 was created for the construction of an expanded Church School area; to build a separate entrance to the Church School; to have a peaked, rather than a flat roof over the wing built in the 1930s; to redecorate the sanctuary and kitchen; and, to install a new heating system. Specifically, the plan called for the extension of the north wall of the wing (toward Central High School) by approximately ten feet, adding a room opposite the kitchen and an enclosed stairway between the first and second stories, completing a second story over the north wing which would contain five classrooms and the installation of a new general heating system providing heat to the auditorium, foyer and all rooms on the second floor of the building. Funds raised in excess of the cost of this plan went to painting the auditorium, new appliances for the kitchen, and the replacement of the supporting beams of the sanctuary. The church secured a loan from the AUA of $18,400 with half the amount interest free; the Rockland Trust Bank also lent money.

However, three years later, in 1957, the church was again at a financial crossroad. According to a pamphlet printed to announce another special three-year fund-raising drive, the church was faced with "an unrealistic budget, insufficient pledges to meet actual church needs, [and a] heavy proportion of 'token giving....'" The new goal was to raise $45,000 for another three-year period. Within six months, in the face of rapid growth in membership, almost $37,000 was pledged providing confidence that the remainder could be raised by a further increase in membership, pledges and Sunday collections. The average weekly pledge for this campaign was two dollars and twenty-seven cents. The fundraising committee appreciated the understanding and cooperation they received from practically everyone contacted during the capital campaign and many people expressed the attitude that the "frank and business-like approach" to the church's real needs "stirred their enthusiasm" which inspired them to significantly increase their pledges. In response, the fundraising committee made clear to the other committees of the church of their responsibility to meet the expectations of the members of the church. The committee took pride in the fact that for the building campaign of three years earlier the church paid a fee of $3,700 to a professional fundraiser in order to raise $32,500, while this committee spent less that $100 and raised pledges amounting to $36,800.

First Parish Church School in the 1950s

The Religious Education program was adapting itself to the explosive growth in enrollment. In September 1952 the Church School had eighty-two children enrolled and twenty-eight staff volunteers. Children had one hour of class work, fifteen minutes of worship, and an hour and fifteen minutes of "creative activities." The 1953-1954 First Parish religious education prospectus stated that liberal religious education at First Parish was "founded on the belief that beginning with the common experiences of every day is the natural way to lead a little child religiously. The ability to know the intangible, invisible and persuasive reality that adults call God comes slowly, but come it will when children are guided to live richly with the common experiences of every day." The school had the following objectives:

- To provide a liberal religious education for the children of religious liberals.
- To accentuate the experiences that have religious significance.
- To link nature with the universe and the natural belief in a universal God.
- To awaken wonder, curiosity and appreciation for things of the Spirit.
- To provide an intelligent, sympathetic, tolerant appreciation and evaluation of the world's great religions and the need of religion for all men.
- To provide an understanding of the Faith of our neighboring Christian Churches and to provide a knowledge of the historical development of Unitarianism.
- To forge the tools to enable our young people to evaluate their own personal religion – their own collection of attitudes – their own habit of thinking within their religion, or growing with it.

Absenteeism in Church School was taken very seriously. Rev. Cooper suggested that a child who had several unexcused absences be dropped from the rolls. The Religious Education Committee agreed that spotty attendance caused the resentment of other classmates and, most importantly, the absent child gained nothing worthwhile. The committee agreed that before a child was removed from Church School the superintendent and teacher would talk with the child's parents. However, classroom learning was not the only activity in the Church School during those years. Other events included a family Thanksgiving Service, a Church School banquet with teachers, an Arbor Day Family Service and Boy Scout and Girl Scout Sundays.

It was a First Parish tradition for many years to open the annual meeting with a hymn and a prayer offered by the minister. Afterward the officers would give their reports and then the various committees would give theirs. In his first annual report at the April 1953 meeting, Rev. Cooper told the congregation that progress had been made the previous year. A sign of the good times was that services were held all year. There was no summer closing and parishioners conducted the services in July and August. There was also an active adult education program and during Lent that year there was a study of the Gospel of Mark. Since April 1952 the church had gained eighteen new members and had four communion services, though they were not held on Sunday mornings.

In 1954 a new Constitution and By-laws were adopted. In an attempt to govern the church more effectively and efficiently there was a change to semi-annual meetings, with one in March, the other in October. Under this new form of governance the chairs of the standing committees became members of the governing Parish Committee, improving communication since all chairs were notified at a single meeting of actions each committee needed to take to better coordinate various Church functions. In what would be described in present day terms as "micromanaging," both the Parish Committee and the Annual Meetings often voted on many mundane issues, even regulating the temperature level in the church building. The 1954 annual meeting voted, "To provide greater comfort and convenience for people using the facilities of our Church, the Parish will authorize the heating of the "Old Sloop Room" and adjacent service areas to a constant 70° on Sunday, Monday, Tuesday and Wednesday only, and restrict the use of the church to these areas and days only, except by special approval of the Parish Committee." That year there was also a motion to join the Scituate Council of Protestant Churches. For reasons not recorded, the motion was tabled.

Star Island, one of a group of islands known as the Isles of Shoals about ten miles offshore from Portsmouth, New Hampshire, is the site of a conference center that has a long history and special meaning for the people of First Parish. From the earliest days of the twentieth century parishioners would go to Star Island for rest, relaxation and for scholarly discussions. Weekly conferences were held with world-renowned speakers talking on a variety of subjects from current events to science. On clear nights stargazers would stand with eyes towards the heavens in awe, seeing planets and stars impossible to observe on the mainland. In the 1950s, for three years in a row, First Parish sent the largest religious education delegation to Religious Education week to Star Island. Because of this dedication, the AUA helped with the costs of sending First Parish children. Other parishioners served as lifeguards, planning committee members and religious education teachers on the island. Bessie Dooley Tufts was such a First Parish Star Island lover that upon her death in 2005 she left money endowing The Star Island Fund, making it possible for the young people of First Parish to spend a week there in the summer. Other dedicated First Parish visitors to Star Island were Jeannette and Bill Muller and Yvonne and John Twomey.

All across the United States religious communities in the post-war era were central to family life. Church membership and attendance were growing in all denominations and faiths. In 1955 First Parish joined with other Protestant churches in town for a house-to-house canvass to determine the religious affiliation of everyone in Scituate. At First Parish, adult activities were lively. The Men's Club met regularly with an average attendance of thirty-six. Some of those meetings were weekend workdays with painting and landscaping. The Men's Club also sponsored activities such as a Halloween Dance, the Christmas Party, and a magazine drive to raise funds for the United Unitarian Appeal. The number of members in the women's groups was beginning to shift as more women began working. The Woman's Alliance, which usually had its meeting during the day, had twenty-four active members and met twice a month. Throughout the 1950's until the 1970's the Alliance had as one of its officers, a chaplain, who led the devotional part of the meeting that included the recitation of the Lord's Prayer. The Unity Club, with twenty-eight members, had dinner meetings and was more active. It was responsible for flowers for Sunday morning worship and contributed toward floral arrangements at Easter and Christmas. The Unity Club held weekend rummage sales and strawberry festivals and because of the financial success of these activities the club was able to contribute to such organizations as the Protestant Guild for the Blind, the Unitarian Service Committee, and to the United Unitarian Appeal.

By April 1955 average Sunday morning attendance had increased fifty percent over the previous year and membership was one hundred fifty-two. The Church School had grown with an enrollment of one hundred and nine children. Part of the increase in school enrollment was due to the church school renovation and added classrooms. All this was good for First Parish and the Scituate community, so it was with great disappointment that Rev. Cooper submitted his resignation in June 1955 after receiving a call to be minister of Unity Church in North Easton, Massachusetts. In his resignation letter, Rev. Cooper wrote, "For the three years we have been in Scituate we have enjoyed the people of the First Parish Church and feel that the Church has a great future before it. Mrs. Cooper and I appreciate the fine cooperative efforts on the part of all our people and trust that you have grown in wisdom and faith."

In October 1955 First Parish extended a call to the Rev. Charles Cooper Donelson, Jr. of Newton Highlands, Massachusetts with a vote of forty-one in favor, nine opposed, one abstention. Donelson was raised in a Lutheran home but he was ordained as a Methodist minister with a degree from the Boston University School of Theology. He had recently left the Unitarian church in Phoenix, Arizona under less than ideal circumstances, but began his Scituate ministry on November 1, 1955 with an initial salary of $3,500 per year. His family lived in the parsonage and the parish paid all utilities including telephone charges (minus personal phone calls.) The church also paid $10.50 per month for the family's medical plan.

At the 1956 annual meeting in March, church president, William Nebe, reported that the financial status of the church had become "poor" due in part to the Sunday school renovation and repairs made to the parsonage to prepare for the arrival of Rev. Donelson and his family. The Woman's Alliance reported that they purchased an "Indian Tree of Life" china service set for one hundred and twenty people at a cost of three hundred seventeen dollars to better accommodate church and community dinners. The dishes are still in use minus a few broken over the years. In his report, Rev. Donelson described the ten-year old parsonage as being "very livable" with an "excellent kitchen" with an electric stove and refrigerator. The countertops were red Formica. The basement "is a honey," large enough to have a washing machine and a play area which included a ping pong table. Rev. Donelson had a "constant rivalry going on" with Rev. Roscoe Trueblood, the minister of the First Parish Church in neighboring Cohasset, as they would take turns hosting ping pong games in each other's parsonage.[8]

On a sunny but crisp May 20, 1956, the congregation observed the 75th anniversary of the church building and the dedication of the church school addition. The celebration began with the church bell ringing for fifteen minutes. The late morning service, with state and local representatives in attendance, started with a reading of a congratulatory letter from Governor Christian Herter.[9] The featured speaker of the Church School dedication was Dr. Ernest W. Kuebler,

---

[8] Donelson report, First Parish files.
[9] Donelson report, First Parish files.

398

who was acting administrator of the Council of Liberal Churches, the organization leading the way towards the merger of the Unitarian and Universalist denominations. Dr. Keubler was also an acknowledged religious education reformer, moving Unitarian Religious Education from Bible-centered curricula to a child-centered program.

Rev. Charles Cooper Donelson, Jr.

Bill Muller, First Parish's Sunday School Superintendent, made these remarks to mark the occasion:

> You've heard of the wonderful progress this church has made in the past ten years as we assemble here today to celebrate another important milestone. This new wing and its attendant improvements have been

made possible only through the physical, financial and spiritual support of our sincere members and friends. From those who constantly prodded our lethargy to think about the future, those loyal men and women who planned and worked so diligently for the building fund, those who helped drive nails and paint walls to stretch our dollar even farther and from those who have and are contributing so faithfully so we may enjoy our new facilities now.... [It] gives me great pleasure to present this blessed event to the people of First Parish Church of Scituate. Let this building and this day inspire us all to constantly continue to improve our facilities to serve as a better place of fellowship and learning for children of all ages.

Sunday morning attendance remained high after Rev. Donelson took over the pulpit. By March 1957 attendance averaged seventy people. The Church choir under the direction of Mary Stenbeck wore new robes. Organist Ruth Tolman's musical skill was appreciated for its excellence. Finances continued to be a concern but not so much as in days past. When he presented the 1957-1958 budget to the congregation, finance chairman, George Lemoine, recalled his coming to First Parish in 1946:

At that time, we had our Services at four o'clock in the afternoon with our part time Minister – Dr. Raymond Johnson. We had 14-20 in the Congregation and about 5 in our Sunday School. We couldn't afford a full time Minister!.... I think our rebirth started that year. After each Sunday P.M. Service, we would congregate at a different church member's house – have coffee and sandwiches and discuss our Church. What we could do to improve it – make it alive again. Progress was slow, but each year we gained new members. Three years ago [1954], we reached the point where our

THE FIRST PARISH UNITARIAN CHURCH
CHARLES C. DONELSON, JR., *Minister*
SCITUATE, MASSACHUSETTS

DEDICATION SERVICE OF THE BUILDING WING
October 7, 1956

THE ORGAN PRELUDE

THE PROCESSIONAL HYMN   458

COVENANT:
    In the Love of Truth and in the Spirit of Jesus we unite for the Worship
    of God and the Service of Man.
Congregation be seated

THE INVOCATION   Reverend Charles C. Donelson, Jr.

THE LORD'S PRAYER (Unison)

JUNIOR CHOIR ANTHEM   "All People Sing Praises"

THE SCRIPTURE READING   Psalm 127

STATEMENT BY DIRECTOR OF CHURCH SCHOOL
    "Ten Years of Progress"   Mr. William Muller

PRESENTATION AND ACCEPTANCE OF OUR BUILDING WING
    Mr. William Nebe, *Chairman of Parish Committee*
    Mr. Wilmot Brown, *Moderator of our Church*

SENIOR CHOIR ANTHEM   "How Amiable Are Thy Dwellings"

DEDICATION ADDRESS
    The Reverend Ernest W. Kuebler
    Director Religious Education Council of Liberal
    Church (Universalist-Unitarian)

HYMN   145

BENEDICTION   Reverend Charles C. Donelson, Jr.

*You are invited to a reception and inspection
of our new facilities at this time.*

Program of Dedication Service for the Religious Education Wing, October 1956

facilities needed expensive repairs. We didn't have enough room for our children, so something had to be done. We started a three-year building program with the aid of professionals.... The results of this drive - at its completion [on] October 1, 1957 - are all around you. We had arrived as a real Church.

Mr. Lemoine ended his report, proclaiming proudly, "We are once more amongst the leaders, as a Church, in our Community and our Unitarian Group."[10]

Bill Muller had served as Superintendent of the First Parish Church School for fourteen years when he resigned in 1958. Under his leadership, the Church School had grown from six to one hundred-eight students! It was anticipated that in the next year enrollment would increase to one hundred twenty-five. His resignation placed a burden on the Religious Education Committee which appealed to parents to volunteer for the school.[11] As the Church School grew so did the responsibilities of its superintendent; so much so that the Religious Education Committee considered paying someone for the position that had previously been voluntary.

PROPOSED ADDITION at the First Parish Unitarian Church, Scituate Center, is shown in an architect's drawing. The two-story addition will provide a modern second floor church school room plus extra rooms for meetings and social gatherings of parishioners. The architect is Robert C. MacArthur of Rockland. The addition will cost about $30,000 and Burnard Pierce of Norwell, the contractor, expects to begin work on the new building this month. A total of $30,500 has been donated or pledged to the church for its building program.

---

[10] First Parish files.

[11] 1959 Religious Education Committee Report First Parish files.

The committee first thought that Mrs. Donelson, wife of the minister, would be well qualified, but there was concern about dual leadership, so the committee sought the help of the AUA in looking for candidates for the director's job.[12] According to committee minutes, the AUA said the likelihood of getting a professional R.E. director was "dismal," as they were scarce and expensive. Even seminary students expected twenty-five dollars per Sunday plus travel expenses.[13] Problems associated with the rapid growth of the Church School continued. At one committee meeting "a lively discussion" centered on several problems: the lack of substitute teachers and the lack of supervision in the church school office due to the superintendent serving as teacher, worship leader, etc.

In 1958 Rev. Donelson went to Washington, D.C. for a National Legislative Workshop on race issues co-sponsored by the American Unitarian Association and the Universalist Church of America. Rev. Donelson reported that both denominations were continuing their long history of social reform and "labor unions, representing people of all religions, have forged ahead with a kind of racial desegregation which does not merely open jobs to negroes but fosters their acceptance as fellow workers, fellow union members and even opens union social events to full participation.... [W]e too hope for a more fundamental integration of America's races than the law demands." With that report, Donelson called for the church to create a Social Action Committee, which was done.

First Parish adopted new articles of association and by-laws at the 1958 Annual Meeting. The purpose of the church returned to a more tradition statement: "The purposes of this church shall be to advance the cause of liberal religion as expressed in our covenant: 'In the love of truth and in the spirit of Jesus, we unite for the worship of God and the service of man.'" Gone was the humanist language of the 1940s. Later, in 1966, another by-law change was made to include the presidents of the Woman's Alliance and the Unity Club as voting

---

[12] Hennessey letter, First Parish files.
[13] First Parish files.

members of the Parish Committee.

1959 was a momentous year. In April, as the American Unitarian Association and the Universalist Church of America moved closer to uniting, First Parish took the matter seriously. Led by the Denominational Affairs Committee, two Sunday morning services were devoted to a discussion of the merger so that an informed vote could be taken. The First Parish Annual Meeting voted to approve the merger with the Universalists at the "earliest possible date." Forty-nine members favored endorsing the merger, with eight opposed and two abstentions.

As the three hundred twenty-fifth anniversary of First Parish approached, Wilmot Brown, chair of the anniversary committee noted at the annual meeting that such an observance "always presents problems for us vis-à-vis our Congregational friends." Brown recommended that First Parish "set our date as far removed from theirs (the Congregationalists) as possible" and suggested the date of celebration be on or about September 18th, the date in 1634 when Rev. Lothrop and members of the Southwark congregation arrived in Boston aboard the *Griffin*.

Just before the celebration, Rev. Donelson announced his resignation. In a letter to the church clerk, he wrote that his decision was difficult since the "Scituate people have been very kind" to him. He expressed his primary interest in ministry: focusing on children in the junior high and high school grades. In the twelve years covering the ministries of Revs. Johnson, Fay, Cooper and Donelson (1946-1958), the church school enrollment plus teachers grew from eleven to 135. Rev. Donelson said he felt "cut off" from the area of ministry for which he was best prepared and for which he had the most interest. It was the interest in the development of children that led him to accept a position with the Falmouth, Massachusetts school system. Once again, following the resignation of a minister, the Religious Services Committee filled the Sunday pulpit with a variety of lay members and visiting ministers.

404

On September 16, 1959 a gala dinner was held to celebrate the three hundred and twenty-fifth anniversary of the church and an Anniversary Service followed. Speakers were the Rev. Dana Greeley, president of the American Unitarian Association and Dr. Samuel Miller, the new dean of the Harvard Divinity School. Dean Miller spoke on "Reason in American Religion," his first public address since becoming dean. United States Senator Leverett Saltonstall was invited but there is no record of his attending the celebration. Later, as part of the celebration, the church and the Scituate Historical Society co-sponsored a lecture by the preeminent historian of Unitarianism, Dr. Conrad Wright of Harvard.

Chapter Seventeen

"The Times They Are A'Changin'" [1]

At a special First Parish meeting on February 14, 1960 the congregation voted overwhelmingly (sixty three to six) in favor of the proposed consolidation of the Unitarian and Universalist denominations. The congregation also voted by a vote of sixty seven in favor and two opposed to call the Rev. Carl Haycock Whittier, Jr. of Sioux City, Iowa as minister. Whittier began his ministry in Scituate on April 15, 1960 and was formally installed as minister on June 5, 1960. His beginning salary was $4,800 plus utility costs for the parsonage not to exceed $400.

Carl Whittier's ministry (1960-1972) was to be the longest since Rev. Sewall's ended in 1848. It spanned the tumultuous "Sixties" and First Parish was as much affected by the societal and cultural transformations as was the nation. Religious life in the United States was still strong and important fifteen years after the end of World War II but that was about to change. Unitarianism, soon to become Unitarian Universalism, transformed itself in the first half of the twentieth from a theistic religion to a faith shaped by humanist thought. The humanist seeds had been planted earlier in the nineteenth century when liberal Christians questioned the Biblical

---

[1] Bob Dylan

accounts of miracles, the trinity and even the divinity of Jesus. God was envisioned as "that Love with which our souls commune." This was a God that was "not necessarily a supernatural or transcendent being. This was a God that might be the expression of the human personality, with religion being strictly a human activity."[2] Two world wars, the brutality of Nazism and Communism and fear of an atomic war, all had an effect on people's belief in God and His benevolence. Unitarianism, based upon a belief in a rational and loving Deity was shaken by these events and moved itself away from divine power to challenging humanity to make the world better. *Time* magazine's April 8, 1966 cover famously asked, "Is God Dead?"

Post-war America was also beginning to understand and recognize its religious pluralism. The Protestant hegemony was weakening as the country elected its first Catholic president in 1960 and Jews celebrated their role in American society and culture. However, along with the acknowledgement of America's diversity came the opening skirmishes of what a generation later would be known as the "culture wars." The first clash came in 1962 when the United States Supreme Court ruled that state sponsored prayer could not be recited in public schools. In Massachusetts, along with the Pledge of Allegiance, school children, for decades, recited The Lord's Prayer. That was no longer permitted and so the Church School, under the direction of Marion Mott (later Marion O'Donnell), made sure its students recited the prayer every Sunday morning. The adults also recited the Lord's Prayer during the worship service but, as Rev. Whittier recalled later, by the end of his Scituate ministry the prayer was no longer a fixed element in the service. This was the case in many Unitarian Universalist churches across the country and in Canada.[3]

On March 16, 1961 one of the strangest incidents in the history of First Parish occurred. Rev. Whittier chronicled the event.

---

[2] Robinson, 143.
[3] Private correspondence to the author.

The sight of a helicopter tied to our 85-foot high church steeple caused many a Scituate resident to blink his eyes in amazement last Thursday. Lots of small and medium-sized children who came out of school to see it were accused by their parents of having watched too much television when they insisted that they had really seen it. To such parents we say, your child really did see such a thing - there was a helicopter tied to the church spire for 15 minutes or so. Perhaps we should have told you it was coming so that you could have joined us, but we are glad you didn't. The traffic jam rivaled town meeting night as school buses trying to take junior high children home became snarled up with cars bearing clergy, selectman, assorted merchants, policemen and parents taking children home. No one was too unhappy for they knew they were part of Scituate's most noteworthy event of March 16th.

The reason for all this as you may have heard by now was the Old Sloop weather vane atop the steeple. Badly damaged this winter by wind and ice, it appeared ready to topple at any moment. It isn't. We now know it to be well attached indeed. The helicopter parked a few feet over it and dropped a man – on a rope, of course – to the steeple. He attempted to free the vane by hand but was forced to put a line on it, go back upstairs, and use first a winch and then the aircraft itself to try to lift it. The rope, carefully chosen to be weak enough to break before damage could be done, broke, leaving the Old Sloop serene as before, its sails still askew, its mast looking weak just as it has looked for a month or more. The helicopter crew decided that they could do no more and flew away. The end result – hundreds of delighted children, many puzzled adults – they didn't know what it was all about – the children didn't either, but being children they didn't care, they just liked it – and a weathervane in whose security we may rest serene – it won't topple into our parking lot. To those who saw it not, we are sorry but we had no way of telling you in advance. There will be no next time – the weather vane will be removed by more conventional means during the summer."[4]

First Parish tradition has it that a member of the church knew someone in the Massachusetts National Guard who was flying the helicopter from Boston to Cape Cod and asked him to hover over the church building to assist removing the weathervane.

Though membership was nearing two hundred, pledges were not sufficient. While the Permanent Fund was growing, by June 1963 the financial situation was so dire that the minister's salary was in arrears and trading stamps, a rewards program distributed mostly at supermarkets, were used to acquire items for the church. Renovations to the building were needed, and despite hard times, the sanctuary was redecorated with improved lighting. The chandelier was removed and recessed lighting was installed. The walls of the sanctuary were painted a pale grey and the oak pews were painted in an off-white with a mahogany rail. The wainscoting and the window frames were painted in the same off-white. The drapes that had adorned the sanctuary windows for many years were removed.[5]

Using money from the Permanent Fund for renovations was controversial and withdrawing funds from the account was cumbersome. The church had been incorporated in Massachusetts under the Act of 1803 and this required a board of trustees, separate from the church officers, to manage its permanent fund. In 1963 the Massachusetts legislature permitted First Parish to incorporate. The

---

[4] Carl Whittier. "The Helicopter and the Church," Whittier file at Andover-Harvard Library.
[5] Bonney papers.

legislation allowed the parish to dissolve the permanent funds trustees by a vote on April 28, 1963. All property of the previous corporation was transferred from the board to trustees to the church as a new corporate entity under statute. A new Investment Committee was formed, and at the October 1965 budget meeting, its report listed the various funds.

- The Charles H. Waterman Fund with $1,000 in the South Scituate Savings Bank earned interest to be used for the maintenance of the church grounds;

- The Harriet S. Foster Fund, originally begun with shares from AT&T, was to be used for the improvement and preservation of church property. It was not to be used for operating expenses. Along with the Ella Gertrude Gardner Trust Fund, also originally a gift of AT&T stock, a portion of these funds was used to repay a loan for the renovated church kitchen.

- The Charles and Ella Waterman Fund began with a $2,000 gift and had $150 withdrawn each year for operating expenses.

- The Cornelia M. Allen Fund, began with a $3,000 gift, was to be used for general worship and was consolidated with funds from other congregations by to the Unitarian Universalist Association to maximize the interest income. The funds are still held by the UUA and First Parish receives regular disbursements.

Years earlier, the Julia A. Neely Fund was established for the relief of elderly women or the education of young women and disbursed by the minister at his discretion. The funds were also held by the UUA for a number of years, but at the request of Rev. Whittier the parish committee voted in 1967 that a more formal scholarship program be started for college bound women who were part of the church family. An award was to be made every other year in the approximate amount of $120. Another standing fund, the Organ Fund, was established in 1965. According to an Investment Committee report that year, the fund had $242.02 in it and the report urged that the fund be better publicized so that additional gifts would be made. Stagnant for many years, the Organ Fund was re-established as the Betty Smith Organ Fund upon her death in 1999, in honor of her love of music. The committee also noted that the funds were being depleted. To preserve them, the committee planned to hold regular meetings to keep a close eye on the funds and periodically evaluate them to see if the church was getting the most out of them.

On November 22, 1963 the church bell tolled following the news of the assassination of President John F. Kennedy.

The church building underwent major improvements from 1967 to 1969. The exterior and steeple were painted; aluminum gutters and downspouts were installed. The remaining carriage sheds, originally built in 1775, were beyond repair and were removed so that a new three bay shed could be constructed. The asphalt driveway in front of the church was re-paved at a cost of $3,000. A survey of the property boundaries was completed and landscaping was done. A new carpet was laid in the sanctuary (dark red with black flecks) and at the back entrance of the building; forty-four foam rubber cushions were made for the pews. The pulpit and the settee were re-upholstered in red velvet; and "oyster white" draperies were installed along the windows for a total cost of $4,000. An acoustical tiled ceiling, as well as new lighting fixtures, was installed in the Old Sloop Room. By order of the town fire marshal all exit doors in the church had to be painted the same and red was the chosen color. To make sure any other changes were considered by the whole congregation, it was voted by the parish that, "No change in color, décor, or basic arrangements of our Church be made without an opportunity for due consideration of the Parish and the considered vote of the Parish Committee." (Despite this, at a later time, the Erdman School, a pre-school renting the upstairs classrooms since 1973, painted four of the doors a different color from red, because the school did not like that color. The suggestion that whoever painted the doors with the unacceptable colors be "drawn and quartered" was deemed inappropriate.)[6]

There were also staff changes at First Parish. Church member Nancy Crafts began as Director of Religious Education in 1966 as the elementary classes in the Church School continued to grow, though there few in the older youth group. By 1968, the school enrolled one hundred-eleven students with an average attendance of eighty. The connection between social reform and the church, in the midst of the civil rights movement and the anti-Vietnam War protests, was being replaced with political action outside of the church by the high school church youth. The societal "generation gap" was evident as First Parish was invited to join other Scituate churches to form a committee to review and criticize movies "for the benefit of the public." The Parish Committee discussed the invitation and rejected it, noting that it was the role of parents, not churches, to decide which movies children should see.[7]

The church continued to be active in the community. First Parish joined a Boston social service ministry, the Benevolent Fraternity of Unitarian Churches (now known as the Unitarian Universalist Urban Ministry). Rev. Whittier was also active in Scituate's Community Action Program, the anti-poverty program that, for a time, had its office in the rear of the Old Sloop Room.

---

[6] First Parish files.
[7] Parish Committee minutes, First Parish files.

Thursday, November 7, 1968   S

THE LADIES OF THE Scituate First Parish Unitarian Alliance have just about completed their many projects in preparation for the parish's annual Christmas Stocking Fair to be held November 23rd at the Church. Workers are Mrs. Russell Wilder, Mrs. Augustus Abbott, Mrs. Louis Cole, Mrs. Philip Schurler, Mrs. George LeMoine, Mrs. William Claus, Mrs. Evelyn Merritt, Mrs. John Gagnon, Mrs. Allerton Bonney, Mrs. Philip Wood and Mrs. Andrew Wyman.

The Fiddidlers (1968)

English as a Second Language classes were conducted there, as well. A newly formed Scituate Community on Human Concerns also met at the church with several First Parish members participating. The group's mission was to survey the town's social service needs and lobby the state legislature to address whatever deficiencies were found. In early 1967 the Parish Committee discussed offering the use of the sanctuary on Friday evenings to Scituate's Jewish community. There is no indication what came of this, but a few years later, a group of Christian Scientists met at the church. In 1967 a community organization of volunteers called "Fish" was started in Scituate. Modeled after similar programs in Marshfield and Cohasset, the purpose was to "demonstrate practical Christianity" by answering calls for a variety of needs such as house

413

calls on the ill or lonely; and, to provide transportation to a hospital or doctor's office. Rev. Whittier served on the governing board, as did a number of women from the church, including Jane Wilder.[8] Rev. Whittier also served on the board of the South Shore Mental Health Association.

Rev. Carl H. Whittier

That same year, 1967, the Parish Committee surveyed members and friends about what First Parish meant to them and what it could be. In response to the question, "What does the Church mean to you?," the responses were enlightening:

---

[8] Parish Committee minutes, First Parish files.

"A place for expressing my spiritual life in fellowship with those of like mind";

"The church is a guiding force in my life. Without it I would be lonely. It means a place too, where I can be closer to God and where my children can learn to find the same peace in their lives;"

"After many generations, it is our church";

"I enjoy the truthfulness of our church most. The fact that I am accepted and my beliefs are respected mean a great deal to me.";
"I look to the church as a place to search, together with others, for spiritual guidance on a personal basis and as a place for understanding and helping to solve on a local level, some of the world problems.... I approve of our church and what it is doing and am only sorry that more of our members do not attend regularly. They are missing a great deal.";

"A great deal or I would not be filling out this silly questionnaire."

The comprehensive survey covered topics like religious services and music, publicity, social outreach, ministerial leadership, religious education and membership. On the whole, the responses were positive, indicating satisfaction with the state of the church. While most of the questions were general, some were very specific, such as how important it was to sing "Amen" after the hymns. A new hymnal had been published and the survey asked about the new hymns. Some commented that the congregation should sing more "singable hymns." As with any survey there were conflicting comments: too much social outreach, not enough; charge tuition for church school; don't.

While the survey responses were optimistic, there was

concern voiced within the parish committee that in 1967 there had been a noticeable decline in church attendance from the previous year. Proposals from the survey for improving attendance included printing a sermon summary in the newsletter; combining advertising with the Norwell and Cohasset churches; appealing for more singers for the choir; and, an organ prelude before the service.[9] The March 1968 Unity Club meeting did its best to bring people into the church, if not on Sunday mornings, perhaps at other times. The meeting's special speaker was an attention-getter who talked about Unidentified Flying Objects. That same year the Unity Club and the Woman's Alliance began hosting monthly birthday parties for residents at the Cardigan Nursing Home in Scituate, a tradition that continued for almost twenty years.

First Parish also attracted attention in 1968 when the church held a four-session sex education program for teens, inviting others from the various churches in the town. The first session got the program off to a successful start with one hundred and sixty young people attending. Discussions on the Vietnam War and the draft were also held at the church in response to the concerns of the church's youth.

In January 1970 the Parish Committee asked Frances and Herb Cole, the church's neighbors to the east, that, should they decide to sell their house, they give First Parish the first option to buy. The Coles replied that they would be "happy" to do so.[10] Sadly, the church never exercised its option. If it had been able to afford the purchase the congregation would have had a larger parsonage and the smaller building could have been used for offices and additional classrooms.

A significant First Parish outreach effort began in March 1971, but not without controversy. Ray Morrison, a parishioner, was a leader in a newly created non-profit organization, the South Shore

---

[9] Parish Committee Minutes, First Parish files.
[10] Cole letters, First Parish files.

Housing Development Corporation (SSHDC), whose goal was to build affordable housing and to rehabilitate existing housing for families whose income levels permitted them, under federal and state law, to buy or rent such housing. After preliminary discussions with the Parish Committee and other members of the church, Mr. Morrison brought a proposal before the Parish Committee asking for a loan to be used as "seed money" to the SSHDC to be repaid to the church upon its request. Although there were some reservations about the proposal, the committee agreed to put the question before the entire congregation for a vote. A special meeting of the parish was held on March 14 to consider the loan and a contentious debate ensued. The Finance Committee opposed the loan as being a poor investment, because almost no return from the loan would be realized. When the vote was taken the congregation decided against loaning the money. As Mr. Morrison later reflected on the debate, he saw the dispute as a classic discussion about the role of a religious institution in society. Well-meaning people took opposite positions on what was best for the church. "There are those who believe," Mr. Morrison wrote, "that [the church] should be 'the church on the hill', far removed from the daily conflict of living. On the other hand there are those who believe that it should be 'the church in the town', intimately involved in the problems of people. What we do not seem to understand is that these options are not mutually exclusive. The church can work toward alleviation of the problems of the outside world and can still remain a place of quiet refuge and understanding."[11]

Following the meeting Rev. Whittier and members of the Parish Committee received many letters. "I am disappointed with our vote...." wrote one member. "People who are in need of this assistance were refused help in order that our church may earn a larger interest with the money.... The bell tolls for us – and we shall die ignobly unless we choose life above money." "Prudence and sound judgment should let the heart rule the mind," wrote a loan opponent. "Monies in the Permanent Fund of the Church should

---

[11] First Parish files.

under these circumstances be put to work and carefully supervised in sound equities with a fair return." Another supporter wrote, "The 'investment' to be made here is in the lives and hearts of others; there is no real 'church' but the church of the heart." [12]

There is an unsigned memorandum in the church files probably written by Rev. Whittier and sent to church members who came to various conclusions about the meeting and the ensuing correspondence. "In the last few years the church has found 'good reason' to decline action of any social moment inside or outside the church," the memo said. "All common effort has been solely limited to the preservation of buildings and grounds and Sunday services. Last Sunday's vote added consistent action to this tradition. Much dissatisfaction with the static position of the church has been manifest in a significant number of the membership. Great discontent has accumulated because all plans for meaningful community social action have met universally with persistent pessimism...." The memo suggested a solution which would allow a member to designate a portion of their pledge to a specific church community project, if one was approved by the parish. Ultimately the controversy came to an end when parishioner Vera Koehring, a retired biology professor, donated $5,000 to the church for the specific use of loaning it to the SSHDC. Other parishioners gave individual donations as well, totally nearly $5,300. A month later, at the 1971 Annual Meeting, the congregation voted to instruct the Parish and the Investment Committees to adopt a policy that would consider "social implications" as well as financial returns when making investment decisions.

At the special March 1971 meeting the congregation amended the by-laws by creating an "associate member" category for persons at least sixteen years of age who adhered to the "spirit and principles" of First Parish. Once they became eighteen they could become full members of First Parish.

---

[12] First Parish files.

In March 1972, after twelve years as minister, Rev. Whittier announced his resignation and his move to a church in Springfield, Missouri. A special meeting was called to accept the resignation and the meeting rose to give thanks to Carl and Sally Whittier for all they had done for the church.

At the 1972 annual meeting the RE Committee reported that enrollment was one hundred and three children but that only half that number regularly attended Church School. The congregation agreed to take out a $5,000 loan payable over ten years at 7.25% for the purpose of retiring other loans and to use $1,500 for repairs to the church and parsonage.

Despite the fact that some of the leadership of the church were older members who had called Rev. Whittier to Scituate, there had been a growing generational divide. The South Shore housing controversy only added to the growing unease of the older generation about the social justice work done by Rev. Whittier and younger parishioners. Many favored Rev. Whittier's activity in many social justice issues, nevertheless, he was caught between both ends of the political spectrum, was criticized by both for lacking resolve in whatever position he took.

Rev. David B. Parke

As First Parish began the search for new leadership, Rev. David Parke, a well-known minister and Unitarian historian, agreed to come to Scituate and serve as an interim minister. He found an active church, but one with financial difficulties. The Church School was a strong part of church life and growing, however, according to the treasurer, the church $6,000 beyond the approved budget of $20,400 to do its work. To help alleviate this situation, Rev. Parke focused his efforts on membership growth during his ministry. At the 1973 annual meeting Parke expressed gratitude to the congregation for making his interim ministry "so pleasant." The congregation felt the same way and expressed how well Rev. Parke worked with its members.

In 1973 the parish voted to lease the upstairs rooms to the Erdman School, a recently established nursery school. The original lease was for five years and, forty years later, the school is still located at First Parish. As the long relationship attests, the bond between the two institutions has been strong. The Erdman School has paid for its heating, an outdoor fire escape, two rest rooms, playground equipment and fencing. The church has paid for other safety costs such as fire extinguishers and fire alarm systems. Some parents whose children attended the Erdman School joined the church.

First Parish called Rev. John Channing Fuller, a close friend and colleague of David Parke, as its next minister. Fuller, a descendant of the great William Ellery Channing, was called to Scituate at a special meeting on May 13, 1973 on a vote of forty-nine to one. He came from Syracuse, New York where he served as minister at the May Memorial Church, a Unitarian Universalist congregation named for the Rev. Samuel J. May, the minister who had served in South Scituate at the same time of First Parish's Edmund Q. Sewall.

Rev. John C. Fuller

Fuller faced major challenges. Problems keeping a permanent choir caused the organist to resign. Church membership had been declining. Income was down and costs were rising with the result, a growing budget deficit. For the 1974-1975 fiscal year the projected shortfall was $7,171, so a special parish meeting in June 1974 voted to borrow $4,000 (through a passbook loan) to help defray the deficit. The church ended the fiscal year $2,300 in the red but apparently the loan was never executed. The minutes of the June 1976 Annual Meeting record a vote taken to rescind an earlier vote, presumably the loan authorization in June 1974, because the vote to rescind followed a vote to borrow $6,000 from Rockland Trust as a fifteen-year loan at seven percent interest.

First Parish's troubles and the typical tasks of ministry became too much for Rev. Fuller. With his energy sapped, his health declined, and so, in November 1974, he resigned his full-time position, which the congregation accepted with "deep regret," and he began to serve part-time. Soon after the change, Rev. Fuller attended a meeting at the church on December 5, 1974. He walked the short distance to the parsonage and later that evening, he suffered a fatal heart attack.

John Fuller's good friend, Rev. David Parke, memorialized Fuller this way:

> John was a minister. He thought long and probingly about existence. He was one of the best ministers I ever knew. He was not the highest paid. He was not the most influential. He did not obtrude himself on his parishioners or his colleagues. He did know how to listen.... He preached from life rather than from books. He took people seriously. His humor was quiet, sharp, droll. His face was made for laughter. His manner in the pulpit was direct and intimate....
>
> There was something of the scholar in him, reflective, critical, unhurried. He liked to take things apart

intellectually and put them together again, ever scrutinizing evidence, probing motives, doubting the validity of a conclusion until it satisfied him all over.

Lives will thrash and fail in the absence of his counsel.[13]

Following Rev. Fuller's death, First Parish appointed a search committee to find "effective, enduring and immediate leadership" without regard as to a full or part-time ministry.[14] Guest ministers and lay people again temporarily filled the pulpit. On January 19, 1975, church member Louise Bates, who was among the first female supervisors at the John Hancock Insurance Company, gave a talk during worship titled "Pray to God and She will help you." The Wayside Pulpit, normally used to announce sermon titles, was employed for a different purpose during this period. Since the Religious Services Committee was never sure who would be the preacher or speaker, the Wayside Pulpit was used for colorful seasonal posters. One February it was red, pink and white and decorated with hearts.

Rev. Thomas Goldsmith was called to be minister of First Parish in a unanimous vote taken at a special parish meeting on June 8, 1975, just after he had finished his studies at Harvard Divinity School. He received a B.A. degree from Queens College in New York and presently serves the First Unitarian Church of Salt Lake City, where he has been the senior minister since 1987.

Upon Rev. Goldsmith's arrival there was renewed enthusiasm in the congregation but financial problems continued to plague the church' and the congregation faced a budget shortfall of almost $2,300. The following year it increased to almost $6,000 due, in part, to the transition from a part-time to a full-time minister. The congregation also looked at ways to improve the First Parish Church School program. Financial support for the school was minimal but

---

[13] Parke eulogy, First Parish files.
[14] First Parish files.

423

the congregation agreed that the poor funding was due to the lack of a clear mission and approach to religious education rather than a lack of commitment on the part of the congregation. The general goal of the Religious Education program, as set forth in a new policy statement was, "to provide for all ages through Junior High School an enriching environment in which to gain understanding of the richness of Judeo-Christian traditions. The environment will provide a sense of community and fellowship to the child and will be sensitive to spiritual and emotional levels of interaction. A feeling of learning and belonging is to be sought." The Church School program centered on three areas: an understanding of church; an understanding about how values determine the decisions a person makes in their lives; and, a forum for discussion of feelings, fears and hopes. Worship was an important component of the Church School. Some Sundays children attended worship with the adults and on other Sundays they has their own worship upstairs in their classroom. Through the work of Rev. Goldsmith and members of the Parish Committee, the church received a $2,000 grant from the UUA. The Parish Committee, after a lengthy discussion about how best to use the money, decided to hire a Director of Religious Education for the 1977-1978 church year. The new Director, Janet (Ellis) Stenkewicz, started in October and served in that position for two years.

In 1976 the United States celebrated the bicentennial of its independence from Great Britain. Scituate marked the occasion with a parade on July 3 (July 4th was a Sunday) and some in the church wanted to build a float, but after two motions to spend $200 from the church treasury for the float, the idea was defeated. In response, several members of the church raised the money on their own, and the church was proudly represented in the parade. The bicentennial provided the congregation and Scituate residents an opportunity to remember the pivotal role that First Parish played in the history of the town. From the founding of the congregation when town and church were one, members accepted as their duty to be active in town affairs. Members of First Parish have served as elected officials, constables, tax collectors, magistrates, selectmen, school committee members, town meeting moderators and on numerous town committees.

Nearly fifteen years after the Massachusetts legislature permitted First Parish to directly control the Permanent Fund (the endowment) – and not through an independent board of trustees – the Parish Committee proposed, in February 1977, creating a General Endowment Fund and an Investment Committee. For a congregation that was almost three hundred and fifty years old, the church's endowment was modest despite the generosity of its benefactors. There was a desire to better manage the endowment with the aim to increase both the fund's valuation and its income. Heretofore, any money bequeathed to the church was normally placed into a savings account with a local bank; the investment firm of Drexel Burnham held about $3,500 from a mutual fund.

The April 1977 Annual Meeting approved the Parish Committee's proposals establishing the General Endowment Fund and the Investment Committee. The Collector and Treasurer would administer the Fund; the Investment Committee was charged with establishing and maintaining an investment policy with the concurrence of the Parish Committee; and, the Parish Committee would recommend to the congregation any disbursements for the parish's approval. Money left over in the Organ Fund, after repairs to the organ, was used to establish the General Endowment Fund. The initial deposit into the General Endowment Fund was $14,000. Soon thereafter, another $2,000 was deposited into the endowment with gifts in memory of the Revs. Cornelis Heijn and John Fuller.

Louise Bates of the new Investment Committee immediately brought up a question about the use of the Endowment Fund that continues to the present day: should the church keep the funds untouched so the principal could grow or under what circumstances (capital improvements, for example) could money be taken from the principal? Under the policy approved at that meeting income from the fund was for general operating expenses; however, the principal was not to be used, except in a "dire emergency," and only for a

425

purpose which had "permanence or substantial durability or long lasting effect;" and, any withdrawal of principal was to be approved by a two-thirds vote of the membership. Restricted funds from benefactors were to be in separate established accounts. Gifts made in the memory of persons, bequests, or life insurance policies were to be deposited into the endowment fund whether directed to do so or not.

At that same annual meeting Parish Committee chair, Gilman Wilder, reported his belief that the general condition of the church was stronger than the previous year due in large part to Rev. Goldsmith. The Third Saturday Suppers, held for fun and fellowship, were praised for the popularity as attendance increased with every dinner. Rev. Goldsmith recalled the dinners as "exquisite" and offered the "best food" of all the church dinners in town.[15] The budget shortfall, which the previous year was almost $6,000, was now down to $1,400. Ray Morrison got up at the meeting to present to the church a check in the amount of $5,200 which represented the return of the gift of Vera Koehring to the church for the purpose of giving the South Shore Housing Development Corporation seed money. These funds were part of the $14,000 initial deposit to the Endowment Fund. Six years after the loan, the Corporation had become a successful operation providing three hundred sixty-five housing units and employing a full-time staff of five. Since the SSHDC had become self-sufficient it no longer needed the seed money. Mr. Morrison expressed the appreciation of the corporation to the church for its financial assistance at the beginning, despite the initial controversy. To the present day the association of First Parish to South Shore Housing has been strong with three members of First Parish serving on the board of directors.

On September 13, 1977, to the shock of the Parish Committee and "with a deep sense of regret," a letter of resignation from Rev. Goldsmith was read. He accepted a call to the First Parish Church in Waltham, Massachusetts. Many in the congregation were

---

[15] Personal correspondence to author.

angry that he left so soon, after only two years, and believed that he used the church as a stepping-stone. That anger apparently dissipated, because twenty years later, he returned to give a sermon at First Parish and many people who were members during his ministry greeted him warmly.

With the resignation of Rev. Goldsmith, the late hiring of a new Director of Religious Education, and a decrease in income from the pledge drive, the congregation again faced a budget deficit for the coming year, portending future deficits that would plague the church. Immediately following Rev. Goldsmith's departure the Parish Committee resolved to maintain the church's positive momentum under his ministry and not slide "back down the hill" to where the church was a few years earlier. The minutes to one Parish Committee meeting end with an editorial comment, apparently made by the committee secretary, "The First Parish Unitarian Church of Scituate has weathered many storms, and we shall weather this one. It won't be easy, but then, what is these days? It will need all of us, pulling together, to keep the momentum that Tom has helped us build."[16]

Rev. Richard Fewkes of the First Parish Church in Norwell, the Ministerial Settlement Representative for the area, assisted the Scituate congregation in looking for a new minister. First Parish immediately selected a new search committee, some of whom served on the committee that had recommended Rev. Goldsmith. While the average time for finding a new minister at that time was nine months, the congregation was hoping to have a new spiritual leader in three to five months. However, from November 1977 to September 1978 the church was without a minister. For several months, the church had lay speakers and the services of the Rev. John Graham, formerly of the United First Parish of Quincy, Massachusetts. Even without a settled minister the church community remained strong.

---

[16] Parish Committee Meeting, September 13, 1977, First Parish files.

On February 6, 1978 an intense storm traveled up east coast and merged with an Arctic cold front at the time of a new moon. The Blizzard of 1978 devastated the town of Scituate. Over two feet of snow fell; winds of 86 miles per hour with stronger gusts blew in from the ocean; and a new moon high tide caused great damage and loss of life. An elderly man and a young child in Scituate drowned when their rescue boat was capsized by a wave. Seven hundred homes were damaged or destroyed. The estimated cost of the storm to the Scituate area was fifty-four million dollars.[17] Scituate residents who became homeless lived in the church's parsonage for a time. All the town's churches helped as best they could, and one lasting institution that continues to this day is the Scituate Food Pantry, which distributes food to people in need, and is administered by the Scituate Clergy Association. For many years the pantry, managed by volunteers from the town's churches, including First Parish, was located at the Foyer of Charity, a Catholic retreat center, but is currently located at the Masonic Hall on Country Way.

The April 1978 Annual Meeting highlighted the problems faced by the church in the wake of Rev. Goldsmith's departure. There was another predicted budget deficit ($3,300) coming at a time when the church needed to make the financial commitment of calling a full-time minister. The building required maintenance and repair; new insulation, new asphalt shingle roofing, along with a fire alarm system were installed.

A month later, at a special parish meeting on May 21, 1978 Rev. Darrell Berger was called as minister by a unanimous vote of fifty-one members. Rev. Berger was born in Toledo, Ohio in 1948. He graduated from Vanderbilt University with a B.A. degree in philosophy and later graduated from Vanderbilt's Divinity School. He and his wife, Jim Anne Howard, an artist, moved to Scituate in July 1978 and were "really excited" to move to the Boston area.[18] While in Scituate, Berger wrote a column in the *Scituate Mariner* called,

---

[17] *Scituate Mariner*, February 7, 2008.
[18] Personal correspondence with the author, March 2, 2007.

428

"Nearly Native;" occasionally delivered commentary on a local radio station, WATD; and was president of the Scituate Clergy Association for five years. There grew an appreciation for the ministry of Rev. Berger and his wife, Jim Ann, in bringing institutional stability to the church, despite the fact that some feared that Rev. Berger, too, would soon leave. Others with unexpressed anger or disappointment about Rev. Goldsmith's departure directed it towards Rev. Berger. However, the prevailing sentiment in the church was positive toward his sermons and the quality of worship music provided by Rodger Vine, a 1971 graduate of Boston University and studied music in France where he once played at Notre Dame Cathedral in Paris. Vine was the church organist until 1992 when he left Scituate to become the organist at Boston's famous Arlington Street Church. Before he left, the congregation held an Appreciation Sunday for him and his wonderful music.

Rev. Tom Goldsmith (l) and Rev. Darrell Berger

The projected Fiscal Year 1979-1980 budget had a $5,360 operational deficit, a clear sign of the church's fiscal situation. Parishioners Barbara and Lou Geyer challenged the congregation in 1981 when the church faced another budget shortfall of $2,525 by offering to donate $300 towards reducing the deficit, if others would contribute as well, within thirty days. When a special meeting was held in May the budget gap had been closed and the proposed budget of almost $40,000 was approved. The minister's salary (including expenses) for that year was $11,400. Finances improved, and by the three hundred and fiftieth Annual Meeting in 1984, the church had a $1,300 budget surplus, having paid off $3,000 in debts. The shuttle bus, which stopped at several locations in town, was revived with the goal of increasing membership and participation in church activities. The Woman's Alliance continued to sew and "fiddidle" articles for the Sea and Snowflake Fairs. However, the Church School did not have a paid Director of Religious Education. In an effort to recruit teachers, two Church School instructors were paid. At the annual meeting, Rev. Berger reported on a humorous, but nonetheless annoying matter. The church's phone number was similar to that of a local business and, as a result, the church was receiving numerous wrong number calls, so the church authorized Rev. Berger to obtain a new telephone number.

Cultural issues and matters of social responsibility were evident at First Parish at this time. Feminist theology came to the church with the UUA's course, "Cakes for the Queen of Heaven," taught by Jim Ann Howard, Rev. Berger's wife. For his part, Rev. Berger was an active participant in the South Shore Peace Coalition that worked to lessen the threat of nuclear war by seeking a freeze on the production of nuclear weapons. He sought to establish a Scituate group. Toward that end, the church hosted a "Peace Pub" in January 1982. The AIDS epidemic was scaring the public at that time and First Parish held Scituate's first educational program about the disease. As it had been doing for many years, the Woman's Alliance continued to host monthly birthday parties for the residents of the Cardigan Nursing Home in the Greenbush section of Scituate.

In June 1979, Vera Koehring, always generous to the church, donated four cemetery plots in the Union Cemetery and the Parish Committee officially accepted the gift pending a vote by the Parish at the Annual Meeting. The property was deeded over to the church but nothing was done with the plots and knowledge of them was lost until the deed was discovered more than twenty-five years later. At the present time, the plots have been offered for sale to church members but no one has purchased them.

The Parish Committee in the fall of 1979 voted to recommend to the annual meeting a change the common name of the church to "The First Parish Unitarian Church," but for all legal and financial matters the church's name would remain as "The First Parish Church of Scituate – Unitarian." At the Annual Meeting in April, 1980 an amendment to the main motion to change the church's name was offered. The amendment proposed to change the church's name to "The First Parish Unitarian Church of Scituate" but it was defeated as was the main motion presented by the Parish Committee.

In a celebration similar to one twenty-five years earlier, the congregation noted the 100th anniversary of the laying cornerstone of the present church building. The principle organizers of the event were Bill Muller and Louise Bates. Unfortunately, Mr. Muller died just before the celebration took place, yet Rev. Berger noted that there was "a rejoicing that most of his last days he was able to give so much to an institution he loved."[19]

There was concern expressed at the April 1980 meeting that the cost of heating oil would exceed a dollar a gallon. Because of the increase in heating fuel costs it was suggested that the church close for one month during the winter, but this was not done as the long-delayed room dividers for the Old Sloop Room were finally installed as a fuel saving device.

---

[19] First Parish files.

In June 1980, the church's neighbor to the east, Mrs. Cole, informed the congregation that she was selling her house and asked whether the church would exercise its right of first refusal to buy the house. It was voted, nine to two, to release Mrs. Cole from her agreement and First Parish lost an opportunity to increase useable space.

By 1981 average Sunday attendance had improved to approximately fifty adults. The endowment fund grew to almost $25,000, increasing significantly in the following year to just under $40,000 because of astute management. Despite this success, the 1982-1983 fiscal year budget was $2,525 in the red, but by 1984 there was a surplus and the treasurer retired some debts.

One of Rev. Berger's earliest stated goals was to reinvigorate the RE program. In 1983, "Chalice Time" started. A story or a lesson directed at children was presented before they were dismissed to their classes. That year thirty-nine children were enrolled in the program with seventeen teachers and aides. In 1987 the church hired church member, Meg Moncy, as the Religious Education Coordinator. Rev. Berger and another church member led the "About Your Sexuality" course, later taught by members, Dr. David Morin, a Scituate pediatrician and his wife, Ellen, a nurse. "About Your Sexuality" was a comprehensive sex education program first developed by the UUA in 1970. The classes covered human anatomy, relationships, sexual intercourse and contraception. It also included a frank discussion of sexually transmitted diseases. The most controversial element of the program was a series of filmstrips with human models illustrating the curriculum.

1983 brought a crisis. One member called it "The Great Unpleasantness;" another described the dilemma as "financial and spiritual." Rev. Berger had asked for a significant increase in his salary as the church struggled with a projected budget deficit of $5,000. The minister's compensation had always been an issue for the church. Now, First Parish was growing and that created additional responsibilities and burdens on the minister. Some members didn't think that the church could afford a salary increase for the minister, though most felt it was deserved. Pledges were down from the year before. This led to much soul searching about the future of the church. A proposal made to the Finance Committee was that the congregation consider a half-time ministry. Some even suggested that the church was unable to sustain itself and should close. Most, however, believed that efforts to keep the church alive should not be abandoned. The Finance Committee presented the half-time ministry proposal to the Parish Committee. At a well-attended meeting to discuss the future of the church, many "frustrations" and much "bitterness," as one long time member described it, poured out. Frustration was high because most of the work of the church had fallen on the minister and a small cadre of hard workers. Some were tired of carrying the burden, others had a hard time reconciling their desire to grow with the reality that the church would never be more than a small to mid-sized congregation; still others were aware of the limitations of a small endowment, a constraint on the ability to adequately pay a minister and staff the church with professional leadership in music and religious education. Most at the meeting believed that their church, having survived numerous crises in its three hundred fifty years, would also survive this period.[20] Nevertheless, there was fallout and for some, their relationship with Rev. Berger was never the same. Finances and church administration suffered. A few members left the church, some permanently, others temporarily. When the dust settled, the 1984-1985 budget provided for a ten percent increase in Rev. Berger's salary.

Other, less dramatic issues arose that year. Filling committee chair positions proved difficult, so four committees were combined into two: Membership/Hospitality and Denominational Affairs/Social Concerns. The church newsletter had for many years been mailed weekly but, in order to save money, the newsletter was mailed bi-weekly. However, as it soon became apparent that there were no significant savings, the annual meeting voted to return to a weekly newsletter. The church steeple was in serious need of repair

---

[20] First Parish files.

and the exterior of the church needed painting. The total cost was $10,580; but, as of June 1985, less than half that amount had been raised. Louise Bates offered to loan the church the balance, but the parish voted instead to get a bank loan. However, a "Save Our Steeple" Fund was established and one hundred contributors made sufficient donations to pay for the repair and painting so no loan was necessary.

There were additional building maintenance problems. A major building repair was necessary after someone noticed that the church sill in the front was sinking, requiring a crane to lift the church about two inches to replace the old, rotting sill which cost $8,400. In 1988 the church and parsonage were connected to the town sewer system with a $10,000 connection cost paid with large donations from sixteen church members. It was at this time the town made an arrangement with the church: in exchange for using one of the church's storage sheds for the town's Housing Authority equipment, the town mowed the church's lawns. Unfortunately, the arrangement lasted just a few years and, until recently, church volunteers did the lawn work. Sparked by a generous donation from a church member the lawns are now maintained by a commercial landscaping company paid through the church's operating expenses.

After more than ten years as First Parish's minister, Rev. Berger contemplated a change. Though both he and his wife liked the Scituate area and considered themselves, "Nearly Native," (the name of his local newspaper column), they never truly felt at home. Adding to the restlessness, other issues were surfacing. Ministerial sabbaticals were becoming a common practice in Unitarian Universalist ministry but First Parish had never granted one to its ministers. Rev. Berger approached the Parish Committee with the idea, explaining that a sabbatical would refresh him, making him a better minister; and, there would be little additional cost to the church. Another matter of professional concern among clergy was a housing allowance. As was common, ministers lived in parsonages and when they didn't, the congregation would compensate the minister for the cost of housing. By the 1980s, the financial needs of ministers changed. Those who lived in parsonages realized that when they left a congregation they had earned no equity from their housing, but ministers who could not afford to buy a home in town with expensive real estate like Scituate, were forced to live in the parsonage, thereby significantly shortchanging their future financial security. Both issues, the sabbatical and housing equity, proved to be sore points within the congregation.[21] As those concerns grew, Rev. Berger accepted a call to the Fourth Universalist Society in New York City and at a special parish meeting on June 18, 1989 the congregation accepted his resignation. Parish Committee Chair Jack Shaw spoke for many in the congregation when he said, "We are a church family and are here to help each other out so I am quite sure we can overcome any problems together."

Following Rev. Berger's departure First Parish went through a UUA recommended self-assessment. The District Executive, Rev. Dorothy Boroush, told the Parish Committee that the congregation had several choices. The church could hire a full-time interim minister; a part-time interim, or all the services could be lay led until a new minister was called. The committee unanimously agreed that it preferred a full-time interim minister. In looking back on the eleven years of Berger's ministry, the congregation found that it had a revitalized Religious Education program and improved the church buildings. Though church membership and Sunday attendance continued to frustrate and disappoint church leaders, the congregation's consensus was that Rev. Berger created an environment for spiritual growth and, because of him, the church enjoyed a positive exposure as the liberal religious community in town.

---

[21] Personal correspondence to author.

435

Rev. Michael Boardman

Rev. Michael Boardman agreed to serve as Interim Minister for the 1989-1990 church year. Rev. Boardman was a graduate of the Starr King School for Ministry in Berkeley, California and had served several Massachusetts Unitarian Universalist congregations before choosing interim ministry as his specialty. In his report to the Spring Annual Meeting, Rev. Boardman said that he had three objectives as Interim Minister: 1) to provide ministerial continuity; 2) to be sensitive to the feelings of the congregation following the resignation of Rev. Berger; and, 3) to help the church with its self-evaluation and ministerial search. Reflecting on his interim year, Boardman observed that the year had been a quiet one with the overall tone being one of maintenance and self-evaluation. However, church finances troubled the congregation and Boardman.

For the first time since the parsonage adjacent to the church had been built, in an effort to increase income, someone other than the minister occupied it. Nevertheless, at the Spring Annual Meeting of 1990, the Finance Committee recommended a budget of $67,328 with a $1,330 shortfall, even with the parsonage rental income. The chair of the Finance Committee noted that it was a "flat" budget. Severe cuts made the year before in contributions to denominational groups like the UUA and the Ballou Channing District continued. On the positive side, the endowment had earned $13,404; rent from the Erdman School increased; and, pledges remained steady, which was a good sign for an interim year. The congregation adopted Rev. Boardman's recommendation that the church change its fiscal year to match the calendar year and that the canvass drive be held sometime between mid-October and early November. This required two parish meetings, one in December to approve the budget and the other, the annual meeting in May, to hear the minister's and committee reports as well as to elect officers. (In 1998, the congregation voted to return to a July-June fiscal year because the calendar year experiment did not match well with the church year cycle because newly elected committee chairs had to develop committee budgets for an assignment they were just beginning to learn.) The annual meeting ended with a resolution expressing the church's gratitude for Rev. Boardman's counsel during a painful period of adjustment.

The mission of an interim minister is to guide a congregation through the transition from one minister to the next. It also is a time for members of the congregation to conduct a self-examination as to who they are as a congregation and what their religious community should be. This process guides a congregation to determine what kind of a minister it wants. Surveys are distributed to the entire congregation, completed and analyzed. Meetings are held. A search committee is charged with reviewing informational material from interested ministers, interviewing them and hearing them preach at

437

neutral locations. From this process, the search committee recommends one candidate to present to the congregation to vote for a call as the new minister. People remember Rev. Boardman's interim ministry as successful, his successor's was not.

On June 10, 1990 First Parish called as its minister the Rev. Steve Stock, with a vote of sixty-nine in favor, one opposed. Rev. Stock was raised in a Jewish home in New York and graduated from Meadville Lombard Theological School in Chicago. His ministry appeared to get off to a good start with Parish Committee chair, Anne Weaver, complimenting Rev. Stock at the October Parish Committee meeting on a "fine opening service." But the relationship among Stock, the Parish Committee and many parishioners collapsed quickly, even as plans were being made for his installation. The breaking point may have been the Christmas Eve service with the church filled with First Parish families and visitors. Complaints about the service were immediately conveyed to the Parish Committee. Some people objected to the length of the service (an hour and a half), compounded by the singing of five hymns and three carols, causing several people to leave during the service. Other people took exception to Rev. Stock's demeanor during the service when he urged people to give to the church because "we're broke."

Rev. Steve Stock

Eighteen people, mostly from the Parish and the Ministerial Relations Committees, met on December 29th to discuss the situation. The purpose of the meeting was to define and air the problem, as the Parish Committee saw it, to the Ministerial Relations Committee. Anne Weaver, who as Parish Committee chair had met regularly with Rev. Stock, relayed his "dissatisfactions." He saw the church as a "dying" congregation, "unfriendly," with a Parish Committee lacking in energy and leadership. In addition, the material the Search Committee sent to all ministerial candidates, was, according to Stock, "misleading." Weaver's recitation of the congregation's views was equally stark. People were dissatisfied, some active members had dropped out; others were not fulfilling their financial pledges because they were "angry, frustrated, discouraged." One person at the meeting characterized the situation as an "unmitigated disaster." The next day the Ministerial Relations Committee met with Rev. Dorothy Boroush, the Ballou Channing District Executive, Rev. Robbie Walsh of Duxbury, (the Good Offices person of the Ballou Channing Minister's Chapter) and Anne Weaver, the Parish Committee chair, to discuss asking Rev. Stock for his resignation. A few days later, this group, along with other interested parties, met with Rev. Stock. It was clear that the relationship between Rev. Stock and the congregation was ruptured, and the situation untenable. In the end, both sides agreed to the terms of a resignation.

The congregation accepted Rev. Stock's resignation on January 27, 1991 at a special parish meeting with fifty-eight people attending. Eight people expressed their concern over what had happened. Three spoke about their belief that communications to the parish about the reasons for the resignation were inadequate. Others voiced confidence that the Parish Committee, the Search Committee and the Ministerial Relations Committee handled the conversations with Rev. Stock and his resignation in a professional manner. The vote was forty-nine in favor of accepting the resignation, seven against, one abstention and one voting "present." Six absentee ballots also voted in the affirmative. The moderator of the meeting, Gilman Wilder, reminded the parish that pursuant to the settlement with Rev. Stock, the minister and his wife, Susan, would remain in the parsonage for a few months and that the parish should treat them in a neighborly fashion. Rev. Stock would go on to serve another Unitarian Universalist church in Alabama, but later he became a Methodist minister serving churches in Alabama and Florida. He died in 2010.

At another special meeting in March 1991 a new Ministerial Search Committee was elected to find a new minister for First Parish. Over the next few weeks, the services were a mixture of lay and clergy led. Then the Parish Committee asked Rev. William "Bill" Gardner to be interim minister. Rev. Gardner was a well-regarded retired minister who was first ordained as a Universalist minister after graduating from Crane Theological School at Tufts University. The agreement between Rev. Gardner and First Parish called for Gardner to be part-time, preaching all but one Sunday a month, and to be available for afternoon meetings and pastoral calls on Sundays. Even with a part-time schedule Gardner immediately went to work effectively and compassionately healing the congregation after Rev. Stock's abrupt departure. However, a national political controversy soon disrupted the era of good feeling. On January 17, 1991 a coalition of military forces, led by the United States, began bombing sites in Iraq to force Iraq to remove its troops from neighboring Kuwait. The church was divided, as was the country, on the necessity of the war. On February 24, a special parish meeting was held and it voted to place yellow ribbons on the church's front doors to symbolize the church's support for the troops fighting in Kuwait and Iraq. As symbols often have different meanings to different people, some in the congregation saw the ribbons as a symbol of the church supporting the Gulf War itself, and not just the troops. The controversy reminded people that while First Parish members may be religious liberals, all are not necessarily political liberals.

At the Annual Meeting in May, 1991 the chair of the Finance Committee reported that due to Rev. Gardner's part-time status, the church had a projected surplus of $5,679, but warned that a budget crisis loomed if the church decided to call a full-time minister because the current level of pledging could not financially one. On the positive side, the endowment continued to grow with a value at the end of March 1991 of $95,176.

During the difficult year of 1991, the Membership and Hospitality Committee became inactive, and the Nominating Committee strained to find people to accept the positions of Parish Committee Chair, Vice-Chair and Secretary. Nevertheless, there was the usual activity in other areas of church life. The Unity Club membership was thirty. It held four dinner meetings and continued to sponsor its weekly yoga exercise led by parishioner Barbara Koelsch. It also sponsored attendance by youth at Star Island and contributed to Renewal House, the shelter for women and children run by the Unitarian Universalist Urban Ministry in Boston. The Woman's Alliance continued its lunchtime meetings with members giving travelogues. Church historian, Margaret Cole Bonney, regaled the group with stories of the "good old days." There were potluck dinners, Christmas caroling, a Greek Dinner, a Yankee Auction, an occasional coffeehouse concert; and, church organist Rodger Vine organized classical and Broadway musical concerts. At the May Annual Meeting, the church faced a budget shortfall of $5,000 but there was the expectation of increased pledge income with the anticipation of a new minister. Parish Committee chair, Anne Weaver, rose to commend the congregation for its courage in handling the very difficult situation with Rev. Stock, while maintaining a high level of commitment and caring for the church community.

In June 1991 Betty Eason passed away. She and her mother, Maybelle, were longtime members of the church and were very active in and loyal to it. Betty, who had no family, left a large portion of her estate to First Parish. By the end of 1991 the Endowment Fund had a valuation of $104,370. The income derived from the growing endowment ensured that First Parish could afford a full-time minister.

At the May 1992 Annual Meeting, Rev. Gardner announced that, with a new minister beginning September 1st, he would resign effective August 31st, but that he would still be available to the

441

congregation during the summer recess. Peter Leavitt, president of the Parish Committee "expressed the profound feelings of gratitude the entire committee has for Bill's help...."

Rev. Bill Gardner

Over the summer of 1992, the building was spruced up for the new minister. A room where office equipment was kept was converted into a minister's office with a new bay window. A wall separating the men and women's restrooms was taken down converting the area into one wheelchair accessible room. At the front entrance to the church a wheelchair accessible ramp and doorway were installed as well as a new fire escape for the upstairs school area.

Recent Benefactors of First Parish

Betty Eason

Dorothy Brown Wood

Louise Bates

Chapter Eighteen

"A beacon to guide us to truth and wisdom;
A vessel to carry us toward justice and love;
A safe harbor in times of trouble."[1]

The Rev. Richard Myles Stower was called by First Parish to be its new minister on April 12, 1992. The search committee stated its belief that Rev. Stower would "bring warmth, positivism, vitality, and a deep understanding and concern for people." The parish vote was sixty-one in favor, six opposed.[2] Like his predecessor Rev. Stock, Stower was a native of New York City and grew up in a Jewish home. He was attracted to Unitarian Universalism in his thirties and became an active member of First Parish in Concord, Massachusetts where former UUA President Dana Greeley was senior minister. Stower entered the ministry after serving as a teacher in an elementary school in the South Bronx, New York; working at Benton & Bowles, a major advertising agency in Manhattan; as a sales representative at a New Hampshire television station; and, working in the New Hampshire Division of Welfare. He was hired by the United States Department of Agriculture's Food and Nutrition Service,

---

[1] Written by Larry Litten of the 1993 Long Range Planning Committee, First Parish files.
[2] Parish Committee minutes, April 12, 1992, First Parish files.

working first in Washington, D.C. and then at the agency's regional office in Boston. He received B.A. and M.A. degrees in History from the George Washington University and earned his Master of Divinity degree from Harvard Divinity School in 1990. Prior to being called to Scituate, Rev. Stower served the Kearsarge (New Hampshire) Unitarian Universalist Fellowship as a part-time minister; and, at the Keene (New Hampshire) Unitarian Universalist Church as interim minister. Because of the generous bequest of Betty Eason, the Scituate congregation was able to call Rev. Stower as a full-time minister. Rev. Stower was the first settled minister whose family did not live in the parsonage since it was built following World War II. Nancy Richards-Stower was an attorney and former chair of the New Hampshire Human Rights Commission. Their son, Jonathan, was a sixth-grader at the time of their move. During the first year of his ministry the Stowers rented a home in Scituate and the following year they purchased a house on Whittier Drive, about a mile from the church. For many years they would host a New Year's Day open house for members and friends of the church.

At the suggestion of Rev. Stower, the Parish Committee created a Long Range Planning Committee that began work in the spring of 1993 to assess the future needs and opportunities for the church. The committee was made up of five people who had been church members from two to twenty-eight years. The committee was steadfast and met thirty times over twenty-one months. To better prepare for their work, the committee talked with members of other Unitarian Universalist churches who had done similar long range planning. Church members were interviewed in groups and twelve Scituate residents, not parishioners, participated in telling the committee how First Parish was viewed in Scituate at large. The committee identified six goals: enriched worship, programs and services for members; greater participation in church activities; more involvement in social action programs; a strengthened financial base; improved facilities and grounds; and, a strengthened and effective governance process. To meet those goals the committee made numerous recommendations, most of which have been accomplished over the years.

Rev. Stower initiated several new rituals into the worship service at First Parish. In June 1993 the church year closed with the Flower Communion. This service was created in 1923 by the Rev. Norbert Čapek, founder of the Unitarian Church in Prague. In place of bread and wine found in orthodox liturgy, Rev. Čapek asked people to bring flowers from the Czech countryside to share with each other. In September 1993, the church year began with a Water Ceremony during which people were invited to pour into a common bowl a small sample of water from their summer travels, near and far, and relate the significance of the place for them. Once a month the congregation was asked to share a joy or a concern with the congregation, "something that brings a smile to our face or a tear to our eye," as Rev. Stower would introduce the moment in the service. Another tradition Rev. Stower started had children lighting the chalice flame at the beginning of each Sunday service, creating the symbol of Unitarian Universalism's search for truth along the spiritual path. As a child lit the chalice flame they said, "May we have eyes that see, hearts that love, and hands that are ready to serve." Rev. Stower said that his reason for including the children were to provide a safe and sympathetic setting for them to gain confidence speaking in front of a group of people, mostly adults; and, to acknowledge their importance in the church community.

In the late 1990s the church experimented with having two Christmas Eve services because of overcrowding in the sanctuary. The earlier service was intended for families with young children and both were identical except that the choir sang only at the later service. This lasted a few years until attendance at the earlier service dwindled. For many the Christmas Eve service was the highlight of the church year with wonderful music, stories read by children, and candlelight. Nancy Richards-Stower decorated the sanctuary with greens on the windowsills and wreaths hung from the windows and behind the pulpit. Prior to Christmas, Rev. Stower conducted quiet vesper services to bring stillness to a hectic time of year. On New Year's Eve, 1999 there was a gathering at the church to welcome in the new millennium. At midnight Rev. Stower and children rung the church bell as people watched fireworks in the sky over Cohasset.

Rev. Richard M. Stower

Music has always been an important part of the First Parish worship service and to church life. The congregation is blessed to have a sanctuary with pleasing acoustics. One year, a local newspaper rated First Parish as one of the best places to hear music on the South Shore. Talented church members and classically trained musicians have served as organists, choir directors and music directors over the years. Ian Lodge, a Berklee College of Music student from England, became music director, also in September 1992. An incident involving Mr. Lodge during Rev. Stower's candidating week earlier that spring launched it with a humorous and tension relieving start. Having been introduced to the congregation as the search committee's recommended candidate, Rev. Stower preached the same Sunday as the beginning of Daylight Saving Time. Mr. Lodge, newly arrived in the United States from England, was unaware of the time change and arrived at the church in the middle of the service, very embarrassed, as this was his audition as well. In spite of his error, Mr. Lodge, a jazz pianist, was hired and his organ playing of classical music was greatly appreciated by the congregation. After two years he left the church to pursue a music career in Los Angeles.

A new Unitarian Universalist hymnal was published in the spring of 1993. Member Robert Hansman donated the purchase of forty hymnals. It is not unusual for parishioners to criticize a new hymnal when it is introduced. Such was the case at First Parish. Though most of the hymns were familiar, others had words changed to make the hymns gender neutral; still other hymns were just plain "un-singable."

In September 1994, Ian Lodge recommended as his successor, Mika Pohjola who was from Finland and was also a Berklee College student. Pohjola was hired as the new organist. He was trained in classical music in Sweden but his first musical love was, like Mr. Lodge, jazz. Since Pohjola didn't have a car, Rev. Stower or members of First Parish met him at the Braintree T station and then, after the service, brought him back to the station for his return to Boston. For special services and Christmas Eve, Pohjola invited soloists from Berklee to sing. One was Johanna Grüssner. Both have since pursued music careers and have made a number of successful and highly regarded recordings. Following Mr. Pohjola's resignation in December 1995 the church invited several people to provide music while the search for a permanent organist was under way. Some of the guest organists were very good; others were not.

One guest organist forgot to turn off the blower to the organ, thus burning out the ninety-year old motor. The estimated cost to replace the motor was very high so members, Peter Tolman, a licensed electrician, along with Ray Morrison and Gil Wilder, removed the burned and fused wiring around the armature and manually rewound the yards of wire to return the motor to operating condition.

In the fall of 1997 First Parish hired Gerald Peters as its organist. Playing beautifully on the Hook and Hastings pipe organ, Mr. Peters quickly became a beloved member of the First Parish community. He revived the church choir and organized several memorable concerts by classical and jazz pianists, as well as vocalists. One evening he gave an inaugural concert on a harpsichord he built. The quality of the worship music improved under his leadership. Unfortunately, Mr. Peters abruptly resigned during a dispute over salary and benefits and tragically took his own life a few months later. The church was heartbroken, and at the invitation of the Peters' family, the First Parish choir sang at his memorial service at the Methodist Church in Marshfield.

The church searched for another music director to play its organ and lead the choir. For a brief time Tom Handel, the Dean of Students at the New England Conservatory, served as music director. Mr. Handel was an exceptional organist and led the expanding church choir into new areas of choral music. However, he resigned after only four months expressing that he preferred to play in a more liturgically based church. His replacement also served briefly. In contrast with Tom Handel, the congregation and choir were not pleased with her musicianship. Into the breach came Beth Hilliard, a church member, who was a classically trained pianist and teacher. Ms. Hilliard began playing piano pieces during worship but soon added the organ to her repertoire. She enjoyed playing it so much that she took organ lessons to improve her skill. Hilliard also gave patient direction and encouragement to the choir which grew and thrived. Her talented children often played the flute and cello to supplement the worship music. All at First Parish were sad to see Ms. Hilliard leave the church when her family relocated to Wisconsin in 2006. However, her legacy is still heard, enjoyed and celebrated in the church today, as her family donated a grand piano, which graces the front of the sanctuary. Ms. Hilliard recommended the current church organist, pianist and choir director, Elizabeth (Beth) Dubuisson, called affectionately by some, "Beth II." Ms. Dubuisson took over the position of music director seamlessly and has provided wonderful music and choir leadership for worship services. Her two daughters, skilled musicians in their own right, have played during worship.

The report of Long Range Planning Committee also recommended an improvement in the programs and services to church members. Office tasks advanced with the use of a computer. The First Parish newsletter was given the name, *"The Sloop's Log,"* by Nancy Richards-Stower. Eventually, church members were given the choice to receive the newsletter by way of electronic transmission, thus cutting down the cost of paper and postage. Periodic e-mails kept the congregation informed about church matters. A website was created to share information and promote First Parish. By 2010 social network media was used to keep people informed of events at the church.

New members and regular visitors were invited to a "Tea With the Minister" during which Rev. Stower gave a history of Unitarian Universalism, First Parish, an overview of how First Parish governed itself and, the responsibilities of membership. Adult Education programs including "Movie Night" which showed films with religious, moral and ethical themes which were discussed following the movie. A Spiritual Autobiography class guided participants in an exploration of their personal spiritual journeys. Another program, "Evensong," provided a small group to share thoughts, experiences, doubts and religious beliefs over eight weekly gatherings. Other thought-provoking classes were "The Greater Meanings Book Group," where theological works and novels were discussed; and, there was a weekly Bible Study group. In addition to Barbara Koelsch's on-going yoga exercise class, there were occasional meditation sessions.

While not a new initiative, the church's Caring Committee improved services to members who were ill suffered or a death in the family. The committee sent flowers and organized the home delivery of prepared meals. Transportation to doctor's appointments for people who were too ill to drive themselves or trips to the grocery store were provided. Members of the Alliance and Unity Club prepared collations in the Old Sloop Room for a church member following a funeral or memorial service.

Another Long Range Planning Committee recommendation, increasing participation in church activities, required the painful retirement of once popular, but well-worn activities such as the Goods and Services Auction and the Sea Fair. The Sea Fair, for nearly fifty years, was a well-liked First Parish event that featured a roller coaster, games, a yard and food sale, and horse-drawn rides. However, it was a very labor intensive event, much more so than the winter Snowflake Fair, and by the early 1990s, the Sea Fair was not much more than a summer edition of the Snowflake Fair, and so, by the mid-1990s the Sea Fair was no more. Later it was replaced by a more modest Plant, Bake and Barn Sale, which was later trimmed to just a Plant and Bake Sale in early June. Nevertheless, participation in these events was high and contributed to the building of a community spirit as did other events such as potluck and theme dinners as well as Family Game Nights. Dinners to kickoff the annual canvass pledge drives were also well attended, as certain parishioners were honored, often in humorous ways, for their dedication to the church. More recently, parishioners were awarded the "Lothie," named after Rev. Lothrop, for their church work.

Another effort that required a major commitment and coordination by members of the congregation was the annual Bottle and Can Drive. In 2000 the Town of Scituate permitted non-profit organizations, during a given month, to sort out redeemable bottles and cans at the town transfer station, deliver them to a redemption center, and retain all of the money. One year, in order to recruit members to spend a shift at the dump, Toni Eubanks and Chris Berkeley sang musical parodies at the start of the Sunday service. During the drive, coffee was delivered to the volunteers as the bottles as the bottles and cans were sorted. Continuing to the present, this work has been the second largest fundraiser for the church, after the Snowflake Fair, bringing in at least $3,000 each year.

The annual Snowflake Fair was the major fundraiser for the church. On the Wednesday before the fair, the aroma of balsam fir wreaths and boughs filled the church vestibule and the Old Sloop Room courtesy of member Erica Boyle who brought them to the church from Vermont. A joyful group then decorated the wreaths and boughs for sale. In recent years, Barbara Koelsch and Libby Burbank made and sold boxes of fudge. Roxanne Griem and Kay Shaw sold previously owned jewelry and many others brought their baked goods and other food items to sell, with that table managed by Gail Anderson, Anne Weaver and Alma Morrison. A recent addition was a variety of gift baskets created by Cathie McGowan, Mary McRae and others. Items raffled were Red Sox tickets, photographs and blankets knitted or crocheted by Barbara Leavitt's mother. For years the Alliance sold items that the "Fiddidlers" sewed and knitted.

The Fiddidlers (2012)

Memorable items included Libby Burbank's stuffed animals and Bessie Dooley Tufts dusters made of a stuffed cloth garden glove on a stick adorned with a bejeweled ring. By the early 1990s the Fiddidlers ended and the Alliance table receipts were diminishing, mainly because of the aging and passing of Alliance members. But happily, in 2010, Kim Ryan and Gail Anderson revived the Fiddidlers, who met weekly to create items to sell at the Fair.

Throughout the history of First Parish, worries about church finances were always at the forefront. Finances during the early years of Rev. Stower's ministry were tight though improving. There were some occasions when Rev. Stower was asked to delay depositing his salary and housing checks because there was not enough cash in the church's checking account. Within weeks of his arrival, Dorothy Brown Wood, another long-time and active member of the church (and daughter of Wilmot Brown) died. Dot, as she was known, was also very generous to the church and left over $114,000 to the congregation, significantly increasing the Endowment Fund. The generous bequests of Betty Eason, Dot Wood, and later, Louise Bates (who died in 2003 and instructed the church to place the nearly $310,000 in net proceeds from the sale of her house into the Endowment Fund) would eventually produce at least $30,000 annually into the general operating funds, thus, easing the financial pressure. With better management, the Endowment grew and by 2008 it was valued at nearly $900,000. Then, the global banking crisis and recession reduced the endowment funds by over twenty-five percent. The endowment regained most of its losses, and by May 2011 it was close to $875,000 in value. The endowment had become large enough for the congregation to borrow from it for large capital projects.

A more deliberate approach to the annual pledge drive, along with an increase in membership, and increased rental income from parsonage tenants and the Erdman School helped. Some years brought an increase of five-to-seven percent in pledges over the previous year. Keeping expenses down was not a problem; however, getting income to steadily increase would be a challenge. Nevertheless, income from pledges did increase from an average of $522 in Fiscal Year 1994 to $1200 in fiscal year 2010. Attentive financial stewardship, particularly under treasurer Christine Berkeley, who facilitated the transition from manual to computerized bookkeeping, kept the budget in balance, or with a manageable deficit. By 2008 First Parish was able to apply some of the surplus towards the following year's budget and to pay down the loan from the Endowment Fund for capital expenses. In addition, Louise Bates provided in her will that the Parish Committee was permitted to withdraw up to $10,000 per year from the principal funds from her bequest for operating expenses. She also left $10,000 in cash which was placed into the church checking account. Ms. Bates' gifts were the largest bequest in the history of First Parish. She so loved the church that her ashes were interred in the First Parish Memorial Garden.

"The goal of world community with peace, liberty, and justice for all" is one of the core values of contemporary Unitarian Universalism. It is the inspiration for much of the social justice and social responsibility work of First Parish. Throughout the years the church has been active in social justice and humanitarian issues, locally, nationally and internationally. Beginning in 2005, the congregation sponsored a Social Justice Award that provided a graduating student at Scituate High School a $250 cash award for submitting the best essay on a social justice theme. In the Greater Boston area, First Parish and the Unitarian Universalist Urban Ministry have had a long association. Rev. Stower served on the Urban Ministry's board of directors for fourteen years. Member Andrew Culbert also served. Speakers from the Urban Ministry's Renewal House, a shelter for battered women and children, often visited First Parish to talk about Renewal House's work. In response, the church has been generous with financial contributions, clothing and household items over the years. An offshoot of the Urban Ministry was the Tuckerman Coalition. Founded in the late 1990s, the Tuckerman Coalition, named after the social reformer and

Unitarian minister, Joseph Tuckerman, had as its mission advocating for families and children living in poverty in Massachusetts. With support from the federal government decreasing, Massachusetts, like other states, was taking on more responsibility for human services. The Coalition, run by a steering committee of ministers and lay people, sought to lend a liberal voice to the legislative debate in the Massachusetts General Court by hiring a highly-regarded social services lobbyist, Lisa Simonetti, to inform the Coalition about legislative proposals of interest and to act on its behalf. After some initial legislative success, such as the creation of the Newborn Home Visiting Program, a preventative program for first time parents under the age of 21. (The Coalition later worked to expand the program from the original 18-year-old age limit, as well as the expansion of funding.) Other policy issues and legislation the Coalition worked on were low-income feeding programs in public schools, juvenile justice and the prevention of the reinstitution of the death penalty in Massachusetts. On behalf of the Tuckerman Coalition, Rev. Stower testified before a legislative committee which was considering changes in the Children in Need of Services Program (CHINS), a state service to help families in crisis. After these initial successes and efforts, the Tuckerman Coalition floundered because it was unable to maintain sufficient funding and it dissolved.

In November 2003, the Massachusetts Supreme Judicial Court ruled that the Massachusetts constitution mandated the freedom to marry for same-sex couples. The lead plaintiffs were Unitarian Universalists, Hillary and Julie Goodridge, as were two other plaintiff couples. Thus, in May 2004, Massachusetts became the first state to grant marriage licenses to same-sex couples. Over the next three years there were various legal and legislative efforts to overturn the judicial decision or amend the state constitution. Rev. Stower personally lobbied Scituate's legislators to support the marriage of gay and lesbians and to oppose a proposed constitutional amendment to revoke the state Supreme Court's decision, even though Sen. Robert Hedlund and Rep. Frank Hynes voiced support for the amendment. Many First Parish members signed letters and petitions to their legislators supporting equal rights for same sex couples. In June 2007, the Massachusetts Constitutional Convention, made up of both houses of the legislature, overwhelming defeated the proposed constitutional amendment that would have overturned the Goodridge ruling. The previous month, at the 2007 Annual Meeting, First Parish had voted to seek recognition by the Unitarian Universalist Association as a "Welcoming Congregation." In order to be so acknowledged, the congregation spent a year educating itself and engaging in self-reflection on gay, lesbian, bi-sexual and transgender issues. To celebrate the successful designation, the church, in March 2008, placed an enormous rainbow banner, made by Claire Sherman, across the front facade of the church for a month. A more permanent welcoming symbol, a rainbow flag, was hung at the church entrance.

The "Welcoming Congregation" Celebration March 23, 2008

In the aftermath of the sexual abuse scandal in the Boston Archdiocese of the Roman Catholic Church, legislation was proposed in the Massachusetts General Court requiring financial disclosures for religious institutions and charities. This was particularly aimed at the Catholic churches, because the Boston archdiocese had been transferring money from a priest pension fund to a special account to pay for sexual abuse lawsuits, but the legislation would have affected all religious institutions in the state. Rev. Stower spoke with members of the Scituate legislative delegation in opposition to the proposal, citing the prohibitive annual cost of audits and other financial reports that could cause small congregations to close. Rev. Stower explained to the legislators that churches that have congregational polity (that is, independent and self-governing) did not have the same fiscal framework as hierarchical churches, since the congregation is fully aware and in control of its own funds. Under pressure, the proposed legislation was withdrawn.

First Parish has, over the years, been generous in its humanitarian efforts, starting with the Ladies Sewing Circle which made bandages for the Union soldiers during the Civil War. In 1995 a tragic fire in Scituate killed three children and severely injured others in the family. The whole town, including First Parish, responded by raising money to help the family restore the material goods they lost. Hurricane Mitch, in October 1998, devastated Honduras and Nicaragua, and killed over eleven thousand people; the December 2004 Indian Ocean tsunami killed over one hundred thirty thousand people; Hurricane Katrina flooded New Orleans, Louisiana and other Gulf states in August 2005. In response to these natural disasters First Parish donated over a thousand dollars to the Red Cross and the Unitarian Universalist Service Committee relief funds. When there was a fire in May 2010 at the Barnstable Unitarian Church, the congregation founded by Rev. Lothrop and others from Scituate, First Parish raised funds for the church. Church members also distribute food to the Scituate needy at the local food pantry and members have delivered "Meals on Wheels" to Scituate's elderly and disabled. In 1996 First Parish began a relationship with Heifer International. Based in Little Rock, Arkansas, Heifer seeks to end hunger and poverty in a sustainable way throughout the world by donating the funds for livestock for farming, food and fur and wool for income to villages and families. Offspring of the livestock are then given away to other nearby villages for their use. Over the years First Parish, led by the children of the Church School, has raised thousands of dollars to purchase water buffalo, sheep, pigs, rabbits, llamas and bees. Church member Frank Kilduff and Rev. Stower, on separate occasions, visited the Heifer International headquarters and farm to see how the organization operates. The Appalachian Service Project is a community effort in which First Parish high school students and parents have participated since 2005. Along with members from other churches in Scituate and Cohasset the group travels each summer to Tennessee or West Virginia to build new homes and repair existing homes for low-income families.

In 1995 Meg Moncy resigned as the Religious Education Coordinator and Rev. Stower, using the vacancy as an opportunity, recommended to the congregation that the job title be changed back to "Director of Religious Education (DRE)"; and, that the hours of the position be increased with an accompanying raise in compensation of thirty-seven percent. The recommendation passed unanimously. A former member of First Parish and student at Harvard Divinity School, Jeanne Melis Mills, was hired to restructure the RE program for one year. Ms. Mills assisted in creating a new vision for the RE program. Following Mills, church member Pam Molinari became the DRE. She built on the structure that Mills had developed and after a few years Molinari put her own stamp on the successful program. In 2003 a registration fee for Church School students was introduced to offset the costs of school classroom materials. Children learned about Unitarian Universalism, other religions, ecology, and social justice. Older children took field trips to other houses of worship and to Concord, Massachusetts to view the homes of Ralph Waldo Emerson and Louisa May Alcott and to Sleepy Hollow Cemetery where Henry David Thoreau and Nathaniel Hawthorne, the Alcotts and Emersons are interred. Easter egg and scavenger hunts at the church and apple picking at the home of Jack and Kay Shaw were fun activities. For the first several years of his ministry, Rev. Stower was the advisor to the High School Youth Group which Pam Molinari took over.

After thirteen years of service Molinari resigned a few weeks before Church School started in September 2008. Stepping into the breach were volunteer teachers Cathie McGowan, Sue Duff, Kim Ryan, Laura Smith and others, who worked together to put a successful program in place. At a ministers' meeting in the spring of 2009, Revs. Stower and Jan Carlson-Bull of First Parish of Cohasset agreed to share Cohasset's DRE, Jim FitzGerald, with both churches splitting the expenses. Both congregations accepted the collaboration, but it had mixed results. Most of the effort came from the Scituate church. The "Our Whole Lives" class, an age appropriate sexuality course, was attended by middle school students from both congregations but the two popular instructors, Veronica Amelang and Michael Feeney, came from Scituate. Other combined activities met with lesser success. FitzGerald, a Catholic, resigned his position to increase the hours at his other job at Call to Action, a progressive Catholic organization. Christine Bulman, a member of First Parish Unitarian Universalist Church in Duxbury, who grew up in Scituate, was hired as DRE and she began in August 2010. After significantly improving the RE program she resigned in 2012 to pursue an educational business opportunity.

The First Parish church building, parsonage and its grounds continued to be maintained and improved. In 1993 the Wayside Pulpit was relocated. Since it was first installed in the 1920s, people read the posted message as they went to town hall or the high school (when both were across the street.) As First Parish Road became a major thoroughfare for cars and trucks, the messages on the Wayside Pulpit, parallel to the road, were difficult to read. Member Jack Shaw repositioned the Wayside Pulpit, with two observable sides, so that it was perpendicular to First Parish Road. The east-facing side posted thought-provoking sayings and the west-facing side posted the title of the Sunday sermon.

The First Parish Memorial Garden was created in 1994. One of the organizers in its development was Anne Thome, who died before its completion, and who was the first person whose ashes were interred in the garden. Sadly, the grand cherry tree, in the center of the garden, estimated to be two hundred years old, became diseased and was taken down in 2009. Over the years Nancy Richards-Stower has tended to the garden lovingly. A granite bench was placed in the garden to mark the ministry of both Rev. Stower and Nancy Richards-Stower but most fittingly for gardening work of the latter.

In March 1994 the church voted to approve a bank loan of $25,000 for painting the church's exterior and installing gutters and downspouts. Thermal windows were put in the Old Sloop Room and the sanctuary was painted for the first time in decades covering water stains on the ceiling. The old furnaces were replaced thanks to a gift from Gail and Arthur Anderson of Anderson Fuel Company. Twelve years later, the church building was repainted with a new roof, front, side and rear doors installed. Interior electrical wiring and lighting were updated and a modern fire and smoke alarm system was also installed. To the relief on many, the pothole ridden dirt driveway around the back of the church was paved with asphalt. Donations by John and Yvonne Twomey provided for the periodic refinishing of the Old Sloop Room wood floor. In February 1997 the front of the church was illuminated by the "beacon for the deacon," a memorial to Michael Strzelecki who served many years as head usher and who was tireless in making minor repairs around the church. In 2001 the sound system was improved through the generosity of member Bessie Dooley Tufts, in memory of her son, Brad. A severe nor'easter in 2010 blew off much the vinyl siding on the eastern side of the church. The siding, which was installed in the early 1970s, was replaced with new wooden clapboards and the whole façade was repainted. In 2012, Frank and Leslie Kilduff, out of concern for the environment and their devotion to First Parish, approached the congregation with a proposal to install solar panels on the church's roof, which would decrease the cost of electricity to the church. The congregation approved and the use of solar energy serves as a prominent example of First Parish's commitment to social responsibility.

1996 brought the loss of many long-time members of the church including Carolyn Locklin Cohen who grew up in the church, whose parents were active members and Michael Strzelecki, "the Deacon," husband of Jean Cole Strzelecki, whose work around the church was legendary. Within weeks of his arrival in Scituate, Rev. Stower came home to the house his family was renting to find Strzelecki mowing the lawn. "The minister shouldn't have to mow his lawn," Strzelecki said. On another occasion, Strzelecki and Gil Wilder, both in their seventies, were high up a ladder, with chain saws, confidently pruning branches off the large cherry tree in the Memorial Garden. Strzelecki and Wilder chuckled as the much younger Stower nervously held the ladder, concerned for his elderly parishioners.

Gladys Wright, an active member of the Alliance also passed away in 1996, as did social activist Marge Giffin. Then word came from Florida that former member Beulah LaVangie died. Bill Terzis, who served on many church committees including finance, died too. With the passing of these long-time members First Parish mourned, but the vibrancy of the church continued with the addition of fourteen new members, the most people to join in a single year in many decades. Most of the new members had children so the Church School grew as well.

Community groups began using the church at an increasing rate. Barbara Koelsch for many years led her community yoga class in the Old Sloop Room from which she donated a portion of the proceeds to the Unity Club until the class ended in June 1999. A union held meetings at the church in an effort to organize the workers at a local nursing home. Scituate High School held its Peer Leadership Training sessions at First Parish. The Girl and Boys Scouts met in the church, as did the town's No Place for Hate® Committee, two Alcoholics Anonymous groups, the Scituate school system's diversity training and the Scituate Town Charter

Commission. Concerts in the sanctuary featured local and nationally known musicians and were open to the public. Jay Unger and Molly Mason, who wrote and played the background music for the Public Broadcasting Corporation's *The Civil War*, played twice at the church. Molly Mason played the old bass viol crafted by the Merritt brothers in 1823 much to the delight of church members in the audience.

As a student of history, Rev. Stower immersed himself in the history of First Parish and every January he gave a sermon on some

Bartlett Professor of New England Church History at Harvard Divinity School, to mark the church's three hundred and sixty-fifth anniversary. In addition, at Rev. Stower's invitation, two presidents of the UUA preached from the Scituate pulpit, Revs. John Buehrens and William Sinkford. Rev. Stower also dressed as a Pilgrim for Scituate's Heritage Days and gave talks to visitors on the history of First Parish.

During his ministry Rev. Stower was active in community affairs. He served as president of the Scituate Clergy Association for five years and under his leadership the clergy formed a cordial inter-faith relationship that was felt throughout the town. The Clergy Association held community Thanksgiving services and baccalaureate services for graduating Scituate High School students. In 1993 Stower worked with a group to develop a network of parents who pledged to each other to provide adult supervision for their children's house parties. In the fall of 1999 he spoke before the Scituate Board of Education and the school councils at the Hatherly and Cushing schools to recommend a conflict resolution program for the schools in the wake of the shooting deaths of twelve students and one teacher at the Columbine (Colorado) High School earlier that year. He was often asked to give the invocation at Scituate's Citizen of the Year dinners; and he represented the Scituate clergy at a memorial service for Pope John Paul II at St. Mary of the Nativity Church in April 2005. Rev. Stower and Rev. Jerry Smith of the First Trinitarian Congregational Church led a community service in the wake of the

September 11, 2001 attacks on the World Trade Center towers in New York City and the Pentagon in Washington.

In May 2008, clergy and civic leaders formed The Scituate Collaborative (with Rev. Stower serving as convener) in an attempt to better coordinate information about and delivery of social services to those who could use them. In the aftermath of a severe winter storm in late December 2010 which destroyed Scituate homes by fire and flooding, the Collaborative began an effort to make disaster relief to Scituate citizens more effective and efficient by coordinating local groups like the Scituate Council on Aging, the Scituate Food Pantry, Scituate Community Christmas and the American Red Cross and the Federal Emergency Management Administration (FEMA.) In 2012, the group was renamed SANDS (The Scituate Alliance of Natural Disaster Services.)

As part of the covenant between First Parish and Rev. Stower there was a provision that allowed Rev. Stower to take a sabbatical every five years. A Sabbatical Committee was formed in 1998 to plan for Rev. Stower's four-month absence. Committee members were responsible for administrative and pastoral matters during his leave and Rev. Stower arranged for guest ministers and speakers to fill the pulpit. In January 2000 the congregation gave Rev. Stower a "Bon Voyage" party before his trip to Nepal, Thailand, and the island of Bali in Indonesia. On his return he stopped in London to begin his research of the history of First Parish for this volume. At the British Library he held and read the original tracts written by Henry Jacob four hundred years earlier. He visited the Southwark Local History Library in the area where Jacob and Rev. Lothrop and the Southwark congregation met in worship and communion. In 2007 Rev. Stower took a second, shorter sabbatical during which he travelled to Little Rock, Arkansas to visit Heifer International headquarters learning how it operates around the world in helping people and their communities become self-sustaining. He also spent a week at Pendle Hill, a Quaker retreat center near Philadelphia for a time of rest and reflection. In 2009, he and his wife, Nancy, traveled to Eastern Europe to explore the cities and towns where their grandparents were born. They also travelled in England and stayed in Kent where they visited Rev. Lothrop's parish church in Egerton and the town of Tenterden, home to some of the earliest Scituate settlers.

Gordon Lothrop, UUA President Bill Sinkford, Rev. Stower

In September 2008 First Parish began its celebration of the 375th anniversary of its gathering. To mark the arrival of Rev. John Lothrop, his family and some members of his Southwark congregation, a special dinner was held in the Old Sloop Room. Rev. Stower made a presentation, as did Rev. Bill Sinkford, president of the UUA, and Gordon Lothrop, a direct descendent of Rev. Lothrop. Other members of the Lothrop family attended. In January 2009, the congregation gathered for a special worship service modeled after a seventeenth century worship with readings from the Geneva Bible used by the Pilgrims, and the singing of hymns without instrumental accompaniment. Rev. Stower wore appropriate Pilgrim attire (on loan from the Plimoth Plantation museum). The anniversary was also marked by the attendance and congratulations of town, state and UUA officials. A proclamation entered into the *Congressional Record* by Representative William Delahunt; letters and citations from United States Senators Edward Kennedy and John Kerry, State Senator Robert Hedlund, and State Representatives James Cantwell and Garrett Bradley were read.

There were other activities celebrating the anniversary. In the fall, 375 daffodil bulbs were planted at the base of the Wayside Pulpit and $375 was donated to the Scituate Town Library. Pictures of the church's communion cups, reproductions of old postcards with pictures of the church and commemorative bookmarks were created and sold. Another highlight of the anniversary year was a dinner held at Plimoth Plantation that featured an early seventeenth century meal as First Parish's forbearers would have enjoyed. Entertainment was provided by a quartet of singers and actors, in period dress, who serenaded the gathering with period songs and engaged the dinner guests in seventeenth century conversation. Articles about the anniversary appeared in the *Boston Globe*, the *Patriot Ledger* and the *Scituate Mariner*. In the fall, former ministers Tom Goldsmith, Darrell Berger and David Parke returned to First Parish to preach from their old pulpit.

Mindful of the connection between the Scituate and Barnstable parishes, Rev. Stower accepted an invitation to speak at the rededication of the Lothrop Bible at the Sturgis Library in Barnstable along with members of the Lothrop family and the ministers of Barnstable's Unitarian and Congregational churches. The personal Bible of Rev. Lothrop was carried by him on the voyage to Massachusetts and, while at sea, some candlewax burned holes in some pages. Lothrop repaired it and wrote in the missing verses by hand from memory. The Sturgis Library was once Lothrop's home and the place where he and his congregation worshipped and there one can view the Bible in its new display case.

Further strengthening the bonds between First Parish and the Lothrop family, in January 2011, Gordon Lothrop presented First Parish a check for $3,500 from the Lothropp Family Foundation for the maintenance of the church building and church records. Rev. Stower is presently the chaplain of the Lothropp Family Foundation.

In June 2010 Rev. Stower announced that he would step down as minister in the summer of 2011. The congregation and Rev. Stower had a year to say good-bye to each other, but there was still work to be done. For about seventy-five years the Parish Committee governed the church (with the entire parish membership the ultimate authority.) The structure had become outmoded. Too often the reports of the various committees would turn into a discussion of a particular committee's work, turning the Parish Committee into a Committee of the Whole for that committee. With busy schedules it was difficult for people to volunteer to lead a committee. A new governance model was needed, so a Governance Task Force was created and charged to research how other Unitarian Universalist churches were governed and to report its recommendations to the parish. After months of dedicated work the Task Force presented its report to the congregation for its consideration in May 2012. The task force recommended that the Parish Committee be reconfigured, comprised of seven members: two co-chairs, the treasurer, secretary and three at-large liaisons who would be responsible for three areas. The Administration and Leadership Liaison would report to the Parish Committee on matters concerning buildings and grounds, finance and development, nominations and by-law revisions; the Membership and Outreach Liaison would report on public relations, membership, hospitality, social justice, denominational affairs and social programs; and, the Parish Life Liaison would be concerned with matters relating to religious education, religious services, and the Committee on Ministry. The Minister would continue to serve on the Parish Committee as a non-voting, ex-officio member.

In the spring of 2011, the Parish Committee hired the Rev. Stephen Cook as the interim minister for a two-year period. Rev.

Cook was most recently the interim minister at the Wellesley Hills Unitarian Church.

In the final months of Rev. Stower's ministry the mutual affection between him and the First Parish congregation was clearly evident on several occasions. At the kick-off dinner to the annual canvass, master of ceremonies, Dave Berkeley, accompanied by the church choir gave Rev. Stower a good-natured roasting. Frank Kilduff brought down the house with his rock star impersonation. Rev. Stower received several personalized joke gifts including an oversized dollar bill with his picture and the motto, "In Rich We Trust," and matching Wal-Mart greeter vests for him and his employment lawyer, activist wife, Nancy.

Overlooking Scituate Harbor on a beautiful spring evening, First Parish members, Scituate clergy and other Scituate citizens, as well as Unitarian Universalist ministerial colleagues of Rev. Stower, enjoyed a delightful dinner party held at the Satuit Boat Club catered by church member, Claire Sherman. On this occasion it was the former pastor of the First Baptist Church in Scituate, Stephen Trimble, who entertained the gathering at Rev. Stower's expense.

At his final service as minister of First Parish on June 19, 2011, Rev. Stower reminisced about his nineteen years in Scituate and how much the church, the congregation and the town meant to him and how much they transformed him. As a parting gift to the congregation Rev. Stower presented an illuminated work of calligraphy listing of all of First Parish's ministers beginning with Rev. John Lothrop and the sites of First Parish buildings.

A Personal Epilogue

It was a cold winter's day in January 1992 when I turned onto First Parish Road and headed east. East where the sun rises over the ocean every day. Coming to the crest of the hill to my left was First Parish church with Lawson Tower next to it. I had seen pictures but here it was, right in front of me. There was a man standing in front of the door and my stomach did a tumble as I drove up the driveway, got out of the car, and met Ray Morrison for the first time. Ray welcomed me and we went inside the church and he showed me around. Then I met with the Search Committee. We had a nice conversation at lunch, then the next day the committee heard me preach at the Universalist Unitarian Church of Brockton. A couple of weeks later I was told that the committee was prepared to recommend me to First Parish and did I want to come to First Parish as its minister. I said yes and on April 12,1992 the congregation voted to call me and I accepted. A new chapter in my life was beginning; and on June 19, 2011 another chapter ended.

A few years ago I was driving around town and as I drove along Front Street in the harbor, Betty Crowley, then the coordinator of the Scituate Food Pantry, shouted out to me, "Hello Rev. Stower!" I passed where the Front Street Book Store used to be and thought of Pam Giovannini and the wedding I did for her daughter Beth. I drove past Bailey's Liquor store where Maryanne Hennessey Bailey worked behind the counter. I officiated at her sister's wedding and the memorial services for her parents, Carol and Joe Hennessey, active members of the church in the 1950s and 1960s. Her son Phil was a school friend and baseball teammate of Jonathan's. I hugged the harbor, passed the Bates House, which Yvonne Twomey has given to the town and maintained by the Historical Society. I drove along Hatherly Road, past what was then called "Dad's Store" up the street from where, on a snowy day years earlier, I married Chris and Dave Berkeley. Making a turn onto Gannett Road I passed Vicki and Ken Davis' house and then past Gil and Jane Wilder's. Jane was on my Search Committee and, of course, whenever I think of Gil, I always smile. Gil is the embodiment of a New England Yankee. Always on the move, always thinking of doing things better, and most importantly, being civic-minded. So, as I headed back home, along Country Way, I said to myself, "This is my town." Not in an imperial way, but it a way that only comes from love. And where is my heart? Here.

We Americans like happy endings where all the threads of a plot come neatly together. I remember taking my father to a French movie in the 1960s where time was not relevant and the plot did not move in a linear fashion. He hated the movie. "I like something with a beginning, a middle and an end," he said. I think all of us would agree, but life is not like that. It can be cyclical and circular; life can be two steps forward and one step back. We make U-turns; go down a one-way street the wrong way. Rarely what we want to do in our lives is finished when we come to our end.

Moses never crossed on over into the Promised Land, but he went as far as it was possible for him to go. For forty years he struggled with a stubborn people; members of First Parish are not stubborn, cantankerous sometimes, but not stubborn. For forty years Moses dwelt in tents and lived off the land; for forty years he was a pilgrim; and all to one end: that he might reach the Promised Land! At last that day arrived! He stood on Mr. Nebo and gazed longingly into the Promised Land. But, we are then told, God said, "I have let you *see* the Promised Land, but you shall not yourself cross over into it." And there, hardly a stone's throw short of his life's goal, he died!

But, again, that is life. Knowing he would not enter the Promised Land, Moses prepared Joshua for the great task ahead. And so it is for those whose life is wrapped up in ministry. We strive to provide the foundation for leadership of those who succeed us, for the concern of a minister must always be the welfare of the congregation he or she has led.

The truth for us all, every one of us, is that the journey is what counts most, not the destination. The forty years that Moses led his people wandering in the desert was a trial for all of them. But what did they learn? Moses learned about leadership. The Israelites learned patience, even amidst the grumbling. They even learned that sometimes things happen – good and bad - that are beyond their control and so the journey through the desert transformed both Moses and the Israelites. We humans are always on the go; we're not static and lifeless like rocks. We are pilgrims, sojourners, and only so do we stay alive; and that being the case, it is the journey we should enjoy; it is the journey that gives the deepest meaning to our lives. And so it is with me. I enjoyed my time, my journey, with the people of the First Parish Unitarian Universalist Church of Scituate.

I do not have the eloquence of Rev. Sewall's words of good-bye. So allow me to quote him as if they were my own words.

"Permit me to dwell in your own and your children's remembrance as one who wished and strove to do all he could to advance your and their highest happenings."

Blessings on our beloved First Parish.

Rev. Stower, Nancy Richards-Stower and the children of First Parish
June, 2011

Name	Scituate Ministry	College or Seminary
John Lothrop (1584-1653)	1634-1639	Queen's College, Oxford
Peter Saxton (1573?-1651)	1640-1641	Trinity College, Cambridge
Christopher Blackwood (1608?-1670)	1641	Pembroke College, Cambridge
Charles Chauncy (1592-1672)	1641-1654	Trinity College, Cambridge
Henry Dunster (1609-1659)	1654-1659	Magdalen College, Cambridge
Nicholas Baker (1610-1678)	1660-1678	St. John's College, Cambridge
Jeremiah Cushing (1654-1705)	1691-1705	Harvard College
Nathaniel Pitcher (1685-1723)	1707-1723	Harvard College
Shearjashub Bourn (1699-1768)	1724-1761	Harvard College
Ebenezer Grosvenor (1738-1788)	1762-1780	Yale College
Ebenezer Dawes (1756-1791)	1787-1791	Harvard College
Nehemiah Thomas (1765-1831)	1792-1831	Harvard College
Edmund Q. Sewall (1796-1866)	1831-1848	Harvard College
Ephraim Nute, Jr. (1819-1897)	1848-1851	Harvard Divinity School
Fiske Barrett II (1816-1879)	1852-1859	Harvard Divinity School
William G. Babcock (1820-1911)	1860-1865	Harvard Divinity School
William S. Heywood (1824-1905)	1865-1867	Did not attend a seminary
H. L. Cargill (1869-1912)	1869-1870	Boston School of Ministry
Nicholas P. Gilman (1849-1912)	1872-1874	Harvard Divinity School
Sheldon C. Clark (1846-1928)	1875-1877	Meadville Theological School
Nathanael Seaver, Jr. (1836-1919)	1882-1886	Harvard Divinity School
H. A. Whitman (1843-1911)	1888-1889	So. Baptist Theological Sem.
William H. Spencer (1840-1923)	1890-1891	Harvard Divinity School
Watson Weed (1849-1905)	1892-1896	Cazenovia Seminary
Fred H. Gile (1860-1938)	1897-1899	?
Joseph C. Allen (1869-1955)	1900-1901	Harvard Divinity School
Stanley M. Hunter (1870?-?)	1901-1903	Meadville Theological School
George A. Hathaway (1875-?)	1904-1908	Harvard Divinity School
Hilary Bygrave (1847-1921)	1909-1911	?
Robert P. Doremus (1879-?)	1912-1913	Meadville and Harvard Divinity
Henry W. Pinkham (1864-1947)	1914-1915	Newton Theological School
George W. H. Troop (?-?)	1915	Harvard Divinity School
William W. Locke (1858-1945)	1915-1922	Harvard Divinity School
Cornelus Heijn (1891-1968)	1923-1930	Meadville and Harvard Divinity

Robert Lewis Weis (?-?)	1931-1933	Meadville and Pacific Unit. Sem.
Robert C. Withington (1904-1995)	1933-1937	Meadville Theological School
Lewis W. Sanford (1878-1947)	1937-1942	Harvard Divinity School
Walter Reid Hunt (1867-?)*	1942-1943	Harvard Divinity School
Alfred Schenkman (1919-1984)	1942-1945	Meadville and Univ. of Chicago
Raymond Johnson (1885-1951)	1945-1948	?
Leon C. Fay (1913-2003)	1948-1951	Crane Theological School
Henry G. Cooper (1919-1984)	1952-1955	Meadville and Univ. of Chicago
Charles C. Donelson, Jr. (1919-?)	1955-1969	Boston Univ. Sch. of Theology
Carl H. Whittier (1929-)	1960-1972	Harvard Divinity School
David Parke (1928-)*	1972-1973	Meadville Lombard Theo. Sch.
John C. Fuller (1921-1974)	1973-1974	Meadville Lombard Theo. Sch.
Tom Goldsmith (1949-)	1975-1977	Harvard Divinity
Darrell Berger (1948-)	1978-1989	Vanderbilt Divinity School
Michael Boardman (1937-2007)*	1989-1990	Starr King Sch. for the Ministry
Steve Stock (1945-2010)	1990-1991	Meadville Lombard Theo. Sch.
William Gardner (1912-2000)*	1991-1992	Tufts College Sch. of Religion
Richard M. Stower (1946-)	1992-2011	Harvard Divinity School
Stephen M. Cook (1949-)*	2011-	Bangor Theological Seminary

* Interim Ministers

Bibliography

This bibliography lists the primary and secondary material mentioned in the text. Some of the sources noted in the text are minister's files located the Andover-Harvard Library at the Harvard Divinity School in Cambridge, Massachusetts. Most of the Sewall family correspondence can be found in the Thoreau-Sewall Collection at the Huntington Library in San Marino, California. The Martha Strickland letters are located in the Labadie Collection in the Special Collections Library at the University of Michigan in Ann Arbor. Other files, including some of Margaret Cole Bonney's essays, as well as First Parish minutes of its various committee, are in the First Parish archives. Older church journals from the eighteenth century are kept in the Scituate town archives at the Scituate Town Hall. Newer church journals from the past one hundred and fifty years are in the church's archives.

Acheson, R. J. *Radical Puritans.* Guilford: Globe Pequot Press, 1990.

Adams, Brooks. *The Emancipation of Massachusetts.* Boston: Houghton Mifflin and Company, 1887.

A Second Series of Letters Concerning the History of the First Parish in Scituate. Boston: J. Munroe, 1845.

Ahlstrom, Sidney E. *A Religious History of the American People.* New Haven: Yale University Press, 1972

Allen, William . *An American Biographical and Historical Dictionary.* Boston: William Hyde & Co., 1832.

Anderson, Robert Charles. *The Pilgrim Migration: Immigrants to Plymouth Colony, 1620-1633.* Boston: New England Historic Genealogical Society, 2004.

_____. *The Great Migration Begins, Vol. II.* Boston: New England Historic Genealogical Society, 1995.

Appleton's Cyclopedia of American Biography. New York: D. Appleton and Company, 1886.

Bacon, Edwin M. *The Book of Boston: Fifty Years' Recollections of the New England Metropolis.* Boston: The Book of Boston Company, 1916.

Bailyn, Bernard. *The New England Merchants in the Seventeenth Century.* Cambridge: Harvard University Press, 1955.

Beale, David. *The Mayflower Pilgrims: Roots of Puritan, Presbyterian, Congregationalist, and Baptist Heritage.* Greenville: Ambassador-Emerald International, 2000.

Benedict, David. *A General History of the Baptist Denomination in America and Other Parts of the World.* New York: Lewis Colby and Company, 1848.

Bloomfield, Edward H. *The Opposition to the English Separatists, 1570-1625.* Washington: University Press of America, 1981.

Boast, Mary. *The Mayflower and Pilgrim Story.* London: Southwark Libraries Department, 1995.

Boston Evening Post, March 1, 1756.

The Boston Medical and Surgical Journal, Vol. XVIII, "Epilepsy Cured by Trepanning," ed. Smith, J.V.C. 1838.

Bonney, Margaret Cole. *My Scituate.* Privately Published.

_____. *Scituate's Sands of Time.* Privately Published.

Bonomi, Patricia. *Under the Cope of Heaven.* New York: Oxford University Press, 1986.

Boston Daily Globe, May 2, 1917.

_____. June 11, 1917.

Brachlow, Stephen. "John Robinson and the Separatist Ideal." In *The Puritan Experiment in the New World*, The Westminister Conference, 1976.

Bradford, William. *Bradford's History of Plymouth Planation*, ed. William A.T. Davis, 1908. Reprint, New York: Barnes & Noble, 1971.

Bremer, Francis J. *The Puritan Experiment.* Lebanon: University Press of New England, 1995.

Burrage, Champlin. *The Early English Dissenters* (2 volumes), 1912. Reprint, Paris; The Baptist Standard Bearer, Inc.

Cambridge Public School District. "Maria L. Baldwin Biography," http://www.cpsd.us/BAL/history_baldwin.cfm

Carlson, Larry A. "Bronson Alcott's Journal for 1838", Part Two, in *Studies in the American Renaissance.* 1994.

Carpenter, Dorothy. *William Vassall and Dissent in Early Massachusetts.* http://home.gwi.net/~sscarpen/vassall/Vassall.pdf, 2004.

Chalkin, C. W. *Seventeenth Century Kent.* London: Longmans, 1965.

Chaplin, Jeremiah. *The Life of Henry Dunster*. Boston: James R. Osgood, 1872.

Cheever, George B. *The Journal of the Pilgrims*. New York: John Wiley, 1849.

The Christian Register, August 27, 1831.

_____. October 4, 1845.

_____. July 13, 1850.

_____. September 29, 1866.

_____. September 6, 1934.

_____. August 1945.

Christian Watchman, May 10, 1833.

Connick, Charles. "Boston Stained Glass Craftsmen," in *Stained Glass*, Summer 1933.

Cooke, George Willis. *Unitarianism in America*. Charleston: Bibliobazaar, 2006

Cowing, Cedric B. *The Saving Remnant*. Urbana: University of Illinois Press, 1995.

Dale, R. W. *History of English Congregationalism*. London: Hodder and Stoughton, 1907.

Damon, Daniel E. "History of Scituate and South Scituate" in *History of Plymouth County, Massachusetts*. Philadelphia: J. W. Lewis, 1884.

Daniels, Bruce C. *Puritans at Play*. New York: St. Martin's Griffin, 1995.

Deane, Samuel. *A Discourse on Christian Liberty*. Cambridge: Hilliard and Metcalf, 1825

_____. *History of Scituate, Massachusetts, From Its Settlement to 1831*. 1831. Reprint, Scituate: Scituate Historical Society, 1975.

Dinkin, Robert J. "Seating the Meeting House in Early Massachusetts" in *The New England Quarterly, Vol. 43, No. 3*. September, 1970.

Earle, Alice Morse. *Child Life in Colonial Times*.1899. Reprint, New York: Dover, 2009.

_____. *Home and Child Life in Colonial Days*. New York: Macmillan, 1969

_____. *The Sabbath in Puritan New England*. 1898. Reprint, Williamstown: Corner House Publishers, 1969.

Ebert, Sarah. *Louisa May Alcott on Race, Sex and Slavery*. Boston: Northeastern University Press, 1997.

Eliot, Samuel Atkins. *Heralds of a Liberal Faith, Vol. 3*. Boston, American Unitarian Association, 1910.

Emerson, Dorothy May, editor. *Standing Before Us: Unitarian Universalist Women and Social Reform, 1776-1936*. Boston: Skinner House Books, 2000.

Field, Peter S. *The Crisis of the Standing Order*. Amherst: The University of Massachusetts Press, 1998.

History of First Parish of Norwell, Massachusetts. http://www.firstparishnorwell.org/history.htm

Forman, Charles. "Elected Now By Time," in Conrad Wright, editor, *A Stream of Light: A Sesquicentennial History of American Unitarianism*. Boston: Unitarian Universalist Association, 1975.

Foster, Stephen. *The Long Argument: English Puritanism and the Shaping of New England Culture, 1570-1700*. Chapel Hill: The University of North Carolina Press, 1996.

Fowler, William Chauncey. *Memorials of the Chaunceys*. Boston: Henry W. Dutton, 1868.

Fraser, Antonia, *Cromwell*. New York: Grove Press, 1973.

French, Allen, *Charles I and the Puritan Upheaval*. London: Allen & Unwin, 1955.

Furness, Jr., Horace Howard, Editor. *The Letters of Horace Howard Furness*. Boston: Houghton Mifflin Company, 1922.

Gardiner, Samuel Rawson ed. *Reports of Cases in the Courts of Star Chamber and High Commission*. Westminster: Nichols and Son, 1886.

Gaustad, Edwin and Leigh Schmidt. *The Religious History of America*. New York: Harper One, 2002.

George, Timothy. *John Robinson and the English Separatist Tradition*. Macon: Mercer University Press, 1982

Gilman, Nicholas P. " The Personal Ideal of the Unitarian Faith," in *The Unitarian Review and Religious Magazine*. February 1878.

_____. "Socialism," in *Meadville Theological School Quarterly* Bulletin. April 1912.

Godfrey, Dennis. *Clink! The Story of a Forgotten Church*. London: Darwin Press

Godbeer, Richard. *Sexual Revolution in Early America*. Baltimore: The Johns Hopkins University Press, 2002.

Greene, George Sears. *The Greenes of Rhode Island, with historical records of English ancestry, 1534-1902*. New York: The Knickerbocker Press, 1903.

Groth, Barbara. "Ephraim Nute," http://www25.uua.org/uuhs/duub/articles/ephraimnute.html

Gura, Philip F. *A Glimpse of Sion's Glory: Puritan Radicalism in New England, 1620-1660*. Middletown: Wesleyan University Press, 1984.

_____. *American Transcendentalism*. New York: Hill and Wang, 2007.

Hall, David D., editor. *Puritans in the New World: A Critical Anthology*. Princeton: Princeton University Press, 2004.

Hall, Timothy D. "The American Revolution and the Religious Public Sphere," http://revolution.h-net.msu.edu/essays/hall.html

Harding, Walter. *The Days of Henry Thoreau*. New York: Dover Publications, 1982.

Hodges, R. M. *The Ministry of Pain*. 1866.

Hunter, Stanley Mercer. "Is There a Science of Character?" in *The Phrenological Journal of Science and Health*, September 1895.

Huntington, E. B. ed. *Genealogical Memoir of the Lo-Lathrop Family*. E. H. Lathrop, 1884.

The Independent, July 19, 1877.

Jacob, Henry. *A declaration and plainer opening of certaine points, with a sound confirmation of some other, contained in a treatise intituled, The divine beginning and institution of Christes true visible and ministeriall church*. 1612.

_____. *An Attestation of many divines that the Church-government ought to bee alwayes with the peoples free consent*. Middelburg, 1613.

_____. *Divine Beginnings and Institutions of Christ true Visible ... Church*. Leiden, 1610.

Jacobs, Carolyn. "Friends & Allies Paper: Martha Strickland Clark: Reformers and Liberal Thinkers: The Men in Strickland's Life." Unpublished, 2006.

Jessup, Frank W. *Kent History Illustrated*. Maidstone: Kent Education Committee, 1966.

Johnson, Claudia Durst. *Daily Life in Colonial New England*. Westport: Greenwood Publishing, 2008.

Richard Brigham Johnson, ed., "The Diary of Israel Litchfield," *New England Historical and Genealogical Register, CXXIX*. April, 1975.

Jordan, W. K. "Social Institutions in Kent, 1480-1660." In *Essays in Kentish History* ed. by M. Roake and J. Whyman, London: Cass, 1973.

King, Henry Melville. *The Baptism of Roger Williams*. Providence: Preston & Rounds, 1897.

Koopman, Louise Osgood. "The Thoreau Romance," *Massachusetts Review*, IV. 1962.

LaFountain, Jason David. "Reflections on the Funerary Monuments and Burying Grounds of Early New England" M.A. Thesis, University of Maryland, 2004.

Lechford, Thomas. *Plain Dealing or News from New England*. Boston: J. K. Wiggin & Wm. Parsons Lunt, 1867.

Lerner, Gerda. *The Majority Finds Its Past: Placing Women in History*. Chapel Hill: The University of North Carolina Press, 2005.

The Liberator, May 12, 1837.

_____. May 1854

Lockwood, Frank C. "Professor Gilman's Literary Activities," in *Meadville Theological School Quarterly Bulletin*. April 1912.

Maltz, Earl M. *Fugitive Slave on Trial: The Anthony Burns Case and Abolitionist Outrage*. Lawrence: University Press of Kansas, 2010.

Marshfield [Massachusetts] Mail, December 24, 1937.

Mather, Cotton . *Magnalia Christi Americana*. Hartford: Andrus and Son, 1855.

McKenzie, Alexander. *Lectures on the History of the First Church in Cambridge*. Boston: Congregational Publishing Society, 1873.

McLoughlin, William Gerald. *New England Dissent*. Cambridge: Harvard University Press, 1971

Miller, Perry. *Orthodoxy in Massachusetts, 1630-1650*. New York: Harper and Row, 1973.

Moore, Susan Hardman. *Pilgrims: New World Settlers and the Call of Home*. New Haven: Yale University Press, 2008.

Morgan, Edmund S.. *Visible Saints: The History of a Puritan Idea*. Ithaca: Cornell University Press, 1963.

Morison. Samuel Eliot. *The Intellectual Life of Colonial New England*. Westport: Greenwood Press, 1980.

Morning Oregonian, September 29, 1895

Morton, Nathaniel. *New England Memorial*. 1669. Reprint, Boston: Congregational Board of Publication, 1855.

Nason, Elias. *A Gazetteer for the State of Massachusetts*. Boston: B. B. Russell, 1874.

Natick [Massachusetts] Bulletin, August 20, 1975

Neal, Daniel. *History of the Puritans, Vol. I,* 1863.

New York Times, May 29, 1854.

_____. June 5, 1854

_____. "The Strike of the Massachusetts Shoe-workers," February 24, 1860.

_____. November 5, 1911

_____. January 9, 1930.

_____. May 9, 1930

_____. May 20, 1936

Nute, Jr., Ephraim. *"The Leaven of Liberty,"* in *The Liberty Bell*. 1851.

Perkins, Keith W. "John Lothropp," http://www.cumorah.org/libros/ingles/Regional_Studies_in_LDS_History_British_Isles_-_Various_authors.html

Petrulionis, Sandra Harbert. "Swelling That Great Tide of Humanity": The Concord, Massachusetts, Female Anti-Slavery Society, *The New England Quarterly* Vol. 74, No. 3. September, 2001.

Pinkham, Henry Winn. "English and German Sailors Dine Together," from the Henry Winn Pinkham Collection at the University of Denver (Colorado) Penrose Library

Powers, Edwin. *Crime and Punishment in Early Massachusetts, 1620-1692: A Documentary History*. Boston: Beacon Press, 1966.

Pratt, Harvey Hunter. *The Early Planters of Scituate*, 1929. Reprint, Scituate: Scituate Historical Society, 2005.

Prior, Charles W. A. *Defining the Jacobean Church: The Politics of Religious Controversy, 1603-1625*. Cambridge: Cambridge University Press, 2005.

Proceedings of the Grand Lodge of the Most Ancient and Honorable Fraternity of Free and Accepted Masons of the Commonwealth of Massachusetts. Boston: Rockwell and Churchill, 1878.

Prynne, William. *History of the Troubles and Tryal of the Most Reverent Father in God and Blessed Martyr, William Laud, Lord Arch-Bishop of Canterbury*, 1694.

Quincy, Josiah. *History of Harvard University, Vol. I*. Boston: Crosby, Nichols, Lee and Co., 1860.

Quincy Patriot Ledger, May 1951.

Raysor, T.M. "The Love Story of Thoreau," in *Studies in Philology, XXIII*. October, 1926.

Robinson, David. *The Unitarians and Universalists*. Westport: Greenwood Press, 1985

Richardson, Peter. *The Boston Religion*. Rockland: Red Barn Publishing, 2003.

Salmans, O. R. and J. M. Auld. *Cripple Creek: A Standard Handbook of the Mines and Mining Companies*. Colorado Springs, 1901.

Scituate [Massachusetts] Herald, May 10, 1918.

_____. September 4, 1936.

Scituate [Massachusetts] Mariner, March 27, 2003

Shaw, William. *A Sermon Preached November 14, 1787, at the Ordination of the Rev. Ebenezer Dawes to the Pastoral Care of the First Church in Scituate*. 1788.

Shurtleff, Nathaniel B. *Records of the Governor and Company of the Massachusetts Bay, Vol. III*. Boston: William White, 1854

Sibley's Harvard Graduates Vol. II. Cambridge: Charles William Sever, 1881.

Smith, Harmon. *My Friend, My Friend: The Story of Thoreau's Relationship With Emerson*. Amherst: The University of Massachusetts Press, 1999.

South Scituate [Massachusetts] Herald, May 20, 1881.

_____. November 1932

Spencer, Anna Garlin. Papers, Swarthmore College Peace Collection

Spencer, William Henry. Spencer Family Records in the Anna Garlin Spencer Papers, Swarthmore College Peace Collection.

Staloff, Darren. *The Making of An American Thinking Class: Intellectuals & Intelligentsia in Puritan Massachusetts*. New York: Oxford University Press, 1998.

State of Colorado Roster of Elected Officers. Denver: The Smith-Brooks Printing Co., 1911.

Stewart, Shawn. "Transcendental Romance Meets the Ministry of Pain: The Thoreau Brothers, Ellen Sewall, and her Father" by in *The Concord Saunterer*, Vol. 14, 2006.

Stout, Harry S. *The New England Soul.* New York: Oxford University Press, 1986.

Tolmie, Murray. *The Triumph of the Saints: The Separate Churches of London, 1616-1649.* Cambridge: Cambridge University Press, 1977.

The Unitarian: A Monthly Magazine of Liberal Christianity, Vol. IX, 1894.

"Unitarian Pacifist Fellowship Newsletter." May 1947.

Valdespino, Stephen R. *Timothy Hatherly and the Plymouth Colony Pilgrims.* Scituate: Scituate Historical Society, 1987.

Vital Records of Scituate, Massachusetts: to Year 1850, V.2. 1909.

Waite, Clarence M. *Congregationalism in Scituate.* Scituate: First Trinitarian Congregational Church, 1967.

Walker, Williston. *The Creeds and Platforms of Congregationalism.* Cleveland: United Church Press, 1991.

Waters, Robert Edmond Chester. *Parish Registers in England: Their History and Contents with Suggestions for Securing Their Better Custody and Preservation.* London: Fred. J. Roberts, 1883

Watts, Michael. *The Dissenters; From the Reformation to the French Revolution.* Oxford: Clarendon Press, 1978

Webb, Jr., Seth. *The Monthly Journal of the American Unitarian Association,* November 1860.

Weir. David. *Early New England: A Covenanted Society.* Grand Rapids: Wm. B. Eerdmans Publishing, 2005.

Wight, Jr., Daniel. *Church Manual: or the History, Standing Rules, Discipline, Articles of Faith, and Covenant, of the First (Trinitarian Congregational) Church of Christ in Scituate, Mass.* Boston: William S. Damrell, 1844.

_____. *Document of the Pilgrim Conference Containing an Historical Sketch of the First Trinitarian Congregational Church of Christ in Scituate, Mass.* Boston, 1853.

Willison, George F. *Saints and Strangers.* New York: Reynal & Hitchcock, 1945.

Wilson, Walter. *The History and Antiquities of Dissenting Churches, Vol. I.* London: W. Button and Son, 1808.

Winslow, Ola Elizabeth. *Meetinghouse Hill, 1630-1783*. New York: W. W. Norton, 1972.

Winthrop, John. *History of New England, Vol. I*. Boston: Phelps and Farnham, 1825.

Woodhead, Linda. *An Introduction to Christianity*. Cambridge: Cambridge University Press, 2004.

Woodworth, Samuel. *The Poems, Odes, Songs and Other Metrical Effusions.* New York: Abraham Asten and Mattias Lopez, 1818.

Wright, Conrad . *Congregational Polity*. Boston: Skinner House Books, 1997.

Wright, Stephen. "Sarah Jones and the Jacob-Jessey Church: The Relation of a Gentlewoman," 2004. http://www.bl.uk/eblj/2004articles/pdf/article2.

Young, Alexander. *Chronicles of the First Planters of the Colony of Massachusetts Bay*. Boston: Charles C. Little and James Brown, 1846.

ILLUSTRATION CREDITS

Courtesy of John Salmon: 20
Courtesy of the Victoria and Albert Museum, London, England: 29
Photograph taken by Richard Stower: 35
Surrey Congregational History by John Waddington: 38
Courtesy of First Parish Unitarian Universalist Church of Scituate: 119, 163, 286, 327, 344, 348, 365, 382, 393, 401, 429, 436, 438, 442
Courtesy of the Philadelphia Museum of Art, Philadelphia, Pennsylvania: 173
Courtesy of the Andover-Harvard Library, Harvard University: 227, 240, 251, 256, 275, 281, 285, 291, 303, 306, 314, 363, 379, 385, 391, 399
Courtesy of Alan Donaldson: 270
The Book of Boston (1916) by Edwin Monroe Bacon (p. 447): 289
Courtesy of the First Church in Belmont, Massachusetts: 300
Courtesy of Cornelus Heijn, Jr.: 339
Courtesy of Betty Mencucci: 354
Courtesy of the Unitarian Universalist Church of Nashua, New Hampshire: 389
Courtesy of the First Unitarian Universalist Church of Columbus, Ohio: 414
Courtesy of Yvonne Twomey; Nancy Richards-Stower: 443
Courtesy of Rev. David B. Parke: 420
Photograph taken by Annemarie DeSmet: 447
Photograph taken by Nancy Richards-Stower: 452, 464
Photograph taken by Jonathan Stower: 456
Photograph taken by Britain Davis: 471

Index

A

Abbot, George, (Archbishop of Canterbury), 40, 42, 46
Act of Uniformity, 8, 10
Adams, John Quincy, 222, 223
Adams, William C., 298
Adler, Felix, 283
Alcott, Bronson, 190, 214, 221, 244
Alcott, Louis May, 181, 190, 274, 458
Allen, Cornelia 325, 410
Allen, Joseph Cady, 291, 292
Allen, George M., 178
Allen, George O., 272, 289, 297, 333
Allen, Morrill A., 179
American Unitarian Association (AUA), 231, 232, 293, 298, 305, 312, 313, 315, 325, 328, 330, 332, 333, 339, 343, 347, 351, 354, 356, 359, 366, 372, 374, 375, 377, 386, 392, 396, 403
Ames, Charles, 302
Ames, William, 27
Anderson, Arthur and Gail, 297, 452, 453
Annable, Anthony, 59, 61, 65
Antioch College, 256

B

Babcock, William Gustavus, 238-241, 243, 246-249
Bach, Karl, 362, 364-367
Baker, Nicholas, 63, 89, 109-112, 114-115
Baldwin, Maria, 361-362
Ballou, Adin, 250
Bancroft, Richard (Archbiship of Canterbury), 22, 24
baptism, 17, 32-33, 61-62, 65-66, 68, 71, 75-78, 80, 95-97, 99-102, 105, 125, 152
Baptists, 32, 36, 62, 68, 78, 89, 101, 134, 150, 168, 172, 182, 185, 246, 259, 303, 305-306, 319, 320, 326, 338, 361, 367, 369, 373, 376, 467,
Barbone, Sara, 37, 41, 46
Barnes, David, 136, 138, 144, 152
Barnet, Humphrey, 37, 38, 42, 43
Barnstable, Mass., 50, 61, 65, 67, 366, 457, 465
Barrett, Fiske 233-236
Barrow, Henry, 13, 14
Bates, Louise, 423, 425, 431, 434, 443, 453, 454
Berger, Darrell, 428-436, 465

Berkeley, Chris, 451, 454, 469

Berkeley, Dave, 467, 469

Bethune, Mary McLeod, 318

Blackwood, Christopher, 63, 68

Boardman, Michael 436-438

Boivin, Bertram D., 301

Bonney, Edith, 316, 321, 357, 361

Bonney, Margaret Cole, 2, 322, 338, 366, 371, 441, 474

Book of Common Prayer, 8, 9, 10, 17, 34, 35, 71

Bourn, Shearjashub, 129-131 136-137

Bradford, William 27, 60, 75, 86 87, 90, 91

Bradford, Edith, 361

Bragg, Raymond, 378

Branigan, William, 291

Brooks, George, 350

Brooks, Walter, 359

Brown, Dorothy Wood, 322, 380, 443, 453

Brown, Eleanor, 366

Brown, John, 232

Brown, Wilmot, 322, 342, 361, 375, 376, 380, 404, 453

Browne, Robert 13

Buck, Isaac, 114

Bulkeley, Edward, 86

Burbank, Libby, 374, 452, 453

Burns, Anthony 243-246

Bush George H. W., 56

Bush, George W., 56

Bygrave, Hillary 299-301

C

Calvin John, 8, 14, 168

Cambridge Platform, 54, 90, 136, 150, 154

Čapek, Norbert, 446

Cargill, H(enry) L(orenzo), 252

Carver, John, 60

Channing, Wiliam Ellery, 164, 179, 182, 190, 219, 220, 257, 273, 421

Charles I, 32-35, 63, 71

Chauncy, Charles (1592-1672), 55, 59, 61, 63, 65, 66, 69, 70-77, 79-85, 87-95, 100, 102, 105, 111, 122, 124, 157

Chauncy, Charles (1705-1787), 134

Cheriton, 5, 20

Chittenden, Isaac, 114

Civil War (U.S.), 231, 243, 248, 255, 259, 260, 277, 280, 284, 298, 307, 457, 462

Civil War (English), 8, 32, 68, 87

Clapp, Thomas, 140

Clapp, W. T., 328

Clark, Sheldon C., 2, 259, 260, 262, 264-266

Clark, Martha Strickland, 260-265

Clarke, James Freeman, 330

Clarke, Samuel F., 233

Clement VII, Pope, 7

Clink Prison, 7, 13, 22, 37

Cobb, Henry, 59, 61, 65

Cohasset, Mass., 145, 179, 180, 200, 217, 226, 259, 273, 398, 413, 416, 446, 458, 459

Cole, Enoch, 173

Cole, Frances and Herbert, 342, 386, 432

Cole, Harold, 342

Cole, Louis, 326

Cole, Mary Ann, 162

Cole, Marian, 326

Cole, Rena, 318, 325, 377

Cook, Agnes, 338, 343, 361

Cook, Alden, 338, 343, 361, 364

Cook, Stephen, 466

Cooper, Henry George, 390, 391, 394, 395, 397, 404

Cornish, Louis, 315, 330, 331, 356-358

Court of High Commission, 37-49 71-74, 79, 80

Cranmer, Thomas (Archbishop of Canterbury), 8

Creelman, Alan, 338, 367, 369,

Cromwell, Oliver, 33, 92

Crowley, Elizabeth (Betty), 468

Cudworth, James,1, 56, 59, 60, 61, 63, 65, 102, 103, 113, 171

cummings, e.e., 362

Cushing, Jeremiah, 122, 124

D

Daughters of the American Revolution (DAR), 320, 322, 323, 349

Darrow, Clarence, 265

Davis, George, 375, 376

Davis, Ken and Vicki, 469

Dawes, Ebenezer, 153-157, 158, 167

De Normandie, C. Y., 271

Deane, Samuel, 1, 2, 50, 61, 63, 67, 80, 81, 85, 86, 87, 88, 91, 92, 109, 111, 112, 113, 125, 142, 148, 155, 157, 166, 169, 170-171, 179, 180

Delemar, Abigail, 45-46

Dod, Henry, 37, 39-40, 43

Donelson, Jr., Charles, 351, 397-400, 403, 404

Doremus, Robert Proudfit, 302, 303

Dubuisson, Beth, 450

Duff, Sue, 459

Dunster, Henry, 55, 63, 94, 95-103, 105, 109, 171

Duxbury, Mass., 75, 85, 86, 90, 91, 179, 226, 274, 320, 323, 439, 459

Dyer, Mary, 103

E

Eaton, Samuel, 37, 41-44, 49

Edward VI, 8, 9

Egerton, Kent, 5, 34, 35, 57, 464

Eliot, John, 83, 85,

Hathaway, Rufus, 173, 174, 320, 323
Hatherly, Timothy, 1, 56, 59, 60, 61, 68, 76, 79, 81, 83, 87, 103, 171
Hayden, Lewis, 244
Hayes, J. A., 310, 315
Hayward, Dr. George, 193, 195
Hazlet, Rev., 154
Heijn, Cornelis, 334-340, 342, 343, 346-351, 355, 357, 375, 425
Helvie, Clara Cook, 372
Henry VIII, 7, 8, 9, 20
Heywood, William S., 201, 249-252
Higginson, Thomas Wentworth, 225, 244, 245, 246, 381, 383
Hilliard, Beth, 449, 450
Hingham, Mass., 109, 122, 128, 136, 145, 179, 189, 266, 324, 351, 374,
Hodges, R. M., 200, 201
Holmes, John Haynes, 313
Holmes, Jr., Oliver Wendell, 56
Hooker, Thomas, 76
Howard, Bezaleel, 152
Howard, Zechariah, 152
Howard, Jim Ann, 428, 430
Howse, Pennina, 37
Hunt, Walter R., 377
Hunter, Stanley M., 293-296, 301
Hutchinson, Anne, 49, 89, 100

J

Jacob, Henry 2, 4, 5, 14, 17-34, 47, 57, 58, 59, 317, 463, James
Jacob, Sara, 37
James I, 16-18, 31, 34, 35, 51, 52, 62, 70
Jenkins, Charles, 271
Jenkins, Daniel 141
Jenkins, David, 155
Jennings, A(llan) G(ay), 266, 271, 272
Jessey, Henry, 48, 49
Johnson, Raymond, 381, 383-387, 400, 404
Jones, Sarah, 37, 41, 47-48
Jones, Jenkin Lloyd, 282
Judson, Adoniram, 152

K

Kent, England, 4-6, 9, 16, 20, 35, 57, 61, 68, 135, 136, 464
Kifton, William, 36
Kilduff, Frank and Leslie, 458, 460, 467
King Philip's War, 60, 112-114
Koehring, Vera, 418, 426, 431,
Koelsch, Barbara, 441, 450, 452, 461

L

Ladies Aid Society, 276, 284, 286
Ladies Sewing Circle, 248, 260, 275, 276, 297, 318, 457

Laud, William (Archbishop of Canterbury), 34-48, 71, 72-74

Lechford, Thomas, 104, 108

Leiden, Netherlands, 27, 28, 58, 59, 75, 170,

Lemoine, George, 400, 402

Leonard, Abiel 137-138

Lindsey, Theophilus 164

Litchfield, Israel, 141-146, 165, 166

Locke, William Ware, 249, 315-317, 319, 322, 324-334, 337, 338, 356

Lodge, Ian, 447, 448

Longfellow, Henry Wadsworth and Samuel, 56

Lothrop, Gordon, 464, 466

Lothrop, John, 59, 60-66, 68, 72, 75, 80, 81, 83, 88, 94, 345, 353, 365, 366, 404, 451, 457, 463, 464, 465, 467

Luther, Martin 8, 13, 14, 168

M

Maglathlin, Edward B., 274

Magnalia Christi Americana, 67, 114

Manson, Edmund Sewall, 259

Manson, John, 259

Manson, Thomas, 272

Marshfield, Mass., 86, 112, 153, 158, 179, 266, 274, 279, 280, 284, 296, 301, 302, 303, 373, 413, 449,

Mary I, 9

Massachusetts Bay Colony, 49, 51, 54, 57, 58, 62, 66, 74, 75, 79, 83, 84, 85, 86, 87, 89, 90, 94, 101, 102, 104, 106, 108, 112, 123, 127, 135, 296,

Mather, Cotton, 67, 74, 92, 93, 96, 99, 114

May, Samuel J., 181, 190, 195, 221, 223

Mayesville, South Carolina. 317

McGowan, Cathie, 452, 459

Meadville Theological School, 257, 260, 291, 293, 334, 390, 438

Melborne, Elizabeth, 44

Men's Club, 318, 319, 396,

Merritt, Asa, 162, 385

Merritt, Evelyn, 338, 366

Merritt, Henry, 272, 273

Merritt, Shadrach, 162, 385

Metacom, 112, 113

Middelburg, Netherlands, 24, 31

Millenary Petition, 16-18

Miller, Leo, 261-264

Mitchell, Jonathan, 95, 96, 102

Morrison, Alma, 452

Morrison, Ray, 416, 417, 426, 449, 468

Morse, Jedidiah, 164

Morse, Samuel F. B., 164

Muller, Bill, 396, 399, 402, 431

Muller, Jeannette, 380, 396

Roosevelt, Franklin Delano, 56

S

Sabbath, 11, 70, 106, 212, 124, 143, 145, 172, 196, 228, 273,

St. John, Charles E., 293

Salem, Mass., 112, 181, 291, 360

Sanford, Lewis W., 372-376, 378

Sassamon, John (Wassausmon), 112-113

Satuit Christian Union, 287

Saxton, Giles 67

Saxton, Peter, 67-68

Schenkman, Alfred, 377-383

Scituate Historical Society, 3, 143n, 297, 322, 341, 342, 385, 405, 469

Seaver, Jr., Nathanael, 274, 275, 277, 296, 301, 303, 333

Second Parish, Scituate, 87, 88, 110, 111, 112, 116, 129, 136, 144, 170, 179, 180, 181, 182, 195, 226, 227, 266

Separatists, 4, 13, 15, 19, 21, 24, 26, 27, 30, 31, 32-35, 38, 40, 45, 59, 60-62, 78, 104

Sewall, Caroline (Ward), 181, 186, 193, 203, 204, 215, 223,

Sewall, Charles Chauncy, 179

Sewall, Edmund Quincy, 181-190, 192-202, 203, 206, 209-213, 217, 219, 220, 221, 223-227, 257, 272, 316, 406, 421, 470

Sewall, Jr., Edmund (Eddie) Quincy, 187, 193, 194, 203, 205, 206, 209, 210, 211

Sewall, Ellen, 2, 181, 186, 192, 200, 203-218, 223, 273,

Sewall, George, 181, 203, 206, 209, 210

Sewall, Henry Devereux, 181

Sewall, Samuel, 181

Shepard, Thomas, 76, 94, 95, 97,

Sinkford, William (Bill), 462, 464

slavery, 219, 220-225, 228, 232

slaves, 120, 131, 190, 220, 222, 243, 247, 317

Smith, Betty, 411

Smith, Laura, 459

South Scituate, Mass. (Norwell), 89, 136, 138, 152, 179, 181, 190, 227, 252, 272, 278, 421,

South Shore Community Forum, 378, 382

South Shore Housing Development Corporation, 416, 426,

Southwark, 2, 4, 5, 6-7, 9, 13, 15, 17, 22, 28, 29, 30, 31, 32, 36, 38, 41, 47, 48, 49, 55, 56, 57, 59, 61, 62, 317, 404, 463, 464

Airborne attempt at repairing church weathervane, 1962

www.ingramcontent.com/pod-product-compliance
Lightning Source LLC
Chambersburg PA
CBHW061559110426
42742CB00038B/1521